ALSO BY JAMES CURTIS

*Spencer Tracy: A Biography*

*W. C. Fields: A Biography*

*James Whale: A New World of Gods and Monsters*

*Between Flops: A Biography of Preston Sturges*

*The Creative Producer* (editor)

*Featured Player* (editor)

# WILLIAM CAMERON MENZIES

# WILLIAM CAMERON MENZIES

## The Shape of Films to Come

## JAMES CURTIS

PANTHEON BOOKS, NEW YORK

Published in the United States by Pantheon Books,
a division of Penguin Random House LLC, New York, and distributed in Canada
by Random House of Canada, a division of Penguin Random House Ltd., Toronto.

Pantheon Books and colophon are registered trademarks
of Penguin Random House LLC.

Library of Congress Cataloging-in-Publication Data
Curtis, James.
William Cameron Menzies : the shape of films to come / James Curtis.
pages      cm
Includes bibliographical references and index.
Includes filmography.
ISBN 978-0-375-42472-4 (hardcover : alk. paper). ISBN 978-1-101-87067-9 (eBook).
1. Menzies, William Cameron, 1896–1957.   2. Motion picture art directors—United States—
Biography.   3. Set designers—United States—Biography.   4. Motion picture producers and
directors—United States—Biography. I. Title.
PN1998.3.M4645C88 2015 791.4302′5092—dc23 [B] 2015011482

www.pantheonbooks.com

Jacket image sources include: the Menzies Family Collection; the David O. Selznick
Collection at the Harry Ransom Center, the University of Texas at Austin;
the New York Public Library; and two private collections
Jacket design by Janet Hansen
Book design by Soonyoung Kwon

Printed in the United States of America
First Edition

2 4 6 8 9 7 5 3 1

*Frontispiece:* William Cameron Menzies poses with artwork developed
for *The Devil and Miss Jones,* 1941. (MENZIES FAMILY COLLECTION)

For Pamela Lauesen and Toby Antles,
without whom this book could not have been written,
and in memory of Suzanne Menzies Antles

# CONTENTS

# INTRODUCTION

*He Loved Doing the Job*

Richard Sylbert was on the line. Used to expressing himself in bold lines and stark imagery, he was recalling the first time he met William Cameron Menzies. "It was at the Hotel Westbury on Madison Avenue, near the Carlyle. In his hotel room. I remember what he was wearing, how he looked. He was the same height as my father, and he dressed the way his pictures looked. In other words, he was silver-haired. No, not silver—*steel*-haired. You know? And he wore his uniform; I had mine, even in those days, and he always had his, which was gray tweed, gray flannel, black shoes, black tie, white button-down shirt, black pullover sweater. He looked like a black-and-white image."

The year was 1952, and Menzies had come to New York to make the pilot for a TV series based on the Fu Manchu stories of Sax Rohmer. Sylbert, at age twenty-three, was already the veteran of more than a hundred telecasts. "Bill was my first mentor," he said. "He was the director; I was the designer . . . which is not a bad way to start. We got along beautifully. Unfortunately, he died five years later. He died at sixty—he was very young—and he was a terrific guy. He's very important in the field of motion picture design; maybe the most important. Did you ever read that letter Orson Welles wrote? He's not just the father of production design, he's the only one who ever did it in his own time. Anton Grot got reasonably close, but nobody has ever repeated what Menzies did. You couldn't do it, meaning you couldn't have control over Sam Wood—who, as Menzies said, didn't know where to put the camera anyway—and draw all the shots for him. There's no director alive today who would do that."

Along with Ken Adam, who also worked with Menzies at the beginning of his career, Dick Sylbert was probably the most influential of all modern production designers. I had asked the Society of Motion Picture and Television Art Directors how to reach him, and Karen Jacobsen, a tremendous help, gave me the Palm Desert number of Sylbert's agent, Phyllis Rab. I called on a chilly Tuesday morning in January of 2001 and left a message. Within half an hour, Sylbert was back to me.

I suggested that Menzies was one of the great unsung figures of motion picture history. "Oh he was sung," Sylbert responded in his native Brooklynese, "but he was overshadowed by the credit mongers like Cedric Gibbons who worked for the major studios and called themselves supervising art directors and didn't do a fucking thing. When Gibbons died, he had a thousand credits. He had thirty-nine nominations and eleven Oscars. When William Cameron Menzies died, he had one Oscar. The difference between production design and bullshitting is right there."

I hadn't asked about Cedric Gibbons, the autocratic enforcer of the gloss long associated with Metro-Goldwyn-Mayer, but Sylbert scarcely needed prompting. The matter of Gibbons was particularly vexing because he knew that in nearly forty years of designing for the screen, Gibbons saw to it that Menzies never worked at M-G-M. "Do you know that people wouldn't make a movie until they got Menzies? That's how powerful he was at one time. Alexander Korda, when he was making *Thief of Bagdad,* got the actor he wanted, got the director he wanted, because Menzies was going to do the picture. And you know Menzies got credit on it, but Vincent Korda took over because Menzies was still busy with *Gone With the Wind* and [he] got screwed out of both of them. Korda got a nomination for *The Thief of Bagdad,* and Lyle Wheeler, another phony, got an Oscar for *Gone With the Wind.* And all Menzies got was a stupid little plaque.

"He didn't want to play the game. He used to say to me, 'Those fucking stock clerks out in California . . .' They'd go to the stock bins and pull out scenery, because they used to have huge sets standing at all the studios. And he was the only one who never became a supervising art director *because he wanted to do the job.* These guys didn't do the job; they talked about it. Some of them were quite interesting; Grot was interesting, and [department head] Hans Dreier over at Paramount was interesting, and Richard Day [at 20th Century-Fox] would try to be a working designer, but how can you be a designer if you're doing twenty-five pictures a year? You'd need roller skates.

"So they didn't do the job. Menzies wanted to do the job, because Menzies' whole interest was as a dramatist, not a designer, in the sense of an art director, as they called these guys. *He wanted to do the job.* You couldn't do the job if you were running a studio. You just came in in the morning. It was so disgraceful. Gibbons had a heart attack in the mid-forties, showed up occasionally in the next ten years, and got two more Oscars! Because Louis B. Mayer and he set it up—they institutionalized credit stealing. M-G-M and Fox were the biggest studios, so they always got the most votes. No matter how you cut the pie up, Anton Grot I don't think ever won an Oscar. So you can imagine what the game was. The game was: I'll vote for the guys who can give me a job. And that's what happened for forty years. So the decent men like Menzies and Grot and Dick Day, who was between them, got shut out.

"'One picture is worth a thousand words' is what Menzies realized—that you could actually draw this movie out—only because that was the kind of person he was. *He loved doing the job.* He loved the idea of structuring a movie. Did you ever see a little picture called *Ivy*? It's a perfect Menzies picture. There isn't one frame of that picture you can't see him drawing. *Ivy* is pure Menzies—not a great movie, but it's *Menzies*. A black-and-white Menzies movie in which he is in total control. Like he was on most of Sam Wood's films.

"When we used to sit in that room and he would draw, he would draw angles, and he was very, very economical. He didn't care what was outside this one shot. 'The way to do this,' he would say, 'is to shoot down. It's cheaper and it'll look more interesting.' Or you shoot up. Or you do this. We did everything in black-and-white. Black, white, or gray. He did the same thing in *Androcles and the Lion,* he told me once. He couldn't get shadows that were dark enough for the sand, so he put black sand on the shadow. Everything he thought up, he wanted it *pure*. That's why *Ivy* is interesting to look at. It's a pure negative. He knew what he was going to get when it was over.

"I did seventeen black-and-white pictures—I won an Academy Award for black-and-white—but I did them in color. So that I was actually trying to develop these black-and-white ideas, but I was never quite sure how it was going to come out. You know, it wasn't a big deal, but it never had that clarity that Menzies got when he did his own stuff in black-and-white. When he did his color, it was different. It's his black-and-white pictures that tell you the most about him, if you ask me. *Gone With the Wind* is terrific, but with *Gone With the Wind* he began to see what I saw later, which are musical ideas. He has movements in *Gone With the Wind.* There are moods, big passages of what in a symphony would be: slow, fast, slow. He would do it with colors. You know—a whole section of grays and browns and then move on to another. He was an artist, and a lot of these other guys were just architects. Architects are fine—nothing against architects—but he was the artist."

I brought up the films Menzies had directed, such as *Invaders from Mars,* and the largely indifferent results he got as a director. "He was not a great director,"

Sylbert conceded. "Even on *Things to Come,* which is a wonderful picture. Menzies could never have had a career as a director, because he just didn't have that *thing.* What he had was the visual dramatics. He couldn't get the emotional dynamics. You know what I'm talking about. In other words, his narrative structure was entirely in pictures. When I started designing for Kazan, the last thing in the world anybody talked about was pictures. What they talked about was the emotional dynamic of the narrative. So it swung to actors. By the fifties it had become an actors' medium—still is, as a matter of fact, except on rare occasions. But it wasn't then. It was much more visual. When Anton Grot did those pirate movies, they didn't need actors—they could have had dummies. Those pictures could have been silent movies and they would have worked. But it changed in the fifties, when Bill had trouble getting work.

"I only spent a couple of months with Menzies—we did two black-and-white pilots of *Fu Manchu* together—Sax Rohmer was still alive—and the cast was brilliant: Cedric Hardwicke, John Carradine, Melville Cooper, John Newland, Rita Gam. It was the first thing done in a studio on film in New York, independent of anything else, for television. It was just a bunch of people from television who got together with Herb Swope, the producer, and rented the old Gold Medal Studio, which was a mess, and did this thing in nineteen-hundred and fifty-two. That was between my doing *Hamlet* for Maurice Evans on television and *Richard II.* I took a break. They were the two biggest live television shows there were up to that time. Menzies didn't know that I was doing *Richard II* next, but after it aired I got a call from him and he said to me, 'I knew you did that show before I saw the crawl.' Which I'll never forget, because Menzies had a fingerprint.

"The best thing he ever said to me didn't mean as much at the time as it means at this point. I used to live in a fifth-floor walk-up on West 85th Street, and he'd come puffing up the stairs. And he looked at the drawings and he said to me, 'You know kid, you ought to go out to Hollywood. You've got a lot of stuff.' Hollywood—you know I never thought of it? He said, 'Yeah, you should go out to Hollywood and put a little *dignity* back into the business.' That's exactly what he said. That's how he felt about it. *It had lost its dignity.* These stock clerks and credit mongers and bullshit artists had taken control of the business.

"And I know what he meant, because when I went out there we started the New York Revolution. We blew the place up. It's back now, in many ways, to the way it used to be, but it's much improved because there are no more supervising art directors and there are no more companies. There are no studios that anyone works in permanently. . . . I came in at the end of studio, with Marty Ritt and Sidney Lumet, and when you come in that way, you've got to find a way to take control. Which I have obviously done. It's very different than Menzies. It has much more to do with patterns. And with musical structure, rather than with individual shots. You don't get into a room with Kazan and three great actors and tell him where to put the camera. Because he's waiting for those actors to tell him where to put the camera. So what I worked out over the years, a little bit here and a little bit there, is to actually sit down and write a recipe for a movie before it's ever shot. And I've proven it again and again and again. I know it works, and it's another version of structural control, which is really what Menzies was after anyway. He wasn't interested in chaos . . . Menzies was a classicist. You can use that word. In other words, he *formalized* a picture."

Menzies burst upon the Hollywood scene in 1923 with his startling designs for the original *Thief of Bagdad*. Trained as an illustrator rather than an architect, he created a fantasy world that was integral to the action and not merely a backdrop. He gave the film size, and with it came a sense of wonderment. That picture made Menzies, and over the next six years he refined a technique that pre-visualized a film compositionally, recasting actors as graphic elements and teasing out the dramatic values of tone and texture. Occasionally he had a canvas as big as for his initial triumph—*The Hooded Falcon* (for Valentino), *The Beloved Rogue, The Dove, Tempest,* and for the latter two he was awarded the first Oscar ever given for art direction. He brought the illustrator's eye to the camera and graphic validity to an art form that was all too often theatrical rather than cinematic.

The natural course of Menzies' career took him to directing, but he lacked the ability to extract a performance and displayed no sense of pacing. Paired, as was common in the early days of sound, with a director to handle the actors, Menzies managed an uneven slate of pictures, excelling at films that traded in thrills and fantasy. His *Alice in Wonderland* hewed too closely to the drawings of John Tenniel, but *Things to Come* became a visionary masterpiece, hobbled only in terms of the stilted dialogue imposed on the picture by its author, H. G. Wells. Producer David O. Selznick engaged him in 1937, and by the following year he was in charge of the overall look of the decade's most important production, *Gone With the Wind*.

Selznick's plan was to have Menzies compose and sketch every shot in the movie prior to filming, giving it a bold visual style that hid the fact that multiple directors were employed in its making. The technique also gave the producer ultimate control of the production, saving money while permitting him to effectively direct the film himself. Of the hundreds of actors, writers, artists, and craftsmen who contributed to the making of *GWTW,* only two were on the picture from its earliest days through to the last shot—Selznick himself and William Cameron Menzies. The film won eight Academy Awards, including one for Lyle Wheeler for color art direction, but there was no category for what Menzies had done, and so a special award was created for "use of color for the enhancement of dramatic mood." On screen, there was similarly a special credit: "This production designed by William Cameron Menzies."

One of the uncredited directors on *Gone With the Wind* was Sam Wood, a generalist who was fascinated by the continuity boards Menzies and his staff developed for *GWTW,* and soon Wood formed a creative partnership with Menzies that resulted in some of the most memorable films of the 1940s. Since Wood had no visual sense of his own, he gave Menzies full rein over the look of their pictures, preferring to concentrate instead on matters of story and the performances of his actors. Together, the two men constituted one great director, and their output was singular in terms of range and technique—*Our Town, The Devil and Miss Jones, Kings Row, Pride of the Yankees, For Whom the Bell Tolls, Address Unknown* (directed by Menzies, produced by Wood), and the aforementioned *Ivy.*

Five years after the collaboration ended with *Ivy,* Bill Menzies urged Dick Sylbert to go to Hollywood to put a little dignity back into the business. In 1956, Sylbert made the jump to the big screen with Elia Kazan's *Baby Doll.* Eventually he designed over fifty films, including such seminal titles as *Splendor in the Grass, The Manchurian Candidate, Who's Afraid of Virginia Woolf?, The Graduate, Carnal Knowledge,* and *Chinatown.* Sylbert never stopped exploring the process of addition and subtraction, a form of structural problem solving Menzies had taught him, and he never stopped paying tribute to the man who had revolutionized the look and technique of American motion picture production.

# WILLIAM CAMERON MENZIES

# Atlanta Burning

Preparations for the inferno had been under way for weeks when the night of December 10, 1938, finally arrived. Culver City, home to the RKO-Pathé Studios, had never seen anything like it. On a cluttered patch of land due south of the main lot—called "Forty Acres" but only twenty-eight acres in actual area—a crowd of some 250 awaited nightfall with a palpable sense of anticipation and a little dread. Arrayed before them were the broad makings of the Atlanta rail yard as it would have appeared on the night of September 1, 1864, when a Confederate ordnance train was torched by fleeing troops, setting off a series of explosions that shattered every window in the city. The life-size re-creation of this event, a scene that would normally have been accomplished in miniature, would mark the start of filming on the most eagerly anticipated movie of the decade.

Bill Menzies, clad in overcoat, sweater vest, and one of his trademark bow ties, was attending to details, his whitening hair glistening under the weak afternoon sun. He lit a Lucky Strike, one of the dozens he would smoke that day, and continued dressing the foreground, a gang of studio grips at his command. Strategically positioned around him were six Model D Technicolor cameras—all that were available—and two black-and-white cameras to shoot silhouettes and promotional footage. Two of the color cameras had been dedicated to recording the fire in widescreen, an effect producer David O. Selznick wanted for the first-run houses and the New York World's Fair.

The spectacle entailed considerable risk, as the studio was surrounded by a residential neighborhood and had already endured a devastating fire in the mid-1920s. It was Menzies' idea to burn some of the standing sets on the backlot when he learned they would have to be cleared for the construction of a massive brick car shed—the best known of Atlanta's wartime monuments—and the fictional plantation house, Tara. He enlisted studio production manager Ray Klune in the effort to convince Selznick of the viability of the plan, over the fierce objections of M-G-M studio manager Eddie Mannix, who predicted the burning of the sets would not prove to be of "any substantial photographic value" in the Atlanta fire sequence and instead wanted Tara built on his own lot two miles away.

In collaboration with Klune and unit art director Lyle Wheeler, Menzies had studied the backlot and selected as kindling leftover sets from the biblical epic *The King of Kings*. They fitted these with profiles and false fronts that suggested period warehousing, a water tank, a foundry, and populated the foreground with tracks, a string of freight cars, and packing crates of Enfield rifles, ammunition for Napoleon and Blakeley guns, and fixed cartridges. Weathering on the brick-red cars had been accomplished with skilled brushwork and augmented with scrupulously authentic markings—W.&A.R.R., A.&W.P.R.R., M.&W.R.R., and GA.R.R. A gigantic wall, used in the Skull Island scenes of *King Kong,* was similarly dressed, cut from its supports, and laced with cables that extended down through a metal pulley block and several hundred feet to a powerful tractor.

Now, with darkness approaching, Menzies intently made last-minute arrangements of the foreground details, darting from one camera position to the next, adding disabled field pieces of the proper vintage, some old wagons, discarded furniture, piles of cross ties, and, at one crucial point, a mud puddle. A miniature of the redressed sets had been constructed and the camera positions worked out in advance. "We planned the whole thing sort of as a football rehearsal," Klune would later recall.

Working with screenwriter Oliver H. P. Garrett, Menzies had prepared an amplified script of the fire sequence and a detailed continuity that visualized the entire episode in thirty-three drawings: "For all scenes marked 'Transparency,' it is proposed we will shoot backgrounds for those on the night we shoot the fire. For all scenes marked 'Cosgrove Split Screen,' we will shoot the sky material that night, and scenes not marked 'Transparency' or 'Split Screen,' we will shoot straight with the real fire as background."

Initial estimates called for one hundred extras (fifty soldiers and fifty civilians) but then Menzies and playwright Sidney Howard (the original scenarist) reasoned the town would probably have been abandoned by nightfall, and other than a few roughs, sentries, and straggling soldiers, Rhett Butler, Scarlett O'Hara, and the others would have been the last of the refugees. Director George Cukor agreed that this would add a sinister note to the scene, and suggested a few other changes to "increase the feeling that they are trapped in the fire, to have the fire behind them and, as they drive into the foreground, a burning beam falls in front of the horse, forcing them to turn off. Added to the business of losing control of the horse, this gives added justification as to why they are forced to drive through such an intense fire."

Selznick reviewed these suggestions and sent word for Menzies to make new sketches "with particular emphasis on a constantly mounting violence in the shots and the fire getting greater and greater as [Scarlett and Rhett] drive through the streets, climaxing in the panoramic effect* on which we are working." Menzies' revised script and boards for the sequence were delivered on December 2 and rehearsals began promptly—first on the model, then on the lot itself. A final run-through was conducted on Friday, December 9. Fire tests were made on foreground structures, and light meters were held at various distances. Both of the stunt doubles for Rhett Butler, each clad in light linen suit and panama hat, were put through the same set of actions, with bits of physical business worked out between the horses and the drivers as they went. A chill wind blew ominously.

In working out the logistics, it was decided that instead of changing lenses—which, according to Klune, "was a brute of a job on those Technicolor things"—the cameras themselves would have to be moved. Positions were marked on the miniature and numbered sequentially. "We'd move the camera from position one to position five—different lenses on each camera because we wanted to get a medium shot, a long shot, and a close shot from almost every position." Since two of the cameras were allocated to the widescreen effect, and a third was a new high-speed camera designed to catch the collapse of the burning wall in slow motion, just three were left to record the action with conventional Technicolor lenses. Each of the six cameras would be assigned a crew of three—supervisor, operator, technician—responsible for making the specified shots according to Menzies' drawings, reloading the camera after ten minutes of film had been exposed (a complicated process involving three discrete film elements), and moving the outsized camera from one position to the next—all while the fire raged before them.

Given the fact it would be impossible to stop the fire once it had been started,

---

* Black-and-white experiments had been conducted with an anamorphic lens, which compressed the image and allowed the camera to capture more picture information, but Selznick was advised it wasn't feasible to use such a lens with the Technicolor process. Cinematographer Winton Hoch then figured out a way of achieving the effect with two cameras and a mirror.

Klune turned to a man named Lee Zavits ("the best special effects man in the business") to devise a way of at least slowing its progress and affording the company some measure of control. Zavits designed a network of pipes studded with nozzles that could deliver fuel to the flames or dampen them as needed. Three 5,000-gallon tanks fed the system with centrifugal pumps. Two of the tanks contained a mixture of gasoline and distillate; the third was filled with water.

Carbon arcs, white- and red-gelled and some amber, were mounted on tall platforms and trained on the set. Positioned at a microphone in the center of it all was Eric Stacey, assistant director and the man responsible to Menzies, Klune, and, ultimately, Selznick, for ensuring that everything went smoothly. Off to one side were three identical horse-drawn farm wagons and two sets of doubles representing the characters of Rhett and Scarlett. Dummies filled in for other characters: Scarlett's sister-in-law, Melanie; her baby, Beau; and the excitable house servant, Prissy.

Though tests had already been made with a new higher-speed version of the notoriously slow Technicolor film stock, an item was planted in the *Venice Evening Vanguard* advising the local citizenry that "tests of fire and smoke such as would be needed for the burning of Atlanta sequence" would take place that night, with the hope of minimizing the number of onlookers eager to witness the official start of production. Menzies and Klune anxiously followed the weather in the days leading up to the event, and on Friday evening, when the go/no-go decision had to be made, the official forecast read as follows: "Heavy ground fog from sundown on. May lift 100 feet or so during night. Horizontal visibility less than one-half mile." It would be imperative to get all the necessary shots before the fog intervened. The best news of all: NO WIND.

There was scarcely a twilight. It was dark by five o'clock, and work lights illuminated the orderly bustle of property men, cameramen, and electricians as they made their final preparations, casting long shadows as they went. Off-duty firemen from M-G-M and the Culver City Fire Department stood by, ready to take control if the blaze got out of hand. Their ranks were swelled by personnel from the Los Angeles Fire Department, who ringed the area with equipment. Just when everything was in position, supper was announced. The guests made their way to a paved area of the North African village built for *The Garden of Allah,* lined up cafeteria style, and proceeded to gorge themselves on spaghetti, turkey à la king, baked potatoes, salad, pie, and coffee. Making their way back through the adobe dust, most could be observed munching on big red apples.

Now came the wait. Around 7:30, a limousine carrying Selznick and Cukor arrived on the scene. They huddled with Menzies; Jack Cosgrove, the head of the special effects department; Harold Fenton, head of construction; Harold Coles, the property manager; Lee Zavits; Klune; and Yakima Canutt, the principal stunt double for Clark Gable (who would be playing Rhett Butler in the picture). Then Selznick nervously worked the crowd, greeting some and asking others if they thought it would come off properly. All of the studio's department heads were present, and many had brought their wives for the show. Menzies' wife, Mignon, wasn't among them. Not wishing to distract him—and never particularly comfortable around people in the industry—she chose instead a view of the Selznick lot and Ballona Creek from the parking lot of the Westside Tennis Club, where she sat alone in her nine-passenger Cadillac.

Ray Klune went to the microphone and gently asked the crowd, which included the producer's mother, Mrs. Lewis J. Selznick, not to talk during the burn—which was expected to last about forty-five minutes—because relative quiet would be needed to minimize confusion and bring all the carefully rehearsed stunts off as planned. Menzies looked to Selznick to give the word to go, but the producer held off, awaiting the arrival of his brother, agent Myron Selznick. Not only did he want Myron to witness the start of the biggest production of his career, but he also wanted to meet his brother's newest client, a twenty-five-year-old actress who was, as Selznick later put it, "the Scarlett dark horse." By eight o'clock, the temperature had dropped to 55 degrees and fog was starting to roll in. Menzies took his place on the platform, poised to conduct a conflagration of Wagnerian proportions, but Selznick held firm until Ray Klune advised him they wouldn't be able to hold the extra fire and police personnel much longer. And so at 8:20, with his brother nowhere in sight, Selznick gave the okay to proceed.

As Menzies signaled Zavits, Stacey ordered the area cleared and the arcs brought up full, bathing the set in a light so brilliant it was startling. Zavits, from his perch behind a firebreak, cued his men to start the flow of fuel to the pipes, while small fires were lit on asbestos tables in front of some of the lights, giving off trails of thick black smoke. As Wilbur Kurtz, technical advisor to the film, observed, "This smoke, streaming across the field of light, made the background leap in irregular and fast-moving patches of shadow—as if a blaze was in progress in back of the cameras."

When the fuel was confirmed as spraying evenly through the nozzles and coating the wood as planned, Zavits activated a series of electric ignitions and the blaze erupted with a deafening whoosh. In moments the old sets were fully engulfed, the fire roaring up above the buildings and, as in the novel, throwing "street and houses into a glare of light brighter than day, casting monstrous shadows that twisted as wildly as torn sails flapping in a gale on a sinking ship." To Linda Schiller, Selznick's script secretary, "it was just suddenly the holocaust . . . it scared all of us . . . it was like a whole town suddenly going up in flames."

Menzies waited for the effect to build as the crowd stood awestruck. Some recoiled from the intense heat and pervasive smell of gasoline, while others were strangely fascinated and transfixed by the scene. The flames were licking up into the sky as much as two hundred feet when Menzies gave Zavits a cue to momentarily kill the fuel and start the water pumping. As clouds of white steam rose into the night air, he called for the powerful arcs gelled red and amber. The sky exploded in great masses of red and black—hot, violent colors—and with the fire returned to maximum intensity, the backdrop for Rhett and Scarlett's escape from Atlanta was complete. The crews stationed at five of the six cameras began to roll film. Moments later, as stuntwoman Donna Fargo, clad in Scarlett's lavender mourning dress, took her position alongside Yakima Canutt in the wagon, Menzies leaned into the microphone and called, "Action!"

The wagon carrying Rhett and Scarlett scurried into view from an alleyway off Peachtree Street, one of the Technicolor cameras catching a reverse angle of their gallop as they sped toward the fire. They rounded a burning shed, pulling boxes over as they went, and raced westward into the flaming yard. Exploding munitions turned them back and out toward the spectators as the wagon clambered over a section of track and cross ties and got mired in the mud. Leaping down, Rhett tried to budge the horse, then, failing that, signaled Scarlett to hand over her shawl. Wrapping it around the horse's head, Rhett was able to get the animal moving again, but then discovered their pathway blocked by still more fire. Forced back through a gap in the cars, they sped away as dust and smoke swirled furiously around them.

All the mad rearing and plunging were the work of a stunt driver lying prone on the floorboards of the wagon, peering through an opening between Scarlett's legs and controlling the horse with wires running out to the bit. It was all Canutt, an accomplished stunt rider, could do to keep his face obscured from the camera and sustain the illusion he was in control of the thing. Fargo cringed effectively and hid her face, even as she surrendered her shawl. With the fire still raging, Menzies called for another run and the cameras changed positions. Quickly, Yak and his driver got back into the alleyway, again they emerged, and again they faced the wall of flame and veered off into the foreground. This time, on impact with the cross ties, the left front wheel collapsed and the horse, in the chaos and the searing heat of it all, sat down. A gang of grips rushed onto the scene and cleared it for yet another run.

Around the corner, on the back side of the *Kong* set, Clarence Slifer, Jack Cosgrove's assistant, was waiting with the high-speed camera to record the collapse of the giant wall at 72 frames per second—three times normal speed. But since Slifer had barely three minutes of film in the camera and couldn't see what was happening on the other side of the wall, he and his crew had to watch a green light for their cue. And once rolling, there would be a very tight window of time during which a red light could tell them the structure was about to fall.

As the second wagon began its run, the fuel supply to the whole of the wall was brought up and, suddenly, it too was engulfed in flames. From his perspective, Slifer anxiously watched for his signal, but it failed to come as Menzies, momentarily distracted, was busy capturing the footage of the fire and the boiling smoke—angry flames to be optically added to foreground action in scenes later to be shot with the principals.

Meanwhile, the furious light cast on the low-hanging clouds drew scores of cars and thrill seekers, some eager to see what was happening, others convinced the entire neighborhood was going up. Switchboards lit up around the city as people wanted to know where the fire was. (Many thought M-G-M was burning, which handed Selznick a laugh.) With spectators and the noise of the surrounding traffic on the increase, Slifer finally got his cue. Rolling, he waited for the tractor to do its worst as exposed film ticked into the magazine at a ferocious pace. "When our counter reached 700 feet we were beside ourselves with fear that we would run out of film, as a magazine held approximately 950 feet of film."

Seven-fifty, eight hundred, eight-fifty . . . there was less than twenty seconds of film left in the camera when the red bulb came on. The tractor lurched into motion and the skeletal remains of Skull Island, roughly seventy-five feet in height, came crashing down in a spectacular eruption of embers and debris. Moments later, the big blue camera was out of film, but the shot was there. As Slifer and his crew cleaned the movement and reloaded for background plates, firemen with hoses on the periphery of the scene busied themselves shooting blazing fragments out of the night sky as if they were ducks.

With Rhett and Scarlett's run and the wall's collapse now safely in the can, the cameras again shifted positions, and two were reloaded for the process of making background plates. A close-up was shot of Yak in the second wagon, passing a blazing line of fencing. Then the second double took a run past a burning boxcar, the camera trained to shoot through the open doors of the car, but the horse, having galloped into a confined space between the car and a wall of flames, balked at the containment and steadfastly refused to move.

As they gave up the shot, Selznick and Cukor suggested a close-up of some threatened explosives, but the fire was by now on the wane, and they decided they could get it later. It was just then that Myron Selznick, aglow from dinner and a steady flow of cocktails, rolled onto the property, accompanied by Laurence Olivier and his future wife, actress Vivien Leigh. David Selznick took his first look at Leigh in the flesh and knew instantly that she was Scarlett. "Later on, her tests, made under George Cukor's brilliant direction, showed that she could act the part right down to the ground," he said, "but I'll never recover from that first look."

The flames were methodically doused, and Menzies stood amid the ashes and the charred rubble of the set, water dripping from everything, the smell of gasoline still hanging in the air. Exhausted from the strain of it all, he lit yet another cigarette. Selznick came over to him, apologized for ever doubting that he could bring it off, and told him it was one of the greatest things he had ever seen. Nearly 12,000 feet of film had been exposed in less than an hour at a total cost of $26,319.55. As Selznick later wrote, "It was one of the biggest thrills I have had out of making pictures—first, because of the scene itself, and second, because of the frightening but exciting knowledge that *Gone With the Wind* was finally in work."

It is unlikely that David Selznick remembered his first encounter with Menzies' work twenty years earlier, when he was a sixteen-year-old copywriter for Lewis J. Selznick's Select Pictures Corporation and Menzies was the boyish set designer on an Alice Brady picture called *Redhead.* Brady, the winsome twenty-six-year-old daughter of impresario William A. Brady, was principally a stage star who went slumming in the movies, working a fan base comprised almost entirely of women. Since Adolph Zukor, president of Famous Players-Lasky, owned a 50 percent stake in Select, the picture was shot at the old Famous Players studio on 56th Street in New York, where Menzies, recently returned from the war, was a staff art director.

Had young Selznick interviewed him at the time (as he did so many of the writers, directors, and actors who worked for his father), Menzies might well have told him he was born in Aberfeldy, Perthshire, in the Scottish Highlands, within sight of Castle Menzies, a rambling, turreted stone mansion that had stood on the banks of the Tay since early in the reign of Mary, Queen of Scots. But since this was, after all, the boss' son, he more likely would have admitted that the true scene of his birth was an elm-lined street just two blocks from the Yale campus in New Haven, Connecticut, where the most prominent landmark at nearby East Rock Park was the granite Soldiers' and Sailors' Monument that stood at its summit.

Menzies was the second son of Charles Alexander Menzies, a mechanical engineer by trade who was indeed born in Aberfeldy, and Helen "Ellen" Cameron, a descendant of the famous Scottish clan of the same name. They were married in New York in 1892 and settled in New Haven, where Charles had found work with the Robert Morgan Company, a plumbing and heating contractor. In due course, Ellen gave birth to John Cameron, who would continue in the business eventually established by his father, and William Cameron, who was born William Charles Menzies in the family home at 124½ Park Street on July 29, 1896.

Billy, as he came to be known, first caught sight of the castle at the impressionable age of four when his parents took him and his brother to Scotland to stay with his grandparents. The visit lasted a year, long enough for the child to absorb both the romance of his ancestral home and the genuine eeriness of the place. Their modest cottage was at the edge of a wood called Tomchannon and the earthworks among the trees gave evidence of the Covenanter religious battles of the mid-seventeenth century and the Jacobite rebellions of 1715 and 1745. It was a place that abounded in tradition and folklore that had kings, pixies, and shepherds existing on equal planes. "The older people, including my grandfather, believed in bogies, pixies, elves, and little people," Menzies remembered, "and I started to draw—elves, pixies, bogies, and little people." From his boyhood tours of Loch Tay, he developed a druid sensitivity to the language of nature, its shapes, colors, and textures, and the inherent drama they held.

"The child whose early background has an ample spook-ridden, fairy tale element has a tremendous edge on the sophisticated city-bred child when it comes to following an artistic career," he wrote. "The romantic element in even the simplest of conceptions is all a matter of conditioning. When you can see shadows not only as an absence of sufficient light, but as a place [where] things might lurk and jump

The Tomchannon cottage at Weem, near Aberfeldy, where young Menzies lived for a time with his grandparents. The two adjoining Tomchannon cottages are on the same road as Castle Menzies, the seat of the Chiefs of Clan Menzies for more than four hundred years. (PAMELA LAUESEN)

out at you, as you used to think as a child, then you are working with a perpetually stimulated imagination which can add more than a veneer of interest to everyday drama."

Perpetually stimulated or, more properly, distracted, Billy was given to doodling when he should have been paying attention. Enrolled in a day school, he got off to a bad start when he was asked to stand on the first day of class and say his name. When he announced himself "Menzies," the teacher corrected him: "*Mingies.*" The children laughed. The embarrassment of not knowing how to properly pronounce his own name never left him. To American ears it sounds like *Mingus,* but he always made sure that friends and co-workers heard it that way.

Menzies completed his early schooling in New Haven, where his father was a principal in the plumbing firm of Menzies & Menzies. ("Bathrooms remodeled in all the latest styles. Sanitary plumbing a specialty.") He dutifully attended Sunday school at the First Presbyterian Church and compulsively sketched in composition books and on stray scraps of paper. In 1910 he was returned to Scotland to enter the Highland Academy at Amulree. While there, he witnessed the pageantry of a royal visit to Edinburgh by King George V, confirming his abiding affection for "one of the last of the world's beautiful cities."

An indifferent student, Menzies was back in the United States by 1911, and he graduated from New Haven High School in 1914. With his love of whimsical drawing and his portfolio of mastheads and cartoons, it made perfect sense for him to study the practical discipline of architecture at the Yale School of the Fine Arts. Billy was given over to one Mr. Rosenberg, who, for a price, guaranteed success on the entry exams to virtually anyone, and soon his pen-and-ink drawings were decorating the pages of the *Yale Record.*

An incurable daydreamer, Menzies was inspired to a voracious reading habit by his wandering uncle Alec, who had gone off to Peru in his early years to pan for gold. It was Alexander Cameron who taught him chess, philosophy, mythology, and an appreciation for scientific and agnostic writers like Ernst von Haeckel, whose *The Riddle of the Universe* was consumed at an early age. He mastered the fundamentals of architecture, but his heart was with more fanciful forms of expression, and after studying drawing for a time under Edwin Taylor, the famous draughtsman, he declared to his father that he much preferred art to the design of buildings.

Charles Menzies, who had once nursed his own youthful ambition to be a concert violinist, was startlingly supportive. "If you want to be an artist," he told his son, "be a good one. If you show progress, I'll send you to Munich to study. But I don't want the type of artist in the family who gets no farther than drawing labels for tomato cans. And remember—as soon as you earn your first penny by art I'll stop your allowance." Family lore has his mother drawing out her life savings—probably

William Charles Menzies, age fifteen
(MENZIES FAMILY COLLECTION)

all of $500—and giving it to him. "None of them had the slightest clue what Daddy was really about," said Billy's younger daughter, Suzanne, "but they all had such faith in him they were willing to back him."

Menzies left for New York and the Art Students League during the bitter winter of 1915. He found a hall bedroom in an old barn that doubled as a makeshift studio on 58th Street near Columbus Circle, which enabled him, sharing quarters with three other students, to survive on his father's stipend of $10 a week. The League itself was one block over, housed in its own five-story building at 215 West 57th Street. Studying at the League, with its bohemian social traditions and free-form class structure, required a level of self-discipline Menzies hadn't yet developed. "There was no compulsory attendance," he remembered, "so I would spend the days in frivolity and at a late hour at night guiltily make up the time. In winter in New York, with no radiator but one of those mushroom gadgets on the gas jet, I did the old stunt that all freezing writers and artists have done—get everything in the room wrapped around you, punch a hole in the blanket with a pencil and draw through it all." For entertainment, he attended the League dances "equipped with a bottle of so-called Hy-Grade whiskey, which was a fairly palatable bourbon at 22 cents a pint," and, every spring, the Fakirs Ball, a rowdy costumed affair preceded by a parade and a juried exhibition of paintings "faked" from those awarded prizes at the National Academy of Design.

Instructors came to the school at the invitation of the membership, and regular exhibitions in the League's ground-floor gallery permitted the students to survey the range of styles available to them. Menzies chose to study painting with Frank Vincent DuMond and F. Luis Mora, illustration with Charles S. Chapman, and life drawing with George Bridgman. Chapman, whose moody landscapes were defined in bold lines and muted colors, was a particular influence on him, as was the plain-spoken Robert Henri, who began teaching at the League soon after Menzies arrived and whose school of social realism revolutionized American art. Henri's vigorous brushwork and strong contrasting values informed Menzies' emerging style, but it was Chapman who set him on a course to becoming an illustrator rather than a muralist as he had originally planned.

With summer approaching, Chapman told a few of his students—Menzies and Dean Cornwell among them—that he and illustrator Harvey Dunn were opening a school in Leonia, New Jersey. Situated directly across the Hudson River from the Bronx, the Leonia School of Illustration was a converted farmhouse dating from the Civil War. Tuition was $15 a month, with an additional $5 going to rent and kitchen privileges. Dunn was an enormous man with a zeal for teaching, a hard taskmaster who considered art and illustration inseparable. Cornwell, later a painter and mural-ist as well as a famous illustrator, was entranced at Dunn's approach to art: "He taught it as a religion—or awfully close to such."

Dunn had been a student of Howard Pyle, the man who had redefined Ameri-can illustration in the late nineteenth century with his realistic scenes of action and adventure, and he invited some of his old classmates from Pyle's Wilmington school to criticize the students' work. Over the summer, Menzies met—and was critiqued by—the likes of Gayle Porter Hoskins, Frank Schoonover, and N. C. Wyeth. Most of all, he responded to the vivid sense of drama Dunn achieved in his best work, as well as the abandon with which he approached it. "Usually I take two or three days on a picture, getting my facts in like a foundation of form and effect," Dunn said. "Then I tear into it!" He favored wide brushes and palette knives and eschewed lengthy discussions of form and technique. "Paint a little less of the facts," he would say, "and a little more of the spirit."

For his second term at the League, Menzies traded "Filthy-Eighth Street" for a studio apartment on 44th just west of Fifth Avenue. His roommates, equally destitute, were C. C. ("Ted") Beall, later of *Collier's;* John LaGatta, "the greatest painter of svelte women's backs in history"; and, for a while, Howard Darrin, future automotive designer, and his brother Larry. "Thirty-three West 44th, the doggiest address you could have, huddled between the Harvard and the New York Yacht Clubs, opposite D.K.E., cater-corner from Sherry's and a stone's throw from Del-monico's." No one could have known it was a six-flight walk-up and that, in a studio room with two small bedrooms, a kitchen, and a bath, the furniture consisted of two drawing tables, one substantial couch, a trunk that acted as a table, one double bed, and another trunk that acted as a dresser. "In my cubbyhole," said Menzies, "I had a broken-backed Army cot which, if I hadn't been young, would have ruined my kidneys, and the inevitable trunk that acted for dresser, closet, and receptacle for everything loose. In cold weather, the Army cot acquired a mattress of old newspapers."

The lure of extra cash led him to freelancing for *Hardware Age,* where tight little images of doorknobs and hammers brought $4 a drawing. He progressed to children's periodicals and books, and with LaGatta and Beall making money as well, "painlessly" gave up the League. "We were all pretty exuberant and became quite a nuisance, but what an honor to be complained about by Sherry's, Delmonico's, the Harvard Club, and the Yacht Club." Menzies and Ted Beall felt prosperous enough to take a studio apartment on 16th Street opposite New York Hospital where, when they had parties, the windows had to be blanketed so as to not disturb the patients. "Beall and I dabbled in the Village," he said, "but living two blocks north of 14th Street made us semi-uptowners. We knew the Liberal Club, Polly's, the French Bakery, the Black Cat on East Broadway, and all their habitués."

It was about this time that Charles Menzies discovered his son's double life and brought the weekly allowance to an abrupt halt. Concurrently, the jobs on which Menzies had grown to depend dried up, and there was a period of about three weeks when he was compelled to live on a grand total of $8. He managed by sticking to Dow's restaurant in Greenwich Village, which was largely frequented by cabdrivers. "You could get a beef stew, four slices of bread and butter, and a cup of coffee for ten cents," he said, warming at the memory.

In more prosperous times, Menzies and Beall would frequent a German restaurant on 56th Street called Hendricks, which drew its clientele largely from the commercial artists and illustrators who kept studios in the area. It was a great place for picking up freelance work, and it was at Hendricks that the two men made the acquaintance of a Polish artist and designer named Anton Grot, who was working as an art director for the Astra Film Corporation in Jersey City. One day, as America was inching its way toward war, Grot offered Beall a job.

All either man knew about art direction at the time was what Menzies had once observed while studying with Harvey Dunn. Leonia wasn't far from Fort Lee, the center of East Coast film production, and Menzies ran into a chap he knew casually from the League: "He was elated at having a job in the movies for the enormous sum of $35 a week. He read the scenario, noted there was a Louis XVI room, went to the public library, hunted up a good picture of a Louis XVI room, and gave it to the head carpenter, which completed his efforts as art director." Tantalized, Beall

Anton Grot
(AUTHOR'S COLLECTION)

and Menzies made a pact: both would try to enlist, but should only one happen to make it, the other would take the job with Grot. "Beall made the Army," Menzies reported, "and I flunked the Navy with flat feet."

Menzies presented himself at the Solax studio in Fort Lee, where director George Fitzmaurice was making an eight-reel version of the Rudyard Kipling novel *The Naulahka.* In his native France, "Fitz" (as he was called by just about everyone) was a painter, and his subsequent experience as a theatrical set designer enabled him to design his early films entirely by himself. When he hired Grot, late of the Philadelphia-based Lubin organization, he wasn't looking for someone who had come up through the ranks from the construction department, but rather a man who, like himself, had art training and design sense and a flair for the dramatic.

"The first part of the story was laid in India," recalled Arthur Miller, cameraman for the Fitzmaurice unit, "so Anton Grot designed a set representing the interior of a huge Hindu temple, with the foreground thirty feet deep where the action was to take place. The remaining depth of the set was built in what was termed 'forced perspective.' Although the actual depth of the entire set was no more than fifty or sixty feet, it appeared on screen to extend for at least two hundred feet. When Fitzmaurice looked at the test of the set on the screen, he urged Grot to use the same method to build the other sets in the picture. This gave Anton the opportunity to ask for an assistant."

Menzies was twenty but looked a callow fifteen, and Fitzmaurice, when first shown the applicant, fretted he was too young for the job. Still, said Miller, "I did all I could to encourage the idea, not only because I liked Menzies, but also because Anton had been working long hours." Menzies' first contribution to the film was to conjure a tropical setting from the chilly New Jersey landscape for a brief scene between rugged Antonio Moreno and a cabaret dancer named Doraldina. "Palm trees come high in New York," Menzies said, "and as we were working on the well-known shoestring, a real palm was out of the question. One day in the corner of the stage I saw some imitation palm leaf fans. They didn't look much like real palm leaves, but when I got through whittling on them they were a bit better. Then we stuck them up in front of an arc lamp, turned a little wind on them, and there on the ground by Tony and Doraldina were the shadows of palm leaves waving gentle in the tropical breeze. It made a right nice shot, too."

Like most studios of the day, the Solax was built of structural iron and glass, with removable window sashes along the sides to bring direct sun to the floor. The light was controlled with muslin diffusers, which could be rolled back and forth, but the movement of the earth made it impractical for extended periods of filming, and Miller augmented natural illumination with the cold bluish light of Cooper Hewitt mercury vapor tubes. New 80 amp spotlights were revolutionizing cinematography by bringing highlights and shadows to what had been a flat, unmodeled look, and sets with greater depth and character were replacing the crude painted backdrops of just a few years earlier. Though sharp contrasts were difficult to obtain with notoriously slow orthochromatic film stock, stagecraft was rapidly giving way to filmcraft.*

Grot was a meticulous craftsman whose delicate charcoal compositions were carefully executed in terms of both lighting and proportion. He developed his own "diminishing chart," which he used as an overlay in making his drawings, and which gave him the exact proportions an object would diminish at any given distance from the camera when a 40mm lens was used. Grot taught Menzies that a drawing was no good if it couldn't be duplicated in the camera, probably the single most valuable lesson he ever learned.

During the course of production, Menzies designed a harem set using the same technique of cardboard cutouts that had so enhanced the Hindu temple, and he was

---

* Prior to the war, it was French and Italian filmmakers who excelled at production values. Menzies cited *Quo Vadis?* (1912) and *Cabiria* (1913) as specific examples and wondered if the Europeans were more influenced by their paintings than theatrical conventions.

instructed to complete the effect with a nude bather. "I made a date with a model friend of mine and told him to get some girls together for an interview. It was held in his bedroom on 58th and I never will forget the dazed look on the assistant director's face when he saw about six assorted Venuses jammed in a nine-by-twelve bedroom."

Release of *The Naulahka* was delayed some months while Fitzmaurice trimmed nearly three reels of material—almost the entire Western portion of the story—and the company moved on to a Carolyn Wells mystery titled *The Mark of Cain*. Another in a series of Fitzmaurice productions starring Irene Castle, it posed little challenge to Grot and his new assistant, and other than its presence on a handwritten list of early credits, Menzies never mentioned it. Somewhat more memorable was Fitzmaurice's next picture, *Innocent*.

An adaptation of an old Pauline Frederick stage vehicle, *Innocent* was set in China and France, and the resulting design was described as "a marvel" in *Variety:* "[The] sets of scenes in China were works of art and the Parisian atmosphere in Paris was genuine." Despite the enthusiasm it drew, Menzies remembered it chiefly as the film on which he became acquainted with his first genuine movie star, the "perennial juvenile" Fannie Ward, who was forty-five at the time but insistently playing a girl of eighteen.

Menzies, in fact, may not have stayed with *Innocent* through its completion, for not long after the United States entered the war on April 6, 1917, he took another crack at the Navy and, after countless hours of standing on a broom pole, managed to hold his arches up long enough to get in.

# 2

# An Artist of the Modern School

When Mignon Toby first encountered Bill Menzies, it was in the old lunchroom at the Art Students League. Though he had a bad complexion and a girlfriend named Debbie, she thought him "cute." The next time they met was at the 1916 Fakirs Ball, where he was accompanied by a girl wearing nothing more than a coat of blue paint. Again she thought him cute. And this time the feeling was mutual.

Mignon was the daughter of Mr. and Mrs. Edward Toby. He was president of Toby's Practical Business College in Waco, Texas, and Mrs. Nanon Toby was, by her own account, "one of the most successful publicity agents in New York." (She also wrote features for the *New York World* and the *New York Herald*.) When Nan decided her fifteen-year-old daughter had enormous talent, she pulled her out of St. Mary's, a preparatory academy for girls in Garden City, and enrolled her at the Art Students League, where Mignon would spend the next eight years of her life.

Older and taller than Bill, Mignon wore her dark brown hair in a bob. She was not traditionally beautiful, but she had bright brown eyes, a lovely smile, and a light voice that combined her Texas drawl with the beginnings of a New York accent. She was a good dancer who always had men around her and was forever getting her friends dates. One of her partners was Norman Kaiser—later the actor Norman Kerry—whom she had known since he was right tackle on the Hempstead High School football team. Kaiser's friend was a taxi dancer named Rodolfo Guglielmi. One day, Mignon got a call from her mother's boyfriend, a dress extra in the movies, who said they needed some young people for a dance scene and asked if she could round up some friends. She called Kaiser, who asked if he could bring his pal Rudy, and that, according to family lore, was the first time Rudolph Valentino appeared before a movie camera.*

Clearly, Bill Menzies had a case on her, but the courtship didn't go smoothly. He always had to have Ade Scharf, a hard-drinking pal from New Haven, along on dates. That didn't matter much, however, once Mignon discovered that Bill was a "most <u>wonderful</u> dancer." As dancing was a big part of her life, she soon had him working out a routine based on the tune "Too Much Mustard." They auditioned for a spot on the Majestic Roof, and, much to their astonishment, got it. "We were offered the job there," she recalled, "but Mother wouldn't let me do it." By the time Billy—or "Billee" as he tended to spell it—enlisted in the Navy, the two were talking marriage.

Plainly scared of Miggie's stern mother, Menzies put off "the marriage question" as long as possible. Nan begged Edie Smith, her daughter's closest friend, to scuttle the "horrid match," but Edie knew true love when she saw it and let Miggie and Bill use her 23rd Street apartment whenever she and her husband, Walter, went to the movies. Bill shipped out to Guantánamo on July 7, 1917, but the time away made his longing all the more intense. "There isn't any senorita pretty enough to take my mind off you for a minute," he assured her in a letter, "so don't put any worry in on that score." He described his time in Cuba as "fairly active but boring" and began illustrating his letters home with delicate pen-and-ink cartoons of the people of Santiago. "I have been dreaming of you lots down here, sweetheart, and you are always so wonderful after seeing these Cubans."

On March 20, 1918, Bill, still in uniform, wed Mignon at the place where his own parents were married—the Church of the Transfiguration, an Episcopal parish famously known as the Little Church Around the Corner. A hurried five-day honeymoon in Atlantic City followed, with Ade Scharf on hand for breakfast on the very first morning. Then it was off to Pelham Bay, where, on May 18, Menzies accepted office as a provisional Ensign (D) (Deck Duties Only) in the Naval Auxiliary Reserve. Ensign William Charles Menzies of the Merchant Marine was assigned to the collier *Proteus,* which cleared port on July 14. "I was one of the worst Naval officers that ever trod a quarter deck," he later admitted. "I got through Navigation because the instructor had been an extra man and hoped I could help him after the

---

* The film may have been *The Quest of Life* (1916), which featured Maurice Mouvet and his dance partner Florence Walton. Whether it constitutes Valentino's film debut is a matter of conjecture. Valentino biographer Emily Leider suspects he was in Vitagraph's *My Official Wife,* which was made two years earlier. His first confirmed appearance is in the 1916 Famous Players production *Seventeen.*

Mignon Toby, circa 1917, flanked by Bill Menzies and his elder brother, John
(MENZIES FAMILY COLLECTION)

war." His brother, Ensign John C. Menzies, was stationed at the Naval Air Station
in Eastleigh, England. Bill arrived in Glasgow on July 31 and began five months of
gun crew duty, shuttling coal between Queenstown, Brest, Poliac, Bordeaux, and, as
he put it, "all the usual joints."

Discharged on December 20, 1918, Menzies found himself back in New York
with few prospects for work and little money in the bank. Mignon had taken an apartment on West 58th Street, and it was there that they celebrated Christmas. Scouring
the agencies—Sherman & Bryan, H. K. McCain, J. Walter Thompson—he landed
work as an illustrator, but freelance advertising was a tough way to make a living
when clients were famously slow to pay. Mignon, who seemed to know everyone,
introduced him to a director named John Robertson at a holiday party. Then Bill
ran into George Fitzmaurice at the Aker, Merrill and Condit store, and between the
two he was able to get in as a sketch artist at the Famous Players studio, a remodeled
riding academy on 56th Street. "My office," he said, "was an old horse stall covered
with tongue and groove."

Assigned to R. Ellis Wales, an old costume man on his first job as a set designer,
Menzies did most of the heavy lifting on a picture for Robertson called *The Malefac-*

*tor*. He showed a flair for stylish exteriors, rendering a key garden set in the manner of Maxfield Parrish, with a low wall and cypresses beyond a cloud drop and, on one end of the wall, a huge urn with a peacock atop it. "For some reason the property man couldn't get a peacock with a tail," he remembered, "so he wired the tail-less one to the urn and attached a defunct peacock's tail to the end of it." The effect was grand, he said, and might have worked too, if the bird hadn't had more strength than they figured. "Right in the middle of one of [star John] Barrymore's big scenes, the critter jerked loose from the pedestal, jumped straight at John, bumped him to the floor, and, as a souvenir, left its handmade tail wreathed about the famous Barrymore profile."

The picture marked John Barrymore's debut as a dramatic lead after years of playing in comedies. An amateur artist himself, Barrymore was impressed with Menzies' speed and precision, and the two men became friends. When the film was released in April 1919 as *The Test of Honor*, it won Barrymore the following of a true

One of the most elaborate of Menzies' early sets was this Venetian exterior for *A Society Exile* (1919). It took up most of the Famous Players studio on West 56th Street, the former home of Durland's Riding Academy. A foot-deep trough of galvanized iron held the water, while the gondola was moved along the canal on wheels. (ACADEMY OF MOTION PICTURE ARTS AND SCIENCES)

matinee idol and got Menzies raised from $60 to $75 a week. By that point, he had graduated to full status as a "technical" director, designing sets for Famous Players at the rate of two features a month.

Much had changed in the two years since Menzies had served his apprenticeship in Fort Lee. Stirred by the compositions of men like Wilfred Buckland (who aspired "to picturize in a more 'painter-like' manner"), Joseph Urban, and Ben Carré, audiences had come to expect the best movies to be beautiful as well as dramatic. With a man like George Fitzmaurice, Menzies excelled, rising to the demands of a director who had his own keen eye for tone and composition. By the end of 1919, the critic for *Motion Picture Classic,* in his review of *The Witness for the Defense,* would be moved to comment on "the rapidly advancing Fitzmaurice, who attains dozens of singularly beautiful moments and who reveals a surprising knowledge of India."

Production chief Jesse Lasky took note, and Menzies became an advocate of the "artistic" picture—staging a film with an illustrator's values. Giving the director an extra measure of artistry kept him in demand, but the process took more time and imagination than straight photoplay architecture. The challenges of properly photographing an intricate set required the occasional building of models. Then there were the practical matters of blueprints and the overseeing of actual construction, a far cry from the practices of a year or two earlier, when sets were often sketched on the backs of envelopes or on the floors of stages. "In fact," said Menzies, "an early designer of my acquaintance used to design his sets on the palm of his hand if nothing else happened to be handy."

Fourteen-hour days were the norm at Famous Players, and Mignon saw little of her husband, except on Sundays when he could catch up on his sleep. In the spring of 1919, his productivity and resourcefulness led to an offer from Famous Players executive Albert Kaufman to go abroad to design scenery and train an art department for the company's new studio in England. The goal of the venture was to exploit "the personality of British artists, the genius of British authors, the beauty and atmosphere of British settings and scenery" while utilizing the technical knowledge of American artists and craftsmen who had advanced filmmaking techniques while England was at war.

Menzies didn't particularly want to go, but the prestige of the assignment would be good for his résumé, and he stipulated in the agreement that he could not be required to spend more than three months abroad. He negotiated a rate of $100 a week for the duration of the trip and sailed on the SS *Aquitania* on July 16, leaving Mignon, once again, alone in New York. He arrived in London on the 21st, installed himself at the Kenilworth Hotel in Great Russell Street, and proceeded to set up shop at Famous Players' Wardour Street headquarters.

Menzies brought characteristic vigor to the assignment, but was discouraged by an utter lack of anything to do. Kaufman's enthusiasm was premature, considering that even the location for the new facility hadn't yet been settled. "We spent a miserable winter, as England was still on food rations from the war and the only floor space we could find was the interior of an old power house in Shoreditch." Plans were announced to make Marie Corelli's novel *The Sorrows of Satan* as the first of Famous Players' British productions, then that gave way to a play called *The Great Day,* which was presumably selected for the more typically English surroundings it demanded. Yet Kaufman was strangely distant and difficult to see. Menzies took advantage of the lull to visit his grandfather, William Cameron, the greenskeeper at the nine-hole Aberfeldy Golf Club, and his Uncle Alec, who had settled in Northampton.

Though Fitzmaurice wanted him back in New York, Menzies decided the ad game was "really the logical one for me to be in." The picture business was increasingly political and lacked the security of print work. "I suppose there will be more or less of a job at Famous when I get back," he wrote Mignon in early November, "but as far as a contract is concerned, I think I would be better off without one, as they can do anything they want with you when you have a contract and it is a handicap if you have other offers." The new Islington studio was nowhere near being finished when he was sent home—"fired" as he later put it—via the SS *Lapland* on November 27.*

Back at 56th Street, he contributed to Robertson's production of *Dr. Jekyll and Mr. Hyde,* in which Barrymore was playing the dual role, and took over work on an Alice Brady subject called *Sinners.* Watching his salary shrink back to $75 a week wasn't good for his morale, and he was more than receptive when director Raoul Walsh offered to double his rate within a week of his return. A sometime actor who had made his name directing pictures for William Fox, Walsh was going independent with a remake of the Wilson Mizner–Paul Armstrong crime melodrama *The Deep Purple.* He and Armstrong were old friends, Armstrong having been responsible for Albert E. Walsh changing his name to Raoul when the two were a pair of struggling actors. Walsh's wife, actress Miriam Cooper, was set to play the female lead, and Vincent Serrano, a prominent New York stage actor, was to appear opposite her. Funding was coming from the Mayflower Photoplay Corporation, established so directors Allan Dwan and Emile Chautard could make their films in relative autonomy. "Mayflower," said Cooper, "believed that if it had a good director and gave him a free hand, he'd produce good films."

---

* Menzies later learned that when Famous got serious about an English studio, Lasky demanded that he be sent abroad to carry on "the Lasky ideas of settings." In 1924, the studio Kaufman and Menzies established in Poole Street, Hoxton, in the London borough of Hackney, became the home of Gainsborough Pictures.

Menzies joined Mayflower on December 15, 1919, and moved uptown to the Biograph Studios. Freed from the grind of production at Famous Players, he suddenly had the luxury of time to give the old story some gloss and excitement, the film culminating in a flashy cabaret sequence featuring the specialty dancer and Ziegfeld star Bird Millman. *The Deep Purple* took on the look of a major studio production, but Menzies' sets may also have contributed to the static nature of the picture. ("You don't run past a beautiful picture in an art gallery," the reasoning went. "You stop and gaze at it.") The film was unnecessarily episodic—more tableau than driving narrative—and failed to score with either the public or the critics.

Chastened, Walsh gave his wife a choice of material for their second Mayflower production. "It was the last thing Raoul would have chosen," she said. "I had read William J. Locke's *The Idols* and gone completely crazy over it. It was a woman's story, a soap opera if there ever was one. Raoul had it adapted for me and changed the name to *The Oath*." The story of a rich Jewish girl who marries a ne'er-do-well Christian playboy, *The Oath* gave the dark-eyed, white-skinned Cooper one of the meatiest roles of her career. No expense was spared in production or cast. (Actor Conway Tearle was paid $2,500 a week—twice as much as Cooper was getting—to play the supporting lead.) Menzies' lavish settings suggested a world of cold opulence, and Walsh staged the action in stark contrasts of blacks and whites. "There is a fineness of light and shade and real dramatic fire in moments of emotional intensity," said the review in *Variety*. Again, the film flopped miserably at the box office.

In between the Walsh productions, Menzies was lent to other producers. Still, he was carrying just a fraction of his former workload, and finally the time had come to start a family. In the spring of 1920, just as *The Deep Purple* was opening in New York, Mignon discovered she was pregnant. The baby was due in early November—when Bill would be deep in production on *The Oath*—but eleven days late, causing Miggie to spend two anxious weeks at Lenox Hill Hospital "in a lovely large room all to myself" awaiting the birth of their daughter, Jean.

The failure of *The Oath* helped drive Mayflower out of the picture business. Producers were moving to California, where costs were lower and exteriors plentiful. Walsh formed R. A. Walsh Productions, entered into a distribution deal with Associated First National, and decamped to Los Angeles, where he took offices at the Brunton Studios on Melrose Avenue. Menzies briefly considered going back to Famous Players, which had built a spacious new studio on Long Island, but had grown too accustomed to the leisurely pace of Walsh's working methods. He followed, unhappy at leaving the theaters and art galleries of New York City, but seeing no alternative if he wanted to advance his career in pictures.

"Los Angeles, then as now, was the town of conventions," he wrote in 1945, "and there was a Woodsman or an Elk or a Shrine convention going on, and the only room I could get was in a rat-race hotel on Main Street. About the second or third day in Los Angeles, I went out to the old Lasky Ranch to pick a location. Very few roads were paved, and I wore a dark Oxford gray overcoat, a blue serge suit with a starched collar, black shoes, and a bowler. (The New York uniform of the day.) In no time, I was from head to foot the color of adobe before they whitewash it." When Mignon and Jean arrived in Hollywood on April 26, 1921, he was hard at work on a story of romance and revenge in old Spain titled *Serenade.* It was a family affair for Walsh and his wife, with Miriam appearing opposite Raoul's brother George and her brother Gordon serving as assistant director.

Having never been west of Fort Lee, Menzies stuck to his usual routine of referring to books on the architecture of foreign locales, cheerfully exaggerating the characteristics of native design in service of the drama.* For *Serenade,* he could also draw inspiration from the Spanish architecture that dominated the city. Production commenced with key scenes being shot at Mission San Fernando. Cooper loathed working with her Irish brother-in-law, who was sporting an improbable black wig for his role as a Latin lover. "I always dreaded a scene with George," she said. "He was such a lousy actor. He was like a stick." *Serenade* had the production values of Walsh's previous independents and—despite George Walsh's wooden performance—received generally good reviews. It was, in Cooper's words, "most profitable."

Emboldened, Walsh bought the rights to a best-selling Peter B. Kyne novel called *Kindred of the Dust.* An action-packed tale of lumbermen in the Pacific Northwest, it was new stuff to the creative team, with a couple of elaborate fight scenes and an underwater effect leading up to the finale. With too much time on his hands, Menzies may have been guilty of overdesigning the picture. Though the book had been distilled to its essentials, an early review complained that Walsh "tried to encompass too many of the interesting details" and that got in the way of the story. "The director has carried to great lengths the practice of allegorically visualizing the poetically descriptive subtitles."

*Kindred of the Dust* was previewed in January 1922, but by then it was apparent that Walsh would be making no more pictures as an independent. "Raoul was no businessman," Miriam Cooper explained. "He was a capable, hard-working director with a gambling streak who wanted to be a big wheel in the industry, and that was

---

* As Anton Grot once said, "I aim for simplicity and beauty and you can achieve that only by creating an impression . . . the set must be so designed as to blend with the spirit and the action of the picture."

Locked in a secret marriage with a man of a different faith, Minna Hart is beset
by trials that culminate in the murder of her father. The brittle symmetry of
this bedroom interior is violated by the forlorn figure of actress Miriam Cooper.
The last of Raoul Walsh's Mayflower productions, *The Oath* (1921) was spread
over three New York area studios, including the Solax in Fort Lee where Menzies got his start. (ACADEMY OF MOTION PICTURE ARTS AND SCIENCES)

all. As an independent producer he'd been lucky in good times, but in bad times
he, like most others, was squeezed out of business by the high moguls with their
big companies and theater chains. R. A. Walsh Productions had no capital to make
new pictures—we'd spent it—and no chain of theaters to show them in if we made
them. Our distributor, First National, was in trouble, too. And so our company just
died."

Walsh eventually returned to the security of Fox, and Menzies was left—with a
wife and a year-old daughter—to fend for himself in Los Angeles.

·   ·   ·

Bill Menzies expected to land work with another independent when Raoul Walsh closed shop, but he was largely unknown in Los Angeles and his two principal patrons, George Fitzmaurice and John Robertson, were still based in New York. Having given up on the agencies when asked to illustrate an ad for a catarrh remedy ("Do you hack and spit?" the headline inquired), he telegraphed Walsh for help. Headed east on the California Limited with *Kindred of the Dust,* Walsh complied with a letter of introduction to his friend Douglas Fairbanks: "This will introduce Mr. W. C. Menzies, my art director for the past two years. Our association has been at all times pleasant and artistically successful. He is an artist of the modern school and thoroughly understands the technical requirements of motion pictures. I can recommend him most heartily."

The letter got Menzies in at the new Pickford-Fairbanks Studio, where its male proprietor was preparing an elaborate take on the Robin Hood legend. Fairbanks had made a name for himself in lighthearted comedies, but was now sustaining his position as a top draw with a series of increasingly costly costume adventures. Showcasing his enormous charm, effortless athletic prowess, and outsized sense of humor, *Robin Hood* was to outdo *The Mark of Zorro* and *The Three Musketeers* in size and spectacle. Accordingly, the art department had been built up to include Edward Langley, Irvin J. Martin, and Anton Grot under the supervision of Wilfred Buck-land. This extraordinary team created some of the largest sets ever built for a motion picture. Exactly what Menzies did on the picture is unknown, but he was most likely put to work as a sketch artist, a considerable comedown after the on-screen credits he had earned with Famous Players and Walsh. In later years he declined to include it on his résumé.

Nevertheless, *Robin Hood* ensured that he was present on the lot when Mary Pickford started work on an equally ambitious costume picture titled *Dorothy Vernon of Haddon Hall.* At the age of thirty, America's Sweetheart had grown tired of playing adolescent girls and hired the great German director Ernst Lubitsch to guide her "farewell to childhood." She expected Lubitsch, with equal gifts for epic and farce, to impart an air of sophistication she had never before displayed on-screen. Lubitsch then went her one better by proposing instead that she play Marguerite in an adaptation of Goethe's *Faust.*

Although no more alienating a subject could be imagined for Pickford's largely female audience, she went along with the idea to the extent of importing Sven Gade, a Danish stage designer whose startling film version of *Hamlet* with actress Asta Nielsen had taken Europe by storm. Gade began work on the sets, but when Pickford's influential mother, Charlotte, discovered that the plot called for her daughter not only to give birth to an illegitimate child, but to strangle the baby in a key

A late display ad designed by Menzies for the Los Angeles furrier Willard George, a pioneer in the importation of chinchilla pelts. Under the slogan "We search the earth for furs of worth," George became a leading supplier to the movie industry. (MENZIES FAMILY COLLECTION)

scene, the star of *Poor Little Rich Girl* and *Pollyanna* was compelled to drop the idea. Menzies was quietly put back to work on *Dorothy Vernon* so as to make the switch a virtual fait accompli upon Lubitsch's arrival.

Lubitsch, accompanied by his wife and an associate, landed in Los Angeles in December 1922. Pickford sprung the change on him and, predictably, he loathed the idea. After reading the script, a romance set in England in the days of Great Elizabeth and Mary Queen of Scots, he hated it even more. "Der iss too many qveens and not enough qveens," he complained, wondering how Pickford's modest character could make any impression amid the size and grandeur of the thing. He announced that he would not direct *Dorothy Vernon* under any circumstances, but Pickford, rather than giving him a release, proposed a compromise: Edward Knoblock's adaptation of a French play called *Don César de Bazan,* retitled *The Street Singer.* From his earliest days with Fitzmaurice, Menzies had excelled at exteriors. His rooms were straightforward examples of set design—competent, workmanlike—but he was constrained by the conventions of three walls and contemporary decor. It was the play of light and dark and the shifting of the elements that inspired him, and Gade, who got all the attention and most of the credit, was content to leave him to the details of Toledo and Seville in the days of the carnival.* With more money at his disposal than ever before, the Spain Menzies distilled from books and clippings was larger, brighter, more imposing than the real thing, a world that sometimes dwarfed its star, whose director seemed more interested in the romantic plottings of the king than the affairs of a tax-protesting street singer. Nevertheless, Menzies proved equal to the scale Pickford demanded, and the sets, by the account of *The New York Times,* elicited "murmurs of admiration" at the film's premiere. Indeed, Menzies found enough satisfaction in the experience to claim *Rosita* (as the film came to be known) as one of his credits. He particularly relished the experience of working with Lubitsch, who, he later said approvingly, "told his farce with the camera" rather than with titles.

Around this time, Menzies adopted the middle name of Cameron, which he thought would look better on the screen. In the four years since his return from the war, he had contributed to some twenty-five movies, creating settings that ranged from the canals of Venice and the casinos of Paris to British India, the Old South, and Victorian London. His mastery of craft was beyond question, but artistically he was unsatisfied, confined as he was to producing backgrounds for actors, where the

---

* Both Pickford and Fairbanks insisted on authentic costumes and settings for their pictures, but Menzies learned there was such a thing as too much authenticity when he included the campanile of Toledo in one of his early sketches. "Madison Square Garden in New York [had] copied this campanile, and so many people recognized it and asked what Madison Square Garden was doing in the picture that I had to change it."

The town of Seville under construction on the backlot of the Pickford-Fairbanks Studio for *Rosita* (1923)

The completed set with the weight of the centuries upon it. A miniature conceals a nearby stage and continues the illusion of distance to the famed bell tower of the Seville Cathedral. Although Sven Gade posed for stills showing the model of this set to Mary Pickford and Ernst Lubitsch, Menzies placed these photos in his personal album and was presumably the actual designer. (MENZIES FAMILY COLLECTION)

drama was served mainly by pantomime, and mood was more a function of lighting than design. The best experiences came with men like Lubitsch and Fitzmaurice, who understood the physical values of a scene and invested their films with texture and nuance as well as histrionics. He longed for the opportunity to make an American picture filmed with European values, in which graphic design was integral to the storytelling process.

Miraculously, he was about to get that chance.

# 3

# The Thief of Bagdad

The films of Douglas Fairbanks were not so much written as assembled—acrobatic set pieces strung together with the barest shadings of plot, all in service of the trademark Fairbanks personality. They were energetic, high-concept period pieces, for their time the most expensive star vehicles ever made. Fairbanks scrimped on nothing, knowing that size and splendor had become part of the franchise. He was planning to follow the pageantry of *Robin Hood* with an elaborate pirate picture, a significant jump-up in scale if not imagination, and preparations for one were very nearly complete when he strode into a staff meeting one day and said, "Let's do an Arabian Nights story instead."

Having grown a special head of hair for the pirate role, Fairbanks had gone sour on the plot. Exactly what got him excited about the Arabian Nights is a mystery, but he was known to have purchased the American rights to Fritz Lang's *Der müde Tod* (*The Weary Death*, aka *Destiny*), and it may well have been that film's Bagdad sequence, with its brief story of an infidel who loves a caliph's sister, that inspired him. He had, in fact, been tinkering with such a story when director Allan Dwan first sold him on the idea of *Robin Hood*.

Typically, Fairbanks immersed himself in research before going forth on an idea, first sketching the rough elements of plot on the back of an old envelope, then talking it over with a small circle of advisors that included playwright Edward Knoblock, scenario editor Lotta Woods, and his brother Robert. Distilling their input as well as his own thoughts, Fairbanks then hired a writer to draft a treatment—no more than a few thousand words in length—that would form the nucleus of a script. The patchwork nature of the process led to the common writing credit of Elton Thomas—meaning Fairbanks and the collective members of his production staff.

Fairbanks had gotten as far as an outline on his Arabian Nights story (which bore some resemblance to Knoblock's 1911 play *Kismet*) when he began looking for a gimmick, something to propel his character and, therefore, the action. He found it in a quatrain from Sir Richard Francis Burton's literal translation of the *Arabian Nights:*

> *Seek not thy happiness to steal*
> *'Tis work alone that will win thee weal.*
> *Who seeketh bliss sans toil or strife*
> *The impossible seeketh and wasteth life.*

Fairbanks condensed this to the story's simple four-word moral: *Happiness Must Be Earned.*

As work on *Rosita* wound down, it was impossible to ignore the swirl of activity generated by Fairbanks' new, as yet untitled, picture. "He was dickering with a lot of high-powered illustrators and painters," Menzies recalled. Pickford's costume designer, Mitchell Leisen, urged Fairbanks to let Bill Menzies do for Bagdad what he had done so adroitly for Seville, but Fairbanks, who had referred Menzies to Wilfred Buckland on the strength of Raoul Walsh's letter and then forgotten all about him, spent just enough time with him to conclude, as Fitzmaurice had five years earlier, that Menzies was, at the age of twenty-seven, too young for the job.*

Leisen and Knoblock talked Menzies into making some sample drawings to show Fairbanks, and he immersed himself in the project over a long sleepless weekend. "He worked and worked on those paintings day and night," Mignon recalled, "then he asked for another appointment. He went over carrying all those drawings on his head because they were heavy, and he walked into Douglas Fairbanks' office with these boards balanced on his head and said he'd come to show him that he wasn't too young."

What Fairbanks saw bore little resemblance to what most art directors produced at the time. Instead of presenting empty rooms of charcoal or crayon, Menzies had approached the subject as if he were illustrating a storybook, rendering Bagdad in ink and vibrant watercolors and placing Fairbanks' muscular character in the center of each scene. Moreover, the boards were huge—20 x 30 inches—and finished to the

---

* Buckland, by comparison, was fifty-seven at the time and Sven Gade forty-six.

edges. Standing before them, it was easy to be engulfed by the images, their depth and imagination, and hard not to be transported to a fantasy world like no other. Fairbanks, said Leisen, "flipped over them."

Fairbanks had likely seen Edmund Dulac's Art Nouveau illustrations for Laurence Housman's retelling of *Stories from the Arabian Nights,* a 1907 edition that included the tales of the magic horse and the princess of Deryabar. Never, however, had he seen such imagery blown up to such a commanding size. Menzies, too, had likely seen and been influenced by Dulac's intricate drawings, but while Dulac's color renderings conveyed character and an extraordinary sense of detail, they lacked the dark tones and fluidity of movement that came so easily to Menzies' best work. Here were not just scenes from a book, but cinematic ideas conceived and intended for the relatively new medium of the motion picture.

With Menzies' visualizations as inspiration, the writing of the script accelerated. By April of 1923, when *Rosita* was still in production, Fairbanks could describe the film to a reporter in considerable detail: "I am going to make the story of the thief of Bagdad, who loves the Caliph's daughter and then finds that the thing he wants most in all the world is the thing he cannot steal or gain by chicanery. . . . It will, I think, have a wider appeal than anything I have ever done. For the children, there will be seeming magic; for the artist, beauty; for those who seek merely entertainment there will be a swift-moving plot with mystery and suspense."

Bolting from the room, Fairbanks returned momentarily with Knoblock, who was at work on the scenario in an adjacent office. Between them, they carried a portfolio of Menzies' images. "Look at these," Fairbanks enthused, arranging the boards along an office wall. What the reporter saw were "large scenic drawings of startling beauty and originality. One showed the gateway to Bagdad, another a street scene. There was a drawing for a set at the bottom of the sea, another for the bedroom of the Caliph's daughter, showing the thief crossing a long bridge which leads into the moon-flooded chamber. . . . If the plans of the artist and of the star are carried out with fidelity, the remarkable settings of *Robin Hood* will be entirely eclipsed and a new standard for beauty of lighting effects will be set."

Fairbanks went on to describe such visual effects as a winged steed and a magic carpet, both appropriated from Lang. "Three princes will be contenders for the hand of the Caliph's daughter, but this daughter will love the thief. The Caliph will promise his daughter to the suitor who brings the most priceless gift. . . . There will be ten or twelve reels to this film, and every one will be packed full of fancy, glamour, beauty, and a novel plot. The time and location—Bagdad at the height of the glory of the Caliphate—will give an unexampled opportunity for splendor of costumings and backgrounds."

Driven by the seemingly endless stream of visualizations from Menzies' fertile imagination, Knoblock delivered a scenario as thick as the Manhattan directory. Fairbanks seemed to sense they didn't have fourteen reels of script so much as fourteen reels of art direction. "If we don't find a way to defeat that thing," he said, pointing to the massive document as if it were a bomb set to go off, "it will defeat us by its sheer magnitude." He ordered the picture charted from start to finish, detailing the sets and their corresponding action on a scene-by-scene basis, then had the results blueprinted and posted on the walls of his office, which began to take on the look of a war room. Work on the great city of Bagdad would take the longest and would have to start first.

Fairbanks put Menzies in charge of the art direction for *Thief of Bagdad,* but kept him under the watchful eye of Mitchell Leisen, who was a bit younger than Menzies but knew how the boss liked to work. "I designed the costumes in keeping with Bill's sets," Leisen recalled, "and sort of supervised Bill. All of his drawings went over my desk for approval, and I looked on at the construction of the sets. The art director, the set dresser, the costume designer—we all worked together as closely as possible."

As art director, Menzies was charged with overseeing a team of eight associates that included Harold Grieve, Park French, and his old mentor, Anton Grot. Scores of pen-and-ink drawings were made to augment the big color boards, and Fairbanks soon had most of the film in sketch form posted alongside his wall charts. Then detailed models were made of the key sets from which templates could be cut and "scaled up" to the actual size of the set. Pre-visualizing the film became something of an obsession for Fairbanks, and as sets were being erected and test shots made, he was known to shut down arguments by simply bellowing, "To Hell with your perspective—photograph 'em just like the sketches!"

"We worked night and day," Knoblock wrote.

As the sets began to rise up they caused so much comment and admiration throughout Hollywood that visitors from all the other studios kept dropping in to gaze at them in astonishment. The workmen themselves became so keen on their job that when they were taking down the scaffolding of one of the vast buildings, and a new shift of men arrived to take over, the first batch were determined on completing the task so as to be "the first to have a look." The second batch of men insisted on their right to work. The two almost came to blows and finally reached agreement by finishing off the job together. There's enthusiasm for you if you like—the right sort of stuff with which to produce a successful picture!

The sprawling Bagdad set under construction in Los Angeles. For a sense of scale, note the worker at the base of the stairway. (ACADEMY OF MOTION PICTURE ARTS AND SCIENCES)

As the city of Bagdad was taking shape atop some four acres of concrete slab, Fairbanks lamented the ghost gray minarets and keyhole archways and spider balconies. "Those things are anchored to earth," he said. "There's nothing ephemeral about them and we've got to find a way to lift them up." Menzies' solution was to scrap the intricate painting of stonework he originally planned for the foundation, and to instead have the concrete covered with black enamel buffed to a high gloss. Magically, the structure acquired a weightlessness that at last suggested the whimsy of the original paintings. And in the new test shots, the elevations pierced the heavens.

Fairbanks indulged Menzies' zeal for towering interiors by constructing a special stage to contain the boudoir of the Princess, a set that required sixty feet to clear the grid. "The only times we used that stage again," said Menzies, "was when we played badminton." Fairbanks' insistence on absolute fidelity to the drawings led to a genuine pen-and-ink effect on film. The physical structures were all black and white and silver with an occasional accent of gold, and the shadows they cast were

The chamber of the Princess incorporates a sweeping staircase that leads to her domed and canopied bed. The splendor of the room makes it the ideal starting point for a great adventure. (AUTHOR'S COLLECTION)

as key as the spaces they created. Menzies had the insides of the arches blackened to force the perspective; even trees were painted black.

"Here we just played with shadows," Menzies told a visitor as they strolled the latticed bazaars of Shiraz, where the Persian Prince in the story comes in search of treasure. "You can see what the result might have been. . . . Walk through that set. You get a thousand penciled designs, different at every turn. It beats costume. See what we did to those posts? That gives the pen-and-ink effect we strove for. It will photograph like a drawing."

With construction well under way, Fairbanks made the decision to hire Raoul Walsh to direct the film. Under contract to Fox, Walsh was somewhat mystified by the offer, having specialized for so much of his career in "cowboys and gangsters and pimps and prostitutes." It was apparently his early handling of Tom Mix that got Fairbanks' attention, along with the devoted salesmanship of Walsh's agent, Harry Wurtzel. Still, when Walsh went to discuss the project with Fairbanks, he began by saying, "I'm not sure about this, Doug." Fairbanks cautioned him to hold his reservations. "He took me out back and I caught my breath when I saw the sets. . . . [Bill's] artistry was great enough to convince me that I was walking the streets of old Bagdad."

Walsh signed on and embarked with Fairbanks on a daily training regimen that included a brisk half mile jog around the sets rising on the backlot. "When he

For the bazaars of Shiraz, Menzies covered the walkways with latticework. In striving for shadow effects, he proposed to show the top of the set as well as the floor line. (MENZIES FAMILY COLLECTION)

brought the script home," recalled Miriam Cooper, "I couldn't believe the size of it. It was enormous. Everything was worked out to the last detail. 'I guess you won't be writing what you're going to do tomorrow on the back of some scrap of paper,' I said. 'Hell, no,' Raoul said. 'These guys put charts up on the wall telling you what to do each day.'"

The filming of *The Thief of Bagdad* stretched on for months, a constant flow of visitors and masses of extras delivered by the adjacent Pacific Electric line. "The daily audience appeared to put more snap into Doug's performance," Walsh observed, "and he kept his brother Robert, the production manager, busy herding newcomers onto the set to gasp and applaud."

Production was slowed by Fairbanks' dogged insistence that every shot be as identical to its corresponding sketch as humanly possible. As Leo Kuter, who worked in the art department, remembered,

Models of all principal sets for *The Thief of Bagdad* (1924) were built so that Douglas Fairbanks could confirm their fidelity to the artwork. Here he examines the
Cavern of the Enchanted Forest through a special viewfinder that shows what the
camera will see. Menzies, meanwhile, points out the details. (MENZIES FAMILY
COLLECTION)

We used to trace them on glass with wax pencil—set up the glass on the
stage or back lot between the set and the finder on a securely anchored
camera tripod—just so Doug could take a look and satisfy himself that
Menzies' artistry on paper had taken shape in the actual construction of the
set. The sketches, in fact, were photographed and copies distributed to the
cameraman, electrician, and all others concerned to make sure that no facet
of light, mood, or decorative treatment shown in the sketch should escape
reproduction on the screen. Woe be unto the hapless soul who undertook
to shift that well-anchored tripod the least fraction of an inch after Doug
gave his approval.

Design influenced every aspect of the film—acting, writing, direction, cinematography. Leisen's costumes, all flourish and ornamentation, read perfectly against
the clean lines and towering simplicity of the Bagdad sets. Fairbanks himself, clad in

With its undulating features and irregular surfaces, the Bagdad set seemed as if
caught in motion. It challenged Fairbanks and his cast to rise to the standard set
by the film's fanciful architecture. (AUTHOR'S COLLECTION)

the billowing trousers and slippers of the Thief, was, at a trim 150 pounds, so ideal a
physical specimen that he immediately became part of Menzies' fantasy world. The
sets were sized to facilitate his spectacular stunts, with distances carefully calculated
so that any reach or leap by the star would appear effortless on camera. It was as if a
man had wished himself Alice-like into the pages of a storybook, jumping from one

illustration to the next, conquering all obstacles and slaying adversaries as if borne on a cloud, destined for immortality.

To a journalist visiting the set, Menzies paused at a jumble of walls to emphasize how integral the surroundings were to the action. "Fairbanks, in his character of the Thief, smells food cooking up there," he said, pointing to an esplanade.

He sees a fat man asleep in that corner. Steals his turban. Ties one end to the tail of a passing donkey and throws the other end over the balcony rail. Then he boots the donkey, which runs away, pulling Doug aloft to a footing on the balcony.

The Thief steals the food and leaps to the next balcony. He is pursued by the angry housewife. Meanwhile, a fakir below is performing the rope trick. He has thrown the rope into the air, where it remains rigid, without any support, to the astonishment of the crowd. The end of the rope sticking up there is within reach of Doug's hand. As the housewife makes for him, he seizes it. Just then, the muezzin calls to prayer from that minaret. Everything stops and the devout Moslems in the street below prostrate themselves. Down comes poor Doug with a thud in the middle of them.

Menzies paused a moment to marvel at all he had been allowed to do. "I don't suppose I'll ever get a chance like this again."

Fortunately, Raoul Walsh understood how the actors could play off the sets. He populated the palace courtyard with hundreds of Mexican extras clothed to look like Arabs, and embellished the action so the film wouldn't turn into a static showcase of visual splendor. "The rival princes got more than the script called for," he admitted. "Toward the end, I had them running all over the palace searching for the impostor and demanding his head on a platter." Not all of the re-creations were entirely successful, given the flat presentational style that naturally resulted from such fidelity to the illustrations. Menzies' moody visualization of the Cavern of the Enchanted Forest ("a sort of steal from Doré") resisted all efforts to replicate the depth and mystery of the original, and no amount of articulation could keep a giant bat from looking exactly like the plush animal it was. But when the Old Man of the Midnight Sea sends the Thief underwater in search of an ironbound box containing the key to the Abode of the Winged Horse, the ingenuity of a mechanical engineer helped create the superbly effective illusion that resulted on-screen.

"We took a set and cut seaweeds out of buckram and had a series of them hanging down in several places," Menzies explained. "A wind machine was put on so that the seaweeds flapped, but as the scene was taken in slow motion, they undulated when shown on the screen. The camera had a marine disk over the lens and was turned over. Mr. Fairbanks was let down into the scene and went through the motions of swimming underwater. The scene had the appearance of water and gave almost a water feeling. It was a very interesting effect."

Overcast weather impeded filming of the exteriors, and after some seventy days of shooting, the love scenes, the Oriental feast and festival, the spectacle of the Chinese prince's army capturing the city, and the Thief's triumphant return to Bagdad were all still to be done. The most challenging of the remaining effects was the Thief's climactic escape aboard a flying carpet. Merely putting the carpet and its passengers in front of a rolling background wouldn't do for a film that had already exhibited unprecedented scope and sophistication. The answer finally came to Walsh while observing a construction job at Hollywood and Highland: "The steelworkers were topping out, and one of them was riding a load of girders up from the ground level hoisted by a large crane. That gave me the clue. If he could ride the steel, then the thief and the princess could ride the flying carpet."

A carpet with a solid steel frame and cross-strapping was fabricated and connected to wires threaded through an overhead pulley and attached to a hand winch installed out of camera range. On cue, the carpet—on which Fairbanks and Julanne Johnston (the Princess) were seated—was levitated and then yanked toward an open window. "Once the suggestion of impending flight had been thus imparted, the rest was easy enough," Walsh said.

Easy, perhaps, but dangerous as well. "Go to it, Irish," Fairbanks told his director, "but if you drop us on a minaret, I'll come back and haunt you." Menzies devised much of the ensuing action:

> We got a ninety-foot Llewellyn Crane and had the carpet suspended on six wires. There was Doug hanging on six wires he couldn't see. They were each guaranteed to hold 400 pounds, but he said, "I would like something more than a guarantee in a place like this." When the beam was started, the carpet would be left behind a little until the slack was taken up, and it gave us quite a thrill each time it was started. We also had to arrange for a traveling camera (which, by the way, is another thing the art director is involved in), and had a platform built for the cameraman which traveled with the crane. That was the first traveling shot.

When the magic carpet shots were made, Walsh established a local record by populating Menzies' Great Square with 3,348 men, women, and children for a single day. The costumed extras started work on the first of eleven scenes featuring Fairbanks and Johnston at seven o'clock in the morning. Cigarettes and lunch were furnished by the studio, and six cameras covered the action, which continued until the light was lost at four in the afternoon.

Photography on *The Thief of Bagdad* wasn't completed until January 1924, leaving scarcely two months to get the picture assembled, titled, tinted, and scored for its New York premiere. To underscore the magnitude of the event, Fairbanks worked a percentage deal with impresarios Morris Gest and F. Ray Comstock to present the picture at Broadway's Liberty Theatre, where *The Birth of a Nation* had been housed for a historic forty-four-week run. Shown twice daily at a $2.20 top, *Thief* stood to generate an estimated $3,000 a week for Comstock & Gest, who filled the lobby with Hindoo singers and musicians, burned incense throughout the building, and adorned an adjacent billboard with an image of the Thief and his princess soaring high above Bagdad on their magic carpet. On the night of March 18, 1924, a flying wedge of the city's finest cleared the way through a crush of fans for Fairbanks and his wife, and the ovation at the film's conclusion—nearly 11:30—was thunderous. Fairbanks appeared onstage to take a bow, then brought Raoul Walsh up to join him. "Poetry in motion," said Mary Pickford admiringly. "It cost a million, seven-hundred thousand."

Fairbanks, Walsh, and cutter William Nolan had worked long hours to pare the film to fourteen reels for its first public showing. Although the notices were uniformly good—the *Times* called it "a feat of motion picture art which has never been equaled"—*The Thief of Bagdad* undeniably dragged in spots, and the men permitted themselves another four months of thoughtful tightening before the Los Angeles premiere on July 10. Word of the new miracle picture quickly reached the West Coast. The anticipation was palpable—Ernst Lubitsch made a point of seeing the sets before they were pulled down—but Fairbanks tinkered and fretted and refused to show it privately.

Menzies saw Fairbanks' twelve-reel cut for the first time on the night of its Los Angeles opening. Hosting the premiere was Sid Grauman, Doug's pal from San Francisco, whose new Hollywood Boulevard showplace, the Egyptian, would outdo the comparatively tame spectacle of the Liberty. Unlike any of the first-run New York houses, the Egyptian had the real estate to carry its architectural theme to the street with a forecourt promenade flanked by a bazaar of unusual shops. A carnival of street vendors and buskers drew attendees into the world of the Thief, while a Bedouin on the parapet performed the seemingly unnecessary task of calling out the film's title.

Inside, the stage was a riot of hieroglyphics, terminating in a shimmering sunburst over the proscenium arch. Fleurs De Bagdad, a fragrance approximating the scent of a dry martini, perfumed the air as veiled usherettes led the guests to their seats. Members of the orchestra appeared in turbans and robes, and just after eight o'clock actor Milton Sills took the stage to convey the greetings of Douglas Fairbanks, who, he explained, was traveling in France. He went on to introduce the cast members, the key technical crew, and finally Menzies himself, who drew a warm and knowing round of applause from the crowd. Then the curtains parted to reveal a stage crowded with archways, minarets, and hanging rugs as the evening got under way with a lengthy prologue called "The City of Dreams."

It was almost ten o'clock before the movie started, and Grauman had done such an elaborate job of packaging that most films would have seemed lacking by comparison. But Menzies' opening tableau, posed in silhouette against a silvery moonlit desert, in which an old man imparts the story's theme to the young boy at his feet, enveloped the crowd and in moments they were hooked. By the start of the second reel, the audience had assumed an almost childlike appreciation of the images, conquered, in the words of one spectator, "by the spell of some great undreamed of achievement by some marble-white East Indian temple and ivory palace in far Cathay." At the end of the performance, well past midnight, the weary audience had witnessed an audacious injection of European spectacle into the most American form of commercial filmmaking and cheered accordingly.

*The Thief of Bagdad* played legitimate theaters for the rest of the year, a hard card for matinees because of its obvious appeal to children. ("I saw it when it first came out," Orson Welles, who would have been nine years old, remembered. "I'll never forget it.") It was officially released by United Artists on January 1, 1925, and played widely in progressively shorter versions for the rest of the decade. And whatever else Bill Menzies did in his life, he would always be remembered, first and foremost, as the designer of *The Thief of Bagdad*.

# 4

# The Hooded Falcon

"It looks like a dream, doesn't it?"

Menzies was showing off the bamboo wharf where the Prince of Mongols goes in search of treasure rare enough to win the hand of the Caliph's daughter. The water surrounding the Island of Wak had been tinted the color of black ink, its latticework and colonnades a riot of interlacing colors, tile roofs set awry, streets shooting skyward. "No," he lamented. "I don't suppose I'll ever get a chance like this again. But I'm going to do the sets for a picture by Schenck and I'm going to try to get away with a goofy tenement. Perhaps I can."

He had come to regard what he did as "staging" a movie. More than straight architecture, it was a way of prepping a film for the director and the actors, setting the scene for the story to come by enhancing the tone and texture of its individual parts. Neorealism wasn't in Hollywood's vocabulary, certainly not in Menzies'. What he was seeking instead was a kind of graphic truth, layered and nourishing and equal to the formidable capacities of the screen. "Oh, this is the realm of the pictures, isn't it? This is the thing they can do—if they'd only see it. Realism is so unnecessary when we have at our disposal all the resources of the camera to produce effects that can only be rivaled by dreams."

He had been kept on the payroll over the long months it took to commit *The Thief of Bagdad* to film, even as he found himself with little to do in the waning days of production. *Dorothy Vernon of Haddon Hall* had gone on without him—the sets were designed by Harold Grieve—and all he had in the way of new work were the settings and costumes for Eddie Knoblock's new play, a colorful tragedy of nineteenth-century France called *The Lullaby*. Knoblock would remember pulling an all-nighter with Menzies as they designed approximately sixty costumes. "I had a heap of different samples of materials by my side and pinned the appropriate ones on each design as Menzies drew it with lightning speed. He then made the sketches for the scenery—ten sets of them. I don't know at what hour we finished. But we got the work done. I have never come across a more inventive or facile artist than Bill Menzies."

Fairbanks was generous in sharing credit for *Thief*, and items trumpeting Menzies' contributions began appearing long before the picture was ready for release. The film's souvenir program highlighted its design in a section titled "Translating Fantasy into Pictures." Halfway through its premiere showing the audience was applauding every new set as it came across the screen, and the *New York Sun* described the experience as "a sort of orgy of rapture." In January, George Fitzmaurice wired:

HEAR ALL KINDS OF GREAT STORIES ABOUT YOU THAT WILL
PROBABLY BOOST YOUR SALARY WAY OUT OF REACH, BUT IF
YOU STICK TO EARTH MIGHT TAKE YOU TO VENICE AND PARIS
LEAVING EARLY MAY.

What Fitzmaurice had in mind wasn't clear, and Menzies, by May 1924, was at work instead on a brace of pictures for actress Norma Talmadge and another for her sister, Constance. The Talmadge girls were under contract to Norma's husband, producer Joseph M. Schenck, who based his West Coast operations at United Studios, where he owned a controlling interest. Schenck had lost his staff art director, Stephen Goosson, to First National, causing him to seek a replacement. Menzies accepted all three Talmadge assignments on a freelance basis, dispensing with a picture called *Fight* on a Friday and commencing work on the untitled Constance Talmadge comedy the following Monday. *Her Night of Romance,* as it came to be known, was a farce in the Lubitsch tradition, set in England and pairing the youngest of the three Talmadge girls—Natalie, the middle sister, was married to Buster Keaton—with Ronald Colman as a dipsomaniacal nobleman. The third picture of the group, *The Lady,* proved the most challenging, its last-minute choice of director, Frank Borzage, striving for mood in the settings as well as the camerawork, Norma Talmadge rising to one of the best performances of her career as Polly Pearl, the long-suffering heroine of Martin Brown's popular play.*

---

* Exhibitors that year voted Norma Talmadge the nation's top female star by a wide margin.

Then Menzies was on to grander things, the chance to do another picture of *Thief*-like proportions, this time working with his wife's old friend Rudolph Valentino under the aegis of Valentino's new production company. The move was the work of Valentino's wife, a hard-driving woman of Irish descent named Winifred Shaughnessy. At the age of seventeen, "Wink" (as she was known to her family) reinvented herself as the exotic Natacha Rambova, the turban-wearing consort of Theodore Kosloff, Russian-born ballet star and teacher. Soon, Rambova was distinguishing herself more for her designs than for her dancing, and she landed the job of costuming Cecil B. DeMille's *The Woman God Forgot* when she was scarcely twenty. That assignment led to others for DeMille and, eventually, to a stretch as both set and costume designer for Alla Nazimova. It was ahead of Nazimova's production of *Camille* that Rambova initially encountered Madam's choice for the role of Armand. At first, their association generated more tension than synergy, but it was Rambova who was seen on Valentino's arm at the West Coast premiere of *The Four Horsemen of the Apocalypse,* the film that would effectively make him a star.

They weren't married until 1923, delayed by Valentino's inability to obtain a quick divorce from his first wife, the actress Jean Acker. In the meantime, Rambova increasingly involved herself in Valentino's professional affairs, designing his costumes for *Beyond the Rocks* and progressing to art direction on *The Young Rajah.* The latter film particularly displeased her. "Instead of letting the actor who does fine work go on doing it," she raged, "they give him cheap material, cheap sets, cheap casts, cheap everything. The idea then is to make as much money from that personality as possible with the least outlay." At Rambova's urging, Valentino broke his contract with Famous Players-Lasky and the studio promptly suspended him. To earn a living over the time he was enjoined from acting onstage or in movies, he embarked on a seventeen-week promotional dance tour with Rambova that would cover forty cities at a salary of $7,000 a week.

Peace came nearly a year later, with Valentino obligated to Famous Players for two additional films. He would then be free to join a new enterprise, Ritz-Carlton Pictures, the brainchild of one J. D. Williams, formerly the general manager of Associated First National. Working out his commitment in New York, first in *Monsieur Beaucaire,* then *A Sainted Devil,* Valentino and his wife made elaborate plans for his first independent production. "I was conceited enough," Rambova later wrote, "to imagine that I could force the producers into giving Rudy the kind of production which our artistic ambitions called for—productions such as *Robin Hood, The Thief of Bagdad,* or *The Black Pirate.*" Indeed, it was seeing *Thief* at the Liberty Theatre that convinced her that Menzies was "the cleverest dramatic architect in the business today." On April 18, 1924, S. George Ullman, Valentino's manager, wired Menzies in care of the Fairbanks studio in Los Angeles:

ARE YOU AVAILABLE AND WOULD YOU BE INTERESTED TAKING
CHARGE ART WORK ON RUDOLPH VALENTINOS FIRST INDEPENDENT
PICTURE STOP SPANISH ABOUT FIFTEENTH CENTURY ANSWER SIX
WEST FORTY EIGHT STREET.

Menzies spent the summer in New York, conferring with Ullman and the Valentinos while Rudy's two final pictures for Famous Players were filmed at the company's Long Island studio. Working from an original story called *The Scarlet Power,* Menzies envisioned the Moorish Kingdom of Granada as a sleek reinterpretation of Bagdad, tiled and marbled spaces dominated by pools and fountains, symmetrical where Bagdad was anything but, vast in their area and peopled by the elegantly garbed figures of the Muslim aristocracy. As with *Thief,* his renderings were outsized and colorful, and as with Fairbanks, he portrayed Valentino's figure of a young noble throughout.

A full-page ad in the trades announced him as the "creator" of the sets for Valentino's first Ritz picture, which would eventually become known as *The Hooded Falcon.* "Menzies is the magician who designed the famous sets for the wonder scenes of Fairbanks' *Thief of Bagdad,*" the copy blared. "In our first Valentino-Ritz, the exotic sumptuosity of the most extravagant era of human society gives Menzies the opportunity for the chef d'oeuvre of his entire artistic career. We want the industry to know that this will be Menzies' masterpiece." Casting was already under way, with actress Nita Naldi, who was Valentino's leading lady in *Blood and Sand* and *A Sainted Devil,* set for the part of a Moorish princess. Toward the end of production on *Sainted Devil,* the Valentinos also invited director Joseph Henabery onto the project, giving the former Griffith assistant his first chance to make "a big picture—a costume production."

With both *Beaucaire* and *Sainted Devil* out of the way, the Valentinos left for Europe in high spirits, intent on researching ancient Spain and gathering antiquities that would lend authenticity to Menzies' fanciful designs. A full script was being written by June Mathis, who, as the scenarist of *The Four Horsemen of the Apocalypse, The Conquering Power,* and *Camille,* had played an important role in Valentino's ascension. In August, Menzies had a wire from John Considine, Jr., Joe Schenck's general manager, offering him the new Constance Talmadge comedy. After pausing to consider his options, Menzies left for home on the 15th, grateful, perhaps, for a small job against the difficult business of an upcoming spectacle.

When Schenck assumed responsibility for his sister-in-law's career, the year was 1919 and "Dutch" Talmadge was known as a light comedienne, first for Fine Arts, under which she most notably appeared for D. W. Griffith, later for Selznick's Select Pictures Corporation, where she made as many as eight movies a year. Schenck turned her over to the husband-wife writing team of John Emerson and Anita Loos, who conceived a five-reel version of an old Clyde Fitch comedy called *The Virtuous Vamp.* Astonished at the film's success, Schenck rewarded them with a check for $50,000. "Thus began a series of comedies for Dutch," Loos wrote, "in which her career paralleled Norma's and one success followed another. Our pictures were filmed under the happiest circumstances; because the entertainment empire ruled by the Schenck brothers was centered in New York, we worked there instead of Hollywood. Our productions were a family matter, in which Joe's main interest was to keep his mother-in-law happy."

Their collaboration continued after the Talmadge productions moved west, both actresses settling into a comfortable output of two pictures a year. Over time, Emerson and Loos fell away, and the brown-eyed blonde hit a critical and commercial slump. For all its pretensions, *Her Night of Romance* was a box office flop, and again the Emersons were called to the rescue. The result, *Learning to Love,* would be Dutch Talmadge's last genuine hit, a slender twist on *The Virtuous Vamp,* pitting her flirty Patricia Stanhope (aka Pat the Petter) opposite Antonio Moreno, Johnny Harron, and Wallace MacDonald, among others. There was nothing terribly challenging in what Menzies was required to do for the show, as the work of director Sidney Franklin focused on the boisterous interplay among Pat's various suitors, the closing scenes in Paris lending the picture its only real color.

While the Valentinos were away, Joe Henabery met with Adolph Zukor to give notice. He had been with Famous Players, releasing through Paramount, since 1920, and had at all times considered it a pleasant association. Zukor couldn't understand why he would leave the security of a Famous Players contract for a start-up like Ritz-Carlton. Costume pictures hadn't been doing well at the box office, yet Henabery seemed to relish the challenge. "Let me tell you something," Zukor said finally. "We are putting up the money for J. D. Williams' Ritz-Carlton Pictures, and we will release the Valentino pictures." Henabery was thunderstruck. "You could have knocked me over with a feather," he wrote. "I knew the Valentinos would be furious when they discovered they were still tied up with Paramount."

Williams, it seemed, had turned to the only source of financing open to him. And in doing so, he immediately brought to Ritz-Carlton the same financial constraints that had caused the Valentinos to leave Famous Players. Program pictures were to cost no more than $100,000, while no Valentino epic could cost more than $500,000. Yet the new picture, as visualized by Rambova, Valentino, and Menzies, had been estimated at $850,000 to $1 million. This was, of course, cheaper than

Fairbanks' picture, but then Fairbanks largely financed his own productions, and if he wanted to spend $1.7 million on a movie, there was no one to tell him he couldn't. Moreover, the Valentinos were famously profligate with money, unable to manage their own affairs, much less those of a company. And where George Ullman brought fiscal restraint, he also brought a grinding tension between himself and the headstrong Rambova.

Williams' short-term solution was to find another property for Valentino, one that could be filmed quickly and cheaply. Impulsively, and without the knowledge of the Valentinos, he purchased the screen rights to a modern-dress play titled *Cobra,* which had enjoyed a brief run at the Hudson Theatre with Louis Calhern and Judith Anderson in the leads. The role of Jack Race would be retooled for Valentino, who would play Count Rodrigo Torriani to Nita Naldi's Elsie Van Zile. When Rudy and Natacha docked in New York, Valentino sporting a reddish goatee he had grown for *The Hooded Falcon,* Williams informed them of his duplicity. Not only would *Falcon* have to be made for considerably less than its estimate, but it would have to be made in California.

"The Valentinos," wrote Henabery, "were truly babes in the woods in business, because they signed a contract with a promoter without any knowledge as to how and where he was going to get the required finances. I'm sure that had I known the situation earlier, and what it would lead to, I would not have left Paramount."

Williams was behaving as if the film could still be made, and Ullman wired Menzies on the 13th of November:

```
ARRIVING HOLLYWOOD TWENTIETH VALENTINO TWENTY SECOND
STOP START CHIEF DRAUGHTSMAN ON SALARY TWENTY SECOND
```

On the way out by train, Valentino, Rambova, and Henabery read June Mathis' screenplay, which was admittedly written in haste, as Mathis had committed to a string of Colleen Moore comedies for First National. They all agreed the script wouldn't do, and their early days in Hollywood were complicated by a collective effort to fix it. Menzies, meanwhile, assembled a crack team of illustrators, Paul Youngblood, Park French, and Bill Flannery among them. He followed the same technique he had devised for *Thief,* constructing his set visualizations in miniature so as to attain the same qualities of illustration on-screen as they had on paper. "Much could be said about what we did," he later said, "but the most important of all the things we did was the devising of a scheme whereby the artist's design could be projected, to the smallest detail and shadow effect, into the finished set. . . . It was accomplished by reproducing to scale in every detail a model from the artist's

The art team assembled for *The Hooded Falcon* poses with one of the models made to test the "playability" of a set. *From left to right:* Menzies, Paul Youngblood, Fredric Hope, Bob Lee, Park French, Paul Crawley, and Bill Flannery. In 1937, Fred Hope's untimely death would bring Menzies to Selznick International.

original drawing, and from this model cutting templates which were scaled up to the actual size of the set."

Plans went forth until the year's end forced a shift in priorities. "One particularly tough problem confronted us," recalled Joe Henabery, "because the actors and people under contract would soon have to be paid salaries. If we didn't get started soon on the new picture, a lot of money would go down the drain." Valentino was unhappy—not only at the substitution of another story but at the alienation of the woman who "opened the door of opportunity" for him with *The Four Horsemen of the Apocalypse*—June Mathis. "I cannot tell you how sorry I was not to be able to accept her script," he lamented, "but it just would not do, and we were wasting so much time. So we just had to postpone that production. I shall make this modern picture, *Cobra,* while the script . . . is being rewritten."

Menzies and his crew were sent scrambling, and in short order there was a new set of renderings in charcoal and watercolor, interiors distinguished by the richness of their design, opening up the play in their imaginative use of depth and detail. Urged on by Rambova, who was effectively the film's producer, Menzies created settings that were, in Henabery's opinion, too elaborate for the kind of picture they were making. "Mrs. Valentino had great taste and she was a perfectionist," he said, "and expense didn't seem to worry her. In *Cobra,* we had a nightclub set that was larger than any I had ever seen in real life. It required something like 150 Kleig lights, spotlights, and Cooper Hewitts to illuminate it. Even today, few producers would go for such an expenditure."

Shooting got under way in the ancient palace of the Torriani, as settings for the Café del Mare and the later New York segments of *Cobra* were still under construction. The set for an early flashback was simplified considerably, and the mortar simulating Menzies' flagstone floors never completely dried in the cold seasonal air. Valentino later confessed that he despised every minute he worked on *Cobra.* "He didn't like it," said his friend and employee Luther "Lou" Mahoney, "but said it gave his wife a chance to prove her abilities as a head of film production, and as a person who understood such problems that come up in pictures."

With *Cobra* in the can, Ritz-Carlton returned once more to the matter of its original project. Bored "to tears" with a modern story, Rambova was still absorbed in *The Hooded Falcon* when all other resources had turned to *Cobra.* Joe Henabery wanted Anthony Coldewey to do the rewrite, Coldewey having adapted *Cobra* to the screen. Nita Naldi dropped out of the picture, replaced by actress and former Ziegfeld beauty Sally Long. Henabery, who came down with pleurisy during *Cobra* and had to work with his chest taped, dropped out as well, his place taken by actor-director Alan Hale.

The Valentinos fled to Palm Springs with the completion of *Cobra,* leaving J. D. Williams to prepare it for release. No one seemed satisfied with the film, its awkward mix of light comedy and tragedy unlikely to appeal to any particular demographic. Said Joe Henabery, "The female lead was the best part in the play—a vamp. Neither of the two principal parts could be made attractive to audiences—they were both heels." Menzies kept with *The Hooded Falcon,* and sets were reportedly under construction, but then Williams began cutting back on staff, seemingly unable to bring the budget into line with the resources at hand. Arthur Edeson, who shot *Thief of Bagdad,* was contracted as cinematographer, but never officially started. Long's casting was announced in late February 1925, just days before the picture folded.

"When the Valentinos got word *The Hooded Falcon* was to be called off," Henabery wrote in his memoir, "they rushed home upset by the change in plans. It must have been contractual obligations that forced the Valentinos to accept the situation, although I believe J. D. Williams soft-soaped them that *The Hooded Falcon* was far from ready for production, but that it *would* be made after *Cobra*. I feel sure he was fighting for time to solve his problems and did not tell the Valentinos the full story about Paramount's position and Zukor's objection to the costume pictures."

On March 5, 1925, the *Los Angeles Times* reported that George Ullman was in talks with Joe Schenck, who had recently concluded a six-picture deal to bring Norma Talmadge to United Artists and now proposed to do the same for Valentino. "Although nothing definite has been settled yet, Mr. Schenck and I have just been in conference and negotiations are proceeding favorably," Ullman told the paper. "I think a definite announcement may be forthcoming by the end of this week." The item doubled as an obituary for *The Hooded Falcon,* which faded into obscurity, its only legacy being Falcon Lair, the name given the eight-acre estate the Valentinos had purchased in Beverly Hills. "If for no other reason than to have given the public a glimpse at the remarkably beautiful creations of Bill Menzies," Rambova wrote, "it was a pity that this film was never produced."


Menzies returned to Schenck, where he designed the opulent settings for *Her Sister from Paris,* the new comedy for Constance Talmadge, and the considerably more streamlined backgrounds for sister Norma's basilic romance, *Graustark.* He was, by now, in solid with John Considine, and writer Frank Daugherty could remember Considine earnestly introducing Menzies as a "genius." Wrote Daugherty: "As we chatted, I talked a little of Chaplin's sets, if 'sets' they can be called—naming a launch dock in San Pedro, a cobbled street, cheap frames on a studio backlot—and saying I admired their simplicity more than the gaudy and meaningless monstrosities most of the studios are producing. I was a little surprised to find that he agreed with me and could tell me what I was not aware of myself, why I liked them, for he pointed out how the old-fashioned photography to which Chaplin has given grim allegiance accentuates their values and makes them 'realistic' in the best sense of that term."

On July 20, 1925, after fulfilling an assignment for producer Sam Goldwyn, Menzies signed a one-year agreement with Considine and Joseph M. Schenck Productions. The deal called for a weekly rate of $350, whether or not he was actually working on a picture, and half of anything Considine could get for his services on outside productions. Recognizing the logjam logistics of most any production entity, the rate would jump to $400 a week whenever Menzies was required to work on two pictures simultaneously, $500 when his services were needed on three.

The total value of the deal could be upward of $20,000, bringing Menzies, as he approached his twenty-ninth birthday, an unprecedented level of security in a notoriously insecure industry. Within weeks, he had purchased a plot of land in Beverly Hills for $1,500 and was set to build a house entirely of his own design.

Menzies always said that he followed Valentino to Schenck and United Artists, and in a sense he did. Schenck, now a partner in UA, was in the process of ramping up production, and his deal with Valentino represented a significant expansion of his filmmaking activities, which had, up to then, been limited to the pictures of his wife, his sister-in-law, and his brother-in-law, comedian Buster Keaton. George Ullman handled the negotiations, which, at first, had Natacha Rambova's complete approval. The deal would establish the Rudolph Valentino Production Company, and all monies would flow into it. Valentino would receive $7,500 a week and a percentage of the profits from three pictures per year. The principal sticking point turned out to be Rambova's own obsessive involvement in the production of her husband's pictures. Schenck, and particularly Considine, wanted her out of the way. "When the contracts were ready to sign," wrote Ullman, "the Valentinos returned from Palm Springs, and Natacha then discovered that, in order to obtain this contract, Rudy was obliged to promise that she was to have no voice whatsoever in the making of any pictures which it called for."

Ullman credited Rambova with "a great deal of common sense" in yielding "with considerable grace" to the inevitable, "realizing what it meant to her illustrious husband thus to be taken into the fold of United Artists." Lou Mahoney remembered a much different reaction: "That contract was the breaking point for the Valentinos. It was arranged by Mr. Ullman that Mrs. Valentino would have nothing to do with the pictures that were to be made by the Schenck organization. She was entirely shoved out. She was very much upset with Mr. Valentino for signing that contract."

The Valentinos attended a dinner Schenck gave for United Artists president Hiram Abrams in April, and Rudy's first picture for UA was announced the following month. *The Untamed* was a modernization of an Alexander Pushkin novelette, a vehicle devised for Valentino by Rupert Hughes and scripted by Hans Kraly. The picture, Schenck declared in a statement, was to be made "on an elaborate scale," an assertion supported by the evocative designs issuing forth from Menzies' studio, moody charcoal-and-wash drawings that portrayed the dashing figure of a Tartar bandit in the Czarina's reign, a lieutenant of the Imperial Guard turned a Russian Robin Hood by principle and fate.

A Viennese nightclub for the Constance Talmadge comedy *Her Sister from Paris* (1925). Framing the action through a window or a doorway would become a favorite way of suggesting an elaborate interior with what was essentially a partial set. (AUTHOR'S COLLECTION)

Energized by the Zorro-like character—a riff on Fairbanks' similarly masked creation—and the complementary boldness of Menzies' illustrations, Valentino could not wait to begin filming. "There is so much color, so much fire to the part that I hope to make of my role in *The Untamed* the most interesting and vivid of any kind that I have ever played," he enthused, looking forward to a July start date. "The story deals with a people, and conditions, with which we are almost entirely unfamiliar. Just the mere mention of 'Tartar bandit' is enough to conjure all manner of romantic and wildly exotic visions."

Mercifully, Rambova was also at work on a project, and Menzies found himself allocated to that production as well. In an attempt to ameliorate his wife's sense of betrayal, Valentino reluctantly agreed to underwrite a picture for her. "I had previously had a long talk with Rudy, during which we discussed the matter pro and con, realizing its inadvisability," Ullman remembered. "But Valentino assured me that, in the cause of peace and of rest for himself, he must give in and do as she wished. . . . Before I left, it was decided to allow Natacha to try her hand at an independent picture, which she declared could be produced for approximately $30,000." There was surprise all around that Rambova had written a comedy, since she was, in Ullman's words, "almost totally devoid of a sense of humor." Still, he had to concede that *What Price Beauty* was an excellent job, making "clever fun of the agonies women undergo, the time and money they spend in beauty parlors."

*What Price Beauty* went into production before *The Untamed,* and was "all but completed" by the 24th of June. Menzies, who was admittedly "very fond" of Rambova, indulged her whims while doing his level best to keep the settings within budget. Using draperies and black-lacquered floors and artfully frosted mirrors, he accomplished as much with suggestion as hard scenery, permitting the costumes of twenty-two-year-old Gilbert Adrian to assume an unusual prominence. "We did everything we could to save money," said Lou Mahoney, who was helping Menzies with props. "If we needed a prop, I would grab a truck and run and get the prop and even return it the same day to save some of the rental fee. It was just impossible to make the film properly for less than what was spent."

Kyrilla's fortresslike estate in a remote Russian province, where much of the action in *The Eagle* (1925) takes place. As with *Cobra,* Menzies designed sets that were substantial to the point of excess. (MENZIES FAMILY COLLECTION)

Whatever budget that remained went toward a futuristic dream sequence depicting various types of womanhood. "Natacha dubbed me 'the intellectual type of vampire without race or creed or country,'" remembered actress Myrna Loy, who made her debut in the film. "Adrian designed an extraordinary red velvet pajama outfit for me, with a short blond wig that came to little points on my forehead, very very snaky." Rambova intended *What Price Beauty* to show that she could make a commercial picture "at a very small cost" as well as an "artistic" success. When the movie wrapped, however, its cost, according to Ullman, had climbed to nearly $100,000.

*What Price Beauty* was as ethereal and "bizarre" (as Myrna Loy judged it) as *The Untamed*, retitled *The Black Eagle, The Lone Eagle,* and, finally, just *The Eagle,* was solid and earthbound. But where *Cobra,* under Rambova's supervision, was overdesigned, given its featherweight story line, *The Eagle* carried the weight and flair of a Fairbanks picture, a franchise to which Valentino clearly aspired. Filming began on July 19, 1925, the tension with Rambova and the cost overruns on her picture having had a telling effect on its star's well-being, presaging his untimely death from a perforated ulcer. "I remember he had something very wrong with his stomach," director Clarence Brown said. "His breath could knock you over and he was mortified by it, but there was nothing he could do."

*The Eagle* was at once both ornate and chilly from the deliberate lack of color in Menzies' elegant renderings. Appropriately, it was the picture in production when the Valentinos announced a "marital vacation." Rambova left Hollywood for New York and Paris prior to its completion. She and Valentino, as it turned out, would never see each other again.

# 5

# Maturing Period

Joseph Schenck's 1925 move to United Artists was intended, in part, to cover the loss of UA founding partner D. W. Griffith, who had left the company the previous year. Apart from the absence of Griffith's own pictures, there was a general shortage of product that threatened UA's very existence. Neither Douglas Fairbanks nor Mary Pickford could deliver more than one feature a year, and Charlie Chaplin's output had become even less frequent. In the press, it was pointed out that UA, without Griffith, would probably produce no more than three or four pictures a year—not enough to justify a network of exchanges. Even with Schenck, Norma Talmadge's move to UA would be delayed until she had fulfilled her commitment to First National, a process that would take two years. In accepting the chairmanship of United Artists, Schenck agreed to serve without compensation while reserving the right to produce for UA distribution as many as six features a year. To gear up for such a schedule, he formed Art Finance Corporation, which served as the nominal producer of *The Eagle.* Then Art Finance created Feature Productions, Inc. to function as a production entity, and Schenck, in a bold move, assigned it Valentino's contract.

Menzies, as a Schenck employee, would be allocated to the Talmadge pictures as well as Feature Productions. He found his first job under the new pact would indeed be a Talmadge project—the Belasco stage success *Kiki,* for which Schenck had reportedly paid the record price of $75,000. A dispute over the picture rights had stretched years, with Broadway star Lenore Ulric determined to re-create the role on-screen she regarded as her own personal favorite. That Norma Talmadge had never before played comedy made the eventual sale—with Talmadge stipulated as star—a particularly bitter loss for Ulric, who angrily left Belasco's management in retaliation. Spinning the press coverage, Schenck announced "an unprecedented array of technical genius" to collaborate on the picture—Clarence Brown as director, Hans Kraly as scenarist, William Cameron Menzies as designer of "settings and art effects."

That same day, August 30, 1925, Menzies departed for New York and Paris, where he would confer with Belasco's longtime designer Ernest Gros, the man who created the scenery for the original 1921 Broadway production, and study the Aztec motifs of the Exposition Internationale des Arts Décoratifs et Industriels Modernes, the modernist World's Fair that was already revolutionizing the fields of architecture and applied arts.

In Menzies' absence, Schenck announced the first of Feature Productions' new slate of films—the long-awaited screen version of *The Bat,* the phenomenal Broadway stage success that had since become a perennial favorite in dramatic stock. Dubbing it "perhaps the world's most famous mystery play," the *Los Angeles Times* reported the highest price paid that year "for a play or story to be picturized as an independent production." Writer-director Roland West was credited with effecting the purchase, the owners having declined all previous offers because the play had remained such an extraordinary moneymaker. "West put over the coup only after weeks of negotiations and by offering a huge sum," explained the newspaper. Schenck and Art Finance came in on the deal as a source of capital, and West released his share of the rights in mid-November 1925, concurrent with UA's release of *The Eagle.*

By then, *Kiki* was well under way, Menzies having given it a luster unequaled in any of Norma Talmadge's previous vehicles (which tended, despite their prominence, to be low-rent affairs). The story posed no great challenges, though much was made of Menzies' Paris street scenes, which were lauded for their grace and authenticity. The film's set piece was the grand home of the Folies Barbes, a modernist theater that reflected the lines and sensibilities of the burgeoning Art Deco movement. Constructed sectionally, the set would support the lengthy tracking shot that opened the film, taking the camera from the rehearsal of "Deauville Daddy" by the revue's chorus, past stagehands hammering and sawing, sweepers, scenery painters, the old watchman at the stage door, and finally out into the back alley, where the stagestruck gamine Kiki is doing her spirited best to sing along. "Norma was the greatest pantomimist that ever drew a breath," declared Clarence Brown. "She was a natural-born comic; you could turn on a scene with her and she'd go on for five minutes without stopping or repeating herself."

The Art Deco home to the Folies Barbes, as conceived by Menzies for Clarence Brown's production of *Kiki* (1926)

The actual set, dressed and populated, as it appears in the film (MENZIES FAMILY COLLECTION)

Of far greater concern was *The Bat,* which would have to live up to its reputation as a timeless thriller while incorporating effects and enhancements that could only be attained on-screen. Schenck afforded West virtual autonomy in developing the film, having known the younger man since their days together in vaudeville when West was touring a playlet called *The Criminal* and Schenck was acting as his manager. In 1916, they launched their picture careers with *Lost Souls,* a $26,000 feature starring English actress José Collins. After Schenck took charge of his wife's career, West became general manager of production and directed Norma Talmadge in *De Luxe Annie* (1918). That same year, he returned to the stage as coauthor and producer of *The Unknown Purple,* a crime melodrama with fantastic overtones that became a considerable hit.

Working up to a December start date, Menzies strove to invest *The Bat* with a size and scope impossible onstage. What evolved was a mystery of great beauty and elegance, a new way of seeing a genre that had become commonplace in the years since the play opened on Broadway in August of 1920. The story took to the rooftops, an entire city in the background of what had once been the story of the old Fleming mansion alone. Menzies gave the place the sturdy look of a grand manor, its floor space vast, its heights seemingly limitless. Though West failed to take full advantage of the sets, leaving the mise-en-scène largely to the mercy of cameraman Arthur Edeson, the one genuinely jarring difference between Menzies' conceptual illustrations and the resulting film was in the depiction of the Bat himself. Where Menzies visualized a sleekly caped figure lurking in the shadows, suggesting a bat's visage in tone and countenance, West imposed a more literal interpretation, giving the character a grotesque face mask, extravagantly fanged and topped with the ears of a raging chihuahua. Such revisions spoke to West's vaudevillian roots, and kept the picture from emerging as the stylistic triumph it might otherwise have been.

Menzies' influence is most clearly seen in the film's opening moments, when the Bat makes good on a threat to steal the famed Favre Emeralds at the stroke of midnight. The sequence sets the tonal palette for the movie—long shadows, stark shafts of light, towering windows, a brooding sense of dread. The murder of Gideon Bell is heralded by the appearance of a gloved hand at an open window, its shade flapping incongruously in the still night air, the killer's figure framed by the window as he makes his escape, the body of his victim lying crumpled at its base. Menzies sketched this brief prologue, working through a sequence of images on the back of an art board, expressing his thoughts as a series of thumbnails. Refined, they constitute the first time, in all likelihood, that he carried the staging of a scene through to the sequencing of individual shots, a logical progression in technique that was now possible with his status as a salaried employee.

Menzies designed *The Bat* (1926) to a scale impossible to achieve on the stage. Note the similarity of the caped figure at the left of this drawing to Bob Kane's later conception of Batman.
(MENZIES FAMILY COLLECTION)

·   ·   ·

Menzies characterized his five and a half years with Joe Schenck and Feature Productions as a "maturing period" during which he "nearly killed" himself with overwork. In all, he designed the sets for forty-five feature films, either directly under Schenck and Johnny Considine, or on loan-out to other UA producers, Samuel Goldwyn principal among them. Such a workload, he later said, should probably have been allocated to four or five men, but at the time he had only one associate with whom to share the burden, architect and stage designer Park French. Slight and graying, his blue eyes framed by wire-rimmed glasses, French was the more technical of the two, capable of knocking out blueprints as well as renderings, an industrious man who spent his later years designing office buildings. "I never saw him," said his son Charles, then just seven years old. "He went to work early in the morning and came home late at night."

·   ·   ·

The opening of *The Bat* as worked out in a partial set of thumbnails. On the reverse side of this 20 x 15-inch piece of illustration board is the drawing from the previous page. (MENZIES FAMILY COLLECTION)

Rudolph Valentino's second picture for United Artists, *The Son of the Sheik,* looked as surefire as any property could possibly be, a sequel to the actor's first solo sensation, *The Sheik,* which broke New York attendance records when it opened in October of 1921. The original had the effect of settling the Valentino image in the public mind, and when the British author Edith M. Hull penned a sequel, it was obvious that only Valentino could play it. The purchase was finalized in December 1925 while Valentino was in Europe, Schenck claiming the results of a canvas showed that "more than 90 per cent of those who expressed an opinion" favored Valentino in *The Sheik* over his roles in *The Eagle, The Four Horsemen of the Apocalypse,* or *Blood and Sand.* A message from George Ullman caused his client to shorten his European tour and return to California for a March start date.

Considine made every effort to accommodate his star, who was less than thrilled at the prospect of once again playing a part that had dogged him for years. Assigned to direct was George Fitzmaurice, now under contract to Schenck, whom Valentino had wanted for *Blood and Sand* some four years earlier. Frances Marion, one of the screen's top scenarists, was put to work on the script, and Vilma Banky, Valentino's love interest in *The Eagle,* was again his leading lady. Menzies gave his pal Rudy every consideration, and although Valentino was permitted a dual role as both Ahmed and his bearded father, the Sheik of the original film, economies were imposed that showed most forcefully in the scaled-back look of the sets. Where Menzies envisioned a sort of grand Polynesian-style hut as Ahmed's desert retreat, light filtering through slatted openings, what showed in the film was more generically accomplished with bolts of fabric, the set devoid of the structural complexities that distinguished his more artful designs.

On location at the sand dunes outside Yuma, Arizona, the furnacelike heat never abated, even at night. The water was brackish, the flies innumerable, and Menzies found that the shifting light undermined the designs he had so painstakingly worked out. "It is usual to lay out a set to the south," he explained, "because back light is much better. Of course, if you are going to shoot on the set all day, you have to bear in mind the changing position of the sun with relation to the changing action on the set. . . . We didn't shoot the picture until three months later and had forgotten to take the changing declination of the sun into consideration. The result was that the lighting was terrible—it was complete back light, whereas we arranged it for a beautiful cross light." That *Son of the Sheik* seemed less substantial than *The Eagle* reflected the somber fact that the latter film hadn't been the runaway hit it was expected to be, a matter of grave concern to all involved, Valentino in particular.

As Menzies began work on the next Dutch Talmadge comedy, a romantic trifle called *The Duchess of Buffalo,* Schenck upped his quota with United Artists, agreeing to supply eight to ten pictures a year commencing June 1, 1926. When his partners at Art Finance balked at funding an expanded program, Schenck bought them out and formed Art Cinema Corporation to take over the assets. A First National release, *The Duchess of Buffalo* would become the first Schenck production to be filmed at the Pickford-Fairbanks studio, where Feature Productions would now be headquartered, and where Menzies would occupy a studio on the second floor of a building that sat between the main gate and Douglas Fairbanks' barnlike gymnasium.

March of 1926 was momentous in other ways, for a second daughter, Suzanne, was born to the Menzies family on the 11th, further stressing the space limitations of the two-bedroom apartment they occupied on Harper Avenue. Fortunately, relief was at hand in the form of a spacious new home. Along with his work and travel for Schenck, Menzies had designed himself a house every bit as fanciful as one of his sets, and construction had already begun on the parcel of land he had purchased on North Linden Drive, a short walk from the intersection of Wilshire and Santa Monica Boulevards. He was unabashed in his love of Beverly Hills, calling it one of the most beautiful places on earth. "I can remember when there were pine trees growing down Wilshire Boulevard as far as the Old Soldiers' Home," he reminisced in 1954. "Those trees were later offered for sale for ten dollars apiece—and all those huge pine trees you see around town were once planted on Wilshire." With work on his house under way and *The Bat* now in release, Menzies prepared to tackle the most ambitious assignment Considine had yet given him, an all-encompassing job on the scale of *The Thief of Bagdad* and *The Hooded Falcon,* another one of those chances he never again expected to get.

One evening in the spring of 1926, Joe Schenck called on John Barrymore at Los Angeles' Ambassador Hotel. UA's golden patina had dulled somewhat with the departure of Griffith, but there was still power in the names of Chaplin, Pickford, and Fairbanks, and no better affiliation for an actor of Barrymore's artistic and commercial stature. When he left that night, Schenck was pocketing a contract that committed the star of *The Sea Beast* and *Don Juan* to two pictures at a rate of $100,000 per, a coup in that Barrymore, coupled with the magic of the Vitaphone, was soon to be recognized as the biggest name in movies. Yet Schenck would not be paying the Great Profile a weekly salary, as had Warner Bros., and knew he would need to keep his new star happy in ways other than strictly monetary. At Barrymore's behest, Schenck agreed to bring his director, Alan Crosland, to Feature Productions and pledged that Barrymore's first picture for UA would, in terms of production values, be on a par with *The Thief of Bagdad,* thus making *The Beloved Rogue* the third Barrymore "special" in a row.

An attraction also was the opportunity to work again with Menzies, whom Barrymore had known at Famous-Lasky and who would now be re-creating fifteenth-century Paris on the backlot at Pickford-Fairbanks. Menzies tore into the assignment with unusual zeal, even when the writing of the script lagged as Barrymore, Crosland, and assistant director Gordon Hollingshead repaired to Hawaii. According to Barrymore's biographer Gene Fowler, several scenarists endured the development process before writer-director Paul Bern became the author of record.

Jack Barrymore's spirited take on Villon, "poet, pickpocket, patriot—loving France earnestly, French women excessively, French wine exclusively," led Menzies to conclude the character was a little mad. The look of the picture, he therefore decided, should reflect that madness, the sets appearing as Villon himself might have perceived them. Nothing outside the King's palace would be plumb or symmetrical, as if the walls and rooflines of Paris were active participants in the action, leaning in at times as if to express disapproval and visibly buckling under the weight of the snow. It was an organic sort of architecture, subjective and malleable, a celebration of Villon's emotional attachment to the city of his birth.

"France in 1451, when François Villon held forth in Paris, is classified architecturally under the Gothic period," Menzies noted,

> and this period signifies a wild, grotesque, bizarre type of construction. The tendency of that age leaned toward long roof lines, sharp angles, twisted stairways, and fantastic sculpture and carving. Cold, harsh, austere lines accentuated the somber feeling of the period, and because of this harshness, it was a peculiarly wild and fanciful type of interesting beauty. . . . I have endeavored to give the entire background atmosphere personality and character. True, I have diverted somewhat in some instances, from the ethical construction of the period and branched into the mythical, but this was done to enhance the dramatic value of a scene or scenes. For example, in the public square of Rouen, at the time when Joan d'Arc is being burned at the stake, the buildings look down upon the crowd, their frowning eaves throwing a veritable defiance at the King. Again, in the sequence in the kitchen of the Inn, where an atmosphere of comedy prevails, the ovens and the chimneys are of a rounded, rather squatty and rotund design, typifying a light trend of thought—comedy. And in some of the highly dramatic exterior scenes driving snow augments the realism of the setting.

Menzies would share a card with Bern in the opening titles for *Beloved Rogue*, the twin functions of plotting and design linked as the collaborative enterprise they ideally were. By stepping away from the mash of technical credits in which he typically

For much of *The Beloved Rogue,* the contours of Villon's Paris are shrouded in snow—it shields him, embraces him, nurtures him. Here, the King's provision wagon makes a stopover at a tavern called the Over-Ripe Grape, where the poet and his men will seize the opportunity to commandeer it. (MENZIES FAMILY COLLECTION)

found himself, Menzies also worked free of his usual "Settings" credit, advancing to the more formal title of Art Director. It was a major move forward, an acknowledgment that what he did was part of the storytelling process and not simply arrived at in a vacuum. For *Beloved Rogue* he supervised the fabrication, texturing, and painting of the sets, remaining with the picture, as he had with *Thief of Bagdad,* through a production schedule that stretched twelve weeks. When completed, *The Beloved Rogue* was a masterpiece of craft and synthesis, one of the most distinctive pictures to emerge from Hollywood in the waning days of the silent film.

*The Beloved Rogue* was in production when Menzies took occupancy of the house on Linden Drive. Suzanne Menzies, then an infant, later described the place as "French Normandy in design, English Tudor in reality." It was, in fact, a marvel of architectural salvage, incorporating a huge pair of doors from the set of *Cobra* as well as a number of decorative features, relief plaques, and curved finials that had first been conceived of for the sets of his movies. "Daddy was so proud of that house," said Suzie.

They had just finished it; it was a charming house. He was out in the yard one day, and Anton Grot drove by. And stopped to talk. Daddy invited him into the house, and Grot said, "No thank you. I don't like the outside, and I *know* I wouldn't like the inside." Daddy was just crushed.

He and Bill Flannery, who had worked for him [and who was trained as an architect], designed it. Totally impractical. For instance, when you had all the dining room windows open, you couldn't walk around the dining room table because they all opened in. And in 1926 the kitchens were pretty awful. Not enough bathrooms. . . . But it was a great house to give parties in. The living room, which was originally supposed to be his studio, was out of this world—beamed ceilings, window seats. Very warm, very inviting. Everybody loved it. Lon Chaney built a house next door, but he didn't live there very long. I don't think Mother ever talked to his wife. She was always scared that he would pop out of the bushes with one of his makeups on and scare my sister. Mother could always anticipate the worst of anything.

The following year, Menzies designed a fanciful cliff dwelling for Mary Pickford and Douglas Fairbanks, an eight-level seaside retreat gripping an almost vertical plot of land at Solana Beach, the construction of which costed out at $125,000. It was lovely, Pickford noted, but wholly impractical. Later, John Barrymore, contemplating marriage to actress Dolores Costello, would ask Menzies to supervise the design of a six-room addition to his Tower Road estate. ("Just in case I want to have a larger house," the actor hedged.) In general, Menzies seemed to regard architectural design in the same way he did set design, hewing toward the beautiful and the visually arresting and giving short shrift to the demands of livability. Of the small number of structures he designed that were never intended to be seen on a motion picture screen, the house at 602 North Linden would be the only one ever built.

The settling of the family homestead coincided with a relatively easy job, the staging of a modern-dress *Camille* for Norma Talmadge. Schenck had high hopes for his wife's last First National release, a sop to the matinee trade. ("I want Norma to catch fire in this picture," he declared as he trashed a draft scenario by Frances Marion.) Menzies delivered the opulence of Marguerite's famed bedroom and bath, the Mataloti ballroom, and the casino adjacent. The picture would hit its mark,

Menzies' interiors for *The Beloved Rogue* were in harmony with the action, squat and rounded in lighter moments, dense and forbidding at times of peril. "There will be no need for new experiments in camera angles in the filming of this picture," the editors of *Motion Picture* magazine concluded, "for the curious angles are supplied by the sets themselves."
(MENZIES FAMILY COLLECTION)

returning a domestic gross of more than $800,000, but the crucial result for Joe Schenck and United Artists would be his wife's very open affair with her younger leading man, the darkly handsome Gilbert Roland.

Talmadge and Schenck had always been regarded in Hollywood as an odd couple, Norma cool and slightly bored with it all, the squat, homely Joe resembling, in the words of Gloria Swanson, "a second-hand furniture salesman." She was, according to Anita Loos, never really in love with Joe, although she did allow him the privilege of adoring her. "Together," said Loos, "they looked like Snow White and an overgrown dwarf; Joe's figure was portly, he was beginning to go bald, and he suffered a cast in one eye that gave him a permanent squint. But these were only surface faults; in every other way Joe was most engaging; he had the subtle masculine allure which so often accompanies power, and he used his power with the greatest consideration for others."

All of this might have cast a pall on Talmadge's long-awaited arrival at UA, but Schenck, refusing the offers of his gangster friends to rub out his rival, decided instead to double down, returning Roland to his wife's arms for a second picture and giving Menzies carte blanche to create yet another land all its own for the film version of Willard Mack's Broadway melodrama *The Dove*. Facing foreign government protests and the threat of a boycott, the locale for the picture was shifted from rural Mexico to the mythical country of Costa Roja ("somewhere on the Mediterranean coast") where Dolores, the dance hall gal known widely as "The Dove," works a cantina called the Yellow Pig. With license to distance the story from its original setting, Menzies created a sort of Bagdad by the Sea, harsh and magical and otherworldly, and yet unmistakably Mexican in tone and texture. Complementing the flair and color of the designs would be the outsized performance of Noah Beery as Don José María y Sandoval, the brutish caballero who lusts after the Dove and frames her sweetheart, a gambler named Johnny Powell, on a phony charge of murder in his drive to possess her.

For the picture, Menzies found himself working once more with Roland West, who again permitted him to design and essentially direct an opening sequence as he had earlier done for *The Bat*. The nighttime scene opens on a bakery and the

The house Menzies built on North Linden Drive was as distinctive as it was impractical.

The grand caballero's hacienda for *The Dove* (1927). The Mexican locale of Willard Mack's famous play, changed for political exigencies to a mythical land on the Mediterranean, helped win for Menzies the first Academy Award ever presented for art direction. (MENZIES FAMILY COLLECTION)

entrance of Gómez, one of Sandoval's lieutenants. A beggar attempts to steal a loaf of bread, his starving wife in the background urging him on. Gómez takes in the scene, stops the man, and grandly loads his arms up with bread. As the recipient, quivering with gratitude, turns to make his exit, Gomez draws his pistol and shoots him dead. "I have been kind to the poor fellow," he reasons, holstering the weapon. "He will never be hungry again." A deep focus shot completes the prologue, the story told, after the manner of a three-act drama, on three planes working from back to front: the figure of the hysterical woman grieving over her husband's body in the background, the killer and the clerk chatting amiably in middle distance, and a bug sprayer dominating the foreground, a skull and crossbones and the word VENENO gracing the metal can, the lines of composition drawing these elements together in a low-angle tableau of casual brutality.

The scenario was primarily the work of Wallace Smith, a newsman and novelist who held the rank of colonel from his campaign days in Mexico and Central

America during the time of Pancho Villa. Having also illustrated Ben Hecht's *Fantazius Mallare* and *The Florentine Dagger,* Smith spoke the same artistic language as Menzies, and the two men effected a shorthand collaboration as the movie took shape. In the end, it was Menzies' design of the film that earned the most plaudits, with Talmadge's lackluster performance and Gilbert Roland's obvious miscasting noted in most every review. Menzies would later stress the importance of setting in the dramatic impact of a picture, especially in an instance where the actors weren't pulling their collective weight.

> The art director and the cameraman, with their many mechanical and technical resources, can do a great deal to add punch to the action as planned by the director. For example, if the mood of the scene calls for violence and melodramatic action [as in the opening of *The Dove*], the arrangement of the principal lines of the composition would be very extreme, with many straight lines and extreme angles. The point of view would be extreme, either very low or very high. The lens employed might be a wide-angled one, such as a twenty-five millimeter lens which violates the perspective and gives depth and vividness to the scene. The values or masses could be simple and mostly in a low key, with violent highlights. . . . [W]hen the tempo of the action is very fast, there are usually rapidly changing compositions of figures and shadows.

Nineteen twenty-seven would be another big year, with the release of *The Beloved Rogue* in March and work on six additional pictures—*Topsy and Eva, Two Arabian Knights, Sorrell and Son, Sadie Thompson, Drums of Love,* and *The Garden of Eden.* For the independently produced *Two Arabian Knights,* Menzies recycled sets from *The Son of the Sheik* and consulted on location work in the snows at Truckee. With *Drums of Love,* he began a four-picture association with D. W. Griffith, a seemingly momentous occasion of which he never spoke. ("He was receptive, a good man, though he was then past his peak," cinematographer Karl Struss, who shot the film, said of Griffith.) In some cases, as with *Topsy and Eva* and *Sorrell and Son,* Menzies designed the necessary settings and was uninvolved in the shooting of the films. For others, such as *Sadie Thompson,* where he was reunited with Raoul Walsh, he consulted on the script and was present throughout production—to his mind the ideal arrangement.

"In the first place, although not customary, it is of great advantage to the art director to know something of the story as it is being constructed," he said in describing the development process.

Very often he will have many valuable suggestions to offer. . . . When reading the scenario, notes are made, and if there is sufficient time rough sketches of the separate scenes are prepared. After consultation with the cameraman and director and the incorporation of their suggestions, the art director works up his sketches into presentable drawings. He considers such things as point of view, nature of the lens to be used, position of the camera, and so forth. If he is concerned with intimate scenes, he concentrates on possible variations of composition in the close shots. If he is designing a street, or any great long shot, he considers the possibility of trick effects and miniatures, double exposures, split screens, traveling mattes, and so forth. When the drawing is finished, the director, cameraman, and designer confer again, and when all interested are satisfied with the drawing, it is projected through the picture plane, to plan and elevation. This process reproduces the composition line for line, and retains all the violence or dramatic value of the sketch, even with changed point of view. The finished plan and elevation is blueprinted and sometimes transposed into a model and turned over to the construction department.

Improvements valued at $2 million were nearing completion on the Pickford-Fairbanks lot, soon to be renamed the United Artists Studio, when John Considine announced the purchase of an additional sixty acres in nearby Culver City for an "auxiliary plant." Considine was also beefing up the contract talent, signing writers such as Donald McGibeny and F. Scott Fitzgerald to term agreements, and adding actor Michael Vavitch to a stock company that now included Estelle Taylor, Gilbert Roland, and Walter Pidgeon.

UA was so short of releasable product that Schenck gave a distribution contract to the fledgling producer Howard Hughes, who had no track record to speak of but could finance his own films. It was through his attorney, Neil McCarthy, that Hughes met John Considine, and it was Considine who led him to director Lewis Milestone. A former cutter, Milestone had a good sense of pacing and an exceptional eye. *Two Arabian Knights* wasn't as costly as it looked, the casting of actor William Boyd its only true extravagance, but the jaunty comedy was a surprise hit, a critics' darling, and a genuine credit to UA in a year when only four movies carried the firm's imprint.

Considine soon had the Russian-born Milestone back for a second picture, a Corinne Griffith comedy after the fashion of Dutch Talmadge, whose own career was winding down. *The Garden of Eden* was again by Hans Kraly, but Milestone, teamed with Menzies, proved a stronger visual stylist than Sidney Franklin, certainly more collaborative. He delighted in posing problems to be solved with a camera angle, an adroit grouping of actors, or the design of a set to make a comedic point or serve as a visual punch line. "The set itself often causes a laugh," Menzies noted. "In . . . *Garden of Eden* there is a place where a couple starts an argument after they are in bed and every time they sit up to argue they turn on the light. There was a man living across the court, and he noticed the light going on and off and thought somebody was signaling and began to flash his light on and off. Then other people saw it and did the same. We made a miniature of the complete side of a hotel and all the windows were flashing lights. It caused a great laugh."

Menzies sketched gags for Milestone, rendering them "almost in the mood of caricature." Stylistically, his individual panels resembled storybook illustrations, the compositions accomplished with figures rather than structural forms, a significant advancement from his earlier work. It was the closest he had yet come to actually directing actors, and the exercise betrayed an inclination to see them more as graphic elements than fellow artists. "With all due respect to Miss Griffith," wrote William K. Everson in program notes for a 1957 screening, "perhaps the real star of The Garden of Eden is William Cameron Menzies."

Less ambitious in terms of design, yet certainly one of the year's most notable pictures was *Sadie Thompson,* the Gloria Swanson vehicle in which Raoul Walsh would be costarring as well as directing. Walsh hadn't acted in a film since 1915 (the year he played John Wilkes Booth in *The Birth of a Nation*) and would doubtless want Menzies on hand when shooting scenes that required him to be in front of the camera. Filming began in July 1927, with the pace of work hampered by the replacement of cinematographer George Barnes when he was recalled by Sam Goldwyn one week into production. Robert Kurrle replaced him at first, then Oliver Marsh took over from Kurrle when the latter's interior work was found wanting. Menzies' principal contribution was the weary, rain-soaked hotel in Pago Pago where much of the action takes place, a tropical exterior built on a stage at United Artists. "We covered the floor of the stage with dirt, grass, and leaves to give the effect of the ground outside the hotel," he recalled, "but when we turned on the rain effects it was all washed away and we had to cast the whole thing in cement."

Plaster and cement had become the basic textural elements of movie sets, able to catch and cheaply replicate an endless array of surfaces. "Texture is a rather interesting subject," Menzies said at the time.

All our straight plaster textures are cast in sheets nailed to a frame and then pointed or patched with plaster. Brick, slate roofs, stone work, and even

Toni Lebrun's debut at the Palais de Paris in Budapest . . .

. . . is sabotaged when a light switch is thrown backstage. This is one of the many sight gags devised by Menzies for *The Garden of Eden* (1928). (MENZIES FAMILY COLLECTION)

The *Sadie Thompson* company spent a month on Catalina Island, where the Pago Pago wharf scenes were filmed. While on location, Menzies took part in Sadie's arrival as an extra. Here he poses in costume with director Raoul Walsh and Gloria Swanson. At far right, ignoring it all, is Lionel Barrymore. (MENZIES FAMILY COLLECTION)

aged and rotted wood are casts taken from the original thing, made in sheets and applied. That is, if we have a stone wall, we get a lot of stone and build up a wall about six feet high, put the plaster cast on it, and peel it off like you do a cast from a tooth. You can cast any number of pieces of wall from that. The painting is usually done by air guns, and in many cases the light effects are put on by expert air gun operators.

He finished out the year with total immersion in another far-off land, a task rendered all the more difficult by the fitful shifting of personnel. When first announced, the John Barrymore vehicle *Tempest* was an original story by Mme. Fred de Gresac, the French playwright who had previously shared an adaptation credit on *Son of the Sheik* and had taken Frances Marion's place on the Talmadge version of *Camille*. Directing the script, touted as providing Barrymore his first modern screen role in five years, would be Frank Lloyd, late of Paramount. The title stuck, but little else did. Lloyd fell away sometime over the spring of 1927, as did Mme. de Gresac's material, and Russian émigré Viktor Tourjansky, under contract to Metro-Goldwyn-Mayer, replaced him. The new story, set at the time of the Russian revolution, was supplied by Vladimir Nemirovich-Danchenko, Tourjansky's mentor at the Moscow Art Theatre. It was Tourjansky who selected the Russian actress Vera Voronina to be Barrymore's leading lady and imported actor Boris de Fas (from his own *Michael Strogoff*) for the role of a wild-eyed Bolshevik. As veteran scenarist C. Gardner Sullivan got down to work on a screenplay, Menzies began the process of illustrating key sequences with Tourjansky.

Filming commenced in October but didn't go well from the start. "Tourjansky was a perfect delight to work with," said cameraman Charles Rosher. "He had a camera eye, great taste, and a fine imagination. But he wasn't fast enough." Voronina fell ill after two weeks, shutting down the production. Then it was announced to the trade that Lewis Milestone was going to lend Tourjansky "a helping hand." Actress Dorothy Sebastian was borrowed from M-G-M to replace Voronina, but then Considine pulled the plug when it became apparent that Milestone and Menzies were, in effect, doing Tourjansky's job for him. Sebastian was sent back to Culver City, to be replaced, it was hoped, with the German actress Camilla Horn, for whom the part of the Princess Tamara had supposedly been written. (Horn, said Rosher, was Joe Schenck's mistress at the time.) Production resumed in December with the unlikely choice of Sam Taylor as the new director. "I don't know anything about Russia," the former gag man for Harold Lloyd admitted to Considine. "That's all right," the producer assured him, confident that Menzies had already done most of the heavy lifting.

Taylor had no visual style to speak of, but he had a way of injecting sly comedy into otherwise breathless drama that appealed to both Barrymore and Considine. Taylor scrapped all but a single Tourjansky sequence and began anew, working far more closely with Menzies' illustrations than with the script Sullivan had fashioned. "You get your perspective while you're working," Taylor said, "and only then. You can't build convincing climaxes on paper. They develop of themselves." Three weeks into filming, Camilla Horn finally reached Hollywood, and Taylor found himself directing her through an interpreter.

For *Tempest*, Menzies rendered a less stylized version of Russia than he had for *The Eagle*, but one far more comprehensive. He would later speak of the importance of setting and lighting in securing a desired effect, and how, in many cases, authenticity was sacrificed and architectural principles violated for the sake of the response being sought. "My own policy has been to be as accurate and authentic as possible. However, in order to forcefully emphasize the locale I frequently exaggerate—I make my English subject more English than it would naturally be and I over-Russianize Russia."

The picture began with a bird's-eye view of Volinsk, a garrison town near the Austrian border, an elaborate miniature constructed on a giant turntable, the camera closing in on the midnight quarters of Sergeant Ivan Markov. Moody images of Imperial Russia in its final days, sturdy, low to the ground and smothered in snow, were contrasted with scenes of pomp and ceremony, capturing the brittle world of the aristocracy and melding seamlessly with later shots as seen through the bars of Markov's prison window. Menzies once estimated that he made more draw-

The wedding of Ivan and Princess Tamara, one of three finales reportedly shot for *Tempest* (1928). Menzies positions the characters so their surroundings influence the emotional temperature of the scene. A line of shadowy witnesses in the foreground adds depth, while the eye is drawn to the distant figures by the sunlight streaming through a church window. What director Sam Taylor added must have been negligible. (MENZIES FAMILY COLLECTION)

ings for *Tempest* than for any previous film, and the consistency of its look belies the fact that it had multiple directors, a trio of leading ladies, and a well-earned reputation for being, as the *Los Angeles Times* put it, a "bad luck film," ill-starred and seemingly as doomed as the czarist era it portrayed. Its final cost came to $1,041,048—extraordinary for the period.

As with all of his assignments, Menzies drew heavily from an ever-expanding library of reference books, oversized volumes, rebound in some cases, culled from thrift shops and studio libraries, all lavishly illustrated. *The English Interior* by Arthur Stratton. *In English Homes* (three volumes) by Charles Latham. Books on costumes (*Robes of Thespis*) and furniture. *Folk Art of Rural Pennsylvania, Die Alte Schweiz* (cities of old Switzerland), *Provincial Houses in Spain, Portuguese Architecture.* A useful series of books published by Brentano's included such titles as *Picturesque Mexico* (1925) and *Picturesque Yugo-Slavia* (1926).

At the finish of *Tempest*, John Barrymore, believing it out of all of his pictures "the one thing that is any good at all," gifted Menzies with "a peculiarly hybrid of artistic junk" for his library. "The books on architecture are in no way a suggestive reflection on your own magnificent craftsmanship," he said in an accompanying note, "but I thought perhaps you will find in them a possible idea for a semi-detached urinal for Agua Caliente!!"

# 6

# I Could See the Future Clearly

Within the space of a few weeks, *The Dove, Sadie Thompson, Drums of Love,* and *The Garden of Eden* all went before the viewing public, all drawing mixed notices but all garnering praise for their exceptional production values. Credit got scattered among the respective cinematographers and directors, only occasionally extending to the designs of William Cameron Menzies. One Los Angeles reviewer proclaimed *The Dove* "hardly less a triumph for William Cameron Menzies than it is for Norma Talmadge." Yet Mordaunt Hall, writing in *The New York Times,* laid its "real atmosphere" to Roland West. "He has not produced a picture since *The Bat,* but judging from his work on *The Dove,* he has learned a great deal. He knows how to tell a shadow story and how to use his camera without interrupting the various thoughts. His lights and shadows are particularly good." Hall didn't mention Menzies at all.

It was hardly any different for *Sadie Thompson,* and Griffith took the lion's share of the credit for the lovely but listless *Drums of Love.* On *The Garden of Eden* Menzies' contributions were perceived as directorial touches, with Milestone drawing the praise. If the seeming lack of public recognition irked him, Bill Menzies never let on. But where audiences and the press were frequently clueless on matters of who contributed what to a movie, the governors of the newly formed Academy of Motion Picture Arts and Sciences, comprised of five artistic and technical branches, were not only aware but intent on drawing more attention to matters of artistic excellence in an industry frequently maligned by politicians, church groups, and the press. In

July 1928, scarcely more than a year into its existence, the Academy announced a plan for conferring "awards of merit" for the most distinctive achievements in acting, writing, and directing, as well as in the production and technical divisions. The principal award would be in the form of a statuette "emblematic of the profession, to be designed by a sculptor of recognized standing and reproduced in bronze." Honorable mentions, in the forms of "diplomas and similar trophies," would be awarded in each class "whom the judges consider entitled to them."

To get the ball rolling, the Academy defined a narrow window of just three weeks for the nomination of potential recipients, a prospect that sent the 370 members of the organization scrambling. Each would be entitled to make five nominations in a total of twelve categories, drawing from pictures released in the United States between August 1, 1927, and August 1, 1928. Still warmly remembered for his work on *The Thief of Bagdad* and *The Beloved Rogue,* Menzies had seven features that met the qualification: *Two Arabian Knights, Sorrell and Son, The Dove, Sadie Thompson, Drums of Love, The Garden of Eden,* and, most significantly, *Tempest,* which had been playing New York since the middle of May and would open in Los Angeles on July 26, just as Academy members were struggling to complete their ballots.

Widely praised by reviewers, *Tempest* was hailed as much for its looks as for the flawless performances of its principals—Barrymore and Camilla Horn in particular. Interest in the picture kept it at capacity business during the crucial nomination period. Once the August 10 deadline had passed, five judges were appointed from each of the five Academy branches to sift the results, the goal being to submit a group of three nominees for each classification to a central panel of judges charged with the selection of the actual winners and runners-up, a process that would take five months to complete.

By comparison, the movies released during that interval were unexceptional, Norma Talmadge's *The Woman Disputed* being the most notable from the standpoint of design. Once again, Menzies advanced his approach to the physical layout of a film, plotting a stylish opening as well as key scenes and establishing shots, ensuring the pictorial consistency of a film its director, Henry King, later described as "just an assignment." Originally the picture, under its working title, *The Darling of the Gods,* was to have been directed by the Russian-born theatrical impresario Morris Gest, who fell ill as the play, presented on Broadway by A. H. Woods, was being adapted for the screen. The project languished while Talmadge complained of "almost continual changes, and changes again." Less than two weeks before the scheduled start of production, only King, Talmadge, and Gilbert Roland were officially on board.

It appears that Menzies had relatively little interaction with King, who came to the film with the sets under construction and the continuities already approved by

Johnny Considine. For once, Talmadge, thirty-five, would be playing her own age as an Austrian streetwalker. The film opens with an armed chase in the middle of the night, the hunted man jumping a wall, a light fixture shattering at the impact of a police bullet. Rounding a corner, the man is hit in his right arm. Momentarily stunned, he grimaces in pain, then notices a pair of legs in a darkened doorway. The camera tilts up to reveal Mary Ann Wagner, her makeup exaggerated after the manner of a cabaret dancer, her battered hat and polka-dot blouse advertising the fact that she is open for business. A Russian passerby watches as she hides the man, then follows her upstairs. She lights a cigarette in the darkness of her room and finds him standing there. "Judging from your eyes and your voice," he says, "you haven't been in this life long." She takes him to be a customer, but the man tells her that he only wants to talk to her. "I've found the way to escape," he announces and then hands her a card bearing the name of his nephew. "I want you to notify him." Certain he is mad, Mary Ann bursts from the door, the card clutched tightly in her hand. As she races down a labyrinth of a staircase, the oppressiveness of the dingy boardinghouse reflected in its windowless walls and canted ceilings, she hears the report of a pistol.

The extant drawings for this sequence show that Menzies effectively directed it, the setups virtually identical to his visualizations, the body language suggesting the pantomime of the actors. *The Woman Disputed* is full of complex imagery—breakfast on a balcony with the city bustling below, the attack on Lemberg, a traveling shot past the massive columns of a church interior, the battlefield crossing of an Austrian spy through a great jumble of gnarled trees and barbed wire. Repeatedly, Menzies constructed the shot-by-shot opening of a given sequence, then backed off to let King stage his actors—Roland, Arnold Kent, Boris de Fas, Michael Vavitch, Gustav von Seyffertitz. When retakes were deemed necessary, Sam Taylor stepped in to shoot three scenes (according to King) that included a new ending. Again, Menzies' presence on the set ensured a smooth transition, the final shot presenting Talmadge's magdalene from a balcony as a grateful army kneels at her feet, an absurdist conceit made credible by the star's soulful performance, possibly the finest of her career, and the artful culmination of a near-perfect mise-en-scène.

The Expressionist look of the picture was no accident, as Menzies spoke of 1927 as the signal year when German films reached Hollywood in abundance, beginning with the January opening of F. W. Murnau's *Faust* and continuing with a deal to program the Forum Theatre on Pico Boulevard with product from National Film A.G. of Berlin. The arrangement brought such movies as *Aftermath* (*Brennende Grenze*), *The Beautiful Blue Danube* (*An der schönen blauen Donau*), and *Mata Hari: The Red Dancer* (*Mata Hari, die rote Tanzerin*) to Los Angeles audiences, a trend culminating in August of that year with Paramount's release of *Metropolis*. Menzies had seen earlier German exports, specifically *The Cabinet of Dr. Caligari* and *The Golem,* as "very daring and different experiments" that helped forge a new era in pictures. He particularly hailed Murnau's stylistic advances on *The Last Laugh, Faust,* and, with art director Rochus Gliese, on *Sunrise,* concluding years later that Murnau was the director who probably influenced him the most.

Menzies did some experimenting of his own, throwing in on a project initiated by the French journalist Robert Florey, who was functioning as assistant director to Henry King on *The Woman Disputed.* Florey envisioned a Surrealist romance called *The Love of Zero,* for which Menzies would design the simple cardboard and plywood sets. The previous year, Florey, in collaboration with Slavko Vorkapich, had produced *Life and Death of 9413: A Hollywood Extra,* a wry intermarriage of live action and imaginative miniatures. A throwback to *Caligari* in both style and execution, *The Love of Zero* had the same nightmare ambitions but lacked the elements of social commentary that distinguished the earlier film. It did, however, permit its makers to abandon any pretense of reality, a particularly useful step for Menzies in tackling subjects that would soon present themselves. The short, which, the titles boasted, was made at a total cost of $200, had its first public showing before a capacity audience at Hollywood's Filmarte Theater on May 10, 1928. Hearst columnist Louella Parsons acknowledged it had "certainly carried out the 'arty' idea" but lamented that most of those present had to "stand on our heads" to understand it.

With the completion of *The Woman Disputed* and the unremarkable *Battle of the Sexes,* Menzies was loaned to other UA producers while the film that would become *Lady of the Pavements* was in development. He was, in fact, on location on Santa Cruz Island for Sam Goldwyn's production of *The Rescue*—a particularly grueling shoot—when word reached him that his father was dying in New Haven at the age of sixty-two. At the time of his death in September 1928, C. A. Menzies was president of Charles A. Menzies, Inc., one of the city's leading plumbing and heating contractors. For twenty-five years he had been treasurer of the New Haven Caledonian Club and a communicant and elder in the Benedict Memorial Church. It was upon his return from his father's funeral in Connecticut that Menzies for the first time met Laurence Irving, an illustrator and designer for the stage who had been brought to the attention of Douglas Fairbanks by their mutual friend, Eddie Knoblock. Irving had been imported from England to design the sets for *The Iron Mask,* Fairbanks' lavish sequel to *The Three Musketeers.*

"We became friends at first sight," Irving wrote of Menzies.

Our obligations to Eddie were a bond, and my handling of watercolors in the English style was a professional credential that he accepted with generous praise. . . . Bill was ambitious only for scope to exercise his prolific imagination and technical expertise—so marvelously incorporated in a man of boundless energy and with a lively dramatic and comic intuition. This ambition was easily fulfilled. For, even in that philistine stronghold, producers and directors were vying for his services that would inflate their reputations in the eyes of credulous mandarins and undiscerning filmgoers. He had no intellectual pretensions. In all things his heart governed his head. He alluded to his pictured sequences vividly transposed to film as "gags," though many with their rhythmic and emotional content were passages of pure poetry.

Irving would soon discover what Menzies already knew—that synchronous sound was no longer a novelty and that the advent of talking pictures was upon them. Menzies had seen a steady encroachment since *Tempest* went out into the world with a Vitaphone score. *The Woman Disputed* followed with a song attached (the execrable "Woman Disputed, I Love You") and July had seen the New York premiere of *Lights of New York,* a wooden gangster melodrama that nevertheless heralded the arrival of all-talking features. "When I had left [for New Haven]," said Menzies, "talkies were just being talked about. When I returned [a month later] they were an accepted fact. Only talking pictures were being made. And there was I, knowing nothing about them and terrified. I saw my job slipping right away from me. I could see the future clearly, or I thought I could. Talking pictures would be like plays, using only two or three changes of sets. And where would my job be then? I had to do something about it."

Practically all the important films of the new season were to have sound or dialogue sequences, and in some cases they would be all-talking. The sound revolution was altering the landscape of the Metro-Goldwyn-Mayer, Warner Bros., and Fox lots, where new stages designed expressly for the making of talkies were under construction. At United Artists, a new two-story recording building was nearing completion, and M. C. Levee, general manager, had just announced plans for two new soundstages, the total cost for which would run some $250,000. Concurrently, Mary Pickford decided her new movie would be an all-talking version of Helen Hayes' great stage success, *Coquette.*

One of the existing stages on the UA lot was hurriedly adapted to sound, its interior deadened with rolls of dun-colored felt. Fairbanks felt compelled to inspect the results one day while *The Iron Mask* was in production. "When he heard that the stage was wired and blanketed for sound," Irving related,

he took me with him to see what was afoot. That he was dressed and armed as D'Artagnan made our approach more poignant. He paused at the dark entry and said quietly: "Laurence, the romance of picturemaking ends here!"

Under the aegis of Joseph M. Schenck, Menzies shifted from the tableau style of illustration exemplified by his work on *The Thief of Bagdad* and *The Hooded Falcon* to the fluidity of montage and a purer form of cinema. These large-format drawings suggest the extent to which he influenced the first minutes of *The Woman Disputed* (1928). (MENZIES FAMILY COLLECTION)

All the elements of deep focus are present in this tense moment from *The Woman Disputed*. A prayerful Mary Ann Wagner (Norma Talmadge) occupies the foreground, the low angle and leading lines of the floor planks calling the eye to Father Roche (Michael Vavitch), an Austrian spy who towers over her. In the far distance, four detainees ponder their fate, contingent on Mary's decision. This composition, accomplished with the use of a wide angle lens, effectively eliminates the need for crosscutting and keeps the title cards to a minimum. (AUTHOR'S COLLECTION)

Our worst fears were confirmed. The studio, where once in its bright and airy space our sets were built . . . was now as dark as Erebus. Draped with brown felt that lined the walls and hung from the ceiling, festooned with wires and the floor littered with serpentine cables and gadgets that looked like infernal machines, it smelt of a tomb and had the stillness of death.

Contained in such a claustrophobic space, *Coquette* was, by necessity, a modest affair. Directed by Sam Taylor, it required just six sets—yet Menzies said he had trouble designing one that was both pleasing to the eye and could accommodate a microphone (crudely suspended from the catwalks by a rope). Cinematographer Charles Rosher could recall a meeting at which the entire floor scheme had been laid out, with separate camera booths positioned for close-ups and long shots. "Taylor and the sound men must have spent a lot of time laying out those plans," Rosher

The exterior of the Smoking Dog Cabaret, "one of the lowest dives in Paris," for D. W. Griffith's *Lady of the Pavements* (1929). The bold foreground element of the street lantern draws the eye, leading it to an outsized mechanical dog opposite; in the film, Griffith opens on the dog and pulls back to this view. The picture's handsome sets and photography, in the judgment of biographer Richard Schickel, make *Lady of the Pavements* just about the slickest of all Griffith productions. (MENZIES FAMILY COLLECTION)

said. "No consideration had been given as to how the cameraman was to achieve satisfactory lighting." Disgusted, Rosher left the film and was replaced by Karl Struss.

Although the picture was made in the dead of winter, the heat generated by the incandescent lights—as opposed to the sizzling arcs of silent days—turned the closed set into a Turkish bath of sorts. Pickford alone was reported to have lost eight of her one hundred pounds over the course of four weeks, and the camera crew, grinding away in soundproof booths, fared even worse. Apart from the novelty of seeing its star deliver her lines in an exaggerated Southern accent, *Coquette* displayed little of the style or beauty even routine pictures had come to have in the waning days of the voiceless screen.

Ironically, while Pickford was making her talking debut under the most static of circumstances, Menzies and Roland West were overcoming the cumbersome limitations of the new technology with a shrewd hybrid of mobility and voice, boldly applying the conventions of German Expressionism to the demands of the talking screen. Shot mainly as a silent with spoken interludes and the liberal use of sound effects, *Alibi* was a scrupulously planned film, deliberately paced but stark in its imagery, not quite all-talking but masterfully conjuring the illusion of an all-talking production. Menzies spoke to Frank Daugherty of "experimenting with light" on *Alibi,* and Daugherty subsequently praised the chiaroscuro results of those experiments in the pages of *The Film Spectator.* "He described for me the average set bathed in a pure white glow, totally devoid of shadows and contrasts and all that make a mere lamp-lit room, for example, such an interesting composition to the eye."

To counter the flat look of most talkies, Menzies not only invested his images with the deep shadows of a city at night, shafts of light cutting into the compositions with laserlike precision, but he also designed many of the sets in forced perspective, suggesting a depth impossible in the synchronous dialogue sequences, where the actors found themselves clustered around a microphone hidden in a lamp or a telephone. "West," concluded Daugherty, "ran his camera in and out of a city's underworld like an omniscient needle."

It could be said that Menzies went to school on *Coquette* and *Alibi* and was prepared to take the talking film to new places when he was loaned to Sam Goldwyn for *Bulldog Drummond,* the film that would introduce the silky cadences of Ronald Colman to an ever-expanding base of fans. "The acoustical demands in connection with the production of talking pictures have had a very noticeable effect on the design and construction of the settings," Menzies noted.

Too much plain hard surface cannot be exposed unless of a very soft and absorbent texture. We are making very many of our sets of cloth, or of a very porous wall board. Hollow, tunnel-like cavities must be avoided. Also, the set in talking pictures must be lit for long shots and close-ups, which are shot at the same time. There are fewer sets, but more of what might be called single-shot effects. A set prepared for a short and long shot looks almost bare to the eye, but when seen on the screen it has a habit of muddling together. For instance, if the pieces of furniture are close together they look like one mass and you cannot tell what it is. Therefore you have to use it sparingly. The arrangement of the set must also be different for different lenses. A wide angle lens will throw the thing back, which will simplify it and give it some depth and you can naturally have more furnishings; but a narrow angle lens will jam it all up together and consequently you must have greater distance between the furnishings in the set.

Based on a play derived from the first of ten books by the British novelist "Sapper" (Herman Cyril McNeile), *Bulldog Drummond* was calculated to extend Colman's brand beyond the light comedy and adventure roles he played in silent pictures. At first, Goldwyn thought Colman's potential in talkies so great that he tried prying the rights to *Arms and the Man* from George Bernard Shaw, an attempt doomed to failure. He then considered the Sapper property, which he apparently owned and which, mercifully, was not a romance. Burnishing it to the luster of one of Shaw's better works would be a matter of hiring the right adapter, a problem solved when he retained Pulitzer Prize–winning playwright Sidney Howard.

As Menzies remembered it, the initial screenplay was typical for talkies of the time in that it called for a minimal number of sets. Horrified at the stifling prospect of another *Coquette,* Menzies joined forces with Howard and director F. Richard Jones on a revision that ended up specifying a total of sixty-one sets—a significant factor in driving up the film's modest budget. "We have what might be called an added handicap in the necessity of condensing the acoustic properties of the set," he admitted, "but, after a fashion, this tends to a greater and more artistic simplicity." What he sought was an expansion of what he had previously done on projects such as *The Beloved Rogue, Tempest,* and *Alibi*—the "big idea" of coordinating under one man every "art phase" of a production with the goal of heightening the emotional mood of a film. "I took the idea to Samuel Goldwyn, and he saw value in it."

Where before he had plotted individual sequences, leaving the balance of a film to its director and cinematographer, Menzies now proposed to sketch everything—every shot in every scene—with an eye toward rendering a visually exciting movie that would still meet the demands of synchronous sound recording. Where before a set could be realistically proportioned and interesting angles could be achieved by simply moving the relatively lightweight camera to wherever it was needed, now sets needed the effects designed into them, as the camera was contained in an overgrown icebox that was anything but mobile. With thought and preparation, Menzies asserted, composition needn't be determined by the placement of the microphone. In a letter to his mother, Sidney Howard said that he found the work "fascinatingly interesting and difficult without being at all too hard. I mean, the difficulty has been, not driving work, but the adjustment to an entirely new medium and my round about way of telling stories through detailed characterization needs much adjustment to photography."

"The picture was a melodrama," said Menzies, "and I concentrated on the

One of Menzies' boards for *Bulldog Drummond* (1929). Although Wallace Smith is credited on-screen, the film's continuity was effectively the work of the man who also designed its sets.
(MENZIES FAMILY COLLECTION)

camera for melodramatic effects, violating perspective wherever possible. By this I mean that scenes were given photographic perspective the human eye would never encounter, but which was dramatic." When finished, Menzies arrayed the boards, each depicting four shots, in a frieze around his office. Goldwyn, invited to look them over, could scan the walls and see his entire film before him without having yet shot a single frame. "Precision and economy of time were now of greater significance as studio overheads rose exponentially," wrote Laurence Irving. "Bill's method came into its own. Whatever films may have lost on the swings of silence they gained on the roundabouts of a more intelligent appreciation of the art of film design."

Inspired, perhaps, by Menzies' pre-visualization of *Bulldog Drummond,* Goldwyn insisted on a week of rehearsal time for the principal cast—Colman, Lilyan Tashman, Claud Allister, Lawrence Grant, Montagu Love, Wilson Benge, and eighteen-year-old Joan Bennett, who would be making her motion picture debut. Filming began on January 28, 1929, with the cast on set for a 9 a.m. rehearsal. The microphone was placed at 9:50, followed by more rehearsal. The first sound take, recorded on a wax disc, was made at 10:50. Following playback, a second take

Stark prison images comprise the opening moments of *Alibi* (1929). As No. 1065 collects his belongings, the action is played in shadow, the room dominated by a barred window, the illumination courtesy of the world outside.
(MENZIES FAMILY COLLECTION)

was made at 11:05. Moving to the next setup on the storyboard, a rehearsal was captured on wax (no film), followed by playback, more rehearsal, and a take at 12:35. Playback and a second take preceded a break for lunch at 1:05 p.m. And so it went. Everyone worked long, tedious hours, typically to 9 p.m., sometimes past midnight. "At one point," recalled Joan Bennett, "the company worked until three in the morning, with a seven o'clock makeup call for the next day, ready to shoot on the set at nine."

Dick Jones had started as a cutter for Mack Sennett, and his strengths remained those of a specialist in slapstick comedy. When shooting silent, Jones was on comfortable ground, supported as he was by Menzies, cameraman George Barnes, and Barnes' brilliant young associate, Gregg Toland. Menzies indulged his bent for complex visual storytelling, setting action on a distant plane and using a strong foreground atmospheric, such as a lantern, to suggest texture and depth. Barnes and Toland excelled at such deep focus challenges, which could be shot silent and not through the speed-diminishing tyranny of plate glass. The talking sequences, how-

At police headquarters, a seemingly endless line of switchboard operators puts out the call—dead or alive—for Chick Williams, escaped gunman and cop killer. This striking image, which, as Menzies would point out, violates perspective, kicks off the third act of *Alibi*.

ever, had Jones flummoxed and Goldwyn quickly grew dissatisfied with his work. "I vant you to know that ven the director had finished, it vas a lousy film," the producer told Laurence Irving. "Ven he had gone, I tell you, I made all der retakes and dat is vy it is so goot!"

The silent version of *Bulldog Drummond* finished on March 13, and on March 17 it was reported that Los Angeles stage director Leslie Pearce was shooting the "spoken sequences." As with *Alibi,* the picture had been filmed silent when possible to save time, but unlike *Alibi,* sound effects were integrated to complement and, at times, pay off the visuals. A planted news report suggested it took 427 separate and distinct sounds to make the movie "100 percent talking," a contention that counted five different automobile engines, a cuckoo clock, the thump of a falling body, thunder, screams, rain, footsteps on gravel, gunshots, slamming doors, and wind whistles in various keys. Indeed, as if to ring down the curtain on the speechless cinema, the picture opened on the Senior Conservative Club of London, where a sign bolted to the towering doors of the members' lounge demands SILENCE! The image of a

The funhouse perspectives built into the sets for *Bulldog Drummond* serve to amplify a tone
of lighthearted melodrama. The art director, Menzies observed, could "create his design with a
broad arrangement of lines and values, and then apply to these lines and values the realism of
architecture, figures, and properties." (MENZIES FAMILY COLLECTION)

ticking floor clock dissolves to a traveling shot of a liveried attendant making his way
through the club's aged population "with the manner of a graveyard Sexton." As he
sets his silver tray on a table, a spoon clatters to the floor.

"The eternal din in this club is an outrage!" explodes an elderly member.

"You're perfectly right, Colonel," returns Algy, seated nearby. "You ought to
complain." He then addresses a companion crumpled into an adjacent chair. "That's
the third spoon I've heard drop this month."

The figure turns to reveal his face to the camera. "Spoons, my hat!" grouses
Hugh "Bulldog" Drummond. "I wish somebody would throw a bomb and wake
the place up!"

·   ·   ·

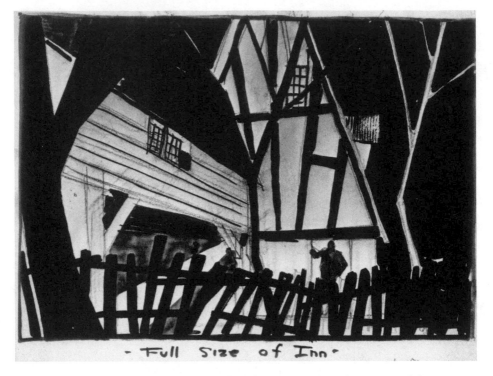

The Green Bay Inn emerged as a riot of conflicting patterns in this conceptual drawing
for *Bulldog Drummond*. Menzies admitted to channeling the Expressionist *Cabinet of Dr.
Caligari* in aspects of his design philosophy. (MENZIES FAMILY COLLECTION)

A few days after filming began on *Bulldog Drummond,* the University of Southern
California, in cooperation with the Academy of Motion Picture Arts and Sciences,
inaugurated a course in motion picture appreciation called "Introduction to the
Photoplay." The lecture series, which was good for two units toward a degree in cinematography, began on February 6, 1929, before a packed house at the university's
Bovard Auditorium, where an exuberant Douglas Fairbanks gave the introductory
address. The weekly talks that followed came from such diverse figures as J. Stuart
Blackton, Paul Bern, Benjamin Glazer, and Irving Thalberg. On April 10, with work
on *Bulldog Drummond* finally at an end, Menzies took the lectern to deliver a speech
he titled "Pictorial Beauty in the Photoplay." (The title was likely inspired by Victor
Freeburg's 1923 survey *Pictorial Beauty on the Screen,* which highlighted the works of
James Cruze and Rex Ingram and the "stylization" of the German Expressionists.)
"As an art director," Menzies began, "I am interested in the photoplay as a series of

pictures—as a series of fixed and moving patterns—as a fluid composition, which is the product of the creative workers who collaborate in production."

He went on to review some of the points made in earlier lectures, expanding particularly on Thalberg's contention that movies reflected the tastes, habits, and sentiments of the times. "The pictorial history of the photoplay is a history of the development of the public taste for beauty on the screen. This taste has been developed by tasting. One artist, in his efforts, has outdone the other, and the public continues, as always, to demand more and more." He ticked off key films in terms of pictorial values (*Cabiria* and *Intolerance*, Lubitsch's *Passion*, *Variety*, and *7th Heaven*), talked about emotional values and how such effects were achieved. "The motion picture technician must have great ingenuity. He must have a knowledge of architecture of all periods and nationalities. He must be able to picturize, and make interesting, a tenement or a prison. He must be a cartoonist, a costumer, a marine painter, a designer of ships, an interior decorator, a landscape painter, a dramatist, an inventor, an historical, and now, an acoustical expert—in fact, a 'Jack of all trades.'"

Menzies gave full credit to the cameraman. ("His responsibility is a grave one, and the art director can often aid him by properly designing the sets.") Sound, however, was very much on the collective mind of the participants, and the addition of speech, he acknowledged, had "disturbed the craft" in all branches of production. "The talkies are no longer a series of mere pictures of people speaking lines, but are rapidly bringing back all of the values, all of the beauty, of the silent motion picture, with sound and speech as a supplement. *In Old Arizona* was probably the first talking picture that did not ignore pictorial beauty. I think that this accounts, to a great extent, for its tremendous success. Several others have had some pictorial interest, but the ultimate in a finished, artistic talkie has yet to be made."

*In Old Arizona*, released in January 1929, was the first feature to take the delicate recording gear—in this case, Fox Movietone—out of the studio and onto location. The results were visually arresting, if not always essential to the ear. The part-talking *Alibi* had just opened to acclaim in New York, and the premiere of *Bulldog Drummond* was less than a month in the future. At M-G-M, King Vidor was making *Hallelujah,* which Thalberg, in his presentation at USC, touted as an "interesting and truthful study of Negro life" that made considerable use of music to heighten the grim drama. In New York, Rouben Mamoulian was shooting *Applause* at Paramount's Long Island studio, a not always successful attempt to meld sound and picture in new and exciting ways. The most popular film of the year would turn out to be *Disraeli,* a talking representation of George Arliss' great stage success, a film that followed all the others into release and yet owed its technique more to *Coquette* than anything Menzies or Mamoulian was attempting.

As I have suggested throughout this lecture, the pictorial quality of motion pictures rests largely with the public. The producers, like many other manufacturers, have awakened to the fact that beauty is efficiency, and that good art is usually good business. They have found that the public is no longer satisfied with the settings, costumes, lightings, and groupings of last year, or yesterday. They have learned that pictures must be well composed, for a well composed picture is one at which the audience can look and see a lot with ease. The eye and the attention of the spectator is attracted to the right point and directed in accordance with the demands of the story. Somehow the idea has crept into many minds that the artistic picture is destined to be unpopular. However, I think that if you will look at the matter fairly you will find that where artistically composed pictures have failed, they have done so not because of beauty, but because of lack of some other necessary attribute.

If the public was seemingly indifferent to the innovations of the talking screen, the critical community and the industry itself were taking notice. On February 17 the results of the Academy's six-month effort to commemorate outstanding achievements in motion picture production were announced to the press in groupings of "first" awards and honorable mentions. Over one thousand nominations had been whittled down to the ten most popular in each category, of which three were selected "in order of their excellence." Following winners in the acting, direction, writing, and cinematography categories, the central board of judges named Menzies as the recipient of the Academy's first-ever award for art direction, the two films cited being *The Dove* and *Tempest*. Honorable mentions went to Rochus Gliese for his work on *Sunrise* and Harry Oliver for *7th Heaven*.

The actual disbursement of the awards took place three months later during the Academy's second anniversary and awards banquet before an audience of some 270 attendees. Vice President William deMille made the announcements as a slightly inebriated Douglas Fairbanks handed out the statuettes and the parchment "diplomas." The principal trophy, designed by sculptor George Stanley, was a male figure in bronze and gold on a base of Belgian marble, the entire assembly standing twelve inches in height. DeMille began with the direction awards, calling upon Frank Borzage (for *7th Heaven*) and Lewis Milestone (for *Two Arabian Knights*) to come up and accept their trophies and certificates. Three honorable mentions followed: King Vidor (for *The Crowd*), Herbert Brenon (*Sorrell and Son*), and Ted Wilde (*Speedy*).

DeMille progressed to the writing awards, then followed with cinematography.

Menzies, at thirty-three, poses with his Academy statuette for cinematographer Karl Struss. (MENZIES FAMILY COLLECTION)

By the time the evening reached art direction, seven statuettes had been presented and nine honorable mentions—four for films Menzies had designed. "First award for the art direction of *The Tempest* and *The Dove* is awarded to Mr. William C. Menzies," deMille announced. Acknowledging the applause (and weaving himself from the effects of several highballs), Menzies made his way to the platform, where he gratefully accepted the award and its accompanying certificate from the man who initially thought he was too young to take on the task of designing *The Thief of Bagdad.* Now they were onstage together, Menzies at the height of his career, Douglas Fairbanks, just days from his forty-sixth birthday, nearing the end of his. There was no acceptance speech, and the presenter's gracious comment went unheard by most everyone other than the recipient himself. "In your hat!" popped Fairbanks, summarily cuing Menzies to return to his seat.

# 7

# Profound Unrest

The reception of *Alibi* marked another crucial advancement for the talking film. Allowances no longer had to be made for the clunky mechanics of recorded sound; the addition of spoken dialogue was celebrated as a genuine enhancement of the screen experience. "It is by far the best of the gangster films," wrote Mordaunt Hall, "and the fact that it is equipped with dialogue makes it all the more stirring. . . . Mr. West has endowed this production with telling direction. He gives to most of his scenes something new, whether he is dealing with glimpses in prison or with those in Police Headquarters. His work possesses color with a minimum of the conventional motion picture flashes." In Los Angeles, Edwin Schallert reported that the picture, with all its pre-release ballyhoo, actually lived up to expectations: "*Alibi* is as skillful a step forward as any that has been taken in this still early day of synchronizations, and will be assured, without the least doubt, of a high popular approval."

The conventions of the part-talkie were still there for those keen enough to notice them, but the integration of silent and talking action was so thoughtful as to take most observers by surprise.* Where the film lacked pacing, it nevertheless provided visual stimulation to an unusual degree. "Talking pictures will eventually be much finer than anything the stage can offer," West said at the time. "Why? Simply,

---

* The same technique, not as successfully employed, would be on display in Universal's *Broadway*, which would open in New York in late May.

the answer is because we have everything the stage has and more. *Alibi* as a play was shown in three scenes. We used a broader canvas, took more sweeping strokes, yet were permitted more detail. We used 30 scenes."

Menzies knew *Alibi* ground to a halt whenever the talking started, and that what seemed new and daring in the spring of 1929 would look creaky in a year or two. "I think that the addition of speech has been a great step forward," he told the audience at USC. "And with the addition of color, stereoptic perspective, and possibly a variety of shape to the screen proportions, we will have attained almost reality itself." Still, the basic language of the motion picture was visual storytelling, and it was essential for the camera—and, by extension, the microphone—to remain the servant of the filmmaker and not the master.

Samuel Goldwyn, his three-camera retakes completed, was so happy with *Bulldog Drummond* he arranged a gala premiere at New York's Apollo Theatre, an event he and Mrs. Goldwyn attended in the company of Ronald Colman and Sidney Howard. (Pointedly, Dick Jones, the film's credited director, was not among the attendees, and Goldwyn was moved to declare that with the coming of sound, the writer was now a more important figure than the director.) The opening images (the stifling old club, the traveling shot among the elderly members, the accidental tinkling of the spoon) told the opening night audience they were in for something special—a talking picture that fully embraced the marriage of picture and sound. Indeed, Colman's lusty performance was so dependent on the way he tossed off the film's dialogue that it would have been utterly impossible to set the same tone without a soundtrack. Some labeled it the talking screen's first genuine satire.

"If it was not all our learned urban dwellers claimed for it," wrote Frank Daugherty, "it at least pointed the way. And it couldn't have achieved even a modicum of success had it not been for the settings of Menzies. For they were wholly of another world, and made the delicious humor of the thing possible. They might have been English backgrounds, it is true—indeed they could have been no other nationality whatsoever—yet surely England never saw those houses, that inn, those mysterious roads. They were at once as English as Buckingham Palace and the Albert Memorial, and as fantastically un-English as the world of Sherlock Holmes. They were, in short, a distinct achievement in the art of creating a background for a picture that could hardly have been changed in even the slightest degree without spoiling the success of the picture."

A spirit of genuine fun pervaded *Bulldog Drummond,* the jaunty pacing something audiences hadn't come to expect from the crude talkies of the period. By pre-composing the film on a shot-by-shot basis, Menzies had effectively pre-edited it as well, enabling it to move at a good clip because the movement had been designed into it. It fell to Colman and the others to simply ride along with it, buying into the good humor of the proceedings while not taking themselves nor the unlikely developments of the plot too seriously. "Goldwyn took a lot of pains with the film," an unsigned review in *Photoplay* acknowledged. "It is intelligently and tastefully done. The sounding is highly expert. Here a rain-drop can be made to act in the sound pictures as a Rolls-Royce. The cutting (one of the drawbacks of the talkies up to now) is finely done. In a phrase, *Bulldog Drummond* is great stuff."

While Mary Pickford thrust herself headlong into talking pictures, Douglas Fairbanks held back, certain, as was his friend and business partner Charlie Chaplin, that little good could come from speaking on-screen. When, as a concession to exhibitors, he agreed to add a talking wraparound to *The Iron Mask,* he did so gamely but without enthusiasm. Numerous takes were required, and once one was seemingly in the can, the playback malfunctioned, distorting a stage-trained tenor that was already ill-suited to the swashbuckling image Fairbanks had created for himself. He talked openly of retiring, though he eventually came around to the idea that he and Pickford should team for a movie, a hope their fans had embraced for years. "Mary's quiet persistence may have shamed him into making a show of defiance," Laurence Irving suggested. "He, too, had won his spurs on Broadway. . . . Why should they not together make the first film that would give utterance to Shakespeare on the screen? And in color, too, for full measure? For some time we weighed the pros and cons of *Othello* and *The Taming of the Shrew.*"

"It was very hard for us to find a play that would give us equally important parts," Pickford explained. "Douglas' leading women have always been just figureheads to be saved in the end. My leading men, with one or two exceptions, have been just the same." When, ultimately, comedy won out over tragedy, Irving was summoned back from England to work in collaboration with Menzies on what would be the most prestigious all-talking picture yet attempted. "Will emphasize light and whimsical feeling of play and maintain spirit of cheerful fun, which must be reflected in settings," director Sam Taylor had cabled. "Have no massive sets, but keep everything intimate and interesting with true feeling of period with sets that are unusual as an artistic impression rather than a mountain of wood and plaster."

The entire enterprise was undermined by the reluctant collaboration of the two stars' respective organizations and the intransigence of their headstrong director. Wrote Irving: "Bill and I, working together in complete harmony, found it difficult to get decisions on what settings were required and harder still to produce designs that would satisfy three minds without a single purpose." While Irving concentrated on costumes, Menzies' hand was most distinctly apparent in the roomy sets and the film's opening tracking shot, the most audacious yet attempted for a talking picture. Opening on a Punch and Judy show, the camera moves back along the street, taking in the scene as the onlookers disperse, then pushes forward toward the center of Padua, its size and bustle suggesting an Italianate Bagdad, a great canyon of commerce and humanity. "We didn't use the sound equipment," explained the cameraman, Karl Struss. "We shot it silent."

If Sam Taylor took the trouble to study *Bulldog Drummond*, his technique rarely betrayed it. There were, at times, as many as four camera booths facing the set, one designated for long shots, another for medium shots, one or two others for close-ups. Menzies wasn't asked to draw the film out, and his compositions were evident only in glimpses. Taylor even resented the presence of Pickford's Shakespeare coach, the distinguished British stage actress Constance Collier. By making long and close shots at the same time, he revisited a problem he had encountered on *Coquette*—the too distant placement of the microphone for close-ups. "The sets for *Taming of the Shrew* were larger," recalled soundman Ed Bernds, "and because the walls and the floors were bare, they were more reverberant . . . [they] were not only high-walled and reverberant; they were architecturally magnificent, so that Sam Taylor tilted his long-shot camera upward to capture the beauty of the graceful arches and dramatic stairways of the William Cameron Menzies sets—and our microphones were forced even higher."

Menzies wasn't present for much of the shooting, having instead been allocated to Goldwyn for work on Ronald Colman's next vehicle, an all-talking adventure yarn titled *Condemned to Devil's Island*. Based on an explosive book by Blair Niles—said to have been the first woman to land on the shores of the famed penal colony—Menzies had the benefit of numerous photographs taken by Mrs. Niles' husband during the course of their government-sanctioned tour of French Guiana. In conception, the film was to have been made by the team responsible for *Bulldog Drummond*—F. Richard Jones, Sidney Howard, George Barnes, Gregg Toland, Colman, of course, and Menzies. Actor Dudley Digges was imported from New York to serve as dialogue director, but Goldwyn's disenchantment with Jones lingered, and the director was off the film, replaced by Wesley Ruggles, by the time the construction of the sets began on the 11th of July.* Again, Howard's script was visualized from start to finish, and the technique so captured the fancy of Ralph Flint, Hollywood correspondent for the *New York Sun*, that what started as a feature article on Goldwyn became a ringing tribute instead to his art director.

---

* Jones, thirty-five, married the Hollywood costume designer Irene Lentz, but never directed another film. He died December 14, 1930.

The Devil's Island setting of *Condemned* (1929) afforded numerous opportunities for what Menzies called "violent and dramatic pattern." (MENZIES FAMILY COLLECTION)

One of the chief assets at Mr. Goldwyn's command for *Condemned* is the assistance of William Cameron Menzies, easily the leading artist at work in Hollywood from the purely pictorial point of view. He has been associated with United Artists these many years, constantly growing in understanding of what should lie back of a well-ordered film in the way of pictorial fluidity and progression. . . . In *Alibi* and *Bulldog Drummond* Mr. Menzies has brought this feeling for dramatic flow in his compositions to a definite head, as anyone with half an eye to such matters can discover for himself. . . . But it is in his designs for *Condemned* that Mr. Menzies has reached the peak of his professional contribution to the screen. I trust that the finished print will realize the entire sequence of drawings that line the walls of his studio on the United Artists lot, for in these drawings lay one of the major secrets for the fashioning of a motion picture. Given a running set of designs such as these to start with, any picture is bound to get off to a head start. Adding whatever else there may be of dramatic value in the way of dialogue, direction, and acting is pure profit if based on such a sure-fire pictorial appeal.

Opening on a powerful storm at sea, Menzies anticipated a sequence of "great violence of action and composition" at the beginning of the picture:

We hold the scene for a few frames of film and then bring the topmast of a ship from the bottom line of the frame. It plunges up through the picture to disclose a man in the crow's nest and continues up until he has disappeared above the upper frame line. Then it plunges down again to indicate that the ship is rolling at an angle of about forty-five degrees, dissolves into the captain shouting orders from the bridge to sailors on the deck, and dissolves again to a point of view of one of the convicts from the cages below decks looking through an open hatch to the bridge. The final scene of this sequence is the close-up of a convict shouting from behind the bars at the captain. As he speaks his lines he swings with the movement of the ship until the close-up is a comparatively long shot, disclosing the lower tier prisoners. Then, as his lines are completed, he swings back into the close-up, and as the hatch cover is slammed down the scene darkens into a natural fadeout.

On *Condemned,* Menzies had the added advantage of a camera freed from the confines of an insulated booth, those "goddamn doghouses" (as Goldwyn referred to them) that prevented movement of most any kind and diminished the quality of otherwise excellent lenses. Menzies had written of the challenge of "applying realistic form to get violent and dramatic pattern" and now such pattern could be varied, enhanced, and vivified with the synchronous tracking shots of George Barnes and Gregg Toland. Despite these and an unusual number of exteriors, the company managed an average of ten and a half setups a day, finishing the picture in thirty-one working days. For Menzies' part, the sets amounted to $36,000 of the film's total budget, with the services of the art director himself, on loan from Feature Productions, costing $2,600.

With a killing workload—twelve features for the 1928–29 season and uncredited work on at least one other—Menzies was also designing a series of musical short subjects, impressionistic one-reelers conceived by Dr. Hugo Riesenfeld, UA's director of music, to feed highbrow content to movie audiences in small, artfully measured doses. Born and educated in Vienna, Riesenfeld had served as concertmaster at Oscar Hammerstein's Manhattan Opera House and was an indefatigable champion of the classics in mass media. "Music," he said, "is the logical partner of the movie. We can get better results than with talking; the waves given off by music are more nearly like the recorded waves of light."

The series, announced over the summer, would consist of once-a-month featurettes built around famous passages of classical and modern music and made "strictly according to United Artists feature standards." The first, *Impressions of Tschaikowsky's Overture 1812,* was intended as a pilot of sorts and screened for an Academy audience in July 1929. Riesenfeld set the premise in a brief foreword, noting the composer's intent to commemorate Russia's defense of Moscow against Napoleon, the "conflict between 'Marseillaise' and 'God Save the Czar' and the burning of Moscow by the self-sacrificing patriots." The maestro assembled an orchestra of seventy-five to play the Overture, simulating a modern performance on the concert stage. Menzies, credited with "pictorial effects," created a stylized war montage to illustrate the music, bells tolling, soldiers marching, peasant women pleading and singing to officers of the invading Grande Armée, silent footage made, in some instances, on standing sets originally built for *Tempest.* "We showed Napoleon on a horse," recalled cinematographer Karl Struss, "and with an arc of unusual power projected his silhouette on an enormous screen, and soldiers marched by with this figure towering over them."

The picture was lauded as much for intent as execution. ("Riesenfeld . . . has not fully found himself in this first experiment," hedged Edwin Schallert, "but the purpose reflects unique possibilities and should have a definite appeal to screen audiences, intensifying their interest in musical works that have a story.") It was two months before Riesenfeld and Menzies could deliver a second entry, a considerable advancement over the first entitled *Glorious Vamps.* A burlesque survey of femmes fatales through the ages, the short was originally planned as a showcase for the vivacious Lupe Velez. Comedienne Christine Maple eventually assumed the job of slipping from one historic guise to the next and, paired with the versatile musical-comedy star Bobby Watson, delivered lively representations of Eve, Delilah, Salome, Cleopatra, Carmen, and Lucretia Borgia. The modern finale, in which Maple warbled a Kipling song set to music, got turned on its head as Menzies superimposed face shots of all types of men—sailors to millionaires—and used split screen effects to shift and scramble a jazzy chorus line.

The result was so exhilarating the decision was made to hold *Glorious Vamps* until the new year, substituting the more sedate *Irish Fantasy* as the second release in the series. Menzies was promptly elevated to co-producer of the featurettes, sharing equal billing with Riesenfeld, and the direction credit was handed to UA production executive O. O. "Bunny" Dull.

The wear, after four years with Schenck and United Artists, was beginning to show. Menzies was continually being overlooked in the reviews of his pictures, with credit for his work often parceled to the director or, sometimes, the cameraman. Only occasionally was a reviewer wise to the extent of his contribution and said as much when the opportunity arose. William Boehnel, the sharply observant critic of the *New York Evening Telegram*, was a frequent advocate, no more so than when he devoted an entire paragraph to Menzies' work in his notice for the otherwise unremarkable *Locked Door*, the first talking picture directed by George Fitzmaurice. "William Cameron Menzies must find it a bit of a nuisance by now to be told over and over again that the designs he makes for the settings of the pictures he is associated with are things of sheer beauty," Boehnel wrote, "but he shall have to bear up under it once more. 'Things of sheer beauty' exactly describes his settings in the present offering. Compositionally, they are well-nigh perfect, and his use of lights and shadows is beautiful and effective. Particularly striking are his creations for the scenes of the party on board the ship just outside the fifteen-mile limit. And so, too, for that matter, are all the other settings in the picture."

Just ten days earlier, Boehnel had caught up with Menzies as "the man behind the scenes" was ending a brief sojourn in New York City:

> The picture as it is projected on the screen is invariably the picture as it flowed through the imagination of Menzies onto his drawing board. From this it would seem that all a director has to do when he gets one of these series of blueprints from Menzies is to shout "Quiet" and turn loose his actors as the drama and the construction detail are both present. It should be apparent, then, that Mr. Menzies plays no little part in the production of motion pictures, and those of you who remember the striking and effective settings he designed for *Bulldog Drummond* can readily appreciate how great a part this is.

Boehnel went on to report that Menzies "hopes eventually to become a full-fledged director of major productions."

It was, Menzies once acknowledged, a long-held ambition. "I had always wanted to direct," he wrote, "but found it difficult to break away from the growing demands for production designing." In August 1929, when his annual deal with the studio came up for renewal, Considine gave him a two-year extension, no options, bumping his weekly rate to $700 for the first year and $800 for the second. He also conferred the title "general production assistant" and announced to the press that Menzies would serve as associate producer on the upcoming Irving Berlin musical *Song of Broadway.* The arrangement, however, was not an altogether happy one, and Considine's unstated concern was that by putting Menzies in charge of his own slate of pictures, other UA productions would go without his unique and valuable talents. As the workload bedeviled him, Menzies would have Mignon drive him to the studio, where she would collect him at the end of a long day, three-year-old Suzie seated in the back and thinking he worked at an oil derrick that stood on an adjacent patch of land. Menzies was set to begin work on *Raffles,* Goldwyn's next project for Ronald Colman, when the release of *Glorious Vamps* brought yet another wave of attention and still more talk of directing.

Christine Maple and her vaudeville Adam, Bobby Watson, cavort in a stylized Garden of Eden for *Glorious Vamps* (1930). Watson would become Hollywood's most unlikely interpreter of Adolf Hitler, a part he would play in ten films, including Menzies' own 1951 production *The Whip Hand.* (AUTHOR'S COLLECTION)

"It didn't run more than ten minutes," said an unsigned review in *Motion Picture News,*

but before *Glorious Vamps* was ended it seemed to us that in William Cameron Menzies, who had considerable to do with its production, here was a director of considerable potential importance. Menzies long has been art director for Joe Schenck. Now he is an associate producer. He should be a director. The one-reeler of which we speak offers sufficient proof. Menzies, for instance, has given this one subject production investiture . . . clever, commercial, and artistic . . . that many features are denied. He knows the camera. He knows his backgrounds. He knows values. In short, he simply knows his stuff and should get a real chance to demonstrate it.

*Condemned* and *Glorious Vamps* were two bright spots in an otherwise dismal season for Menzies. *The Taming of the Shrew* opened to good notices and respectable business, but the results proved unsatisfactory to both its celebrated stars. (Fairbanks would later maintain that *Shrew* was Mary's idea, while Pickford laid the blame on Sam Taylor.) *The Locked Door* was staged at a snail's pace, its only compensation the talking screen debut of twenty-two-year-old Barbara Stanwyck. *New York Nights,* started as a silent, was done over as Norma Talmadge's first talkie, "light and easy" as its star described it, a disappointment at the box office even when featuring the voice of one of the silent screen's biggest attractions. *Lummox,* based on a Fannie Hurst story, had texture and atmosphere, but was starless and depressing. *One Romantic Night,* based on Ferenc Molnár's famous play *The Swan,* seemed a good choice for Lillian Gish, but the resulting film was slow and dull, torpedoed by the selection of Paul L. Stein as director. "He was lacking in all but one of the three 't's so necessary in our world—talent, taste, and temerity," Gish said in a memoir. "One could survive with two, but he had only temerity."

Then there was the matter of *Song of Broadway.* Joe Schenck had an old friend in Harry Richman, the popular star of the *George White Scandals,* and was convinced the Jolsonesque revue singer had a future in talking pictures. Richman's deal was extravagant—$75,000 and 50 percent of the profits. Schenck, eager for a "big score," engaged Irving Berlin to write the script and furnish eight songs for the picture. Richman arrived in Los Angeles on June 17 with the expectation that production would begin in July. No director had yet been assigned, however, and at some point the scenario Berlin delivered was unexpectedly deemed inadequate. The start date was set back to August and Richman, with time on his hands, fell into a rip-roaring affair with actress Clara Bow.

John Considine, who also had ambitions to direct, began reworking Berlin's material, dropping songs and adding in the music of other composers. Menzies found he had little to work with and virtually no authority in his capacity as associate producer. One of the unpublished songs Berlin found in his trunk was the Harlem-themed "Puttin' on the Ritz," and all involved could see its cultural imagery as the basis of a spectacular production number. Another, "Alice in Wonderland," would become the film's Technicolor finale. In August, director Tay Garnett was brought onto the project, and in September, Considine's revised screenplay was awarded the title *Play Boy.* Then Richman fell ill and had surgery. Joan Bennett was added to the cast, as was Eddie Kane, a former vaudeville headliner. Actor-playwright James Gleason was given the job of sharpening Considine's leaden dialogue, then signed on as Richman's devoted friend, Jimmy Tierney. Shooting finally began in October with the English-born Edward H. Sloman serving as a last-minute replacement for Garnett, who, tired of all the waiting around, signed a term contract with another studio.

As usual amid such turmoil, it was the designs and continuities that held the picture together. Menzies was a constant presence on the set, and his influence was apparent in most every scene. The film opened with a difficult tracking shot, the camera starting from the back of a traveling elevator car, peering over the shoulder of Joan Bennett as she scans the inside pages of a trade paper. As the car glides to a stop, it follows her out into the bustling office of a music publisher, where she takes part in an exchange with a mouthy reception clerk and then helps herself to a seat. Resuming its trip, the camera trundles down a hallway toward the end office, taking in a calamitous mixture of piano and voice, the business of commercial music being transacted in a warren of tiny rooms. Finally, it comes to rest on the figures of Gleason and, presently, Richman plugging a song for a less-than-appreciative pigeon, all part of a single two-minute take, synchronous dialogue spoken throughout.

The landmark "Puttin' on the Ritz" number began with Richman, in black tie and tails, taking the stage before a scrim depicting a cartoon cityscape, buildings springing forth astride Lenox Avenue as if grown like stalks of corn. The backdrop rises to reveal a scramble of architectural chaos, windows and rooftops flung in all directions, a billboard hawking CHEWY CHEWY GOOEY GUM, skyscrapers rising in the distance like gigantic masonry dinosaurs, their windows suggesting toothy, malevolent grins, appendages jutting haphazardly from their angular trunks. A chorus of costumed dancers floods the stage, first white, then black, top-hatted in striped pants, gyrating wildly in time with the music. As Richman rejoins the scene, the syncopated population now at its peak, the looming buildings come to life, wagging their fingers and waving their hatlike water towers in one of the most surreal and startling musical tableaux in all of cinema. With the completion of the sequence, Considine's office announced the permanent title of the picture would be the same as the song.

The "Alice" sequence was shot earlier, color being more the novelty than the design, with Joan Bennett cavorting among characters faithful to the illustrations of Sir John Tenniel. Irving Berlin's song was from the 1924 *Music Box Revue,* and the composer brought his family to the set to observe Menzies' handling of the material. "The memory is sharp, freestanding," wrote Mary Ellin Barrett, the Berlins' daughter, not yet three.

I am making my way with my parents, my dark and dapper father, my pale, soignée mother, through a tangle of wires, being lifted over, held on to so I wouldn't get separated in the confusion, the rush of people taking their places, people in costumes representing playing cards, kings, queens, knaves, diamonds, hearts, clubs, and spades, cards come alive, hurrying about. Through the crowd I'm propelled to a central lighted place where a lady with long yellow hair wearing a blue dress pretends to be a child. "That's Alice," my mother says, "and she's in Wonderland." Now my father has disappeared into the confusion. Daddy has gone into Wonderland surrounded by all those ominous figures. I begin to howl. "Daddy will be back," says my mother, holding me fast. "Don't cry. If you cry, we can't take you to all these interesting places."

The filming of the "Alice in Wonderland" sequence would forever be remembered by its participants as taking place the week of October 21, 1929—the same week as the great stock market crash. Berlin, for one, lost a fortune, estimated by some to be as great as $5 million. Schenck took a considerable hit as well, but business—at least in the short term—was holding up. United Artists began 1929 with a $1.6 million surplus, and would end the year with a net profit of $1.3 million. Both *Bulldog Drummond* and *The Taming of the Shrew* brought in billings in excess of $1 million, as did *The Trespasser,* Gloria Swanson's first all-talking picture. Feature Productions, on the other hand, had *Alibi* to its credit and little else. And, despite all the care lavished on it, *Puttin' on the Ritz* would do nothing close to expectations, dependent as it was on a personality with no real screen presence. "I just walked through my part," Harry Richman admitted in his autobiography. "All day long, Clara was on my mind. I couldn't wait to get to her place."

The film had its world premiere in New York City on February 14, 1930. Guy Lombardo and his Royal Canadians performed onstage, and Fannie Brice, Beatrice Lillie, Claudette Colbert, and Rudy Vallee were among the celebrities in attendance. Reviewers generally praised the film's production values and its tuneful score while

With its syncopated chorus of nightmare skyscrapers, the audacious "Puttin' on the Ritz" number drew more attention than any other aspect of the Irving Berlin musical of the same name. In his capacity as associate producer, Menzies prepared continuity boards and oversaw set designs by Park French, Robert Usher (who did the sketches for this sequence), and David S. Hall. French would soon return to commercial architecture, but Usher and Hall, both excellent illustrators, would go on to become Oscar-nominated art directors. (ACADEMY OF MOTION PICTURE ARTS AND SCIENCES)

bemoaning the more grating aspects of the central character and the device of rendering him blind with a gulp of bootleg liquor. It took the urbane Richard Watts, in *The Film Mercury,* to note "that the 'Puttin' on the Ritz' number, from the Harry Richman film of the same name, is the best staged and most imaginative musical number I have yet encountered in a screen musical comedy, and that Mr. Richman, the star, is absolutely no help whatever to the work."

At the time of *Condemned,* Menzies composed an article for *Theatre Arts Monthly* in which he considered the differences between stage and screen design and how he applied the principles of subjective reality to the demands of an analytical camera.

While the cinema designer has the advantage of being able to select his point of view or angle in getting an effect from realistic forms and lighting, it is a handicap of the camera that it does not photograph as the mind sees. If, for instance, you photograph a romantic location such as a picturesque European street, you will have an accurate reproduction—minus the atmosphere, texture, and color. Hence it is always better to substitute a set that is the impression of that street as the mind sees it, slightly romanticized, simplified, and over-textured.

The cinema designer's audience, too, is much more variegated than the stage designer's. He must realize that his effort may be viewed by three or four million people. Among these are some who are artistically inclined, and for these he would prefer to realize broader and more daring effects. But for the majority he must keep a quite realistic and convincing background. This background is a fluid pattern continuously changing, and, as composition is his greatest problem, he must design fundamentally for that. Like the stage designer, he strives hard for economy of effect. Indeed, he strives even harder because, as the composition is continually changing, allowing for but a few moments in which an impression may be absorbed, he must reduce it as closely as possible to one forceful, impressive idea. And there, again, he is at the mercy of the analytical camera, for an effect seemingly barren and simple becomes, on the film, a complicated mass of pattern.

*Raffles,* from the stories by E. W. Hornung, would become the last Ronald Colman feature Menzies would design as he had *Bulldog Drummond*—shot for shot. The cricket-playing "amateur cracksman" had appeared on film as early as 1905, but never had a romantic character more clearly called out for sound and dialogue. Goldwyn kept his core team intact—Sidney Howard, George Barnes, Gregg Toland, Menzies—and added director Harry D'Abbadie D'Arrast, a protégé of George Fitzmaurice and onetime assistant to Chaplin, to the mix. Working in concert with Howard and D'Arrast, Menzies produced some elegant moments, opening, for instance, with a nighttime jewel heist played entirely in silence, the thief's back to the camera, the safe open before him, light emanating from the street outside and passing through the store's Art Deco display windows, a bobby's silhouette making the rounds, a droll working of both shadow and light. Owing to the director's inexperience with sound, Goldwyn mandated four weeks of rehearsal time. "I am enjoying myself in the talkies even if they are harder work," Colman commented in the press. "We take so much more time on preparation now."

Production, scheduled for three weeks, did not go smoothly. D'Arrast, in the producer's judgment, was delivering substandard work. "I think it was all playing too fast for Goldwyn," H. Bruce "Lucky" Humberstone, who was first assistant on the picture, suggested, "and he had trouble making out some of the words. Harry D'Arrast said that comedy had to be played at a certain speed, but Goldwyn didn't think it fit in with Colman's style." D'Arrast was fired and Fitzmaurice stepped in on a day's notice, giving the action a more deliberate pace. The film was finished in four weeks at a cost of $685,000. It would be the last Goldwyn production to be released in both sound and silent versions.

Menzies, by now, had taken to working out his continuity sketches first, then going back to design the settings that would support the demands of each individual shot. It was, he said, the best way for a designer to work, analyzing the scenario scene by scene, considering matters of composition and lighting without the constraints of a predetermined background.

> But one of the peculiarities of the motion picture setting is that a set which is powerful and dynamic in its simplicity as a long shot may be very uninteresting in the semi-long shot or close-up. Hence the necessity of studying each change in the set up of the camera. The talking picture has affected the cinema setting in so far as the dialogue is usually played in a semi-close shot; and because constant dialogue in the earlier talkies resulted in the loss of the silent picture's graphic movement, much more action has been injected into the later dialogue pictures. The solution is to play dialogue scenes in a few key sets and to intersperse them with action shots containing incidental sound. From the point of view of pure design, this is the art director's ideal opportunity—the setting with a single set-up or camera viewpoint. He can now design his composition and reproduce it on the screen without having to satisfy other camera angles. The more perfect the mechanical device of synchronized image and sound becomes, the more personality the actor acquires; and accordingly, as the scene becomes more forceful and convincing, the background may become broader and more impressionistic without being distracting.

When Menzies sat with Frank Daugherty in the spring of 1930, not long after the completion of *Raffles,* it was during a period of what Daugherty saw as "profound unrest," the striving for something less derivative of the other arts and more native to the language of the camera. Describing himself as a "synthetic" American of Scottish extraction, Menzies said he longed to make a walking tour of the English

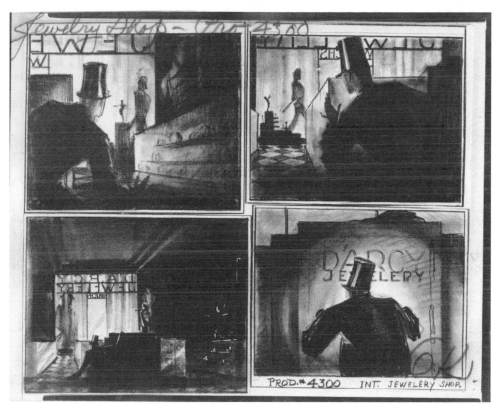

The jewelry store caper at the opening of *Raffles* (1930) plays out in backlight and shadow, the threat of the law a silhouette casually passing on the sidewalk. The point of view is singular, consistent, and takes in all essential graphic elements. (MENZIES FAMILY COLLECTION)

and Scottish seacoast, sketching old castles, idling quiet days, recharging his creative batteries. "It bespeaks," wrote Daugherty,

the painter who is tired of motion picture form and wants to return to the quiet joy of daubing on canvas. But with Menzies it doesn't go very deep, I feel quite sure; and after such a vacation, his curiosity, his knowledge, and above all his desire to perfect himself in the medium of the motion picture would drive him back again. To perfect himself against the day when the motion picture will no longer be a cheap imitation of all the other arts, but a flourishing medium of expression in its own right; and when the motion picture director will be, must be, director, painter, musician, playwright, scholar, rolled into one.

# 8

# A Few Faintly Repressed Bronx Cheers

In May 1930, United Artists announced that the company would produce between nineteen and twenty-one features at a cost of approximately $17 million, up nearly $2 million from the previous year. It was an ambitious schedule, highlighted by releases from all the major partners, including Chaplin, whose last picture, *The Circus,* had dominated the 1927–28 season. Menzies, however, never worked for Chaplin, and the other big hit of the upcoming season, Goldwyn's *Whoopie!* would be designed by the self-taught Richard Day. Menzies was left with a dreary slate of Schenck productions—*DuBarry, Woman of Passion,* which would effectively kill Norma Talmadge's career; *The Lottery Bride,* a stilted musical; *Abraham Lincoln,* D. W. Griffith's first all-talking picture; *Forever Yours,* an aborted remake of Talmadge's *Secrets* with Mary Pickford; *Reaching for the Moon,* a modern-dress musical for Douglas Fairbanks; and Pickford's ill-advised remake of another Talmadge success, *Kiki.*

All carried the distinctive look of a Menzies production, but there was nothing exciting about any of them. Talmadge was beyond caring if she ever made another movie, Pickford was on her way out, as were Fairbanks and Griffith, and *The Lottery Bride* hastened the bankruptcy of producer Arthur Hammerstein. There were still, however, the shorts, which Menzies unabashedly considered his best work. "They're artistic triumphs," he told Florabel Muir of the New York *Daily News.*

"Did they make any money?" she asked.

"They're artistic triumphs, I said. Don't ask me whether they made money. It wasn't my money I was spending."

The most elaborate of the shorts, of which there would ultimately be just six, was based on Paul Dukas' symphonic scherzo *The Sorcerer's Apprentice.* For the visualization, Menzies drew from the imagery of the original poem by Goethe, in which an apprentice is left to conjure a helpmate from a wooden broom, thus summoning magical powers he cannot control. Making elaborate use of miniatures, *The Wizard's Apprentice* managed a rich look on a pauper's budget, its effects limited to puppets and double exposures but nevertheless achieving some striking patterns.* "William Cameron Menzies and Dr. Hugo Riesenfeld have been producing two-reel, non-talking musical pantomimes from time to time that are so good they usually gather more applause than the so-called features," Pare Lorentz wrote in *Judge.* "The best one I have seen is *The Sorcerer's Apprentice* [*sic*]. I advise their owners to give them some money and turn them loose. They probably are the only two men in Hollywood experimenting with movie technique and they know what they are about."

The shorts seemed to inspire a musicality in Menzies' work that seeped into his features, most tellingly in the openings he devised and then invariably saw credited to others. Rhythm, he told Muir, was "a goal that you can reach only after the most laborious and painstaking effort." He illustrated the point with twenty-five drawings that comprised the proposed opening of *Reaching for the Moon:* The Statue of Liberty. Dissolve to Battery Park. Kids playing. Two men sitting on a park bench. Their feet fill the frame. Newspapers obscure their faces. They discuss the market—what to buy, what to sell. The newspapers drop to reveal the men as two bums. The continuity boards would enable the most inept of directors to follow the pyramiding of the gag, which would invariably be labeled a "directorial touch" in the reviews. "My drawings are copyright," he said at the time. "They protect me against the danger of anyone coming around later on and claiming my ideas as their own."

For the beginning of *Kiki,* Menzies designed a camera crane dubbed "the rotary shot" for the near-circular field of vision it could encompass. The device consisted of a caged camera platform fixed to a perambulator that ran on a rail attached to the ceiling of the stage. Operated by six men, the platform could travel in a straight line or a semicircle, as desired, while moving up or down with the aid of a system of weights and pulleys. Updating the memorable traveling shot from the Talmadge ver-

---

* Walt Disney, who was to begin releasing his cartoons through United Artists in 1932, may have been inspired by the Riesenfeld-Menzies shorts to embark on the animated feature *Fantasia* in 1938. Menzies considered Disney the "greatest genius" in Hollywood. "Why? Because he alone has caught the real meaning of rhythm on the screen. I hear a lot of directors and supervisors talking about rhythm, but it's only talk. They don't know what it is nor how to get it. Disney does, and my hat is off to him."

sion of the play, the camera opened on a pair of shoes, crossed on a table and tapping to the beat of a rehearsal. Pulling back, the shot revealed an old stagehand caught up in the rhythm while in the process of sharpening a pencil. It continued past other stagehands, posting bills, hammering, sawing, all working in time to the music, eventually catching the image of a gigantic papier-mâché elephant as it danced into view. Backing up still further, the camera took in the full breadth of the chorus line in mid-routine, ending on a pan to an office door.

On the surface, *Abraham Lincoln,* Griffith's picture, with its obvious parallels to *The Birth of a Nation,* offered the greatest opportunity to do something stirring and original. Menzies thought Stephen Vincent Benét's script "marvelous" but felt it left "great gaps in visualization." Said Menzies: "We had to build up the idea of Lincoln's immortality with pictorial effects. Here's how it was done. We fade in on a log cabin in the wilderness. Then truck up to the door. We see a woman's face. She's working around the cabin, says nothing. Then another woman's face. The first woman says, 'What are you aimin' to call him?' The second woman says, 'Abraham.' In the end of the picture, we shoot back to the cabin and hear that one word—Abraham. Then from the cabin to the inscription on the Lincoln memorial in Washington and dissolve to Daniel Chester French's statue."

Menzies' best efforts notwithstanding, *Abraham Lincoln* was aggressively uncinematic, a theatrical antique within a year or two of its release. "It was straightforwardly shot," Karl Struss acknowledged. "It was an episodic affair by its nature. There wasn't much you could do with it." Griffith himself considered it "all dry history with no thread of romance." Of the season, Menzies' most memorable achievement would be the gleaming Art Deco steamship he created for *Reaching for the Moon,* its entire promenade deck, bridge, and superstructure snugly filling one of only two large soundstages on the UA lot, its interiors occupying the other. *Reaching for the Moon* took shape in the aftermath of the stock market crash, when Irving Berlin was inspired to create a shipboard romance in which Black Tuesday would be the turning point. The project was announced in January 1930, with Berlin already in the process of writing a script and five songs. In March, singer-actor Regis Toomey was reported as likely for the lead—a Wall Street millionaire who gets wiped out in mid-voyage. By May, however, Toomey was out in favor of Douglas Fairbanks, who needed a picture but couldn't sing a note.

Berlin's enthusiasm wavered; he was unhappy being stuck in California, yet musically he felt he was doing some of the best work of his career. (He was particularly proud of a moody waltz that carried the film's title.) Neither *Mammy* nor *Puttin' on the Ritz* had been of particular importance to him—either personally or professionally. Fairbanks' participation ensured a generous budget, and Schenck afforded the production every courtesy. But the screenplay wasn't right, and the size of the undertaking made it an inappropriate choice for John Considine's debut as director. When, in August, actor-playwright and sometime composer Edmund Goulding replaced Considine, Berlin rejoiced, hailing Goulding as "a genius [who] talks my language."

The honeymoon was short-lived. Musicals, which, along with stage plays, had been a mainstay of the talking screen, had fallen into disfavor. "The producers looked forward to an era of revues, operettas, musical comedies, and even talked a little of grand opera," wrote Edwin Schallert in the *Los Angeles Times*. "Today they have turned thumbs down on even the suggestion of most such ventures. The truth of the matter is that the majority of musical pictures were flops at the box office. It

As originally conceived by Menzies, the ocean liner in *Reaching for the Moon* (1931) was a triumph of spatial arrangement and forced perspective. Considerably modified, the actual set was used to stage the boisterous Irving Berlin number "When the Folks High Up Do the Mean Low-Down" and little else. (MENZIES FAMILY COLLECTION)

got to such a stage that filmmakers became positively afraid of such product. They retitled follies shows and shelved other productions that relied for their appeal on melody. Even pictures with incidental music were referred to as 'straight' comedies or dramas, or else other people were featured beside the singing principals."

Filming began in October with a script credited to playwright—and longtime Ziegfeld associate—William Anthony McGuire. Four songs made the cut, and Berlin, in a letter to a friend, reported that the picture "really looks great." Goulding, he added, was "doing a great job on the story. The numbers are well placed." But then something happened to completely change the course of the movie. Likely, that something was *The Lottery Bride,* Feature's second film musical, which was an obvious stiff to preview audiences. Goulding, perhaps under pressure, made the decision to rewrite the script, removing all the song numbers and rendering the movie one of those "straight" comedies Schallert had alluded to just a couple of months earlier. According to Maurice Kussell, the choreographer on the picture, Goulding had a "violent disagreement" with Berlin, who walked out on *Reaching for the Moon.*

The fallout was significant. At a cost of more than $1 million, *Reaching for the Moon* was a guaranteed money-loser. Overextended, Schenck transferred control of Art Cinema to Sam Goldwyn. Berlin went back to New York, not to return until the making of *Top Hat* in 1935. Douglas Fairbanks lost interest in moviemaking, and retired for good in 1934. Considine accepted an offer from Winfield Sheehan to join Fox as a producer and, eventually, it was promised, director. Bunny Dull, Schenck's production manager, followed Considine to Fox as the new unit's business manager. And, on December 15, 1930, Menzies, having obtained a formal release from Schenck, signed with Fox as well, a move that would finally bring him a chance to direct.

Menzies' deal with Fox was for one picture at a salary of $7,500. Strictly speaking, his draw of $500 a week represented a $300 pay cut from what he was making with Schenck, but it was an opportunity he had long coveted and a gamble he was willing to take. "Producers are spending plenty of time fussing as to prospective future stars, feature players, etc., and wasting a lot of money, but they are doing very little in the way of scouting for new directorial material," Harry Modisette observed in a trade paper commentary. "They think nothing of foisting a new face on the public, after having invested several thousand dollars on that particular film, but ask them to give a chance to a fellow who has never directed a picture, but who may have shown his qualifications during a period of years in a thousand ways, and they throw up their hands in horror."

It was a common practice in the early days of sound to pair even established directors with dialogue men who were usually drawn from the stage. When Lewis Milestone directed *All Quiet on the Western Front,* he had George Cukor, a veteran of dramatic stock, to handle the actors, many of whom had no theatrical training. When Cukor himself became a director at Paramount, he was teamed with a man experienced in the mechanics of filmmaking, an editor named Cyril Gardner. And so it was that Menzies, who knew as much about the camera as any director working in Hollywood, was given a codirector in the person of an actor named Kenneth MacKenna. It would be MacKenna, thirty-one, who would coach the performers, leaving the camera work and the physical look of the picture to Menzies. "Wise boy, Kenneth, to direct instead of act," Louella Parsons commented. "I am told he did very well in New York when he produced *Windows* and *What Every Woman Knows.* There are plenty of actors, but few directors, and if Mr. MacKenna has a talent in that direction my advice to him is to direct."

In January, it was announced that Menzies' first film with MacKenna would be *Always Goodbye,* the original story of a "female Lothario" by playwright Kate McLaurin. The picture was supposed to showcase the Italian-born actress Elissa Landi, who had just completed her first picture for Fox. There was a general assumption the ethereal Landi was being groomed by production chief Winfield Sheehan to be Fox's answer to Garbo and Marlene Dietrich—a stretch in that Landi, though beguiling, had none of the smoky mystery that distinguished those actresses. She was, in fact, decidedly at a disadvantage as a man-killer, but her native intelligence—and a set of piercing green eyes—commanded attention. Menzies and MacKenna spent twelve weeks preparing the film, MacKenna exhibiting a flair for literary values that informed his later career as a story editor for M-G-M. The film went into production on March 9 under the title *Red-Handed.*

There wasn't much to be done with the picture, and the script, mostly the work of actor-playwright Lynn Starling, wasn't as cinematic as it was theatrical and witty. Other than a lively jazz party montage at the film's opening—and some smoothly accomplished tracking shots—the burden of the work fell to MacKenna. Dialogue was staged in long takes with relatively few reaction shots. Filming wrapped on April 3 after twenty-three days before the cameras. The result was a conventional caper picture, scarcely an hour in length. Menzies agreed to a contract modification that gave MacKenna equal billing ("A William C. Menzies and Kenneth MacKenna Production") and Fox studio superintendent Sol Wurtzel picked up his option on April 18. Three weeks later, with the film cut and awaiting release, the studio tore up Menzies' old contract and awarded him a new three-picture deal at $10,000 per.

*Always Goodbye* opened at New York's Roxy Theatre on May 22, 1931. The notices were polite, the attendance unexceptional. Judging it "better than average," Irene Thirer of the *Daily News* was the only major critic to highlight the debut team of Menzies and MacKenna. "Give them a hand," she wrote at the head of her review. "The Roxy's film moves smoothly, interestingly, and tastefully for three-quarters of an hour. It doesn't become obvious until the first half has been unreeled. Then its hold on you weakens considerably and you're sure you know exactly how it's going to conclude. And you're right!"

Two Menzies-MacKenna collaborations were announced for the 1931–32 season, both again featuring Elissa Landi and sporting the underdeveloped titles *Cheating* and *In Her Arms*. ("Oriental pride yields to Parisian kisses in a duel of male might and female charm" blared the copy.) Ultimately, the studio had a property better suited to Menzies' sensibilities in *The Spider*, a "play of the varieties" that had notched more than three hundred performances on Broadway. *"The Spider,"* Menzies later observed, "was novel inasmuch as all the happenings occurred on one set, a theatre auditorium, stage, backstage, and dressing rooms." For it, Menzies would be working again with unit art director Gordon Wiles, who had been part of his team at United Artists. Wiles, in turn, would bring forth the interiors of an entire vaudeville theater in the impressionistic strokes Menzies envisioned, eschewing the ornate detailing that had once typified the house style at UA. Actor-playwright Barry Con-

Edmund Lowe, Howard Phillips, and Lois Moran in the backstage thriller *The Spider* (1931) (AUTHOR'S COLLECTION)

ners, an ex-vaudevillian, was brought onto the project to draft a final shooting script. Menzies sat with him and, working from continuity sketches, meticulously detailed the entire visual structure of the film, shot by shot. When filming commenced on June 11, 1931, the picture had been prepared to such an extraordinary degree that a three-week schedule was not deemed unreasonable.

Starring as master magician Chatrand the Great, a role created in New York by John Halliday, would be Edmund Lowe, an efficient if somewhat colorless actor who had been an attraction for Fox since his turn as Sergeant Quirt in *What Price Glory?* Paired with Lowe as the niece of the murdered man would be Lois Moran, soon to conquer Broadway in the Gershwin musicals *Of Thee I Sing* and *Let 'Em Eat Cake*. Imposed on the production as a member of the audience would be El Brendel, the ubiquitous faux Swede who was somebody's idea of comic relief.

Menzies took particular relish in the shooting of Chatrand's stage effects, which included the severing of a human head and the film's climactic séance, during which the shade of the dead man is summoned from the spirit world and the killer with the spider ring is revealed to the audience. Menzies tended to refer to these bits as "devices" as one might refer to a gadget designed to do a specific thing. "It's the way we fool the camera, not the audience," he explained. "The camera is the real heavy because it sees what we don't want it to see and it sometimes picks up what we don't want it to. [In] *The Spider* . . . I wanted to use that gag about the magician's cutting off the woman's head. Remember that old trick? Well, I wanted to do it without cutting, shooting it in a single sequence and keeping the camera moving for the entire scene. Of course, we could have cut it together, but it was more fun to do it the other way just for our own satisfaction."

Throughout, the film was taut and elegantly composed, as handsome and careful a job of staging as anything Fox had managed that season. When Winnie Sheehan screened *The Spider* toward the end of July, he sent Menzies a congratulatory note: "I consider it a 'corking' good entertainment, an excellent mystery melodrama, and everyone connected with the picture deserves credit, to which I herewith subscribe."

Sheehan wasn't the only one taken with *The Spider*. *The Hollywood Spectator* extravagantly praised the work of Edmund Lowe, Lois Moran, Menzies, and Kenneth MacKenna, despairing only at the presence of El Brendel in the cast. "The sustained sequences wherein Lowe and Howard Phillips—a very personable young gentleman, by way of interpolation—try to locate the murderer who is seated in the audience before them, are tense and gripping when they very well might have been boring and ridiculous. The lighting effects and camera technic displayed in these scenes are striking." The New York notices were somewhat more reserved, hampered as they were by memories of Albert Lewis' original staging of the play, where the entire audience effectively became part of the cast. All lauded the film's breakneck pacing, and most all appreciated the intensity of Lowe's hammy performance as Chatrand, a job that reportedly left the actor on the verge of a nervous breakdown. Again, it fell to Pare Lorentz to highlight Menzies' contributions to the picture, which were considerable and obvious to anyone who was paying attention.

"It is entertaining, amusing, well-knit, and, above all, as beautiful to see as *Karamazov, Sous Les Toits,* or any foreign picture we have seen," Lorentz said of *The Spider.* "Fortunately, the semi-supernatural plot allowed Menzies to indulge himself in simple, austere sets—huge Gothic arches, dimly lighted, with his characters in black silhouetted against them—sets that heightened the atmosphere and aided the plot. Besides the architecture, *The Spider* is worth seeing because of its good pace, its easy humor, and its excellent cast. I hope Mr. Menzies gets a crack at another manuscript soon. He is one of the few movie-minded men in all Hollywood."

*The Spider* drew well in places like Minneapolis, where the trades credited word of mouth and "fastidious critics" for the crowds at the Lyric Theatre. At a cost of $311,517, the film went on to worldwide rentals of $519,137, showing a modest profit of $16,052. Following the disappointment of *Always Goodbye,* which drew respectable notices but posted a loss of nearly $70,000, Menzies and MacKenna were finally proving their directorial worth to the management at Fox Film. Sheehan approved separate pictures for both men, assigning MacKenna a racy comedy called *Good Sport* and Menzies another thriller with the working title of *Circumstance.*

Originally published in Great Britain as *The Devil's Triangle, Circumstance* was the work of the prolific English novelist Andrew Soutar, whose particular bent was mystery and spiritualism. Soutar's book was snapped up while still in manuscript, and treatments had already been developed by Kathryn Scola, Doris Malloy, and, of late, the redoubtable Guy Bolton, who was working through a term contract he seemed to regret having signed. When Menzies came onto the project, he took Bolton's September 2 treatment, written in the traditional style of a short story, and recast it as a sixty-nine-page screenplay with an emphasis on action and imagery over dialogue. He broke it down into individual shots and played a key reception sequence as a series of quick lap dissolves. With the filmic structure sketched in, he was given the okay to go to full script with playwright Edith Ellis supplying the dialogue. Menzies' old friend Wallace Smith was subsequently brought in for a rewrite, charged with getting away from the director's fussy shot-specific format. A second draft incorporated yet another set of shot specifications, Menzies and Smith collaborating in much the same way they had in their days together with Schenck at UA.

Production began on October 26, 1931, with Broadway's Violet Heming making her talking feature debut. The English-born Heming, thirty-six, had been signed by Winfield Sheehan during one of his quick trips east, her latest show, *Divorce Me, Dear,* having closed after just six performances. Known for her way with light comedy, Heming understandably felt ill-served by *Circumstance,* in which she was required to play a Russian-born heroine who finds herself wed to a madman. Menzies could be of little help to her, and she played the part with an air of resignation, making no attempt whatsoever to affect an accent. As Capristi, her demented husband, Alexander Kirkland was allowed to run off with the picture, leaving Heming to play most of her scenes opposite Fox contract player Ralph Bellamy (who was nine years her junior).

Menzies kept the film on schedule, devoting considerable attention to Capristi's escape from an English asylum, a bravura piece of Expressionist filmmaking that would come to be regarded as the picture's best sequence. With Kirkland chewing the scenery and Heming giving a dispirited, off-kilter performance, *Circumstance* failed to catch fire dramatically. The rushes weren't playing, and whatever suspense Menzies managed to kindle was more the result of design and camera technique than genuine storytelling prowess. When the picture wrapped on November 18, there was a sense of its having missed its mark, but nobody seemed to know quite what to do about it. Under the title *Almost Married,* it was put before a raucous preview audience on the evening of December 3. The next morning, a devastating account of the event appeared in *The Hollywood Reporter* under the headline "'ALMOST MARRIED' CAN'T MAKE GRADE."

"Although the title suggests a sophisticated comedy drama," the unsigned notice began,

> *Almost Married* is an out-and-out melodrama, with a madman, a harassed heroine, and shadows on the wall. It is so badly done, unimaginatively directed and indifferently acted, that the preview audience last night was openly derisive in spots where they should have been swooning with fright. Not only is the story difficult to follow, jumping as it does from Paris to Russia to London before it finally gets settled, but the director depends for his effects upon numerous closeups of a madman's glaring eyes and the above-mentioned shadows on the wall whenever things seem to be slowing down. . . . The only commendable feature of the production is the photography.

James B. M. Fisher of the Motion Picture Producers and Distributors of America (MPPDA) witnessed the preview. "While it contains nothing contrary to the

Code," he advised in a résumé, "it is another 'gruesome' picture which falls in the class with *Dracula, Frankenstein, Dr. Jekyll and Mr. Hyde,* and *Freaks.* Maybe we are starting a style. We would be pleased to have from New York any advice that can be given to help us to come to conclusions concerning it." The MPPDA's Jason Joy wrote his boss, morality czar Will Hays, the next day: "Is this the beginning of a cycle that ought to be retarded or killed?"

Fox, meanwhile, was in poor shape, with losses mounting and its management in disarray. Heads began to roll with the firing of longtime production manager Theodore Butcher. "This is looked upon as the first in a series of changes among the executives of this company," *The Reporter* noted. "Dismissals, it is understood, will range from the highest to the lowest, no one being too small to be overlooked nor too great to be exempt." Among the first to be sacked were director Allan Dwan, producer-songwriter Buddy DeSylva, and William "Billy" Sistrom—the producer of *Almost Married.*

The studio held firm to a January 17 release date as New York production executive Richard Rowland commissioned a new treatment incorporating more of Guy Bolton's material. But the Fox lot was crawling with auditors, Chase Bank representatives seeking to strictly limit Winfield Sheehan's influence at a time of fiscal crisis. New people were brought in for budgeting and scheduling, and Keith Weeks, the former Prohibition agent who was Sheehan's handpicked studio manager, was given fifteen minutes to clear out of his office. Harley Clarke, the interim president of Fox, had been removed—sent back to Chicago by the same banking interests who had put him there in the first place—and replaced with Edward R. Tinker, board chairman of Chase National, a career banker who freely admitted he knew absolutely nothing about running a studio. On January 7, 1932, word came that Sheehan had suffered a nervous breakdown—an "authentic" one, the trade press reported—brought on, it was construed, by the systematic stripping of his studio authority. While he was reportedly recuperating at a sanitarium near San Francisco, responsibility for the balance of the Fox season fell to Sol Wurtzel, who was charged with bringing the average cost of a Fox feature down to an industry-wide target of $200,000.

Menzies could do nothing other than wait it out, not knowing how extensive the changes to *Almost Married* would be, nor whether he would be permitted to remain on the picture. In February, Bolton suggested a new opening, beginning the convoluted story in Russia instead of Paris and dispensing with Anita's marriage to Capristi with a flashback. Bolton proceeded to incorporate a number of revisions and clarifications into Wallace Smith's October 23 script, a version finalized on March 17 after Menzies had once again inserted his visual notations. In addressing the problem of the actors' performances, particularly Violet Heming's, Wurtzel assigned the Paris-born stage director Marcel Varnel to work alongside Menzies in much the same capacity as had Kenneth MacKenna. By the time retakes were completed in early April, the film's cost had swelled to $267,418 while its running time had shrunk to a mere fifty-one minutes. On April 21, an MPPDA résumé indicated that *Almost Married* again had been viewed, this time in a projection room at Fox. "A number of changes have been made to the picture, including the transportation of several foreign sequences and a new ending. It is our opinion that the revised version is satisfactory [to the Code]." A separate document described the film as "rather well produced—but not outstanding."

The debacle of *Almost Married* effectively ended Menzies' career as a solo director at Fox, even as the studio proved willing to keep him on. Prior to his illness, Sheehan had created several new directing teams in response to John Ford's departure over a salary dispute. Initially, Marcel Varnel had been joined with assistant director R. L. "Lefty" Hough, and together the two men had filmed *Silent Witness*, a small but unusually compelling courtroom drama. Varnel, thirty-nine, could handle

Violet Heming and Herbert Mundin in a chiaroscuro moment from *Almost Married* (1931), Menzies' troubled debut as a solo director  (AUTHOR'S COLLECTION)

actors effectively but had little knowledge of film technique, a circumstance that seemingly made him an ideal fit for Bill Menzies.

Menzies knew from the beginning that making the leap from the drafting table to the stage floor would be an uphill battle, as no art director had managed the feat since the coming of sound.* Fortunately, the failure of *Almost Married* was somewhat mitigated by the release of *The Spider*—and both events were concurrent with the debut of a syndicated radio serial called *Chandu the Magician.* Competition for the new property, being heard on some forty stations, came with the assumption of a built-in audience, and the purchase price of $40,000 was steep. (Fox, by comparison, had paid $27,500 for the rights to *The Spider,* which had proven its drawing power on Broadway.) Edmund Lowe was promptly announced as its star, and assigned to direct was actor-director John Francis Dillon. The deal for *Chandu* was finalized on March 29, 1932, as the retakes for *Almost Married* were being made. Barry Conners and Philip Klein, the prolific team responsible for *The Spider,* were put to work on an adaptation, and the combination of Menzies and Varnel soon supplanted Dillon as directors. Fox Film Corporation formally exercised Menzies' first-year option on May 9; the same day, Irene Ware, a slender redhead, late of *Earl Carroll's Vanities,* arrived in Los Angeles to begin work as a Fox contract player.

While *The Spider* incorporated brief episodes of mysticism, wispy strands of ectoplasm conjuring the spirit world and images of the dead, the picture was essentially an imaginatively filmed whodunit set within the confines of a metropolitan vaudeville house. And for all the earnestness of Edmund Lowe's one-note performance, it was directed with a wink and a nod, its tricks wholly and good-naturedly mechanical. *Chandu the Magician* was something else altogether, an effects-laden adventure in North Africa in which the title character was a genuine yogi with occult powers and an adversary bent on world domination. The story had romance and comedy and a scope approaching *The Thief of Bagdad,* albeit on roughly one fifth the budget. By early June, Menzies was puzzling out the story's visuals and leaving the casting decisions, for the most part, to his colleague Varnel.

Menzies, meanwhile, huddled with cameraman James Wong Howe, who had shot *The Spider* and found the new assignment "much more rewarding" than the Fox programmers to which he was typically assigned. For the Indian rope trick, they would fit a boy with a harness and elevate him with a wire and overhead gear. A full shot of the illusion would be made by staff effects specialist Ralph Hammeras using the Dunning Process to marry the foreground action with a reverse plate of

* In silent days, Hugo Ballin (*Jane Eyre, Vanity Fair*) and Ferdinand Pinney Earle (*A Lover's Oath* aka *The Rubaiyat of Omar Khayyam*) became directors, though Earle had to finance his own picture. In 1934, Cedric Gibbons would become the credited director on *Tarzan and His Mate.*

the temple background. The coals for a fire-walking stunt would be made of broken glass, lit from underneath and rigged for steam and lycopodium flames. The projection of a death ray would be handled by optical effects wizard Fred Sersen "by building a beam against black velvet and drawing a card across the beam exposing it at whatever speed is decided and then doubling this effect on the screen as shot on the set." All stunts, effects, and process shots for *Chandu the Magician* were agreed to and finalized on June 23, 1932.

The 116-page shooting final, dated July 7, 1932, incorporated visual continuity to an unusual degree, expressing graphic values and technical details alongside the traditional elements of dialogue and action. It wasn't ideal; Menzies preferred working off his continuity boards, but the *Chandu* script was the closest he had yet come to one fully integrated document for the making of a movie. With Lowe as Chandu and the promising but inexperienced Irene Ware as Nadji, the picture demanded a truly "evil and menacing" Roxor, the Egyptian madman in pursuit of a death ray. Actor Bela Lugosi, Universal's Dracula of the previous year, had done several pic-

Composition as storytelling: Bela Lugosi holds the foreground in this still posed on the set of *Chandu the Magician* (1932). Edmund Lowe and Irene Ware occupy the middle distance, their path of escape diminishing perilously behind them.
(AUTHOR'S COLLECTION)

The creative team behind *Chandu the Magician:* Co-director Marcel Varnel, Menzies, and cinematographer James Wong Howe. Varnel completed just one more picture for Fox before relocating to England, where he spent the rest of his career directing the likes of George Formby and Will Hay. (ACADEMY OF MOTION PICTURE ARTS AND SCIENCES)

tures at Fox as a freelancer and was secured for the part on a two-week guarantee. Rounding out the cast were veteran character actor Henry B. Walthall and Fox contract players Herbert Mundin, Weldon Heyburn, and June Vlasek. Filming began on July 11, 1932, and continued into early August.

For Menzies, the world of *Chandu* became a wizard's catalogue of split screens and double exposures, miniatures, rear projections, and Tesla coils. Some opticals limited his compositions, while others proved unequal to the film's limited budget. Throughout, a mood of ancient mysticism pervaded, enveloping the performances, lending tone and texture to readings where otherwise there would have been none. ("There's no question that when actors walk into a set of any kind it will affect their performance," he once said.) Seemingly immune to such augmentation, Bela Lugosi proved the lone standout, as potent as any camera trick, his thick Hungarian accent—he hadn't yet mastered English—giving his Roxor a Homeric quality, his orgasmic rant, over visions of the world's great cities falling to his death ray ("All that lives shall know me as master and tremble at my word!") as Shakespearean as anything in the popular cinema of the day.

Immersed in the production of *Chandu,* Menzies was able to ignore the inglorious release of *Almost Married,* which was exiled to Brooklyn for the week of July 22. Mercifully, the New York dailies failed to take notice, leaving its critical drubbing largely to the trades. "Beyond the paucity of screen names," went the *Variety* review, "the film struggles along with a pretty much overdrawn and implausible story. Some of it is quite well handled, and there is sufficient action, but even within the confines of 50 minutes a good deal of the film is slow and draggy. . . . It's pretty complicated, and William Cameron Menzies, turning in his first directorial job, couldn't seem to avoid being buried under the various tangents." The film's November opening in Los Angeles went similarly unacknowledged and was held to the outskirts of the market, playing double bills strictly in neighborhood houses. Worldwide revenues for *Almost Married* were a dismal $228,271, resulting in an eventual loss of nearly $140,000.

The best news for Menzies that summer was *Chandu,* its potential seemingly limitless as it rolled its way toward an aggressive release date of September 18. Due to effects shots requiring lab and optical work, the movie wasn't ready for preview until September 2, nearly a month after production had closed.

*The Hollywood Reporter:*

There are several million kids, more or less, waiting for this picture all over the United States, just as they have been waiting at 7:15, five evenings a week, during the last year for the latest episode of *Chandu the Magician* over the air. Judging from the reception two or three hundred youngsters gave the production last night, even though their elders smiled indulgently at Eddie Lowe's feats of magic, this picture will spread a new crop of black ink on the Fox books. After the exhibitors have played this one, they'll probably start wiring their local Fox exchange to find out when they can book *The Further Adventures of Chandu the Magician.*

Chapin Hall of *The New York Times* hailed the picture as the first of potentially many radio properties to make it to the screen.

The piece has been skillfully handled and, with the story and the setting, used the camera tricks [to] appear to be genuine magic. The screen apparently has not dared use these tricks since the earlier days, when men jumped out of rivers onto bridges for comedy reasons. But Chandu walks through walls, escapes from a coffin at the bottom of the Nile, walks through fire without the slightest discomfort, and does all the glorious things expected of such a hero. An audience of reputedly cynical newspaper fellows hissed the villain and applauded the rescue of the heroine with a sincerity which was remarkable.

Sol Wurtzel authorized a full-page ad in the September 13 issue of *Variety.* Under the headline "PACKED WITH EXPLOITATION MAGIC," the studio heralded the sixty-two stations then carrying the radio *Chandu* and promised local tie-ups with Beech-Nut distributors and White King soap—companies that "spent a fortune in car card and billboard advertising of the broadcast."

It was hard not to buy into the notion that Fox had a monster hit at the ready, and plans were to open the picture in Los Angeles ahead of its New York premiere. Advance press leaned heavily on the radio connection, and early reviews called to mind the same early chapter plays that Chapin Hall remembered so fondly. "As conceived by Fox Films, *Chandu* comes pretty close to being the ideal cameraman's nightmare," Philip K. Scheuer wrote in the *Los Angeles Times.* "So jauntily incredible are its sequences, so pell-mell do they come tumbling forth, that one is all but convinced that he has walked in upon a revival of a 1915 movie. There are only those voices, those unearthly sound effects, to persuade him otherwise. Those, and a really ingenious use of the cinematograph."

Business skewed more heavily to kids than initially anticipated—not a good sign—and the tie-ins with the radio serial reinforced the idea that grown-ups should stay away. Rob Wagner, who, in his magazine *Rob Wagner's Script,* presumed to speak for the adults in the audience, defined the recipe:

Take a bunch of turbans, several crystal balls, a nest of snakes, eight Egyptian mummies, a bag of toads, the Hindu rope trick, and some esoteric Yogi hokum. Add to these good old props of the Mystic East a lot of faked experimental machines and gadgets from the Western Electric Company's laboratories, and the phony science page of the *Examiner*'s Sunday supplement. Stir in a Chinese cameraman, Bela Lugosi, and Eddie Lowe's hypnotic eyes. Then let thirty-two screen-credited authors, laughing in their sleeves at the alleged moronic mentalities of American audiences, stir to the consistency of applesauce. Serve to the accompaniment of screech horns and tom-toms in the key of Asia minor. This is the dish Mr. Fox F. Corp. served at the Beverly Theatre, hoping to mystify and frighten the villagers. But all he got for his and the audience's pains were a few faintly repressed Bronx cheers from the adults, laughter from the adultoresses, and raspberries from the kids.

*Chandu the Magician* was hardly a disaster. Worldwide rentals totaled nearly $500,000, but it never took off in the way the studio had hoped, inspiring awestruck word of mouth and repeat business from followers of the daily radio serial. At a final cost of $349,456, *Chandu* fell short of break-even by more than $50,000, bringing Menzies' record of losses as a director at Fox to nearly a quarter million dollars.

# 9

# Wonderland

As preparations for *Chandu the Magician* went forth, William Cameron Menzies was effectively demoted to art director with Fox's announcement in late June 1932 that he would be designing the sets for *Cavalcade,* Winfield Sheehan's first personal production since his return to the studio. The Noël Coward play, a span of English life as seen from above and below stairs, had first come to the studio's attention when the wife of Fox president Edward R. Tinker saw the author's own staging of the show in London and cabled her husband. The scope of the story, which covered thirty years of British history as seen from the perspective of a single household, would demand the best of Fox's contract talent. Playwright S. N. Behrman and Sonya Levien had been put to work on an adaptation, and Glasgow-born Frank Lloyd, a veteran of more than one hundred pictures, was set to direct. That the film would be a prestige credit was beyond any reasonable doubt, just as it would surely be seen within the industry as a comedown for Bill Menzies.

Chandu provided enough of a respite that Menzies was unable to design *Cavalcade* in the time allotted, and the job eventually passed to longtime Fox staffer William Darling. The final screenplay, delivered between the Los Angeles and New York openings of *Chandu,* called for a "symbolic passage of the war years," and Menzies was assigned the task of covering the whole of the Great War in approximately three and a half minutes of screen time. Scenarist Reginald Berkeley envisioned the sequence "as a piece of impressionism. 1914, 15, 16, 17, 18. Soldiers, in the smart field dress and soft caps of 1914, are marching briskly in unscarred, open country, through a conventional French village, in drowsy summer weather." Berkeley described a steady deterioration of the troops and their surroundings as the years drag on, the mud thickening and the wreckage of war evolving into "one vast cemetery of crosses."

Menzies was allocated to *Cavalcade* for the entire seven weeks it took to shoot the movie, often functioning as Sheehan's executive assistant, particularly when the studio boss was out of town. He was even asked at one point to oversee the shooting of cast stills. Demoralized, he chose to embellish Berkeley's trudge of death—men trailing across the screen and snaking into the distance—with a montage of battle scenes now all too familiar to movie audiences from a glut of pictures about the Great War. His days were consumed with the filming of graphic imagery, endless shots of proud figures marching on treadmills, their faces often filling the screen, the dead dropping from view, the pacing of the cuts quickening as the mindless slaughter continues unabated. *Cavalcade* would go on to become a monster hit, garnering three Academy Awards, including Best Picture and Best Director, but Menzies would never speak of the film and refused to include it among his credits.

His next assignment was yet another venture into the world of conjuring, creating the "technical effects" for the battle royal between magicians that had been known on Broadway as *Trick for Trick*. No longer entitled to a co-direction credit, he would instead be asked to convert the casual sleight-of-hand of the stage show to a series of flamboyant illusions better suited to the size and technical capabilities of the talking screen. Actor-director Hamilton MacFadden would be in charge of the story and the commonplace mystery at its core, leaving the camera directions and the physical look of the film to Menzies and unit art director Duncan Cramer. Employing techniques refined during the production of *Chandu,* Menzies created some genuinely spectacular moments, causing a hall carpet to come to life, a staircase to appear and disappear one step at a time, and the entire floor of a furnished room to vanish. The job, which involved eight weeks of preparation as well as a four-week shoot, was grueling in the hours it demanded, the otherwise impressive results hampered by a weak script and indifferent casting.

With Menzies' assignment to *I Loved You Wednesday,* an odd amalgam of comedy and drama based on a Broadway flop of the same title, it appeared that his fall from grace was permanent and that the studio would likely not be taking up his next option. *Wednesday* began filming on March 27, 1933, with the very capable Henry King directing and Menzies charged with merely framing the shots, his principal responsibility being the design and staging—with dance director Sammy Lee—of a neo-Egyptian riot of a ballet for June Vlasek and Elissa Landi. The sado-erotic "Dance of the Maidens" turned out so well, in fact, that Winnie Sheehan issued instructions that Menzies be given a reprieve of sorts—co-direction credit on the picture.

Several days later, however, Menzies' contract was allowed to lapse and he was summarily taken off salary, even as *I Loved You Wednesday* remained in production. King completed the picture with location work at Boulder Dam, and Landi promptly fled town, her whereabouts and destination unknown.

On September 22, 1932, Lamarr Trotti, assistant to Colonel Jason Joy of the MPPDA's Studio Relations Committee, memoed his boss. Trotti had read of actress Eva Le Gallienne's new stage adaptation of *Alice in Wonderland,* set to open in

The Cubist "Dance of the Maidens" from *I Loved You Wednesday* (1933), a wild interlude in an otherwise routine picture that earned Menzies a co-direction credit. The featured dancers are George Bruggeman and June Vlasek. At right, doing her best to keep out of the way, is Elissa Landi. (AUTHOR'S COLLECTION)

December at Le Gallienne's Manhattan Civic Repertory Theatre, and suggested that Fox, to where Joy, as a production executive, would soon be moving, make a film of it. *Alice* had been in the news for a number of reasons, not the least of which was the centenary of the birth of Charles Lutwidge Dodgson, who, under the pseudonym Lewis Carroll, had written *Alice's Adventures in Wonderland* and its sequel *Through the Looking-Glass.* In the United States, the 1932 commemoration included an exhibition of the original manuscript and a visit from Mrs. Alice Hargreaves, the author's inspiration for the stories.

There had been earlier screen versions of the Alice books, the first dating from 1903. There had, in fact, already been an all-talking version, a primitive independent shot in New Jersey in 1931. The books were in the public domain in the United States, available to anyone, but not in England, where the rights had been tied up by actor Edgar Norton, who had revered the works since childhood and thought

At the Henry E. Huntington Library in San Marino, Menzies, director Norman Z. McLeod, and screenwriter Joseph L. Mankiewicz examine printer George Dalziel's copy of *Alice's Adventures in Wonderland.* (ACADEMY OF MOTION PICTURE ARTS AND SCIENCES)

they would combine to make a wonderful feature. It was Norton who discouraged a Walt Disney version of *Alice* because the entire film, with the sole exception of Mary Pickford, would be animated. Fox Film, at Colonel Joy's instigation, contemplated a live action picture, as did Universal. Mrs. Norton, a onetime Broadway actress and now her husband's manager, took the proposition to Paramount, ultimately settling the rights at the cinematic home of Ernst Lubitsch and the Four Marx Brothers.

In June 1933, the studio announced a worldwide search for the girl to play Alice. Meanwhile, staff writer Joseph L. Mankiewicz was given the task of developing a treatment. Mankiewicz, in his first conference with production head Emanuel L. Cohen, asked Cohen which book he wanted to make "because you can't do them both in one film." Cohen replied, "We own them both. We're going to do them both." Mankiewicz was already at work on a conflation of the two books when Norman Z. McLeod was selected as director of *Alice in Wonderland.* A former cartoonist and veteran of ten features, McLeod seemed an inspired choice for the absurdist world of Lewis Carroll. It was, in fact, McLeod who saw the need for Menzies on such a picture—and for more than just "trick sequences" (as one trade paper erroneously reported). Menzies had staged the "Alice" segment for *Puttin' on the Ritz* using papier-mâché masks to duplicate the original character designs of Sir John Tenniel.

With the concurrence of associate producer Louis D. "Bud" Lighton, it was agreed that Tenniel's illustrations would be used as a basis throughout. As Mankiewicz worked ahead on his scenario, Menzies began illustrating the film, intent upon developing a hybrid form of script that incorporated dialogue, technical directions, and action within a fully visualized continuity. "[The] idea has been suggested numerous times by artists as a possible economy step," *Variety* reported. "It never reached first base, however, with the studios unable to get the artists and directors to see each other's side of the argument." Working with pencil on yellow scrap paper, Menzies would make a freehand border and rough in the shot, carefully printing out the action and any technical notations in his own distinctive hand.

In combining the two books, holding to the Carroll text, and keeping the look of the characters true to the originals, the project came close to embracing the conventions of the Le Gallienne production. Moreover, the actress had been adamant that her *Alice* not just be for children, as past adaptations had been: "The story as Carroll wrote it is enjoyed as much, if not more, by adults than it is by children, and that's what we mean the play to be." For the filmmakers, this translated into seeding the cast with as many big names as possible, creating for the adults a sort of guessing game of who exactly was impersonating whom. Bing Crosby for the Mock Turtle. Charles Laughton for Humpty-Dumpty. Mary Boland for the White Queen. The challenge was in creating rubber masks for these players that would allow their facial

The beginnings of a fully integrated screenplay for *Alice in Wonderland* (1933): Working from Joe Mankiewicz's outline, Menzies would rough in a composition, writing out the action and adding technical notes. The shooting final was three inches thick, contained 642 illustrations, and weighed six and a half pounds. (MENZIES FAMILY COLLECTION) expressions to come through. To this end, Paramount's Wally Westmore partnered with Max Factor to create a sufficiently flexible latex foundation, using comedian Jack Oakie (who was to play Tweedledum) as his guinea pig. As of late July, the masks were satisfactory in terms of looks and functionality, but they put off such an offensive odor it was impossible for Oakie to wear one for more than a few minutes.

By August 11, optical effects specialist Farciot Edouart had reviewed all 276 pages of yellow script and identified a total of forty-four process shots—nineteen projection (rear screen) transparencies and twenty-five blue screen transparencies—in addition to miniatures and a number of purely mechanical effects. Menzies, by then, was producing finished pages, conscious of the need for the Steno Department to eventually trace those images onto mimeograph stencils. Mankiewicz crammed everything he could into the story, sending Alice down the rabbit hole to Wonderland as well as integrating episodes from the world behind the looking-glass. A prologue, which would come later, would complete the melding of the two works, with Alice, bored on a winter's day, stepping through the mirror above the fireplace in order to see the reverse room on the other side.

Casting went forward as the film's September start date approached, with most roles being filled by Paramount contract players. Ford Sterling, Skeets Gallagher, Raymond Hatton, Polly Moran, Sterling Holloway, Roscoe Ates, Alison Skipworth, Lillian Harmer, Richard Arlen, Jackie Searl, Charlie Ruggles, Baby LeRoy, May Robson, Alec B. Francis, William Austin, Edna May Oliver, and Roscoe Karns were all set for parts by the end of August. Up in Wally Westmore's studio, Newt Jones, who had started with Menzies as a blueprint boy in 1928, was kept busy spraying rubber masks. In early September, Gary Cooper was assigned the role of the White Knight. Louise Fazenda was brought in to sub for Mary Boland (who was on location in Hawaii), and W. C. Fields was tapped to replace Charles Laughton as Humpty-Dumpty. Also added to the cast were Leon Errol, Edward Everett Horton, and Ned Sparks.

Production opened on September 11, 1933, with Leon Errol in a brief turn as Alice's uncle Gilbert, but with no firm decision as yet on Alice herself. The company laid off for two days as Norman McLeod made additional tests, but the picture was already ten days behind schedule, and Manny Cohen ordered the director to have a girl selected by the 15th. With the list of choices narrowed to three (only one of whom, seventeen-year-old Ida Lupino, was actually English), McLeod dropped the decision into the collective lap of Cohen's executive team and went back to making process shots with Menzies.

Management was anxious to get the film finished so prints could be in England and its possessions—where *Alice* had become a holiday institution—by Christmas. (It was feared that going in after the holidays would result in a 50 percent drop in potential revenues.) On Friday, September 16, the last-minute selection of nineteen-year-old Charlotte Henry, a bit player who had previously appeared for Paramount in *Huckleberry Finn,* was announced in the trade press. With the cast largely complete, shooting began in earnest the following Monday with Menzies and McLeod working side by side, Menzies guiding the camerawork and overseeing the effects while McLeod handled the actors. The massive 646-page screenplay containing Menzies' illustrations turned out to be too huge to give the players, and a more traditional 200-page version, sans the drawings, was submitted to the MPPDA and used by the film's nontechnical personnel. Still, it was Menzies' illustrated screenplay that everyone who came on the set wanted to see, and the *Los Angeles Times* reported that three publishers were bidding for the rights.

As the film came together—particularly the optical effects as they were returned

*Alice in Wonderland* brought the drawings of John Tenniel to life, but at the cost of obscuring its actors under pounds of latex. Typical were Jack Oakie and Roscoe Karns, preparing to do battle here as Tweedledum and Tweedledee. As in most scenes, the presence of Alice (Charlotte Henry) serves to amplify the film's grotesqueries. (AUTHOR'S COLLECTION)

from the lab—there was unanimous delight over what was sure to be an enormous hit. The only sour notes were sounded by the actors who found themselves encased in rubber with only their voices left to register an impression. "The costumes and the headpieces were so heavy that the actors couldn't carry them," remembered Joe Mankiewicz, "so they had doubles walking through all the master or long shots." In costume, an actor could only take nourishment through a straw, and the stage, when lit, was hellishly hot. One day on the set, seventy-year-old Alison Skipworth, playing the Duchess, fainted dead away from the heat.

"The only part I ever asked for was the Mad Hatter in *Alice in Wonderland*," recalled Edward Everett Horton, "and I was sorry. They made everyone wear such heavy makeup and such cumbersome costumes, nobody could be identified. . . . Why, everyone knows I look exactly like the Mad Hatter and Charlie Ruggles' face with his little whiskers is just right—as it is—for the March Hare. Well, they just ruined the whole picture." It's possible, in fact, that Menzies' well-known disdain for actors came from his experiences with them on *Alice.* Suzanne Menzies could recall a day in October 1933 when she and her sister, Jean, were allowed to visit the Paramount lot. Their host, a studio functionary, asked if they'd care to meet Humpty-Dumpty. Led onto a darkened soundstage, they observed a grotesque figure in a canvas chair, an egg-shaped prosthesis glued to his head and a set of spindly legs dangling lifelessly from his chin. "I guess it was W. C. Fields," she said. "He was evidently drunk, sitting there and bellowing something. We were ushered out quickly."

Work on the screenplay was finally finished on October 19 when revisions to the Tweedledee and Tweedledum sequence were filed with the Hays Office. Casting, however, wasn't fully settled until early November—seven weeks into production. Bud Lighton had been unsuccessful in convincing either Bing Crosby or Russ Columbo to play the Mock Turtle, and Paramount contract player Cary Grant, who had played the music halls in his native England and could sing passably, was assigned the part. With three or four weeks of work remaining, there was no room for emendations or mishaps. In the interest of time, the garden of living flowers and the looking-glass insects from the second book were eliminated from the schedule. And when, in late October, Norman McLeod fell ill with the flu, Menzies stepped in as director.

For Alice, the end of the looking-glass world comes with a climactic banquet for the looking-glass creatures, a crown upon her head, the drowsy White Queen seated to her right, the equally drowsy Red Queen to her left. "I rise," Alice tells the assemblage—and literally she does, suddenly lighter than air. Following the book's lead, Menzies created a nightmare spectacle of drunken birds, rodents, rabbits, and frogs, objects taking flight as candelabras burst into fireworks. "Something's going to happen!" the White Queen warns. "Something's going to happen!" In the script, Menzies called for one-foot flashes of the various characters, repeatedly underscoring a tempo of malevolence.

"With music, screaming, and the sputtering and boom of fireworks as a hellish background, Alice finds herself rising once more. Rising with her, on all sides, are bottles equipped with wings . . . both Queens are busy screaming constantly and monotonously and hear nothing . . . Alice, hanging uncomfortably in the air, watches with fear as several decanters fly past her." The dinner roast appears in the chair beside her, issuing a cheery greeting. With a mad laugh, the White Queen disappears down a tureen of soup, gurgling loudly as she descends. "The musical and vocal backgrounds have by now reached a veritable madhouse of discord . . . All the animals turn and glare balefully at Alice . . . As one man, they now climb upon the hopelessly messy table and start toward her . . . Frankly, completely, and utterly terrified, she waits for her doom . . . Down the table toward Alice come the animals on their menacing march. Through smoke and eerie lighting, each growling, grumbling, or squeaking ominously—they advance. Stepping on plates, crashing into carafes, upsetting dishes, on they come."

The final image in this frenzied assault on the senses is that of the Red Queen, her hands wrapped murderously around Alice's neck, seemingly choking the life from her, a shocker of a switch on Lewis Carroll, who had Alice shaking the mischievous Red Queen "into a kitten" only to awaken from the dream and find a real kitten—her own—in her hands. In the twist engineered by Menzies and Mankiewicz, the sequence is infinitely darker, a precursor of sorts to the English portmanteau masterpiece *Dead of Night,* which also builds, in the words of Martin Scorsese, to "a crescendo of madness."

*Alice in Wonderland* closed on November 8, 1933, and previewed in Riverside on the evening of the 26th. Retakes were ordered, delaying Charlotte Henry's departure on a ten-thousand-mile promotional tour of the United States and Canada. Another sneak took place in Santa Monica on December 4, after which trims were ordered. Eliminated were Father William and Son from the episode of the caterpillar, the trial of the Knave of Hearts, the marionettes portraying the Jabberwocky and the Frumious Bandersnatch, and an epilogue featuring actress Jacqueline Wells as Alice's sister. At a final running time of seventy-six minutes, the picture was viewed by the Hays Office on December 9, 1933. In conferring approval, Dr. James Wingate complimented the studio on an excellent job. "We trust that, in addition to the satisfaction of having produced one of the most notable pictures of the year, Paramount will also find that the picture will measure up at the box office to its outstanding production quality."

For Menzies, credit on the picture was an uncertain matter. From a French liner crossing the Atlantic, screenwriter Paul Perez wrote to say that he had read the fully illustrated *Alice* script and that his pal Bill really "did wonders" with it. "I do hope it proves successful and gooses you even further up the ladder of deserved success. I do think you're an awful mugg, not insisting on joint scenario credit with [Joe]. Anyone seeing the scenario will think you merely did the illustrations, not realizing the difficult technical problems you so cleverly solved. Of course, Paramount knows how much you did, but unless they give you a better break in the title credits—which they won't, unless you put up a man's-size bellow—the Industry will tip its hat to McLeod and Mank, not to Menzies."

As it turned out, Perez's well-intentioned pep talk wasn't necessary, for when the studio submitted corrected credits to the MPPDA, Menzies was indeed awarded co-screenplay credit on the picture. Plans were to open *Alice* on December 22 in 120 cities in the United States, twelve in Canada, and fifty in Europe and Asia.* Yet, opinions had been wildly divergent on the subject of the picture's quality, some objecting to the harshness of its tone, others to its bizarre mash-up of two distinctly different books. (Exiting a studio preview, one viewer was heard to say: "I'd like to have their losses on this one.") To children, particularly, the film was more scary than charming, as wondrous and uninvolving as an intricate windup toy. The December 16 issue of *The Hollywood Reporter* carried the headline: "ALICE" PARA. HEADACHE. "The execs have to date met all divided opinions on the picture with the answer, 'Yes—but no matter what they say about it we'll clean up a million on the Christmas trade with the kids.'" But now, the trade paper reported, the studio was seeking to put Mary Pickford onstage at its flagship Times Square theater to protect its Christmas week business, a turn for which the actress was demanding a $20,000 fee.

The next day, Philip K. Scheuer of the *Los Angeles Times* weighed in, suggesting the picture would strike the regular filmgoer, used to realistic live action fare, as "quasi-fantasy" or only half an illusion. "He will resent it because he can't believe it—and besides, he will be too busy trying to identify the actors' voices with the masks worn by most of them, and both voices and masks with the characters they are supposed to represent, to care much. The fact that many attending the [preview] showing responded only to the animated cartoon sequence (Walrus and Carpenter), which I found dull, proves that this is still the only form in which—as far

---

* This entailed the shipping of five "lavenders" (fine grain positives) via separate flights to the Paramount lab on Long Island. Printing negatives were to be struck and shipped to France, England, Germany, the Netherlands, and Scandinavia.

A rendering of the "Dream City of the Ancient East," in which Menzies sought to bring the stark value contrasts of pen-and-ink illustration to the screen. Intricately detailed surfaces of white and silver were punctuated by the deep blacks of openings and archways. (MENZIES FAMILY COLLECTION)

Menzies used strong verticals to emphasize the extreme height of the gateway to the walled city of Bagdad. This outsized painting, early and speculative, may have been one of the originals shown to Douglas Fairbanks in Menzies' pursuit of the assignment. (BARRY LAUESEN)

A soaring pattern of ornate grillwork stimulates interest in the Thief's midnight approach. "They let me take one detail and feature the devil out of it," Menzies said. "That's the way to get effects into pictures—height. That's the one dimension that lets loose the imagination." (MENZIES FAMILY COLLECTION)

The color and spectacle of *The Hooded Falcon* were to be on a scale equal to *The Thief of Bagdad.* In playing a Spanish prince of the fourteenth century, Valentino wanted to reproduce parts of the Alhambra, "the most perfect pearl of all Muslim art and culture," but the backers decreed that no Valentino picture should cost more than $500,000, effectively scuttling the project. (JEREM C. HUTCHESON)

Menzies' original rendering of Ahmed's desert retreat for *The Son of the Sheik* (1926). Economies scotched the design, a shame considering it would be Rudolph Valentino's final film and a formidable commercial success. (PAMELA LAUESEN)

François Villon's fifteenth-century Paris as devised for *The Beloved Rogue* (1927). By using architecture to convey mood and character, Menzies took the film a step beyond *The Thief of Bagdad*. (PAMELA LAUESEN)

In *Tempest* (1928), the events of the Revolution parade past the dungeon cell of Ivan Markov. Menzies places the critical action in the far distance, where the exodus of prisoners leaving for the front is portrayed more forcefully through suggestion than spectacle. The foreground is dominated by rigid patterns of iron and stone. (MENZIES FAMILY COLLECTION)

Menzies wasn't the credited art director on Ernst Lubitsch's *Eternal Love*—Walter Reimann was—but as head of the art department at United Artists he was occasionally called upon to work in behind a colleague. Here he offers a dynamic alternative to the film's somewhat confused ending. (MENZIES FAMILY COLLECTION)

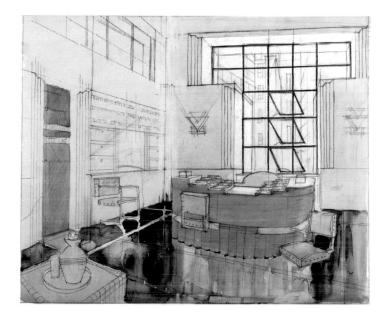

*Reaching for the Moon,* Douglas Fairbanks' first noncostume picture in a decade, was to be "startlingly modern," a 1930 production designed, according to the advance press, "in the spirit of 1932." *Above:* Larry Day's Art Deco office, with its tiered, gadget-laden desk and chairs of tubular steel (MENZIES FAMILY COLLECTION)

An early illustration project never completed by Menzies. From a children's book about a girl who gets caught in a snowball, it survives today in the form of twenty-six color drawings, of which this is number 12. (MENZIES FAMILY COLLECTION)

A late watercolor rendering of Tara, David O. Selznick's "dream house" for
*Gone With the Wind* (1939) (DAVID O. SELZNICK COLLECTION, HARRY RANSOM CENTER)

as fantasy is concerned—they are willing to go all the way. It's the Silly Symphony influence."

The coordinated openings brought forth a tidal wave of notices, most of them mixed. *Variety* lamented a painful lack of story progression. ("Nothing grows out of anything else in this phantasmagoria. It's like reading a whole volume of separate four-line gags. It takes super-human endurance.") And Rob Wagner dubbed it "one of the worst flops of the cinema." On the other hand, Mordaunt Hall, in *The New York Times,* found many things to praise: "If the film is disappointing in some essentials, it must be said that it is a masterpiece of camera wizardry. The manner in which Alice grows tall and then becomes tiny is accomplished splendidly, and likewise the stage settings designed by William Cameron Menzies will delight grown-ups and youngsters, for there are huge sets to dwarf some of the fantastic characters and others that are in miniature to give a contrasting effect."

Business started out strong in New York, Paramount and Pickford having come to terms, and the studio's Times Square flagship topped $50,000 for what had always been a traditionally difficult week. (*Variety* credited Pickford, rather than the movie, with "providing most of the draft at the boxoffice.") In Los Angeles, the downtown Paramount added a series of morning kid matinees, pulling a tidy $17,200 for the same period. The picture did even better in San Francisco, where Charlotte Henry was appearing onstage three times a day. In all, the film did respectably, limited as it was to the single Christmas week—no holdovers—and comparing unfavorably to the touring Le Gallienne version, which appeared to hurt its chances with the carriage trade. The bad news for *Alice in Wonderland* came from England, where the studio expected to recoup most of its $600,000 investment. Reservations were voiced over the melding of the two books and complaints that the Brooklyn-born actress playing the title character wasn't British. *Alice* had to be yanked from London's Plaza Theatre before it had completed its scheduled run, and did only marginally better in the provinces, where there wasn't time for the inevitable word of mouth to do its damage.

By Christmas Day, *Alice in Wonderland* was being widely acknowledged within the industry as an international disaster . . . albeit a well-intentioned one.

Before the commercial fate of *Alice in Wonderland* was fully known, Menzies pulled another assignment. Under Manny Cohen, the studio was moving away from the practice of paying two directors to make one film. Teams still under contract were being dissolved, and individuals unable to make the grade were being dropped once their contracts were up. The latest to go solo was Alexander Hall, an editor whose primary strength was in the pacing of action. Given the Rupert Hughes story "Kidnapt" to film, Hall stepped away from a project he was to have made in tandem with his frequent collaborator, a former dialogue director named George Somnes. *The Man Who Broke His Heart* was originally to have starred Gary Cooper, later Randolph Scott, and, for a brief while, Charles Bickford. When Menzies was paired with Somnes to direct the picture, Preston Foster and Victor McLaglen were set for the male leads. Actress Carole Lombard had been expected to join them until her breakout hit in *Bolero* made her too valuable for what was essentially a programmer. Instead, Lombard was assigned *We're Not Dressing* opposite Bing Crosby, and an eighteen-year-old novice, Dorothy Dell, was dropped into the role of Toy, a sweet-natured prostitute.

A melodrama of the San Francisco waterfront, *The Man Who Broke His Heart* got under way on January 4, 1934, affording Menzies little chance of influencing the design of the sets. Fortunately, the cinematographer on the show was the prolific Victor Milner, who had been Dutch Talmadge's cameraman on *Her Night of Romance* and *Learning to Love,* and who had shot *The Wanderer,* an early job at Paramount for which Menzies had created a sort of biblical Bagdad at the behest of Raoul Walsh. He and Milner collaborated seamlessly, giving the picture, shot entirely indoors, a rich atmospheric texture. Under Somnes' direction, the Mississippi-born Dell, a former Miss Universe, emerged as the film's dominant personality, a young Mae West with a style and range all her own. When the picture finished ahead of schedule, Menzies pronounced her genuine star material, a judgment shared by studio management and a Westwood preview audience, which saw the picture under the title *Wharf Angel* on the night of February 25.

"Miss Dell is chockful of sexy personality," *Daily Variety* affirmed, "and handles her part like a veteran. She warbles a blues number in a café dive after she goes straight that stamps her as an excellent entertainer." Upon its Los Angeles opening in March, Philip K. Scheuer praised the work of the film's leads and "a capital reproduction of the San Francisco docks atmosphere." The following month, when *Wharf Angel* played the New York Paramount, Mordaunt Hall of the *Times* faulted the material more than anything. "It is like a short story drawn out to novel length," he wrote. "The picture, however, has been ably directed by William Cameron Menzies and George Somnes, but while admiring their work one wonders why they put so much effort into such a thankless yarn." By the time Hall's words appeared, Dorothy Dell had completed a second picture, *Little Miss Marker,* with Adolphe Menjou and Shirley Temple, and was at work on a third, Wesley Ruggles' *Shoot the Works.* Scarcely six weeks later, having just witnessed a sneak preview of the latter picture, she was killed in a late night auto accident at the age of nineteen.

. . .

Upon the completion of *Wharf Angel,* both Menzies and George Somnes were left idle, presumably until their respective contracts ran out. Somnes, who had been with Paramount since 1929, returned to regional theatre and would never direct another film. Menzies, who was widely credited with the raffish look of the movie, eventually drew another assignment, directing Carole Lombard as Frederick Irving Anderson's lady jewel thief Sophie Lang. Menzies would have considerably more time to prepare the picture, and once again he would be working with unit art director Robert Odell, as he had on *Alice in Wonderland.* The script, by producer Bayard Veiller's son, Tony, was a smart and funny take on Anderson's 1925 book, shrewdly tailored to Lombard's gifts as a deft comedienne. In all respects, *The Notorious Sophie Lang* looked to be the ideal vehicle to establish Bill Menzies, at long last, as a solo director.

Lombard's removal, coming just days before the start of production, seemingly derailed the entire enterprise. After having been part of the package for nearly a

Menzies and co-director George Somnes during the filming of *Wharf Angel* (1934). Preston Foster plays a scene with Alison Skipworth, while Victor McLaglen awaits his entrance.
(NEW YORK PUBLIC LIBRARY)

month, she was shunted to a picture opposite Gary Cooper as a result of her splendid work in *Twentieth Century.* The May 5 start date was moved back as Menzies and Veiller hustled to find a replacement. On May 7, it was announced that singer-actress Gertrude Michael would step in, having just completed her role as Calpurnia in Cecil B. DeMille's *Cleopatra.* While not an even trade for the luminous Lombard, Michael would bring wit and authority to a part deceptively difficult to pull off.

Filming began on May 9, but Michael was ill with grippe, and Menzies was forced to shoot around her, picking up an expository scene in a police inspector's office with actors Arthur Byron and Paul Cavanagh. Michael appeared on the set for the first time on the 10th, ill with bronchitis but functional, and work began on the Harris and Hardie jewel heist, a brisk introduction to Sophie Lang and her criminal methods that was to set the tone for the rest of the picture.

Then disaster struck.

Having completed three full days of filming, Menzies was driving home late on a Friday night when he plowed into a car parked near the intersection of Melrose and Sweetzer, about three miles west of the studio. The owner of the car, who was standing beside it when the collision occurred, sustained bruises, lacerations, and a mild concussion. Denying that he was drunk, Menzies was taken to Hollywood Receiving Hospital, where a doctor administered a sobriety test and pronounced him incapable of operating a motor vehicle. He was booked and fingerprinted by the police, and spent nearly four hours in jail before a $500 bond could be posted. News of the arrest and the counts against him made the Saturday papers.

Menzies' drinking had long been an issue, and there were times when it may even have hampered his career. In a letter to his mother in late 1928, he referred to "that terrible telegram" from the Goldwyn company, apparently sent after he was forced to leave the set of *The Rescue.* "I am afraid I have been rather poisonous to my family," he conceded, "but this business just about drives me crazy." Mignon, a lifelong teetotaler, worried about him at parties, where a physical intolerance for liquor made him an easy and sometimes dangerous drunk. "He was such a responsibility," she lamented. "They called him 'two-drink Menzies.'"

The *Sophie Lang* company worked Monday, Tuesday, and at least part of Wednesday, giving the picture a total of seven days before the camera. What happened next is unclear. If Menzies missed a day of shooting on a picture that was, due to Gertrude Michael's illness, already behind schedule, there may have been pressure on Bayard Veiller to pick up the pace. Was there another incident? Did Menzies perhaps miss a second day due, in part, to a court appearance? Whatever the reason, sometime on Wednesday, May 16, he was taken off *The Notorious Sophie Lang,* and by Friday it was known that Ralph Murphy, newly signed to a Paramount contract, would replace him.

Reported in the press as ill due to a "laryngitis attack," Menzies was assigned to work with optical effects expert Gordon Jennings on a battle montage for *Cleopatra,* a task that would take up the remainder of the time left on his Paramount contract. He began work on the five-minute sequence on Tuesday, May 22, 1934, and continued for nearly a month, proposing, in places, new footage based on DeMille's dictated notes. The result was a frantic assemblage of new material, stock footage, and miniature work so striking it put Menzies' earlier tableau for *Cavalcade* to shame.

Aware he was in his last days at the studio, Menzies put out word that he was seeking a new engagement, but his drinking and his drunk driving arrest had become too widely known for anyone to take a chance on him. In desperation, he requested—and received—a generous letter of recommendation from DeMille, who stated that he had known the bearer for "about twelve years" and considered him to be "an artist of unquestioned standing and ability." Nothing, however, seemed to help. When Menzies checked off the Paramount lot on June 17, 1934, DeMille followed up with a second letter, dated June 19, in which he expressed his thanks for his "splendid work" on the montage scenes of *Cleopatra.* "The assistance rendered was timely and needed, and I appreciate your fine work and cooperation."

With a family to support and no prospects in sight, the summer of 1934 must have been brutal. It wasn't until August 9—eight long weeks after his termination at Paramount—that the following item appeared in *Daily Variety:*

### Korda and Menzies in London Deal

Alexander Korda is negotiating with William Cameron Menzies for a picture deal in England. If salary differences are adjusted the director will sail next week. Film intended for Menzies is based on an H. G. Wells yarn.

# 10

# The Shape of Things to Come

Exactly how William Cameron Menzies came to the attention of Alexander Korda isn't known, but it's easy to imagine an initial word coming from any of several Americans then working for the man who had single-handedly made the British film a viable international commodity. There was, for example, cinematographer Harold Rosson, who was in London shooting *The Scarlet Pimpernel* for Korda. And the visual effects wizard Ned Mann, who had first worked with Menzies on *The Thief of Bagdad.* And then there was Douglas Fairbanks himself, who was appearing for Korda in what would be his final film, *The Private Life of Don Juan.* Knowing that Korda was intent on making *The Shape of Things to Come,* which would depict the future as imagined by H. G. Wells, Fairbanks may well have suggested the artist who had so successfully envisioned Bagdad as the perfect man to bring Wells' Everytown to the screen.

Menzies left Los Angeles via the Chief on Sunday, August 12, 1934, with passage booked on the *Ile de France* for the following Saturday. It took two days to get to Chicago by train. "Stopped in Newton and was interviewed by a lady from the local paper," he wrote Mignon. "It's too bad my credits lately aren't more imposing." On the trip over, there were about 180 passengers on a ship designed to carry 600. On board were director Al Santell and his wife, Jack Alicoate of *The Film Daily,* director William Beaudine and his wife, and Lady Peel (the comedienne Beatrice Lillie). Menzies' commitment to Korda was to keep him in London until at least January, but at the time of his departure there was nothing more from Wells than the original book, a didactic work of prophecy published in 1933, and a treatment bearing the singular title *Whither Mankind? A Film of the Future.*

Menzies was anticipating trouble with his labor permit, but there was none. He settled into a flat in Albemarle Street, Piccadilly, where the rent was mercifully cheap—five guineas a week (about US $25, including service). "It looks as if at worst it's co-direction with Korda and the biggest picture in English history, very difficult but right up my alley. . . . I feel I'm going to be a hit here, and at least for the moment I'm simply insane for the place. The people are lovely. Maybe it will pall, but I doubt it. London is still full of hookers and pansies, but everyone is so polite and friendly."

There were friends to see: Laurence and Rosalind Irving; the American art director Jack Okey, who had been brought over by Korda to design a new studio complex; Hal Rosson; Paul and Molly Perez. One weekend, Menzies blithely hired a taxi to drive him to Aberfeldy, a distance of some 450 miles. "Things move terribly slowly here and I get very upset worrying about it," he wrote, "but when I spoke of it to Korda, he said he had nearly gone crazy when he first came over, but after a while you get to expect it." On a night in October, he dined at Korda's with H. G. Wells, who held sway over the project to such an extent he spoke frequently of it as "my film." A portly little man with an unnaturally high-pitched voice, Wells was engaged in the prentice effort of revising his initial treatment, and Menzies felt their exchange that evening "accomplished a lot." Wells followed up with a handwritten note: "The film is an H G Wells film & your highest & best is needed for the complete realization of my treatment. Bless you."

Menzies responded in the only way he could, sketching ideas based on the fragments afforded him, then taking them round to Wells' flat at Chiltern Court, where they would be summarily rejected or returned for further refinement. "I am still running back and forth to Wells' and still seem to retain my standing," he reported in early November. "I have seen very little of Korda lately. Must get over to the other studio and see him this week." The place at Albemarle was dark and depressing, and in November Menzies took a new flat, light and cheerful, at Marble Arch, where the surrounding streets reminded him of New Haven. The change of scenery had only a momentary effect on his mood swings though, and within days he was despairing again of ever getting the picture into production. "I feel very low today," he admitted in a letter to Mignon on the 23rd of November. "I suppose from the cold, but I'm not very optimistic about conditions for picture making here and, sub rosa, Korda is very nice but very changeable. It's too bad movies are such a worry, because I could certainly enjoy life if it wasn't for the ever-present miserable worry about making money."

Korda was incrementally sending his production personnel to the United States to keep abreast of the "latest movements and methods of film production," leaving the impression he wouldn't be needing his entire staff until the anticipated completion of the new studio in April. Laurence Irving, meanwhile, felt it was the designs Menzies was contriving of a collapsed civilization—and the news from Germany that seemed so much like a prelude—that drove him to seek the solace of the bottle. "After dining with us one evening, he had found release from his tensions to such an extent that I felt I should see him safely to bed at Mount Royal, a vast apartment hotel building. He had forgotten the number of his room. So, in close embrace, we explored one tunnel-like floor after another, as I propped him up at the end of each corridor and sought whatever number he was inspired to suggest. After what seemed hours of trial and error and several altercations with angry residents roused from sleep, I left him safely bestowed in his cell-like quarters."

Wells acknowledged the collective help of Korda, Menzies, and the Hungarian playwright Lajos Bíró (who essentially functioned as an uncredited scenarist) in developing the treatment from which the film would be made. "They were greatly excited by the general conception," he wrote, "but they found the draft quite impracticable for production. A second treatment was then written. This, with various modifications, was made into a scenario of the old type. This scenario again was set aside for a second version, and this again was revised and put back into the form of [a] treatment."

The design of the picture proved as much a challenge as its screenplay. Alexander Korda's youngest brother, Vincent, would create the settings for the present-day sequences and for the scenes of desolation after decades of war. The rebuilding of Everytown, however, and the views of the city one hundred years hence would require the eye of a true visionary. At various points, futurist painter Fernand Léger, the urbanist architect Le Corbusier, and abstract photographer László Moholy-Nagy were consulted. None proved up to the challenge—Le Corbusier, after reading Wells' treatment, declined to become involved—and so, as work moved forward, Korda, in consultation with Menzies and Ned Mann, derived much of the film's futuristic look from an array of published sources, beginning with the descriptions Wells himself had provided.*

Vincent's son, Michael, could remember his father "busily ransacking the libraries for avant-garde furniture designs, architectural fantasies, helicopters and autogyros, monorails and electric bubble cars, television sets and space vehicles. The nursery at Hampstead became a repository for his rejected design models, and while other children were playing with trains and toy soldiers, I was playing with rocket ships, ray guns, and flying wings."

---

* A detailed analysis of Vincent Korda's various influences and inspirations can be found in Christopher Frayling's *Things to Come* (London: BFI Publishing, 1995).

Gradually, it became clear to Menzies that Alexander Korda expected him to direct the picture entirely by himself. Ned Mann described a working relationship far more collaborative than what he usually saw in Hollywood: "Vincent Korda, the art director, outlined his conception of the ideas contained in H. G. Wells' script. I added my suggestions to those of William Cameron Menzies, the director, and Georges Périnal, in charge of the cameras, and others. And when all points of view had been considered I was able to decide how the desired effects were to be produced." André de Toth, who would later work with the Kordas, recalled Vincent as "the most unassuming human being I met. He would put his rumpled hat on, a cord to tie up his pants. He was a happy man. He was a true artist. He really didn't belong to the picture business."

Menzies bonded with Vincent Korda in a way he couldn't with Alex, the master salesman who brought all the sparkle to the trio of Hungarian brothers (director Zoltan Korda being the third member of the triumvirate). "I have gotten to be great friends with Vincent Korda," Menzies wrote in February 1935, "which is a good break for me." The "trick stuff" (as Menzies put it) was already under way at Consolidated Studios, Boreham Wood, but casting was still to be settled, the only name mentioned thus far being Robert Donat, who had drawn notice for his work in *The Count of Monte Cristo.* Wells, noted Menzies, seemed to like the early effects footage, although "it's always tough for laymen to understand uncut stuff."

By then, Menzies had settled into a thoroughly cosmopolitan lifestyle, acquiring a car, a new wardrobe, and a mistress. "I'm sorry our pals can't see me in my trick English clothes," he said in one letter. "I resemble a well-dressed prize fighter with the very square shoulders and small hips. My suits came out very well too. The suits cost about $65 apiece and the shirts about $7 and [are] the <u>best</u> in London." Yet the picture was going so slowly by Hollywood standards that insecurity nearly consumed him. "I expect Korda to blow up any day and fire us all, but we are doing all we can. The expense, of course, is terrible. At least I would get home, but I'm afraid if it did blow up it wouldn't do me any good. I have worried about the thing ever since I got off the boat, which is one of the things that has made me unhappy in England."

On the first of March, with Wells on his way to New York, Menzies recounted "a very pleasant interview" with Korda that helped ease his anxieties. He was set to move to Worton Hall, Isleworth, to begin shooting, but there were problems with the costumes—specified, detailed, and often rejected by Wells. "I miss you terribly," he wrote Mignon, "and if it wasn't that I thought this picture will make me, I'd have gotten myself fired a long time ago. I still think it will be a sensational picture if we ever get it done, and Korda is undoubtedly the whitest man I have ever worked for.

I can do practically anything I want." Two weeks later, he felt the return of "the old Hollywood strain, fluttering guts and everything, as I am trying to put over something new, and you know how I worry. I did a sequence in drawings that Korda liked immensely, and am shooting it next week. It's just with extras and atmosphere, but it's the kind of thing I do best."

Story changes were proposed, but Wells, upon his return, would concede nothing easily, and progress, complicated by financing problems, came at a snail's pace. By April Menzies was "absolutely concentrated" on making *Whither Mankind?* a great picture, the kind of picture that would secure his future and that of his family. "This is the one big thing in my life now, and I think the results will warrant it. I have a tremendous advantage over here in my general knowledge of pictures, as I can do most of the things myself. My sets, my lighting, compositions, continuity, etc." Yet he dreaded getting into the dialogue scenes, not only because of his discomfort around actors, but also because of old Wells, who was driving director Lothar Mendes mad on a concurrently shooting picture, *The Man Who Could Work Miracles.* In May, the company traveled to Blaina, South Wales, to shoot battle footage for which two hundred unemployed miners were issued uniforms and dummy rifles and arranged according to Menzies' continuity sketches. On June 7, fierce winds laid waste to the Everytown set, which was under construction on what would become the studio backlot at Denham. A painter was killed, and five other workers were injured in the collapse.

A cast was gradually assembled, beginning with Raymond Massey, the Canadian-born actor who had been a memorable Chauvelin in Korda's *The Scarlet Pimpernel.* "I had read Wells' novel," he recounted, "fascinated by its humor and the earthy humanity of its characters. . . . But when I saw Wells' script I was appalled. Every trace of wit, humor, and emotion, everything which had made the novel so enthralling, had been cut and replaced with large gobs of socialist theory which might have been lifted from a Sidney Webb tract. Although Wells often declared he was not a teacher or a political theorist, this was exactly what he had become."

For the part of the dictatorial Boss, who continues to wage war amid the wreckage of an Everytown bereft of resources, Korda selected Ralph Richardson, relatively new to films but soon to become a genuine star of the West End. For his wily consort Roxana, Korda cast London Films contract player Margaretta Scott, who remembered Menzies as "a delightful person to be with and frightfully good."

The opening montage was shot mostly on a vast stage at Worton Hall, Vincent Korda's contemporary city anticipating Christmas 1940 amid the signs and shoutings of imminent war. A visitor from *The Scotsman* observed a huge set "representing the width of a street in the West End of London, with a luxury hotel on one side, and on the other a super cinema. Buses, taxis, cars, and bicycles filled the roadway, while the pavements were crowded with people. . . . On an adjoining stage was a set of a street from the East End of London, where cameras had recorded the effect of a bomb explosion during an air raid of the future war. Everywhere carpenters were busy constructing modernistic buildings of lath and plaster. Cameramen, electricians, and experts for this and that were moving about. There was a suggestion of intense, purposeful activity."

Vincent Korda, meanwhile, was at work in his studio amid sketches of giant beetlelike tanks and houses and buildings of the mid-twenty-first century representing a style of architecture "as distinctive as that of Greece or of the Renaissance." Said Margaretta Scott: "I think Menzies and Korda worked very much as a team, and the back-up people were terrific." In addition to Korda, Périnal, Ned Mann, and the others, Menzies also acknowledged a "funny collection of Cockney prop men" he taught to shoot craps and who, he said, would "absolutely go through Hell and high water for me." As decades of battle ensued, the advanced city of the present became the battered ruin of Everytown 1970.

"Well, Darling, everything is unbelievably jake," Menzies advised Mignon in an uncharacteristically jubilant letter. "I am absolutely (at least for the moment) the white-haired boy, and yesterday's dailies really gave me a thrill. I have two marvelous actors in Richardson and Massey, and Margaretta Scott is marvelous and is photographing like a million. Korda and Wells are both mad about the stuff, and everyone thinks it's going to be the great picture. . . . I realize now what an awful thing Johnny [Considine] did to me when he started me off co-directing. If I had been on my own from the start, I don't think I would ever have had the last awful three years."

Nighttime exteriors took fourteen days (instead of the scheduled five) to complete and put Menzies on a regimen of box lunches and two or three hours of sleep a day. "Alex, I think, got to like the stuff better," he said, "but I had the horrors as it was so slow and dawn came so fast." Daytime brought its own set of worries, including endless waits for the sun to appear. ("We are shooting the desolation sequence, so we are full of ruin and anemic people.") Raymond Massey, playing aviator John Cabal, one of the "last trustees of civilization," remembered Wells as a constant presence on the set, though his involvement appeared to be limited to the close attention he paid the costumes adorning the female members of the cast. Menzies, however, was the frequent recipient of handwritten notes from the Great Man, generally pointing out how he had failed at the staging of an unplayable scene.

"Those final scenes of Cabal with the dead Boss & with Roxana will not do," Wells said in a typical missive. "What is wrong with the Boss scene is Cabal's delivery of his last line. He stands up & <u>speaks</u> it. But he ought to say it <u>clearly & calmly</u> to himself. Massey is an emotional man. That is his dangerous quality & here he has been allowed to be emotional almost to the point of shouting hysterically." Wells went on to hammer the point, concluding that Menzies was focusing on all the wrong things. "All the Cecil de Mille effects of crowds & milling about & so on that you are spending so much thought & time & money upon do not matter a rip in comparison with the effective handling of this essential drama. They are very effective in their way, but they are <u>not this film</u>."

In truth, however, they were. The striking visuals on which Menzies and his colleagues were laboring so hard were coming to define a film that was otherwise lacking in dramatic values. "The picture was fantastically difficult to act," Massey stated in his autobiography. "Wells had deliberately formalized the dialogue, particularly in the later sequences. The novel's realism had vanished from the screenplay in which we delivered heavy-handed speeches instead of carrying on conversations. Emotion

The death of the Boss in *Things to Come* (1936) illustrates the collaboration between Vincent Korda and William Cameron Menzies. The set is doubtless Korda's work, but the composition, Cabal towering in the middle distance, the Boss' crumpled figure in the foreground, is clearly Menzies'. (AUTHOR'S COLLECTION)

had no place in Wells' new world." Though Wells admitted to "a state of fatigue" as filming dragged on, he diligently kept at Menzies and Korda and, sometimes, even the actors, convinced his film would suffer without a vigilance that bordered on the obsessive.

"Alex has gone away," Menzies told Mignon on the 26th of August, "but I have been wrestling with Wells this week. I have pretty well finished the longer sequence I was on, but I have lost my perspective and I don't know whether it's good or not. I most certainly will be the happiest man in the world when it's finished. . . . I am beginning on the really future, future world next week, and it might give me a new interest. The picture has a strange, believable reality that might make it terribly successful. I think generally my work has been good."

By September 1935, the picture had been seven months in production and the end was only vaguely in sight. Alex Korda was meeting with United Artists executives in New York and Los Angeles and talking up a planned slate of thirty-six features in the press. He was, he told Eileen Creelman of the *New York Sun,* preparing to direct his own production of *Cyrano* with Charles Laughton in the title role. He added that he was eager to get back to England, where an American director, William Cameron Menzies, was finishing *The Shape of Things to Come.* When a press agent interrupted him with a reminder that the title *Whither Mankind?* had been changed to *100 Years from Now,* the producer shook his head insistently. "No, no; it is *The Shape of Things to Come.* I have just had a peppery wire from H. G. Wells and he says it must be that."

In England, Wells had written composer Arthur Bliss: "We are really getting the film in shape at last. In about ten days time I shall be able to show you the first two-thirds and up to the opening of the New World part continuous. Then you and I and the Director and the Sound Expert and the Cutter ought to sit down and look at it hard. Then you and the Sound Expert ought to do some fruitful discussion. The final part is being shot but at present no continuity is possible."

At the time, Menzies was finishing up the desolation sequence and preparing to shoot the first scenes set in 2036, an episode that ends with an angry mob attempting to stop the firing of the Space Gun—a device out of Jules Verne that proposes to shoot a manned capsule into space as an ordinary firearm might shoot a bullet. Menzies had come to consider Vincent Korda impractical and knew it would fall to him to give the Space Gun the weight and drama it lacked as a miniature. "I felt a little better about the stuff today," he wrote on September 7, "as I had a good day with beautiful clouds and damn near finished my exteriors. The particular set I am in has nearly driven me crazy—it's been a jinx from the go. My main worry now is when the hell we will ever get this lousy picture finished. I saw a list of the first set of the new world, or rather the 'Moon Gun' sequence, and it was lousy, but like I always have to do, I am going to try and save it, but that's what takes the time."

Raymond Massey credited Menzies for the "swift and orderly progress" of the picture. "*Things to Come* was a difficult job for all of us," he said. "We were always the puppets of Wells, completely under his control. Like all socialists, in his forecast of man's future Wells saw nothing but authoritarianism. A bad dictatorship would be followed by a benevolent one. A benign big brother was bound to be a bore. He was the fellow I played in the futuristic part of the film. I could only act Oswald Cabal as calmly and quietly as possible and, as the saying goes, 'Everybody was very kind.'"

A "puppet" who didn't fare quite as well as Massey was fifty-six-year-old Ernest Thesiger, perhaps the most experienced actor in the cast. Thesiger's role, as the rebel artist Theotocopulos, was to rile a mob of followers against the machinery of the modern age, to "talk all this machinery down" in a discourse over the televisor.

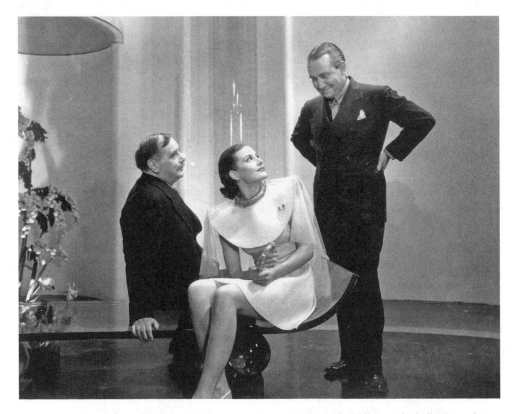

Redemption on an international scale: Menzies poses with H. G. Wells and the ballerina and actress Pearl Argyle on the set of *Things to Come.* (AUTHOR'S COLLECTION)

Thesiger certainly seemed to fit the part, dramatically flourishing a great cloak as described in the text, but his scenes, when cut together, failed to establish him, in the author's mind, as someone capable of rallying a group of ardent followers. Contending the character's voice needed more *vox humana*, Wells demanded that Thesiger's scenes be reshot with another actor, and when Korda returned to London he complied, engaging the younger—and somewhat more substantial—Cedric Hardwicke for the part.

As Menzies glumly reported in his letter of November 13, "I am more or less buried in retakes. Korda is a hound for them and, personally, I don't think they are any great improvement. . . . I have been terribly worried about the picture lately, but I hope it's just staleness. It's at the point where you can't tell much about it. Korda blows hot and cold too, which is rather discouraging and nerve wracking. I can't seem to get back to my old gayness lately, but this thing is a terrible thing to have on your mind." His mood wasn't improved by a chance encounter with Douglas Fairbanks, who was all of fifty-two but looked "very old." Wells, meanwhile, had gone to America, where he hoped to induce Charlie Chaplin to play the title role in his *History of Mr. Polly.* Sardonically, Menzies noted that Wells had published his treatment (under the title *Things to Come*) and had taken an awful panning for it. "We are all glad he has left," he said of Wells. "Hollywood can have him, and I hope they like him."

Retakes for the film's final act were made at Worton Hall during one of the most savage of English winters. As the temperature hovered near zero Celsius, Raymond Massey found himself working on unheated stages in "abbreviated skirts and Tudor-like doublets of foam rubber and pleated buckram." Mercifully, the scenes with Cedric Hardwicke, augmented by long shots still containing Ernest Thesiger, went quickly, Menzies having assumed a perfunctory attitude toward the bits and pieces remaining.

Here it is another Monday and the headaches still carry on. I have had a lot of re-takes, principally because I am so tired mentally I can't think with any originality. Korda is a very difficult taskmaster, and is greatly affected by his yes-men. . . . I am nearly driven insane by delays, and Korda is getting rather sarcastic and ugly again. . . . It is maddening to have to work as I have this year and have nothing to show for it. But I think the picture will make it jake for me from now on. . . . Ray Massey is chafing at the bit. He is doing a play in New York. His wife has been there for several months. I would like to see the damn thing thru and, if it was just a question of a few days, see the premiere here, as I deserve a little kick out of all this work, and it being the biggest.

By the last of November, Massey had been given his release and Korda, who had been away, was screening the footage Menzies had shot in his absence. "Fortunately, so far he has liked it," Menzies said in a letter to his family, "but he is looking at it in small pieces, which is a little like slow torture. He seems to be feeling swell. Naturally he is on the crest of the wave. He likes my modern world stuff a lot. Most of the stuff he gave me hell for he is gradually coming around to like. . . . Well, my dears, I start to see the end of it, and I hope I have a successful homecoming. I mean as far as the picture is concerned. It certainly is different and, I think, as well made as possible under the circumstances. They certainly have never made one like it anywhere."

He was planning to spend New Year's Eve at the Chelsea Arts Ball but fell ill instead. "Another reason for feeling low," he added on the 11th of January, "is that Wells is back and is going to run the picture today, so I hope there aren't a million changes. The first part of the picture is in good shape. I'm not so sure of the last." Editor Francis D. "Pete" Lyon, who had been asked to recut and polish the first half of the film while Charles Crichton worked on the second half, witnessed the screening: "When the lights came on after the running, our eyes were on Mr. Wells, of course, because we wanted him to be pleased with our efforts to present his prized creation to the movie world. He slowly rose and paced in front of us for a few seconds, then turned and said, 'There is only one thing wrong with this film—it is five years too soon.' We were all relieved that he didn't take us apart."

With Wells' approval, a preview was scheduled for the week of January 20, 1936, giving Menzies just two weeks to get the last of the effects shots into the picture. Then George V died at the age of seventy, causing the showing to be put off indefinitely. Menzies feared Korda would use the time to start fiddling with the picture again, hindering his best efforts to finally get the thing done. "Korda has the jitters and I suppose the King's death won't help it any, and I have a strong feeling of dog house again. Some of the faults are mine, naturally, for I am tired and sick of the picture, but as usual I take the rap for everything. Sets are never ready, and I have to shoot everything in a few minutes. . . . I have definitely decided to concentrate on getting independent in the next few years, as I really can't take it anymore. 15 to 18 years of this worry and tearing your brain apart is too much, and I must accumulate some money and ease up a bit. I figure 3 to 5 years of hell and concentration on making money, and then some peace of mind. I feel ninety and am beginning to look 100."

The world premiere of *Things to Come* took place on February 21, 1936, at UA's Leicester Square Theatre, the day after the British Board of Film Censors awarded it an "A" certificate at a running time of 117 minutes. The program began at 8:45 with an edition of *World News Bulletin* and a Mickey Mouse cartoon. Recalled Cedric Hardwicke, "My work in *Things to Come* was completed with such speed and lack of ceremony that the actor I had replaced had no idea that his entire performance lay on the cutting room floor. He arrived with a party of expectant friends at the London premiere, an exceedingly fashionable gathering. After his disappointment, I remained pleasantly surprised that he did not become my enemy for life."

What the audience witnessed that evening bore little resemblance to any British movie they had yet seen. The London Film logo, Big Ben chiming against a cloud-filled sky, gave way to a monumental set of credits, unparalleled in size and weight, the portentous music of Arthur Bliss ringing out a grim, dissonant warning of what was to pass in the opening minutes. Up on a bustling Everytown, Christmas 1940, chorales heralding frantic scenes of celebration, the streets awash with traffic. A young boy in stark close-up eyes a toy in a shop window; a joyous couple drive along, a Christmas tree loaded into the back of their sleek roadster; Christmas holly piled high atop a vendor's cart as the ominous image of a *News Gazette* truck pulls into view, its side plastered with the words THE WORLD ON THE BRINK OF WAR. A militaristic march intrudes on "God Rest Ye Merry Gentlemen," the word WAR populating the background, subtly at first, then insistently amid flashes of Christmas turkeys and pantomimes, street vendors and carolers, handbills and posters, their letters progressively larger, more harrowing: RUMOURS OF WAR . . . EUROPE IS ARMING . . . WAR STORM BREWING . . .

It was a spectacular couple of minutes, the sort of thing Menzies had done for others in the past, now on full view as a work entirely of his own, the most flamboyant and unsettling bit of filmmaking he had yet afforded himself, the work of a man at the very pinnacle of his powers as a visual artist. Hampered by Wells' declamatory dialogue, he could do little with the early exchanges between Cabal and the industrialist Passworthy, the latter disparaging the possibility of war even as forces are mustering and an air attack is on the way. Another urgent montage set the tone for the film, sequences of astonishing size and pattern alternating with tedious rounds of dialogue, fine, stage-trained actors struggling with words better left read than spoken. The fortification of Everytown and the subsequent air attack, effectively depicting the London blitz as happening within four months of its actual occurrence, was accompanied by music so intrinsic that Wells had wanted it recorded in advance of production. "This Bliss music," he insisted, "is not intended to be tacked on; it is part of the design. The spirit of the opening is busy and fretful and into it creeps a deepening menace."

As the film progressed, it became evident that the strength of *Things to Come* lay in its sweep and vision, its hundred-year dream of rebirth having overwhelmed any hope of dramatic validity. The years of war come to desolation and the rule of a petty despot, while the wandering sickness ("a new fever of mind and body") afflicts the populace. Into the scene flies an aged Cabal, his garb and demeanor presaging a utopian future. ("And now for the rule of the Airmen," he intones over the dead body of the Boss, "and a new life for mankind.") Little more than an hour into the picture, the reconstruction of Everytown begins, a process that stretches from 1970 to the year 2036 and reveals a vast cavernous city anticipating the atrium hotel designs of John C. Portman. Wells called for "one of the high-flung City Ways" displaying "the very bold and decorative architecture of this semi-subterranean city and the use of running water and novel and beautiful plants and flowering shrubs in decoration. In the sustained bright light and conditioned air of the new Everytown, and in the hands of skillful gardeners, vegetation has taken on a new vigor and love-liness. People pass. People gather in knots and look down on the great spaces below."

Menzies' influence on Vincent Korda was most readily apparent in the point of view he imposed on a scene, giving the muscular streamline that dominated the lat-ter part of the picture a grace and energy all its own. Though the designs may well have been Korda's, their lines filled the frame by way of Menzies' compositional eye, and he favored deep perspectives and low angles, ensuring his figures would "read" against walls, ceilings, or cloud-filled skies, building the strength of his compositions on suggestion as much as actual detail.

The architecture of the future Everytown came in concentric circles, automated work crews assembling the great city as one might an elaborate layer cake. "Only the lower part of that set is real—up to and including the third platform," Ned Mann pointed out at the time. "The figures on and above the fourth platform are dum-mies attached to a model. All the curved background is in miniature." What Mann described was, in fact, a "hanging" miniature—a model suspended a few feet in front of the camera and carefully registered with the partial set in the distance. The film made use of many such models, which gave it the richest possible look without the expense of actually building the sets they represented. The climactic firing of the Space Gun, for example, was accomplished with a series of miniatures.

"On the screen this gun appears gigantic, reaching up into the clouds and domi-nating the surrounding landscape," said Mann.

But the model for a long shot was no more than 20 feet high and made of thin sheet metal. The clouds and the direction of lighting required special care. The clouds were not painted on a backcloth, which would have looked flat and stagy. They were created out of smoke, so that the sky was a min-iature of the real thing. Sunlight streaming in from one side we imitated with a spotlight. For the closer shot of the Space Gun we used a larger scale model; for, with the detail so enormously magnified, absolute accuracy was essential if a crude result was to be avoided on the screen. In this case we employed similar smoke clouds, and a powerful spotlight casting sun shadows to give greater depth and relief to the picture.

The film ended on an uncertain note, the latter-day Cabal and Passworthy following the progress of the space bullet on the giant mirror of a telescope and debating the eternal struggle of human advancement. "My God!" exclaims Passworthy. "Is there never to be an age of happiness? Is there never to be rest?"

"Rest enough for the individual man," Cabal responds. "Too much of it and too soon, and we call it death. But for Man no rest and no ending. He must go on—conquest beyond conquest. This little planet and its winds and ways, and all the laws of mind and matter that restrain him. Then the planets about him, and at last out across immensity to the stars. And when he has conquered all the deeps of space and all the mysteries of time—still he will be beginning."

"But—we're such little creatures," Passworthy says. "Poor humanity, so fragile, so weak—little, little animals."

"Little animals—And if we're no more than animals we must snatch each little scrap of happiness and live and suffer and pass, mattering no more than all the other animals do or have done . . . All the universe is nothingness . . . Which shall it be, Passworthy? Which shall it be?" And then the chorus rises on the infinite display of deep space before them: WHICH SHALL IT BE? WHICH SHALL IT BE? WHICH SHALL IT BE?

H. G. Wells, perhaps sensing the mixed reaction of the audience, was dismayed. While willing to assume some of the blame for his "mess of a film," he disproportionately blamed Alex Korda, who had afforded him unprecedented influence, and Menzies, who was, in reality, responsible for much of what the audience seemed to respond to and like. "For me it was a huge disillusionment," Wells wrote privately not long after the premiere.

It was, I saw plainly, pretentious, clumsy, and scamped. I had fumbled with it. My control over the production had been ineffective. Cameron Menzies was an incompetent director; he loved to get away on location and waste money on irrelevancies; and Korda let this happen.* Menzies was a sort of

---

* Unfamiliar with film terminology, Wells apparently considered anything not contained within the walls of a soundstage to be "location."

The extraordinary Christmas Eve montage that opens *Things to Come*. "It's just with extras and atmosphere," Menzies wrote, "but it's the kind of thing I do best."

Cecil B. De Mille without his imagination; his mind ran on loud machinery and crowd effects. He was sub-conscious of his own commonness of mind. . . . The most difficult part of this particular film, and the most stimulating to the imagination, was the phase representing a hundred and twenty years hence, but the difficulties of the task of realization frightened Menzies; he would not get going on that, and he spent most of the available money on an immensely costly elaboration of the earlier two-thirds of the story. He either failed to produce, or he produced so badly that ultimately they had to cut a good half of my dramatic scenes.

When Wells wrote of his "dramatic scenes" he meant, of course, the endless speeches that brought the action to a screeching halt. As the author, he could not recognize nor acknowledge the essential contribution that Menzies—and Vincent Korda and Ned Mann and Georges Périnal and their associates—had made in keeping the film consistently interesting, if not necessarily involving. The critics who had previewed the film the previous night, however, had little trouble in doing so.

"When America sees this film it probably will regard it as the most important ever to come out of a British studio," predicted the London correspondent for the *Motion Picture Herald*. "From such dispassionate viewpoint as a British reviewer may claim, it seems that America will be right. . . . The audience found the glimpses of the future breathtaking and applause was prolonged for individual sets and effects. Women and some men criticized the lack of 'story.' Objection to the arid Wellsian world was common; but its picturization was thought 'marvelous.'" The *Variety* report was even more damning of Wells while praising the film's technical properties. "William Cameron Menzies is the director, and for lavishness of treatment and decor, and skillful mixture of illusionary devices of expert camera tricks and sound necromancy, it surpasses in scope anything which has come from Hollywood. . . . Because it is a departure from routine paths, and as such is to be commended, it will be viewed as an experiment successful in every respect except emotionally. For heart interest Mr. Wells hands you an electric switch."

*Things to Come* fared better in the secular press, where nationalistic pride in the sheer scope and magnitude of the £256,000 picture—by far England's most expensive—drew plaudits from most of the London dailies. "It is a leviathan among films," said Sydney Carroll in *The Times*.

It makes Armageddon look like a street row. It shows science flourishing the keys of Hell and Death, and creating from the ruins of Everytown crazy labyrinthine cities radiant with artificial light, teeming with crowds

The subterranean Everytown of the year 2036, probably the most famous single image from *Things to Come*. Generally credited to Menzies, who would have influenced the composition, it is more likely the work of Vincent Korda, who drew upon a range of influences to produce what Christopher Frayling has called "a grandiose fusion of Le Corbusier and American streamlining." (AUTHOR'S COLLECTION)

of art-starved people craving for old excitements and former thrills. A stupendous spectacle, an overwhelming Doréan, Jules Vernesque, elaborated Metropolis, staggering to eye, mind, and spirit, the like of which has never been seen and never will be seen again. When twenty minutes of repetition have been cut from it, it should obtain a wide world sale. It makes film history.

Alistair Cooke, writing in *The Listener,* broke with the herd in a somewhat dismissive notice that took Wells to task for bad acting, dialogue, and psychology. "In a film showing the death of a nation and its rebirth in a new age of sight and sound, the only people who must have imagination are the scene designer, the direc-

Passworthy and Cabal stand before a telescopic mirror at the conclusion of *Things to Come,* observing the progress of the bullet fired from the Space Gun. For a film built on bold graphic ideas, going big with this final set was an imperative. (AUTHOR'S COLLECTION)

tor, and the cameraman. And the achievement of *Things to Come* is no more and certainly no less the ingenious hours spent around little white models by William Menzies, Vincent Korda, and Georges Périnal." Yet C. A. Lejeune found such criticisms petty, considering that for the first time the medium had been used to state "a hard and fairly complex argument" with force and beauty. "It is very easy to nag at *Things to Come,*" she wrote. "When a thing is so big that the imagination cannot quite embrace it, there is always a picking and scrambling at the detail. At a dozen points the film is vulnerable, and I have no doubt at all that it will go out into the world stuck full of Lilliputian arrows. But not one of them will measure its stature nor impede its power."

For the next few weeks, it seemed that all business in London was directed at two United Artists releases—Chaplin's *Modern Times* and *Things to Come.* Early into its run, it was decided to trim the film by a full reel—nearly ten minutes—in advance of a wider release pattern. Menzies may have had input, but by this point he was en route to New York aboard the *Bremen*, where, accompanied by Ned Mann, special effects assistant Lawrence Butler, and editor William Hornbeck, he would give Korda's partners at UA their first look at the finished product. "We ran the show for United Artists and the opinion was divided," Menzies recounted in a final letter to California, "altho all agreed it was too long. I hope Korda will agree to cuts, as I think they are right. . . . I am a little worried that the picture is a great technical achievement rather than a dramatic success. However, I don't think it can do anything but help me. Damn that old fool Wells."

Menzies was another six weeks in New York, overseeing the cutting of the picture to a final running time of ninety-six minutes. Eager to see his family, he stopped just short of attending the premiere at New York's Rivoli Theatre, instead boarding a Transcontinental and Western DC-2 bound for Los Angeles. On the morning of April 19, he arrived home after a grueling eighteen-hour trip that included refueling stops in Chicago, Kansas City, and Albuquerque. Gathered to meet him were Mignon; Jean, now fifteen and in high school; and Suzie, who was just eight when her father left for England. After an absence of nineteen months, his Scottish mother, effusive as ever, greeted him with a handshake.

Awaiting him also was an urgent cablegram from Korda:

RETURN BY NEXT PLANE.

# 11

# What I've Wanted to Do All My Life

Korda backed off, permitting the director of *Things to Come* to attend the Los Angeles premiere of his own picture. The film was getting a lot of advance play in the local press—more, it seemed, than it had in England—and Menzies hoped all the hype would reestablish him as a viable director of American movies.* The reviews from New York were more mixed than the British notices, Wells not being the national treasure he was in the U.K. (No one in England, for instance, dared label the film "solemn and dull and depressing" as had Norbert Lusk, a correspondent for the *Los Angeles Times.*) "Picture has been cut 16 minutes since its first showing in London," reported the stateside *Variety* notice, "and can stand 10–15 minutes more clipping." Happily, Menzies was generally given his due, Frank Nugent in *The New York Times* recalling "a pessimistic, frightening, yet inspiring picture . . . which does credit to its maker, Alexander Korda of London Films; to its director, William Cameron Menzies of Hollywood, and to its cast and technical crew."

Business on Broadway was reassuringly sound, with lines trailing six abreast around the corner from the box office and stretching an entire city block. Over the first three and a half days of its run, 47,312 patrons purchased tickets to see *Things to Come,* billed on the marquee as "The Most Amazing Picture Ever Made." In Los Angeles, Menzies basked in the kind of glory he never again expected to see in his adopted hometown.

* Specifically, Menzies talked of going with Mary Pickford and Jesse L. Lasky, who had formed a new production company releasing through United Artists.

"*Things to Come* is mechanically brilliant," Philip K. Scheuer proclaimed.

The destruction of "Everytown" on Christmas Eve in 1940, with its contrasts, sharp and bitter, between the quick and the dead, is unforgettable. Then desolation and ruin—the Wandering sickness—the rise of "The Chief," small-time dictator—the arrival of the Scientist, and his challenge: Law and Sanity vs. Brutes and Fools—war, and the Gas of Peace—the city of tomorrow, with its simple spaciousness and pleasant whirring sounds— the race to the Space Gun, and finally the flight into darkness . . . these are depicted on a scale as grand as it seems practical. The players are no more impressive than figures seen through the wrong end of a telescope. Story threads are picked up and dropped, as in the inconclusive episode of the Chief's woman. Occasionally dialogue halts progress. And with it all, I emerged convinced that I had seen the first real motion picture in a dog's age.

Menzies tried lining up another Hollywood movie to direct, but all he was offered, by his own account, was a single "very class 'B' one." Korda, evidently, was the only producer in the world who was willing to entrust him with a major production. Indeed, while he was still in New York, trimming *Things to Come* for the American market, Korda had announced him as co-director (with actor-playwright Miles Malleson) of *Hamlet,* a first for the talking screen with Robert Donat in the title role. Having no comparable offers at hand, Menzies reluctantly left for England again on May 4, having spent exactly two weeks in the company of his family.

"I don't think Mother wanted to go to begin with," Suzanne Menzies said of Mignon's reluctance to accompany him. "She didn't want to leave her nice house and her girlfriends. They had a big fight and he said, 'Well, don't go.' And she said, 'Okay, I won't go.' She took that opening and used it as an excuse for not going, which we heard about for the rest of our lives. 'He told me he didn't want me.' I know Ned Mann took his family over . . . the Americans were taking their families over. So we stayed here, for which I was very glad, although I missed him."

Menzies had feared he might be making a mistake in not leaving immediately upon receipt of Korda's wire, and it turned out he was right. The Donat project having quickly evaporated, Korda was urgently seeking Menzies' return to direct Stanley John Weyman's *Under the Red Robe* with Conrad Veidt, Annabella, and Raymond Massey as Cardinal Richelieu. But upon his arrival, he found the picture had already been given to another director, leaving him with no story and no prospects for a speedy return. "I don't know whether he was put out or not," Menzies said of Korda. "I'm afraid I'm a little inclined to vacillate and it's lousy in business. However, maybe

I'll get something better, but I'm afraid I will be definitely longer. The studios are enormous, and I feel a little lost after the small one."

The new studios at Denham were indeed enormous, but far from complete. It was, in fact, a non-Korda production, Max Schach's *Southern Roses,* that became the first to shoot there. Still, one could walk through the well-kept gardens adjoining the old country house that contained Korda's offices, along a woodland path bordering the River Colne, and peer across the water at the gray battlements of the castle built for *The Ghost Goes West.* In a distant field, the tower used in the Space Gun scenes for *Things to Come* still stood, as did, close by, the weathered remains of Everytown. "There seems to be a gentle air of gloom around the studio," Menzies reported on May 23. "I don't think things are going so smooth and of course they expect to lose money on [*Things to Come*].* I have a story to read, but it's terrible, I think. I have only seen Korda once, and he was very friendly, but I have a hunch I may be a little in the dog house. Seems to be my doom."

The "terrible" story was titled *Troopship,* and it was to be the second film produced under Korda's aegis by Erich Pommer, the onetime head of production for Germany's UFA. Korda himself was preparing to direct Charles Laughton in *Rembrandt,* another in London Films' series of historical biographies, and needed the help of men like Pommer to keep the new studio complex busy. *Troopship* was oddly suited to Menzies in that the setup had the various members of a British regiment returning home after a long stretch of foreign service, only to learn they had just six hours with their loved ones before deploying once more. The early material was from Wolfgang Wilhelm and Henry Koster, both, like Pommer, German émigrés, and Korda didn't seem to like anything they produced.

Ralph Richardson recalled Korda as a man beaten down by construction delays and the dual onslaught of two simultaneous pictures with H. G. Wells. "His manner to me was mostly one of ironic weariness," the actor said. "He gave me the impression that I slightly bored him—very likely I did—but at the same time he drew me towards him." Menzies struggled with *Troopship,* the portmanteau concept defeated by the weakness of its individual stories. "I have been practically suicidal since I got back here," he admitted in a letter home after a month's work. "The only saving thing is the visitors, but they have made it so expensive that that is spoiled. . . . It sounds as if I have a marvelous time, but just think of the lousy, lonesome, boring days in between. Hours of story conference and hanging around to worry about cast, etc. . . . They are still working on the script, and they are getting some new

* Its early performance notwithstanding, *Things to Come* didn't do well. Worldwide revenues amounted to US $1,121,881 on a total cost of £256,028 (US $1,257,098 at the time).

writers. I may have Bill Lipscombe and Clemence Dane, both very good, before we shoot. I have no idea how long it will take, but it should be very interesting, along the lines of 'Grand Hotel.'"

Pommer had another American director, William K. Howard, for his first film under Korda, an Elizabethan drama called *Fire Over England*. "Pommer is so involved in getting Bill Howard started that I haven't seen much of him lately and the story seems to be progressing very slowly," Menzies wrote in July. "They have never gotten a new labor permit for me and mine has been out for about a month, so I suppose I will be thrown out of the country soon, and the way I feel tonight, the sooner the better. . . . I wish I could quietly make a great picture and get out, but that isn't the way they do things over here. . . . Once in every few days I get the horrors and the homesick blues and this is one and a Monday. . . . I hope that things will work out and that I get on with the picture soon."

Howard began shooting a few days later, and Menzies, concurrently, got War Office permission to use an actual troopship. The plan was to sail it, with his cast and crew, to Alexandria, Egypt, and come back with real soldiers. "Things still seem very wobbly at the studio," he fretted. "I don't know where the money comes from that they are pouring in." On July 29, he glumly observed his fortieth birthday: "I hear about all the boys doing well in Hollywood. This one becoming a producer and that one becoming a director and it makes me go nuts marking time. . . . I passed forty without any pain, but it does seem as sort of [a] turning point in your life. I'll never be the boy art director again." In a nostalgic mood, he lunched with writer Tom Geraghty and they talked of the old Fairbanks days. "Doug is here," he wrote Mignon. "I saw him at a restaurant the other night. [His new wife, Sylvia] Ashley looked very attractive, Doug old."

By the middle of August, Menzies had half a new *Troopship* script by Ian Hay and Clemence Dane. "It's a lot better and, all things being even, I may be able to make a good picture. I like Pommer in spots, but I think he is fair." Then, having put three months' work in on the film, he was abruptly shifted to Korda's latest enthusiasm, an ambitious filming of Robert Graves' 1934 novel of the Roman Empire, *I, Claudius*. Korda had originally intended to direct the picture himself, but the process of developing a screenplay had seemingly defeated him, as had the prospect of once again directing Charles Laughton, this time in the role of the lame and stammering Tiberius Claudius, grandson of Mark Antony and uncle of the murderous Caligula.

Graves later blamed Korda's reliance on Hungarians "who were not altogether qualified for the jobs which he gave them, especially in the English department." Specifically, early drafts of the script had been written by Lajos Bíró and his frequent collaborator, Arthur Wimperis. "I was eventually shown a bit of the . . . a bit of some sort of a script in which a character comes in, I think it was Caligula comes in and says, 'My armies are revolting,' which . . . seems rather odd use of English. There was a lot that was revolting in the script besides." At one point, Graves himself was commissioned to write a screenplay, which he said was apparently "filed somewhere." When Menzies came aboard, the scenarist was Carl Zuckmayer, the German playwright who had written *Rembrandt.*

Just as Menzies had put across the majesty of the reborn Everytown in *Things to Come,* so would he, in Korda's mind, do the same for ancient Rome. Within days, he was on his way to Italy with Laughton and costume designer John Armstrong, toting a Leica he had borrowed from Vincent Korda. On the train, Laughton seemed to delight in attracting attention and then reveling in Menzies' discomfort. "You know, I can cry on demand," the actor said at one point, and then proceeded to do so. In Rome, he sat himself in front of a statue of Claudius and emoted enough to attract a small crowd, Menzies cringing and no doubt wishing he could disappear.

"The Fascisti thing is terrible," Menzies said in a letter to Mignon. "Everyone saluting + bragging about Mussolini + on every wall writings or posters 'Vive il Duce.' They seem very well off + the best looking people as a rule (especially the women)." They visited Tivoli, site of the famous Villa d'Este, attended a cocktail party with the Ministry of Cinema and Propaganda, toured the Vatican Museum, and spent a full day studying the Forum and the new excavations in the hills around it. They drove on to Naples and Pompeii, the words "Vive il Duce" on practically every tree along the way.

"Charles loves Americans + I made a great hit with him. He is one of the nicest people I have ever met + I don't think [he] has any strange practices outside of eating too much. I have made a great hit with him which will be easier for me during production." The party left Naples in time to put Laughton on a train for the south of France. "I fell on my face in bed after we saw Chas off + the next morning we were rushed out to see the sets for a huge Italian picture principally made by the gov't.* The sets were enormous but not very good. They are using 18,000 people in one scene." On the whole, the whirlwind trip had given Menzies "a new viewpoint on the script and sets" although, he said, he had "never worked so hard" in his life.

Production was set to start in September, the principal cast, apart from Laughton, comprised of Emlyn Williams, Flora Robson, Alan Aynesworth, John Clements, and, in the role of the scheming Messalina, second cousin to Claudius, Merle Oberon. The dark-skinned beauty, who had blossomed into Korda's only true female star, was in Los Angeles working for Samuel Goldwyn. It was Oberon's absence—she

---

* According to Catherine Surowiec, this was *Scipione l'africano* (1937).

was shooting *Beloved Enemy* with Brian Aherne and David Niven—that forced a delay of two months, prompting additional work on the script and a return to Rome for Menzies, this time in the company of Vincent Korda. "I feel alright," he wrote on the 26th of October, "but never high, and the atmosphere about the lot is a bit depressing and I feel so sort of guilty that 'Things to Come' didn't clean up for them. I will be shooting in a week or so and altho that will probably mean temperamental difficulties, I think it will snap me out of it. Vincent Korda has been a great help, as he is usually cheerful and very philosophical. I certainly have acquired a great deal of knowledge of ancient Rome; at least movie life is an education."

Oberon returned to London in early November, unhappy with the part of Messalina but eager to get on with it. Predictably, given Korda's patterns, there were additional delays, and she filled her time traveling—Paris, St. Moritz, Northumberland, Wales. The waiting continued to weigh heavily on Menzies until one day he asked Harry Ham, Korda's production manager, to tell Alex he was taking the next boat home. Korda's reaction to the news was instantaneous. "He was amazed that I was so upset + said he was giving me a promotion + I was crabbing so I agreed to direct, produce, shoot, write + cut two pictures for him. It's what I've wanted to do all my life + if the company doesn't fold up in the meantime I think it will be a great break. . . . They are completely mine + the credit will be produced + directed by William Cameron Menzies. I am terribly excited—for the first time I can do my own stuff + they are melodramas with one sort of whimsical character running thro. That's why it will be a series, something on the Charlie Chan type, only better I hope!" He assured Mignon the pictures wouldn't take as long to shoot as *Claudius*—likely less than two months. "I am terribly glad to be off Claudius as I am afraid it's going to be an unpleasant set-up. Anyway, I had two nice trips to Italy."

Korda put him together with a British novelist and film critic who dabbled in American-style thrillers. The idea, at least at first, was for Menzies to develop the initial entry for a series, a franchise that could become a reliable, albeit modest, source of income for London Film. "I am getting definitely excited about my story," he said on November 27.

Unbelievable as it seems, the writer is very intelligent and altho I have to help him plenty, he is very sound. If you can, you might get his book thru [Beverly Hills bookseller] Marian Hunter. It's called "A Gun for Sale" and his name is Graham Greene. It's very low key, but very exciting. We went out the other night and started at Paddington and walked and drove the whole route of the story thru Soho and ending up on the river at Wapping. It's amazing how many ideas we got from the trip. In a way, I don't care what happens as I want to get home, but I would like to do this one entirely on my own, as then I'd know whether I really have something on the ball or not.

Greene was given three weeks to deliver an original story, for which he was paid a fee of £175. "There is a typical Korda snag," Greene wrote his brother Hugh. "The story is a fairly realistic low-life thriller about race gangs, the hero a stool-pigeon. Korda wishes me to write a part for [the British music hall star] George Robey!" The picture, *Four Dark Hours,* was given a start date of January 15, 1937. As Menzies said in a letter, "I am trying to have the other one written by the time I have finished the first, and if either one clicks I should make some money. I don't think the first one will ever win the Nobel Prize, but I think it's entertaining. . . . Korda showed a loss since April of £330,000, or about one-million-five-hundred-thousand bucks, which is nothing like the Fox-Chase loss, but plenty over here, so he may fold before I finish."

Menzies passed another gloomy Christmas in England—his third in a row—and was otherwise focused on script, casting, and continuity boards, the first act somewhat recalling *The Woman Disputed* in tone and structure. "I'm thick in scenario," Graham Greene wrote his brother on Boxing Day. "Medium shots and Insert Shots and Flash backs and the rest of the racket. Korda, I'm glad to say, has given up the Robey idea and seems to be leaving us alone. Casting is proving very different. Menzies finds lovely people with appallingly tough faces, but when they open their mouths they all have Oxford accents."

Menzies later described how he laid out the soundstage with a viewfinder, putting lines down on the floor and only creating sets to occupy the areas within those lines. The technique enabled him to erect four or five more sets on one stage, saving time when moving the company between scenes. *Four Dark Hours* was shot quickly, utilizing the services of Korda contract players Rene Ray and Robert Newton. Heading the cast as Jim Connor, small-time song-and-dance man, was John Mills, not particularly new to films but by no means a box office attraction. There was, Menzies understood going in, no guarantee the movie would be released internationally, but Korda had nevertheless promised a 10 percent cut of the producer's profits in addition to a salary of $1,000 a week. The film's unofficial template became *The 39 Steps,* a successful "wrong man" thriller Robert Donat had made on loan-out to Gaumont British. The twist in Greene's story was that it was Rene Ray's character on the run, falsely accused of killing Newton, with Mills helping her elude the police without knowing she is, in fact, wanted for the murder of his own brother. "We decided to hire an English gangster as an authority and technical advisor," Menzies later recounted. "In a few weeks I learned more about the underworld of

A scene lifted from *Gone With the Wind*, in which Rhett, Scarlett, and the others drive off into the distance as a single lamp is left glowing in the foreground. Menzies' composition confines all the essential action to the lower third of the frame, leaving ample room for the "hideous red glow" of the sky to penetrate the leafy canopy of a narrow street. (ACADEMY OF MOTION PICTURE ARTS AND SCIENCES)

To fill the hours when there wasn't any work, Menzies painted intricate patterns on the walls and doors of the upstairs hallway in his Beverly Hills home. (RON GROEPER)

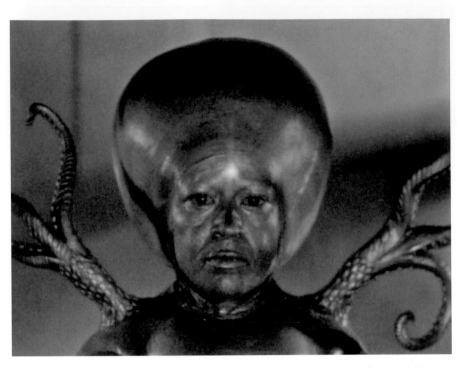

The haunting imagery of *Invaders from Mars* stayed with a generation of young viewers, many of whom discovered the film on television. *Above:* The alien intelligence is probably the most persistent image from the film, a countenance as interpreted by Menzies from a script that described the creature as "brontocephalic." *Below:* The horizon fence had become a leitmotif in Menzies' work, a device that reliably invested a shot with depth and mystery.

*Above:* Dr. Blake's peril is underscored with the inspired use of a Plexiglas sheet that permits her face to be seen as well as the surgical instrument about to implant a crystal at the base of her brain. *Below:* David's jail cell confines him in pattern, the space literally closing in on him at a time when he fears he can trust nobody.

Self-portrait, circa 1952  (MENZIES FAMILY COLLECTION)

London than any other Englishman except the police. My authority was practically festooned with knives and razors, and when the picture came to an end and I had to discharge him, he got a little tough. I had a gone feeling in my stomach, but I got equally tough and said, 'Scram, Slug,' and he went out quite meekly, razors and all."

As carefully as Menzies prepared and shot the picture, its gritty Soho exteriors giving it a somewhat noirish quality before there ever really was such a thing, he was completely unequipped to direct the stage-trained actors in his cast, who were used to the deliberate pace of British filmmaking and unable to adapt to the snappier demands of the downbeat crime melodrama—an unusual genre in the U.K. As a result, *Four Dark Hours*—so titled because all its action took place within that specific time frame—lacked the essential element of urgency. When Korda screened it, he was obviously disappointed, and although it was sluggish almost to the point of tedium, no one seemed to know quite what to do about it. The film, Menzies later told the *Los Angeles Daily News*, was shelved "when the Korda release deal fell through."

*I, Claudius* finally got under way in February with Josef von Sternberg, reportedly at the behest of Marlene Dietrich, directing. Despite a brilliant set of elements—script, casting, Vincent Korda's spectacular sets—the production was every bit as troubled as Menzies predicted, and it limped along for a month, delivering wonderful results while exacting an extraordinary emotional toll on everyone involved. Laughton disliked von Sternberg, Merle Oberon hated her part, and Alex found himself second-guessing every aspect of the process. On March 16, 1937, Oberon was involved in an auto accident—the severity of her injuries exaggerated according to some reports—and Korda seized the opportunity to take an £80,000 insurance payout, canceling the film and disbanding the company. Menzies, with just one unreleased feature to show for his ten months at Denham, left for home aboard the *Queen Mary,* dispirited and unsure of where next he would work. "His experience with Korda," concluded Laurence Irving, "had not been very heart-lifting."

*Four Dark Hours* continued to languish on the shelf until William K. Howard delivered a more satisfactory example of the genre in Edgar Wallace's *The Squeaker.* Inspired, Korda asked Howard to revisit Menzies' unreleased picture, with Howard's screenwriter, Edward O. "Ted" Berkman, attempting a revision. (Menzies had frankly considered the film in its original form "impossible to show in America on account of the broad Cockney.") Sometime late that year, Howard recalled the cast and shot new dialogue sequences, intent on making the picture releasable through United Artists. Menzies had been so reticent in dealing with his actors that John Mills, in his autobiography, could remember only Howard, "happily hitting the bottle," as the director of the film. "Bill Howard had made some excellent movies," he wrote, "but by the time we caught up with him, he was, I'm afraid, slightly over the hill."

In July 1939, British Lion was set to release the picture at a running time of sixty-four minutes. A few months later, it was picked up by 20th Century-Fox Film Co., Ltd., and under the title *The Green Cockatoo,* was released in Great Britain in March 1940. It wasn't, however, until July of 1947, after Mills had won a degree of fame for his work as Pip in David Lean's celebrated version of *Great Expectations,* that it was finally released in the United States.

Just as Menzies was arriving back in New York, David O. Selznick was entering into negotiations to bring M-G-M assistant art director Fredric Hope to Selznick International, the independent studio he founded in 1935. Talks stalled within days when Hope, thirty-seven, underwent emergency surgery at St. Vincent's Hospital for a burst appendix. With two pictures in the queue, the first to start shooting in just eight weeks, Selznick, in a lather, phoned Metro-Goldwyn-Mayer production manager J. J. Cohn. "He said, 'Joe, I need a man so-and-so, so-and-so, so-and-so,'"

Rene Ray and John Mills in *The Green Cockatoo.* "The film's best asset is its players," C. A. Lejeune wrote in *The Observer,* "who act at times as if the piece were credible." (BRITISH FILM INSTITUTE)

Colin recalled. "Matter of fact, he wanted me to go to work there. 'I'll call you, David.' Then I called him back. I said, 'So there's a man on his way back from Europe now. Your brother, Myron, is handling it. Because he'd be ideal for you. I think, David, he's what you want—William Cameron Menzies.' And I knew Bill pretty well. Socially and otherwise. And I had spent time with Bill in England before that. David was very grateful for that."

On April 16, 1937, while Hope was laid up in the hospital, Selznick dictated a memo to corporate counsel and secretary Daniel T. O'Shea: "We haven't settled on the Hope matter, but in the meantime I should like you to find out salary, etc., on Menzies—just as a protection. I would be interested in Menzies if he has given up his producing ideas, as a substitute for Hope . . . if the Hope deal falls through." Four days later, on April 20, Hope died of complications from the operation he had undergone two weeks earlier.

Colin's endorsement—and Hope's death—turned Selznick's attention squarely to Bill Menzies, even as Menzies refused to abandon his dream of producing and directing his own pictures. O'Shea suggested they guarantee him co-direction of one picture a year, on the condition that he "generally do art work for us" at the rate of $1,000 a week. Talks continued into late May, Menzies preferring to freelance, and the contract that resulted was for an initial period, with options, of just three months. Word went out on June 7 that Menzies had been signed in the capacity of "production assistant," a new position created expressly for him. "Menzies will supervise practically all preliminary details of films, in respect to sets, locationing, and other matters," Edwin Schallert reported. "In addition he will direct, and his first film will be associated with Robert Sinclair, the stage director."

Promptly, Menzies was put in charge of second unit work on *Nothing Sacred*, a picture being written in a "white heat"—as story editor Val Lewton put it—by novelist, playwright, and veteran screenwriter Ben Hecht. Conceived as Hollywood's first three-color Technicolor comedy, there was little stock footage for the film to draw upon. Establishing shots, montage clips, effects shots, and process plates would all have to be created from scratch. A week after principal photography commenced under William Wellman's direction, Menzies found himself back in New York, learning the limitations of the new three-color process with Technicolor cameraman Will Cline. A nighttime pan of the Waldorf-Astoria was vetoed by Jack Cosgrove, Selznick's special effects man, because Technicolor was unable to pick up the incandescent lighting in the hotel's windows. Similar shots of Madison Square Garden and Times Square were only possible because neon signs registered better.

He made daylight shots of Rockefeller Center and the Waldorf, caught ocean liners steaming up and down the harbor, filmed customs men at work and society figures at play. Through Selznick's business partner, John Hay "Jock" Whitney, he arranged to pick up a shot of polo players at Meadowbrook, panning down the field with the grandstands in the background. The yachting stuff called for in the still incomplete script was made on the East River with doubles representing Fredric March and Carole Lombard. Selznick praised a shot of a steelworker straddling a girder some forty stories above the city as "startlingly good." Particularly important were morning shots of the airliner carrying the supposedly doomed Hazel Flagg over Manhattan, Menzies and his crew trailing a Lockheed 12 and shooting plates to be employed in the filming of interiors. "Daddy was on that plane with [stunt pilot] Paul Mantz and was absolutely terrified," Suzanne Menzies remembered. "There was nothing to hang on to—not even seats, just the camera—and Mantz was nuts. I think they flew *under* the Brooklyn Bridge." Through it all, Selznick urged restraint with the expensive three-strip color stock, reminding Menzies they could only use a few feet of anything he shot.

"New York is terribly warm," Menzies said in a letter to his eleven-year-old daughter, "and full of very unattractive people all looking at things and commenting on them in very loud and very unmusical voices. . . . For your comfort, darling, you have missed nothing in not seeing New York. It looks more like Glendale on a Saturday night than Glendale, except that it looks more like Redondo than it does like Glendale. Anyway, honey, New York looks marvelous if you know you are leaving it in a very short time."

Back in California, Menzies tackled the montage sequences for *Nothing Sacred* and designed the satiric "Heroines of History" pageant. (The Breen Office rejected five sketches of tentative costumes because they allegedly violated the nudity clause of the Production Code.) He was busy directing night footage in San Pedro—three setups involving nineteen firemen and two policemen—the day the studio announced his first co-direction job with Sinclair would be the Janet Gaynor vehicle *Angel on Broadway.* By the end of August, Selznick, who favored literary classics for picture material, had him sketching the climactic sequence for *The Adventures of Tom Sawyer.*

In a screenplay credited to the poet and literary critic John V. A. Weaver, Selznick had built the third act of the picture around an incident in Mark Twain's novel in which Tom and Becky Thatcher become lost in McDougal's Cave. Using the book's original engravings as a guide, Menzies sketched out a potent nine-minute sequence in which the children are dwarfed by the spectacular caverns, beset by bats, consumed by despair and hunger, a hunk of wedding cake their only food, and threatened by the maniacal Injun Joe, whom Tom, with certain death just inches away, sends plunging into the infinite darkness of a deep ravine. It was strong stuff

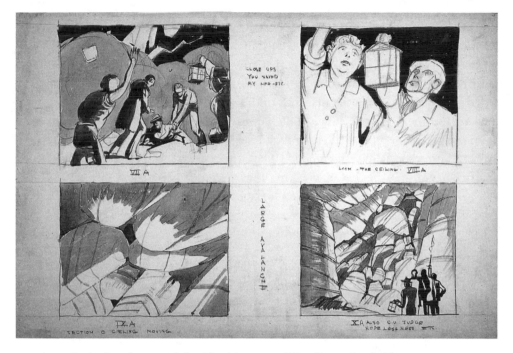

A continuity board prepared for *The Adventures of Tom Sawyer* (1938). The cave sequence proved so effective that preview audiences seemed to think it was, in the words of David O. Selznick, "somehow too horrible for children." (DAVID O. SELZNICK COLLECTION, HARRY RANSOM CENTER)

in the vivid new Technicolor, calculated to send hearts racing among adults in the audience and traumatize kids into sleeping with the lights on.

Selznick, for one, was delighted, and gave Menzies the job of staging the sequence in collaboration with director Norman Taurog. Not long before, he had lamented the inexperience of unit art director Lyle Wheeler, whom he had hired with no previous movie experience, while contrasting it with Menzies' "very wide experience." Preparing to mount a production of *Gone With the Wind,* the rights to which he had purchased the previous year, Selznick began to imagine a much more significant role for Menzies than for Wheeler. "I would like to see him actively take charge of the physical preparation of *Gone With the Wind,*" he wrote of Menzies, "including advance work on the sets, handling and selection of location shots, process shots, etc.; layouts and effects, etc. for the mass action scenes; investigations and suggestions leading to the proper handling of the street scenes without an inordinate expense; and a dozen other things leading to proper organization of the great and troublesome physical aspects of *Gone With the Wind.*"

Two weeks later, his thoughts on Menzies' participation had sharpened considerably. "I think Menzies is going to be invaluable on the montage sequences in *Gone With the Wind*," Selznick mused in a memo to studio manager Henry Ginsberg, "and feel I should go even farther than this and have him do a complete cutting script with sketches from the first shot to the last on the entire job of *Gone With the Wind*. I feel too that he may be the answer to what I have long sought for, which is a pre-cut picture and that with or without the help of [supervising editor] Hal Kern, or some cutter specially designated for the purpose, we might be able to cut a picture eighty percent on paper before we grind the cameras."

Selznick knew the film would be a logistical nightmare to produce, complex and expensive. The only way to gain absolute control over it would be to pre-visualize it through Menzies' technique of continuity sketches. On September 1, as shooting began on the cave sequence for *Tom Sawyer*, he dictated a memo to Jock Whitney and John Wharton, the corporate treasurer of Selznick International, more fully outlining his plans:

> I feel we need a man of Menzies' talent and enormous experience on the sets of this picture, and on its physical production. I hope to have *Gone With the Wind* prepared almost down to the last camera angle before we start shooting, because on this picture really thorough preparation will save hundreds of thousands of dollars. . . . While our script is not completed, and we are not yet certain of what we will have to cut, we know there are a half dozen things . . . such as Tara, the Wilkes house, Miss Pittypat's home, the ball in Atlanta . . . that must of necessity stay in, as well as the streets of Atlanta for the news of Gettysburg and the big evacuation scene which involve great physical problems and which will more than utilize Menzies' time until we can give him a complete script. When he gets the complete script, he can then do all the sets, set sketches, and plans . . . and can start on what I want on this picture and what has only been done a few times in picture history (and these times mostly by Menzies)—a complete script in sketch form, showing actual camera setups, lighting, etc. . . .
>
> Menzies may turn out to be one of the most valuable factors in properly producing this picture. One of the minor problems in connection with this arrangement is the matter of Menzies' credit. Menzies is terribly anxious not to get back to art direction as such, and of course his work on this picture, as I see it, will be a lot greater in scope than is normally associated with the term "art direction." Accordingly, I would probably give him some such credit as "Production Designed by William Cameron Menzies."

# 12

# Production Designed By . . .

Bill Menzies had never read *Gone With the Wind*—it not being one of the "gloomy books" he kept in stacks by his bed—but he certainly knew its impact. First published by Macmillan in 1936, it was an instantaneous hit with more than a million copies in print by the end of the year. The British edition, published in September, was issued in a cautious printing of three thousand just as Menzies, immersed in the trappings of ancient Rome, was preparing to direct *I, Claudius*. At no time did the book, a thick Civil War romance, strike him as exceptional picture material, and he took little notice when its author, Margaret Mitchell, won the Pulitzer Prize in May of the following year. By then, of course, he was dickering with David O. Selznick and knew that Selznick owned the rights, having bought the novel, unread, just as it was gathering momentum.*

There was talk of starting the film in 1938, but the script had not yet been completed, and Menzies saw no reason to believe he would play a crucial role in its making, assuming he was destined to play any role at all.

Menzies' involvement with the film grew over a period of four months as Selznick weighed the advantages of having someone on *Gone With the Wind* who was uniquely qualified to not only manage aspects of its physical production, but to

---

* Selznick paid $50,000 for the rights to the book, a fat price for the time but by no means a record. *The Grapes of Wrath* brought $60,000 and the play *You Can't Take It with You*, which won the 1937 Pulitzer Prize for drama, fetched a startling $265,000.

give it a graphic cohesion lacking in most American films. Sidney Howard had been engaged to adapt the 1,037-page novel to the screen and had been at work on a script since the beginning of the year. George Cukor had been set as director even longer and, together with Selznick, had been focused on casting the picture with a seemingly endless array of names, Clark Gable, Gary Cooper, and Errol Flynn being the top picks for Rhett Butler, and practically every competent actress in town vying for the role of Scarlett O'Hara. Menzies continued his work on *Nothing Sacred* through September, directing retakes and added scenes, store window shots and inserts. He was laid off in October with the understanding he would submit ideas in connection with *Gone With the Wind,* after which Selznick would decide if, when, and under what circumstances he would be engaged for the picture. In the interim, he promised he would start no other job without first checking with the studio, as he wanted the directing work only Selznick seemed willing to give him.

In December, Selznick determined he could likely start *GWTW* much sooner than he originally thought—possibly as early as February—and directed Henry Ginsberg to speak to Menzies about handling the supervision of the art department as well as the "cutting script" (as it was described at the time). Ginsberg was also to ask Menzies what sort of assistance he wanted in the way of a unit art man, Menzies having already recommended Hobe Erwin, formerly of RKO, as set decorator.

"I have finally reached Bill Menzies' *Gone With the Wind* sketches," Selznick informed Ginsberg and Daniel O'Shea on December 15, "and I am completely sold that we should have him on this picture. I have told Bill that until our future plans are settled I do not want to get into any contractual commitments of any size. On the other hand, there is the possibility of our getting word to start production in March, which does not give us any too much time, Lord knows, and we may be wasting precious weeks of preparation that can never be gained again because of any one of several things, such as the [Clark] Gable schedule and the dates that we must take him if we are to have him at all."

On Christmas Eve 1937, Selznick finally confirmed to Ginsberg that William Cameron Menzies would be going back on the company payroll effective January 3, 1938. Production illustrator Dorothea Holt would act as Menzies' assistant.

In the early days of *Gone With the Wind,* there was no complete screenplay, just the novel and the reference materials gathered by Selznick personnel on two trips to Atlanta—photos of old houses, primarily, and the Georgia landscape. Then there was Wilbur G. Kurtz, a well-known architect and painter recommended by Margaret Mitchell as "our greatest authority on the Civil War in this section." Kurtz was introduced to George Cukor on a visit to Clayton County in March 1937, and was subsequently retained by the studio to act as technical advisor to Menzies and the production team. When he came west in late January 1938, Kurtz's first three weeks were spent in the Selznick art department, where he and Menzies conferred on the book and its settings.

"At these conferences," recounted Kurtz,

> we designed Tara, Aunt Pitty's house, Melanie's house and the Atlanta sets which included the big car shed. Twelve Oaks was another matter; the Wilkes estate, as described, is pure fiction, for there never was such a place in Clayton County. However, it was a necessary piece of fiction in that the storywriters demanded at least one glimpse of the traditional moonlight and magnolia atmosphere of the old South. Since Twelve Oaks was a myth in the novel, it was treated as such in the picture—hence those glorious interiors, the monumental stairways, and an atmosphere of opulence that would make a Clayton County farmer rub his eyes. Scarlett, herself, designed her Atlanta house, summoning thereto all of the bad taste of the period and most of Rhett's money. The Art Department let her have her way here, and thereby an effect was achieved that was entirely keeping with the facts.

When they first met, Menzies told Kurtz he had already made hundreds of "shorthand" sketches, presumably from Sidney Howard's draft script dated November 27, 1937. "I'd see him out in the backyard," said Suzie Menzies. "He'd wash his hair and then dry it in the sun. He'd sit with that sketchbook and stare into space. And then he'd draw something; sometimes it was my mother's rear end, and other times it was *Tom Sawyer* or *Gone With the Wind*. He was a great one for staring into space."

As Howard gave Kurtz his own copy to read, Howard remarked: "Here's a four-hour picture. It'll have to be cut to two hours, more cutting than Mr. Selznick and Mr. Cukor will admit at present." As it turned out, Howard's work displayed an excellent grasp of camera technique—when to truck, pan, or shoot direct. From his preliminary boards, Menzies graduated to larger, more finished watercolors of key sequences—exteriors at first—taking Howard's ideas, along with episodes from the book, and refining them into masterful scenes of graphic drama. Kurtz found himself admiring one such rendering, lifted straight from the text and recalled in Howard's screenplay, in which the Union army corps are closing in, one just nine miles away, and a lighted lamp is left behind as Rhett, Scarlett, and the others drive off toward Tara, the sequence ending on the stark imagery of that single camphene lamp.

Owing to the lack of stock footage in the new three-strip Technicolor process, Menzies directed an unusual amount of second unit work for *Nothing Sacred* (1937). Exteriors shot on the Forty Acres backlot included tattoo store and fish stall inserts as well as this impromptu window display attesting to the flash celebrity of Hazel Flagg.

Menzies' sketch shows the wagon and the starved horse—and the rest—in a silhouette against the lighted lamp in front of the open gate of Aunt Pittypat's house. Menzies said that this lone lamp business was one of the most telling touches in the book. . . . I cannot begin to relate in detail the various novel conceptions of Menzies' sketches—dramatic and novel effects are aimed at, and color—always color—must be uppermost, <u>for GWTW is to be in Technicolor!</u> He despairs of red soil—must have it—even if the old spray gun is used, with barrels of red paint splattered on California terrain!

They got to the design of Tara on February 2, Menzies having previously proclaimed himself "afraid" of it. In the art studio where he spent most of his time—he had a formal office and secretary in the main administration building but was rarely there—Tara and Twelve Oaks gradually appeared, roughed out on big sheets of tracing paper. Menzies, Kurtz observed, was gleeful over the covered way to the kitchen, insisting on a variety of building textures toward the rear of the house to break the monotony of white brick. "The ash-hopper was new to him, but he could understand the covered well. He never heard of a scuppernong, looked at me like he thought I was kidding."

Early on, Margaret Mitchell had taken Cukor and the other "Selznickers" through Clayton County, showing them old houses that were built "before Sherman got there" and cautioning them that white columns were the exception rather than the rule. "I besought them to please leave Tara ugly, sprawling, and columnless, and they agreed. I imagine, however, that when it comes to Twelve Oaks they will put columns all around the house and make it as large as our new city auditorium." Kurtz artfully talked Menzies out of columns on three sides of the mythical Twelve Oaks, and eventually Menzies embraced Doric columns over the complex Ionic columns on which he had initially insisted. These were to be only the first of many such renderings, and both iconic structures would evolve over time.

Three days before Wilbur Kurtz was to leave for home, the news on the lot was that Selznick had bought a new story. *The Gay Banditti,* a sly melding of grift and sentiment by the Australian-born poet and novelist I. A. R. Wylie. Selznick needed a picture for actress Janet Gaynor, who had last appeared for the studio in *A Star Is Born.* He also needed to fulfill an eight-picture distribution commitment to United Artists, thus keeping his options open with regard to *Gone With the Wind.* The Selznick Research Department was put on the case, and an adaptation of the London-based story was commissioned from Britain's Charles Bennett, working in collaboration with the American playwright and scenarist Frederick Jackson.

Meanwhile, in a memo to George Cukor, Selznick expressed growing satisfaction with the *GWTW* development process: "I am more enthusiastic than ever about the script and will be calling Menzies in to conferences practically each day so that by the time we finish the script, we will have almost all the physical production mapped out as well." As plans for *The Gay Banditti* (soon retitled *Miss Fortune Leaves It to Them* and, ultimately, *The Young in Heart*) went forward, Selznick had Menzies added to the budget as Lyle Wheeler's supervisor and arranged for him to be copied on all memos regarding script changes.

As a dry run for *Gone With the Wind,* Menzies acquitted himself admirably on *Young in Heart,* functioning as an uncredited assistant to the producer while overseeing set design and personally sketching the continuities of key sequences. For the film's opening on the Riviera where the various members of the Carleton family are

Sample pages from a spiral-bound sketchbook show some of Menzies' earliest
"shorthand" visualizations for *Gone With the Wind* (1939). (MENZIES FAMILY
COLLECTION)

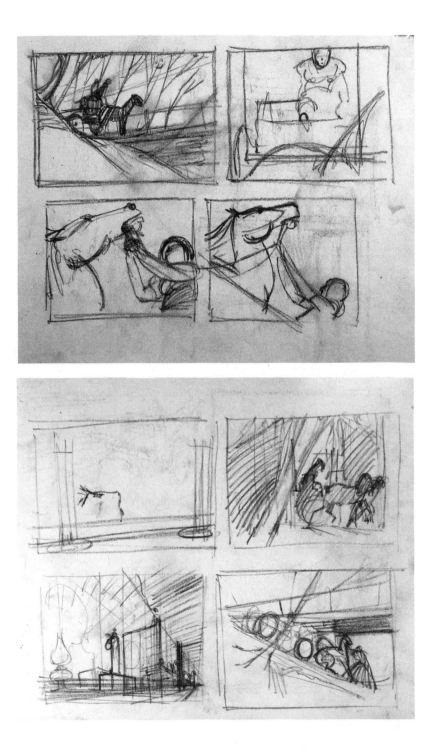

introduced, he and Wheeler created a grand terrace on multiple levels that allowed the camera to flow smoothly from one exchange to the next. The vast showroom of the Flying Wombat sedan, with its twirling display chassis and power train, was matched by the executive office of the British-American Civil and Hydraulic Engineering Co., its walls clad with the muscular figures of industrial workers as rendered by Dan Sayre Groesbeck. Menzies also suggested alternate ways of shooting the train derailment that marks the climax of the first act, proposing to either film it as a miniature or entirely from the interior, as had been done for a dirigible crash in *The Lottery Bride.* Both approaches, he noted, would cost approximately the same.

Production got under way on May 3 with the prolific Richard Wallace directing and Gaynor; Douglas Fairbanks, Jr.; Roland Young; Paulette Goddard; and Billie Burke heading the cast. Menzies' work was principally with cinematographer Leon Shamroy, leaving the amiable Wallace to handle the actors. An efficient shoot, they were done in six weeks, but then retakes and added scenes carried them into September, Lewis Milestone directing nine days of them, Menzies the balance. Menzies also designed and shot the main titles, generic scenes from the story as played in silhouette, the credits laid over the incidental action, a classy opening to a perfectly pleasant picture that was budgeted at close to $1 million.

For Menzies, the real significance of *The Young in Heart* was in his personal credit, for Selznick had been struggling with the matter for months. In February, he had written publicist Russell Birdwell, who, in a draft press release, had portrayed Menzies as something akin to a draftsman on *Gone With the Wind.* "I don't think the word 'drafting' is fair to Menzies," he cautioned.

> This term in motion picture language means simply a draftsman working under an art director. Menzies' task is a monumental one and I am anxious that he receive a fair credit. Actually what he is doing is "designing" the picture and "designing" it in color, if it is to be made in color. If Mr. Cukor for any reason does not like this term, I suggest you get together with him and let me see some alternatives. Whatever phrase is chosen should be satisfactory to both Mr. Cukor and Mr. Menzies, and nothing should be sent out on this announcement that is not seen and approved by both.

Cukor evidently had no objection, and so the credit that was settled upon was the one that Selznick himself had coined in September of the previous year. It became Menzies' handle on *Gone With the Wind,* even though the release of that picture was still eighteen months in the future. In the meantime, Menzies was to embrace the same approximate responsibilities on a pair of more modestly proportioned Selznick productions, and so the producer decreed that the credit so arduously arrived at for *GWTW* would became Menzies' credit on *The Young in Heart* as well: "Production Designed by William Cameron Menzies."

In July, while Menzies was staging the titles for *Young in Heart,* Selznick was urgently pondering the question of who should direct his final release for United Artists. Its basis was Rose Franken's 1937 novel *Of Great Riches*—retitled *Made for Each Other*—and it was to be Carole Lombard's second picture for Selznick International. On a list of possible candidates, the names of John G. Blystone, Sidney Lanfield, Edward H. Griffith, George Fitzmaurice, Elliott Nugent, Irving Cummings, James Flood, E. A. Dupont, Allan Dwan, James Whale, William K. Howard, Frank Tuttle, Rouben Mamoulian, and Wesley Ruggles had all been crossed off. Those with check marks next to them were Tay Garnett, Edmund Goulding, George Cukor, H. C. "Hank" Potter, Ernst Lubitsch, Sam Wood, and Alexander Hall. There were only three names on the list that were circled: John Cromwell, Richard Wallace, and Henry King. It was about this time that William Burnside, a British sales consultant who had worked with Selznick on the U.K. release of *Tom Sawyer,* made a pitch:

> Once before, in conversation, I mentioned to you that Bill Menzies could, in my opinion, if given the opportunity, turn in a swell directorial job. As I am the only person here on this lot who has worked with him in a directorial capacity [on *Things to Come*] and as I have worked with a considerable number of so-called "ace" directors, I can assure you that from my observations Menzies can produce a "joker" for their "ace" every time. . . . I would be the last to detract from either Wallace's or Shamroy's work on *The Young in Heart* but I wonder if even you fully realize the great assistance that Menzies was to both of these men on that picture, both from a point of view of camera angles and practical physical direction.

Selznick didn't select Menzies for the job—he instead chose John Cromwell, the director of two previous films for the studio—thinking, perhaps, that Menzies would too fully have been taken away from *Gone With the Wind* if given the assignment. Moreover, the film, at least at first, didn't require the kind of pictorial fireworks Menzies was used to providing. The intimate story of newlyweds and their day-to-day trials, *Made for Each Other* was an actors' picture, and Selznick arranged to borrow James Stewart from M-G-M to play the role of the young attorney opposite Lombard. Ironically, Menzies ended up spending more time on added scenes and retakes for *Made for Each Other* than he did on *The Young in Heart,* keeping him busy on the picture, between extended bouts on *GWTW,* into January of 1939.

By the end of July, he was back in New York, quartered, as before, at the Essex House and shooting second unit footage. "Another trying hot day," he wrote Mignon on the evening of the 29th. "We got all set to shoot this a.m. but had to call it off as the haze set in again. I'm afraid we won't get any real shooting weather until we get rain. I am afraid I am not as good a wanderer as I used to be, my darling. New York depresses me. It's so boisterous and tough and cheap, and I'm sick of smelling like a gymnasium." Plans seemed to change hourly, and there was no screenplay to work from—just a synopsis. "I haven't been able to get up to New Haven," he added, "as things are in such a mess I felt I should stand by to hear from the coast."

It was a measure of the urgency Selznick felt in delivering the picture that *Made for Each Other* went before the cameras on August 26 with just thirteen pages of script. Veteran screenwriter Jo Swerling worked just ahead of Cromwell and his company, minimizing the value Menzies' continuity sketches routinely brought to a production. Instead, it became Menzies' job to keep Lyle Wheeler on track and ensure the sets were available when Cromwell needed them.* Menzies was also assigned the opening of the picture, in which Selznick wanted stock footage of New York to lead to Stewart's introduction on a busy sidewalk. "The entire effect of this is to be going down through the canyons of New York to pick out any average citizen, and I should like to see it laid out in sketches by Bill, regardless of whether we utilize stock film."

Selznick came to rely on Menzies for moody hospital shots, montage and miniature work, background plates, inserts, and the design of key scenes. All the main titles, neatly establishing the marriage of the two principal characters, were sketched and directed by Menzies, as was Stewart's introduction on the city sidewalk, the camera closing in on the character's listing in the Manhattan phone book as an inexpensive alternative to "the canyons of New York" when no stock footage could be found that proved suitable. "Mr. Menzies should direct this [sequence] if Mr. Cromwell has no objections. Mr. Cromwell can go over this at any time between now and the time it is shot with Mr. Menzies or myself." The real work on *Made for Each Other* came when the picture finished in early October.

The third act centered on the life-threatening illness of the Masons' year-old son, a bout with pneumonia that can only be arrested with the help of a new serum. Located in Salt Lake City, the medicine is unobtainable due to weather, prompting a

---

* "You had better immediately inform Mr. Menzies and Mr. Wheeler to have the café set ready for Saturday morning," Selznick warned in a typical memo to production manager Edward Butcher.

daring flight that has little chance of success. With the principals—Lombard, Stewart, Charles Coburn, Lucile Watson—released, subject to recall, Menzies began laying out the sequence, nearly two reels of material, in collaboration with Jo Swerling.

"This," Selznick wrote in an all-hands memo,

> includes the montage preceding Johnny's visit to [Judge] Doolittle's home [to plead for the money to bring the serum to New York], winding up with the bit in the Salt Lake City airport. . . . The Menzies script should also include the entire development, starting with the aviator refusing to take off, after the money has been raised, and going straight through the storm, the parachute drop, the ride over the bridge, etc. . . . Mr. Cromwell should shoot those two pieces of the respective Menzies sequences which concern the two aviators at the Salt Lake City airport. The rest should be shot by Mr. Menzies, and work should be started with no delay whatsoever on the assembly of stock film, etc., etc., to the end that the shooting of these sequences may commence no later than the day after the picture proper is finished. . . . If it is at all possible, I would like Miss Holt or such other sketch artist as Mr. Menzies wishes to designate to work right along with Mr. Swerling and Mr. Menzies, to the end that I can consider the script on each draft of this material in sketch form as well as script form. . . . It is my hope that we will be able to have a preview of the picture by between October 22nd and 25th.

Previews in November and December resulted in nineteen pages of new scenes and retakes, with Menzies finishing the last of these on January 5, 1939. When the final credits were submitted to the Production Code Administration, once again they included the line: "Production Designed by William Cameron Menzies."

Just as filming was set to begin on *Made for Each Other,* Selznick signed the contracts with Metro-Goldwyn-Mayer that called for the loan of Clark Gable and the release of *Gone With the Wind* through Loew's Incorporated. Gable, who was preparing to shoot *Idiot's Delight* at his home studio, would become available in January, meaning that Selznick would need a finished script, final design approvals on sets and costumes, and a decision on the casting of Scarlett O'Hara. He told his department heads the film could start as early as November 15—a date nobody seemed to take seriously—and that the agreement with M-G-M would in no way compromise its identity as a Selznick International picture. Comparative estimates put the likely cost of the film at $2,250,000; Selznick said that in cutting the script he would aim at holding its cost to $2 million.

By October, Menzies had floated the idea of burning the standing sets on Forty Acres so that room could be cleared for new exteriors, particularly Tara. It was an audacious plan, and Selznick, at first, wasn't sure what to think. "I would appreciate Mr. Cukor working with Mr. Menzies and Mr. Wheeler on those things which will be needed for the first work in the picture," he wrote on the 13th, "so that I know about the plans for them before I leave [for a brief Bermuda vacation] next Friday, Oct. 21st. This should include, particularly, the building of Tara and the plans to photograph the burning sets which will be destroyed to make way for Tara." A few days later, with the starting date finally set, Selznick asked that work start immediately on the remaining set sketches. "I am hopeful that we will have every single set in the picture designed and approved at least three weeks in advance of our starting to shoot—and that stage space will also be all laid out for these sets to the end that there will be no problem whatsoever in connection with the sets during the picture's shooting, except perhaps for set dressing."

A month later, after a number of conferences between Menzies, Wheeler, and George Cukor, twenty-four sets had been okayed in sketch form, another six were awaiting approval, and another seven were being modeled. On November 9, Menzies sent his "amplified" script of the fire sequence to Bermuda for Selznick's approval. "George has seen a detailed drawing continuity of the fire sequence and approves," he wrote. "He suggested a couple of extra shots not included in this scenario, one of which is described by [Margaret] Mitchell of going through a tunnel of fire, which I think I can trick at the same time."

Menzies asked that Selznick approve "actual structural and special effect preparations" that would enable them to shoot the fire sequence on Saturday, November 26. Responding by cable, Selznick declined to approve the preparations "and in any case would certainly not approve this vital sequence until went over in detail with Menzies and saw full sketches." He asked that it be held until his return "in which case would like Menzies prepare sketches in continuity form in great detail, and will go over first day I am back."

Reports from the Selznick art department began on the 9th, with the staff consisting of four draftsmen, two sketch artists, Wheeler (initially listed on the manifest as assistant art director), and Menzies. The first drawings were an exterior of Tara and an interior of its living room, while preliminary drawings were of Atlanta streets (for the fire sequence) and the lower floor of Twelve Oaks. The group of draftsmen soon enlarged to include three additional men and a model maker named Al Simpson. Other early sets in the works: the Atlanta rail station, Peachtree Street, and an exterior of the old *Examiner* office. The typical progression was from multiple sketches to preliminary working drawings, then more sketches, and then the final working drawings.

As Cukor busied himself shooting tests for Scarlett O'Hara and Melanie Wilkes, Menzies and Jack Cosgrove tested the characteristics of Technicolor's new "speed" stock, making night filter tests, a projection screen test, and, finally, an evening fire test at Forty Acres. Menzies also made process tests using a translucent screen. Observed Wilbur Kurtz, who was present for these tests, "This translucent screen is a recent device gotten up as a substitute for the old ground glass screens, which had to be large and were dangerous. Someone might try to walk through one. The test was to see if the same thing could be done properly in Technicolor."

As the night of December 10 approached, there were daily conferences regarding the fire sequence, which, as Kurtz put it, "is still at the top of studio interest. These conferences work out physical sequences as well as the why or wherefore of them, the psychology of them being paramount." On Thursday, December 8, preparations on Forty Acres were nearing completion. The freight cars were almost finished and had been positioned on the wooden rails. The old *King Kong* set had been piped for

December 10, 1938: Menzies confers with producer David O. Selznick
and director George Cukor prior to calling action on *Gone With the Wind*.
(DAVID O. SELZNICK COLLECTION, HARRY RANSOM CENTER)

burning, and the contraption designed to pull it over had been fastened into place. The next night, Friday, December 9, saw the disabled guns in position and the boxcars lettered and painted up.

Despite all the preparation, the countless meetings and the innumerable continuity boards, it was obvious that Selznick still was not entirely comfortable with the plan. "We had a big argument about this," Ray Klune remembered. "He wanted me to call it off and I said, 'No, you're going to have to get somebody else to call it off. I just won't do it.' So he said, 'I won't be there.' I said, 'Well, maybe it's better that you shouldn't be there, but you'll be missing something. Even if it's a disaster, David, why don't you share it with us?'"

Of course, it wasn't a disaster. "We set about eight houses afire in Culver City," Klune acknowledged. "But we had that all organized too. There were firemen there in nothing flat. And I think our total damages were $1,200." Selznick nearly missed out on one of the biggest thrills of his life. When it was all over, and all of the flames had been doused, he sent a wire to Jock Whitney in New York:

SHOT KEY FIRE SCENES AT EIGHT-THIRTY TONIGHT, AND
JUDGING BY HOW THEY LOOKED TO THE EYE THEY ARE GOING TO
BE SENSATIONAL.

# 13

# GWTW

The first rushes were up on Tuesday, and nearly everyone got a look at the spectacular fire footage, wondering how it would all fit together. With the clearing of the site already under way, Menzies turned his attention to a model of Atlanta that was housed in Jock Whitney's office, Selznick, Cukor, and the others gathering to discuss the assemblage of false fronts that would be finalized within days. The producer's mania for detail extended to the proper shade of red for the Georgian clay, and Wilbur Kurtz had a box of it shipped to his Culver City hotel. Essentially finished with *Made for Each Other,* Selznick told Menzies that he would see him anytime, dispensing with the routine of appointments that usually had to be made a day in advance.

Regarding Tara, Selznick wasn't satisfied with any of the drawings produced by Menzies and Lyle Wheeler. "He wants a dream house," Kurtz concluded, "not an architectural monument." Menzies said he would "get right on" another drawing and that he'd do a composition this time rather than a rendering. Cukor, meanwhile, had his own ideas of how the house should look, and Kurtz noted the art department had thrown just about everything into its design of Tara other than round columns. They continued to wrestle with the look of "the most important house in the world" through Christmas. By New Year's Eve, the barrel-vaulted car shed had been framed, part of the roof was in place, and the plaster sheet brick was ready to be applied. Nearby, on a graceful rise of ground, the foundations of Tara had been laid and its framing was finally at hand.

Selznick, meanwhile, was revising Sidney Howard's screenplay in collaboration with Oliver H. P. Garrett. On January 6, 1939, he heralded the completion of the first pages in a memo to the production team:

> Commencing with the first final scenes, which will come through today on *Gone With the Wind,* I will expect Messrs. Menzies, Kern, and [cinematographer Lee] Garmes to meet regularly and lay out their conceptions of the camera angles to the end that we may all know, in advance, exactly what we are going to get in the way of lighting and set-ups; and to the further and even more important end that we may do a job of pre-cutting with the camera that is greatly more economical than has ever been attempted before. . . . I will want Menzies and his staff to sketch for me each angle and before we go into each sequence I will go over these and make any changes that I think are necessary before we go over it with Mr. Cukor.

Selznick was, in effect, preparing to direct the film by proxy, Menzies putting his artistry at the producer's disposal and rendering a mise-en-scène that would essentially straitjacket the director. Over the course of production, literally thousands of conceptual illustrations would be generated by the Selznick art department. Of the larger pieces, which conveyed nuance and color, Menzies did more than his fair share, but just as many were done by Dorothea Holt and Joseph McMillan "Mac" Johnson, both of whom had styles all their own. Yet, when it came to continuity boards, the panels that emphasized composition and the progression of story over detail, most were done by Menzies alone. "The first thing I do in starting a sketch," he said in a 1938 interview, "is to draw in circles for the faces of the actors. I figure out the set as a background to the group, even taking into consideration how many feet an actor will have to walk to get from center stage to exit at left center. So it's really a sort of precutting of the picture."

The exterior of Tara was nearly finished by the 11th of January, when grading was in process and Menzies decided the proper color of Georgia clay could be achieved with ground brick. On Monday, January 16, Henry Ginsberg called a meeting at which he informed the department heads that production would commence on the 23rd—and to a man they all said they couldn't be ready. The Tara interiors were going up on Stage 3, the woodwork a powder blue, and painters were at work on a huge backing that would depict a landscape of fields and pines. Out on Forty Acres, exteriors were nearly camera-ready, and Peachtree, constructed along a rutted roadway over the facades of standing sets, was crawling with workers.

The first one hundred pages of Garrett's script were widely distributed the following day, giving everyone a first look at what was presumed to be the shooting

Menzies poses with the art department staff assembled for *Gone With the Wind*. Looking over his shoulder (in hat) is the credited art director, Lyle Wheeler. (DAVID O. SELZNICK COLLECTION, HARRY RANSOM CENTER)

final. A week later Selznick dispatched a copy of the "so-called Howard-Garrett script" to Jock Whitney in New York.

> The only thing that I can see that might get us into trouble would be for me suddenly to be run down by a bus, so you'd better get me heavily insured. As long as I survive the whole situation is well in hand: the whole picture is in my mind from beginning to end; all the sets for the first six weeks of shooting are approved in detail; all the costumes approved; the entire picture cast with the exceptions only of Belle Watling and Frank Kennedy, who don't work for some time; and generally the picture is, I assure you, much better organized than any picture of its size has ever been before in advance of production.

Filming actually began on January 26, 1939, with a long shot of Scarlett O'Hara running down the steps of Tara and along the walk toward the eventual arrival of her father, the soil appropriately reddened with a dusting of brick and the dogwood blossoms in all their artificial glory. It would be the first of approximately one hundred matte shots made under the supervision of Jack Cosgrove, who had encouraged the extensive use of matte paintings on glass or Masonite as a way of saving money on the building of sets. ("Jack," said Clarence Slifer, "was a great man for spotting opportunities for matte shots and to convince the director that he needed them.") Equipment problems and fog plagued the company that day, and the afternoon was given over to work in Scarlett's bedroom, Vivien Leigh playing her first scenes with singer-comedienne Hattie McDaniel, who had won the coveted role of Mammy, the slave who had been Scarlett's nurse from birth. With the design of the sets settled, attention turned forcefully to how they—and the actors—were being photographed, and shooting was held up nearly an hour as Lee Garmes and representatives from Technicolor debated the amount of light flooding the small room. Leigh's stand-in wilted as sections of wall were alternately erected and taken down, all to make room for lights that may or may not have been necessary.

Frank Nugent, on hand for *The New York Times,* described the situation "an unconscionable to-do" given the crush of resources suddenly brought to a halt.

> William Cameron Menzies, the art director, was running all over the place, squinting through the camera with Lee Garmes, conjuring up a window frame to cast its shadow decoratively across a four-poster bed, bloodthirstily commanding the men on the catwalks to "kill that broad."* Walter Plunkett, the dress designer, had a couple of sketches desperately in need of director George Cukor's approval. Mr. Cukor, oblivious to Mr. Plunkett, was looking for someone called Charlie, and Charlie was busy applying a last-minute coat of paint to the back of a mirror we are sure won't ever appear in the completed shot.

Two days later, Selznick issued a memo deploring

> the conflicting opinions about color among members of the art departments, officials of the Technicolor company, etc., if we are to avoid confusion, loss of time and waste of money through such ridiculously unnecessary things as repainting sets, etc. I should like to reiterate that Mr. Menzies is the final word on these matters and should be the arbiter on any differences of opinion. I hold Mr. Menzies responsible for the physical aspects of the production and for the color values of the production, and any difference of opinion should be settled by him, hopefully without delay or equivocation.

---

* "Broad" was short for "broadside," a type of incandescent flood lamp.

Menzies had worked in color before—the old two-color variety in the 1920s and early 1930s, and the new three-strip process on *Nothing Sacred* and *Adventures of Tom Sawyer*—but only for isolated sequences, never for an entire picture. Now, faced with designing *Gone With the Wind* in color from beginning to end, he abandoned the stark images he favored in black-and-white for a pastel look that lent itself to variations in tone and intensity according to the dramatic needs of a scene. He could also see the progression of the story in terms of what Richard Sylbert later characterized as "musical ideas"—moods and passages of color that brought a symphonic cohesion to the action and built to highpoints in the narrative.

In handwritten notes made after he finished the picture, Menzies described his approach to color values on *Gone With the Wind* and the overriding philosophy that guided his choices. Color was intensified to heighten the drama, lessened to accentuate patterns, times of day, and physical conditions. "No attempt was made to make Gone 'pretty-pretty,'" he wrote. "When unpleasant colors were required to enhance the drama they were used and the spectrum was reduced often to punch up conditions for dramatic effect. Severe red skies & Indigo backings were planned for macabre strong & unhappy atmosphere, as were soft combinations of pleasant colors for an opposite condition. Times of day were, I think, gone farther into in [terms of] color study than ever before. For instance, pre-dawn, dawn, evening, cold days, hazen skies for discomfort & heat, etc."

Practically all the material shot over the first few days of production would have to be done over. Hairstyles were wrong, colors proved unacceptable, and actor Robert Gleckler died before completing his scenes as Jonas Wilkerson. Since the new Technicolor stock required 40 percent less illumination, the decision was made to deliberately underlight the O'Hara family's evening prayer service, an experiment that elicited another memo from the producer deploring photography "so dark as to bewilder an audience." Wrote Selznick: "If we can't get artistry and clarity, let's forget the artistry."

The first truly memorable sequence in the picture was initially not so memorable. It came with Gerald O'Hara's paean to the land, his arm around Scarlett as they regard Tara in the distance. ("It'll come to you, this love of the land. There's no gettin' away from it if you're Irish.") It was a Cosgrove shot, made on the backlot, Tara as situated on Forty Acres, perfectly respectable but pastoral and static. Gerald's hair was all wrong, as was the landscaping, yet a retake showed no real improvement. Six weeks into production, Selznick decided they had been kidding themselves "in feeling that we could get really effective stuff on the back lot that should have been made on location." He thought the walk of Gerald and Scarlett, which came straight from Margaret Mitchell, looked on-screen as though "it were the back yard of a suburban home" and predicted that it would have to be remade. He wrote Ray

Klune: "I'd like you and Mr. Menzies to get together immediately to make sure that our remaining exteriors, such as the exterior of Twelve Oaks and the shot in which Gerald talks about the land being the only thing that matters (even if this is shot on the stage) have real beauty instead of looking like 'B' picture film."

It was while the company was on location at Pasadena's Busch Gardens that Menzies, in consultation with Cosgrove and Clarence Slifer, worked out a fix to the problem by adding motion and depth, the camera retreating to reveal the foreground figures as framed by a massive oak tree, the emphasis on the plantation before them and Scarlett's birthright as Gerald's eldest daughter. "They," recalled Slifer, "were to be in silhouette against a sunset sky (a plate made after [a] big rain storm in 1938) with Tara (matte painting) in the background. I planned this shot to be composited on our new printer, using an aerial [projected] image of the Tara painting." The tree itself was a cardboard cutout.

Menzies later described "the almost imperceptible darkening and enriching of the values and color until we achieve the violent contrast of the pullback shot. Cosgrove painted the distance in what is called close values and cool colors which, against the violent blacks of the tree and the silhouetted figures, gave a very convincing effect of depth and distance." The run-up to the shot was similarly modified. "Throughout the walking sequence, the colors were designed to become cooler and darker (blues and violet), giving the feeling of approaching night. The significant achievement was in going from an idyllic, fairly light scene, when Scarlett and Gerald meet in the meadow, into a strong dramatic effect of darkness to point up Gerald's lines about the meaning of land to the Irish, and blending them without shock."

On Friday, January 27, Menzies directed second unit footage of the barbecue at Twelve Oaks, detailed material that would eventually be deleted from the movie. The next major sequence to be tackled was the Monster Bazaar held to raise money for Atlanta's military hospital, a riot of colors that demanded a less nuanced reading.

In the bazaar sequence, when Scarlett horrifies Atlantans by dancing in widow's weeds, symphonic color had to be sacrificed for a certain degree of realism in order to produce an effect of a ballroom decorated by local folks, yet at the same time its brilliance had to be overdone a bit to contrast with the later drabness illustrating the disintegration of the South. This was also true to a degree in the Twelve Oaks barbecue sequence, where we played a high key of brilliant colors, particularly in the costumes and sunshine effects of the outdoor scenes. The dark silhouettes of Ashley and Melanie in the foreground as they go from the house to the terrace accentuates the bright sunshine and gay costumes beyond. This was done particularly to afford contrast to the scenes at Twelve Oaks when it is in ruins, a shambles in the steely blue-gray dawn.

Cukor worked nearly a week on the bazaar, a sequence that would establish the ferocious attraction between Scarlett and Rhett. He moved on to the "green bonnet" scene that follows Rhett's return from Paris, and then, on February 7, settled in for three days on the "birthing scene." Plenty of objections had issued forth from the Breen Office, most concerning Melanie's anguish during the birth of her son. ("There should be no <u>moaning or loud crying</u> and you will, of course, eliminate the line of Scarlett, 'And a ball of twine and scissors.'") It fell to Menzies to underscore her suffering in profiles of stark black and sharp, knifelike patterns of yellow, no light falling on the shutters or the human figures in the foreground, simply a white backing reflecting the colored glare of floodlamps through the slits. "Orange is a hot color," he commented, "and with black it's violent. . . . That suggested the hot afternoon as well as the violence of childbirth in those days. No scene of this combination can be held long on the screen. It will tear an audience to pieces."

Rhett's arrival at Miss Pitty's house signaled the start of their flight to Tara and the gauntlet of the burning rail yard, but trouble was mounting between Cukor and Selznick, and this would be some of the last footage shot under Cukor's direction. In November 1938 Selznick had written Menzies on the subject of Cukor's perceived extravagances:

> I have always felt that the shooting of two or three hundred thousand feet to secure an eight or nine thousand finished picture is, on the face of it, absurd. . . . On <u>Gone With the Wind</u> a more thorough camera-cutting becomes not merely desirable, but actually almost essential, if we are to bring the picture in at a cost that is not fabulous. This is particularly true because we will find that Cukor will probably eat up a great deal of film—and I need not go into the expense of Technicolor film—through the number of takes, although I have already spoken several times to George about the necessity of his doing more rehearsal where desirable and shooting less takes, to hold down costs, and I intend to watch this very carefully and to go into it with George again and again if necessary.

Selznick's admonitions didn't do much good; Gable, for instance, had to carry Olivia de Havilland down the stairs at Aunt Pittypat's a dozen times before the director was satisfied. And Leslie Howard, in an early letter to his daughter, complained that after seven days of shooting they were five days behind schedule. Cukor, meanwhile, was equally unhappy with Selznick's incessant rewrites, which made advance planning difficult and frequently rendered Menzies' sketches obsolete.

"He had a very good script, written by Sidney Howard, but David kept fooling around with it," Lee Garmes said. "All the preparatory work was based on Sidney Howard's script, but when we started shooting, we were using Selznick's. His own material just didn't play the same. Cukor was too much of a gentleman to go to Dave and say, 'Look, you silly son-of-a-bitch, your writing isn't as good as Sidney Howard's.' He did the scenes to the best of his ability and they wouldn't play."

Matters came to a head on Sunday, February 12, when it was determined that Cukor, by mutual consent, would leave the film. A statement was issued to the press blaming "a series of disagreements" for the rupture and declaring the only solution "is for a new director to be selected at as early a date as is practicable." George Cukor's final day as director of *Gone With the Wind* was February 15, 1939.


"After the first ten days of shooting," remembered Ray Klune, "we only had twenty-three minutes of film—and ten of those had to be re-shot." On February 16, production was suspended at a carrying cost of $10,000 a day. Within hours, Victor Fleming had agreed to be the new director, Selznick's first choice, King Vidor, having turned down the assignment. "When Cukor left," said Lee Garmes, "we closed down the picture for a week or so, and Victor Fleming looked at the tests and the finished stuff. He didn't give a damn what he said to Selznick, because he was on loan from Metro, so he told him point blank, 'David, your fucking script is no fucking good.' He demanded the Howard script back. He got it back."

Fleming had, as the director of *Red Dust,* fashioned Clark Gable's hard-charging screen persona in his own image—except that, in the opinion of many, Fleming, at age fifty, was better-looking than Gable. When production resumed on March 2, he was put to work reshooting a lot of what Cukor had done—Scarlett's introduction with the Tarleton twins, Gerald's walk with Scarlett, parts of the Atlanta bazaar. Several matte shots had been made under Cukor's direction, including Rhett, Scarlett, and the others preparing to flee Aunt Pitty's house, and now Menzies filmed their departure in accordance with the conceptual drawing Wilbur Kurtz had so admired, the single camphene lamp left lighted on the sidewalk. The fire sequence itself was continually being rewritten, incorporating the footage shot December 10, but with Selznick trimming it back when the stunt doubles, to his mind, looked more like doubles than the actors they were supposed to represent.

In time, Selznick came to decide that Lee Garmes' work was much too dark, and a week after Fleming resumed production, Garmes was released as cameraman. "I worked for about ten or twelve weeks," Garmes recalled. "We were using a new type of film, with softer tones, softer quality, but David had been accustomed to working with picture postcard colors. He tried to blame me because the picture was looking too quiet in texture. I liked the look; I thought it was wonderful, and long afterwards he told me he should never have taken me off the picture."

Significantly, Garmes was replaced by a man who had even less experience in color, Warners' Ernest Haller. It was Haller who shot *Jezebel* the previous year, and who would now finish *Gone With the Wind* in tandem with Technicolor's own Ray Rennahan. On Saturday, March 11, Fleming and Haller shot the famous "war talk" sequence in the newly completed dining room at Twelve Oaks, Rhett forcefully breaking with the Southern fervor for war. ("Has any one of you ever thought that there's not a cannon factory in the whole South, and scarcely an iron foundry worth considering? Have you thought that we wouldn't have a single warship and that the Yankee fleet could bottle our harbors up?") At once the rushes crackled with excitement.

Both Vivien Leigh and Olivia de Havilland had protested Cukor's removal from the picture, and few were fond of Fleming or his determination to "make this picture a melodrama." The only direction Leigh said she ever got from Fleming was "Ham it up!" And Marcella Rabwin, Selznick's executive assistant, plainly thought him a bastard. "He did not like Mr. Selznick," she said of Fleming.

> I think he did not like almost everybody in the world except Clark Gable and himself. But he did something—he revitalized the whole theme of *Gone With the Wind.* Suddenly things began to happen. The girls didn't realize that [in] their crying for George Cukor, but what's happening is that the film has spirit and tempo. He was a very, very fine director even though I personally couldn't stand the language that he used on the set, the way he treated Vivien Leigh—he was very harsh with her. I don't wonder that she cried for George because George was a very sympathetic and passive person with her. He allowed her to be what she felt the role should be, but Fleming didn't. Fleming demanded of her that she be the bitch that she was described as.

Leslie Howard, who considered it a badge of honor never to have read the book, returned the week of March 20 to play the scenes representing Ashley's Christmas furlough. For his arrival, Menzies had the Atlanta rail station shot with a blue filter to throw the scene into a "wintery cold monotone," punching up the rigors of life during wartime.* By contrast, the feeling of warmth was boosted for interiors at Aunt Pittypat's house, creating a haven for Ashley and Melanie, one that follows them as they ascend the stairs with yellow-tinged candles, leaving Scarlett in a depression of heavy blacks and cold half-tones. For Ashley's departure the following morning, Menzies wanted an absence of color, the gray uniform against the gray of the fog. "A very light blue filter helped this without really adding color," he said.

By the end of March, Menzies was in Chico, ninety miles north of Sacramento, overseeing Gerald O'Hara's riding scenes with director Chester Franklin and cameraman Wilfrid Cline. In scouting potential landscapes to represent Georgia and, in particular, the terrain opposite Tara, Menzies painted a vivid word picture of what he saw:

> Rolling country in Spring green with plowed red fields, minimum amount of fences, and if possible some large oak trees, dogwood in bloom and pines in the distance. The action entails a ride of a horseman more or less across country, Negroes working in fields plowing and of course no indication of telegraph poles, paved roads, signs or houses, except buildings that might be outlying farm buildings. . . . This will be a shot showing the horseman riding so it will entail considerable area, possibly a 360° panorama. . . . Also required are shots of slave quarters, fruit orchards in bloom, shots of hill roads possible for use for Confederate troops coming home from war, also dramatic type of scenery among pines showing no plowed fields and apparently a good distance from any habitation. The principal requirement is very lush, rolling, peaceful countryside.

Little was peaceful, however, as there was no escaping Selznick. In a wire that found its way to Menzies in his compartment aboard the West Coast Limited, DOS complained of Lyle Wheeler's rendering of Rhett Butler's bedroom, which he described as "shockingly bad." Given the importance of Rhett's house to the second half of the story, he wondered if perhaps somebody else should be called in. In his reply, Menzies diffused the situation by offering his assessment of Major John Bidwell's residence, built in Chico in 1865, and suggesting the mansion's octagonal tower bedroom as a model for Rhett's:

---

* "Blue is a cold, highly dramatic color," Menzies explained. "When it hits the screen in overtones, it makes audiences put on their mental overcoats."

Menzies found opportunities for pattern in the fields of the antebellum South.
(DAVID O. SELZNICK COLLECTION, HARRY RANSOM CENTER)

OUTSIDE WINDOWS CAN BE SEEN BEAUTIFUL OAKS AND MAGNOLIAS
AND OTHER WINGS OF HOUSE. MIGHT EVEN PLAY PART OF DAY OR
NIGHT SCENES ON VERANDA AND NIGHT SCENES CAN BE LIT AND
COMPOSED LIKE OLD ENGLISH CASTLE TOWER ROOM ESPECIALLY
FOR DRAMATIC SCENES.

He sent some rough sketches to Wheeler, and Selznick embraced the idea to the extent that Rhett's bedroom became similarly shaped, although he rejected the idea of windows on all sides as impractical. The eventual set was dominated instead by a huge full-figure portrait of Vivien Leigh.

April found Sidney Howard back at work on the script, but with low expectations and little time to spare. "I shall be finished early next week," he advised his wife on April 8. "The problem arises then: when will [Selznick] read what I have written and clear me? I leave, of course, whether he clears me or not. Then he will put still another writer on my new script which he will not have read and the new man will spend another two weeks re-doing what has been done so often." Selznick, he observed, was "bent double" with chronic indigestion and half the staff "look, talk, and behave as though they are on the verge of breakdowns." Victor Fleming, having jumped without a break to *GWTW* from *The Wizard of Oz,* was particularly quick in showing the strain. "Fleming takes four shots of something a day to keep going, and another shot or so to fix him so he can sleep after the day's stimulants." Scarcely three weeks into Fleming's time on the picture, actor Spencer Tracy visited the Flemings on a Sunday evening and stayed until midnight. "[I] thought I was nervous until I saw Victor," Tracy wrote in his datebook. "Bad shape."

Although he remembered him as "one of the few geniuses I ever met in the picture business," Ridgeway "Reggie" Callow, second assistant director under Eric Stacey, could recall Menzies' own distinctive coping routine: "For lunch he'd have five martinis and wouldn't eat anything. Then at night he'd really start to drink. He had a friend [in] Jack Cosgrove. . . . He was a good sidekick. I'll tell you, between the two of them we had a hell of a time getting them on the set, but once they were on the set they were pros." Journalist Susan Myrick, an advisor on the "speech, manners, and customs of the period" and, like Wilbur Kurtz, an Atlantan, marveled at Menzies' productivity. "Bill knows everything in the world about artistic effects," she said in a column for the *Macon Telegraph,* "and does more work than any other ten men I ever saw. Yet he has time for a joke or a good story, often, and keeps us in gales of laughter with his Cockney-accent imitations and his tales of Scotland. . . . [His] set plans were so accurately scaled that an architect could trace his blueprints from them."

Menzies had worked previously with Fleming, and the two men were, according to Laurence Irving, "old friends and partners" in the production of *GWTW.* "I spent many happy evenings with Bill at his home," said Irving, who was visiting Los Angeles with producer Gabriel Pascal. "Tired as he was after a long day's work, he was exhilarated by his complete fulfillment as a designer in his compositions for the immense canvas of *Gone With the Wind* that was now taking shape."

Irving and Pascal spent time on Stage 14 at Selznick International, watching as Menzies arranged the towering nighttime shadows cast by Vivien Leigh and Olivia de Havilland against the far wall of a set, an effect he achieved with the use of doubles who were required to move in unison with the actresses in the foreground of the shot. "They were shooting the scenes in which Scarlett O'Hara was helping an old doctor in an improvised hospital in Atlanta. The set was a masterpiece—a wooden Presbyterian church, its east window shattered by shellfire, and before the altar a great field-stove was boiling water to sterilize dressings. The floor was carpeted with gray-clad and bandaged soldiers. Bill had rid himself of the restrictive supervision

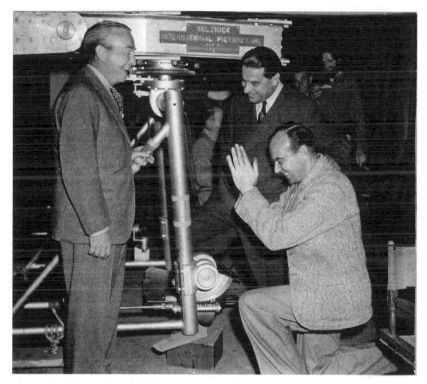

On the set of *GWTW,* Laurence Irving bows to the master as producer Gabriel Pascal looks on. (KEVIN BROWNLOW)

of Technicolor advisors, and, boldly experimenting, had made color his servant to enhance the dramatic impact of his camera setups. Every detail was perfectly contrived."

As Menzies himself noted, the general lighting in the daytime sequence was white, yet "a rather poisonous blue & amber effect was thrown across the faces & beds to increase its unpleasantness. The source of this was indicated by using the usual blue & light amber window of the Victorian church." In the vestry, which had been commandeered as an operating room, he underscored the "macabre effect" with an accent of green. "Remember," Fleming called out to the extras, "this is a hot summer day. This hospital is a filthy place. You are tormented by wounds, mosquitoes, flies, bedbugs, lice. Now everybody sound off in misery . . . I want a perfect litany of pain!"

Six weeks into his tenure on *Gone With the Wind,* Victor Fleming was a physical and emotional wreck. On April 13, Monte Westmore, the unit makeup man, told Susan Myrick that Fleming couldn't possibly last. "I think he is right," Myrick recorded in her diary. "Vic told me today he was tired to death and he was getting the jitters and he thought he would just have to quit." Selznick, who felt it would be "a miracle" if Fleming could shoot for another seven or eight weeks, proposed borrowing veteran director Robert Z. Leonard from M-G-M to act as understudy. Briefly, Fleming rallied, taking on the balance of Olivia de Havilland's scenes and attempting to finish with Leslie Howard so that Howard could start work on Selznick's *Intermezzo.* On Thursday, April 27, after a day of grappling with Melanie's death scene, Fleming began shooting Scarlett's frosty encounter with Belle Watling on the steps of the church.

Drained from the events of the day, Fleming would brook no dissension from Vivien Leigh, who had grown used to challenging him on their sometimes conflicting interpretations of character. Screenwriter John Lee Mahin, a close colleague of Fleming's, was on the set and witnessed their clash. "Vic was feeling very ill," Mahin said, "and he was nervous and tired. He had terrible pain in his kidneys; he had stones, and you could just see that he was drawn. She was getting more and more bitchy, because she was approaching the scene where she was an awful bitch, and she was getting scared of it." Fleming ended the discussion by rolling up his copy of the script and suggesting that Leigh stick it up her "royal British ass." Storming off the set, he vowed never to return.

The next day, it was announced that Fleming would rest a week, and that Sam Wood, late of M-G-M and *Goodbye, Mr. Chips,* would direct until his return. For Bill Menzies, the turn of events could not have been more momentous.

Samuel Grosvenor Wood was a renowned handler of actors, perhaps because he was once one himself. Born and reared in Philadelphia, Wood was the son of a textile manufacturer whose formal education scarcely extended beyond grade school. Tall and athletic, he went hunting for gold in Colorado and eventually landed in Los Angeles, where he fell into real estate. One night, he went to a dance at the Alexandria Hotel and met actress Clara Roush, a gorgeous redhead who also happened to be an heiress. She rebuffed him at first, thinking him beneath her, but Wood, with his piercing brown eyes, was such a handsome specimen she eventually agreed to go out with him. They were married in 1908, and their first daughter, Jeane, was born the following year.

Wood managed well for a while—he later reckoned he spent a decade in the investment game—then, as the proud owner of a cutaway coat, started taking day work in the movies after having "lost a fortune" in real estate. Cecil B. DeMille's right-hand gal was Clara Wood's best friend, and she was able to get Sam an interview with DeMille, who needed an assistant. "I'll have you do everything," DeMille told him, and eventually he was sent out to shoot some second unit footage. C.B. loved the results, and Wood, at age thirty-four, was advanced to assistant director, commencing with the marital comedy *Old Wives for New*. With DeMille's blessing, Wood struck out on his own in 1920, directing the Wallace Reid comedy *Double Speed*. There followed a string of pictures for Famous Players-Lasky, a total of six with Reid and ten with Gloria Swanson, after whom Wood's second daughter was named. By 1939, Sam Wood had more than fifty features to his credit, including such diverse fare as *Peck's Bad Boy*, *Christopher Bean*, and *A Night at the Opera*.

Clark Gable wasn't keen on Wood, having appeared under his direction in *Hold Your Man*, a good picture that unexpectedly turned into a showcase for Jean Harlow. Yet Wood quickly proved himself, jumping in on three days' notice and nearly fin-

Menzies is photographed with Clark Gable and a somewhat distracted Vivien Leigh as they prepare to shoot Rhett and Scarlett's escape from Atlanta. (DAVID O. SELZNICK COLLECTION, HARRY RANSOM CENTER)

ishing with Leslie Howard, then shooting the Belle Watling scene that had brought the previous week's schedule to a halt. Having never before directed a color picture, Wood was duly impressed with how Menzies achieved the night effects on the church steps using a heavy blue filter and a spray of blue light, leaving the strong patterns of color in the church's stained glass windows to suggest the "warm spirit of relief" to be found within. "It was freezing cold that night," Reggie Callow remembered, "and every time that Ona Munson as Belle Watling walked over to get into her carriage, the horses would decide to take a leak. They must have done it fourteen times, until their bladders finally ran out and we were able to get a good take." Said Olivia de Havilland, "I liked that scene, and thought it went well, and was relieved to see that the new hand would guide us wisely."

Wood moved with remarkable speed, tackling the terrifically emotional scenes of Scarlett's return to Tara, where she finds the house in shambles, nothing to eat, her sisters ill, and her mother dead. By midweek, even Gable had revised his opinion of Wood, pronouncing himself "very happy." *Gone With the Wind* continued with Sam Wood at the helm for two weeks, Menzies stepping away to shoot inserts and compositional footage—generally things requiring doubles and not the principal actors—but otherwise remaining close at hand. When Victor Fleming returned on May 15, preparations were under way for what would become the picture's most famous shot, in which Scarlett, in search of Dr. Meade, picks her way through a field of wounded soldiers, the camera pulling up and away until it reveals the full expanse of the Atlanta railway yards crowded with the bodies of hundreds, perhaps thousands, of Confederates.

The image came from a memorable passage in the book, Margaret Mitchell painting a vivid picture of men lying shoulder to shoulder in the pitiless sun, lining the tracks, the sidewalks, and stretching out in endless rows under the car shed.

> Some lay stiff and still but many writhed under the hot sun, moaning. Everywhere, swarms of flies hovered over the men, crawling and buzzing in their faces, everywhere was blood, dirty bandages, groans, screamed curses of pain as stretcher bearers lifted men. The smell of sweat, of blood, of unwashed bodies, of excrement rose up in waves of blistering heat until the fetid stench almost nauseated her. The ambulance men hurrying here and there among the prostrate forms frequently stepped on wounded men, so thickly packed were the rows, and those trodden upon stared stolidly up, waiting their turn.

As it evolved, the shot was seen as encapsulating all the misfortune and misery that had befallen the South in its pursuit of war. In cinematic terms, the treatment

Menzies' rough conception of the wounded crowding the Atlanta railway yards,
working out the camera's reveal of the dead and dying . . .

. . . as the scene progresses into the car barn. (MENZIES FAMILY COLLECTION)

was obvious; what wasn't nearly so evident was how exactly to accomplish such a shot. Menzies had worked out the logistics in consultation with Lee Garmes, Jack Cosgrove, and Ray Klune. In March, just after Garmes' dismissal, Selznick had written Cosgrove in connection with "the shot which you are going to do of the wounded men in the square, with the line of wounded extending beyond the actual bodies and dummies that we will be using, and with the tracks going off into the distance, I wish you would see the reference on page 292 of the book to the 'rails shining in the sun.' I wish you would go after this effect. I am also hopeful that Mr. Menzies will be able to contribute some ideas to Mr. Fleming for ways and means to get this effect of merciless sun and intolerable heat throughout this sequence."

Menzies' sense was to try for "a brazen effect of sky" and a minimum of color in the pale gray uniforms of the wounded, the burnt red of the earth throwing the one bit of color—Scarlett's hat—into prominence, emphasizing the tiny figure against "the massed carpet of wounded." At first, it was thought that the shot could be made while Victor Fleming was away, but then Selznick made the decision to hold it for Fleming, knowing it would be one of the film's signature images. "[Menzies] devised and created the shot," Reggie Callow confirmed, "and it was his suggestion that we use an oil derrick crane in order to pull the camera back to such a high position."

It had been estimated the camera would need to be approximately ninety feet off the ground at its highest point—far higher than for even the largest of camera cranes. Then there was the matter of vibration, a derrick crane hardly being a precision piece of photographic equipment. In the end, the problem was solved by placing the crane, with its tractor treads, on the back of a flatbed truck, thereby eliminating the need for the crane to move under its own power. Said Ray Klune, "We built a concrete ramp about one hundred and fifty feet long—it had to support a piece of steel that weighed ten tons—and these were the days before fast-drying concrete and we couldn't put the damn crane on the ramp for two weeks, but when we finally did, we rehearsed it and the crane slid back down the ramp as smooth as glass while the arm raised and it worked out very smoothly."

Work on the sequence began on Saturday, May 20, and continued on Monday, when Ernest Haller, operator Arthur Arling, and Fleming were sent aloft on a swinging eight-foot-by-eight-foot platform scarcely large enough to accommodate the bulky Technicolor camera. "A diesel engine pulled the truck that moved the crane," Susan Myrick recounted for her *Telegraph* readers, "and as the long arm rose into the air the machine moved slowly backward, showing more and more rows of pitifully clad, crudely tended, wounded Confederates. I had a feeling that the cameraman was about as high as [Atlanta's seventeen-story] Candler Building." Said Clarence Slifer, "The studio used all of the extras that the Guild could supply for wounded soldiers, about 1,500 of them, and added about 1,000 dummies. . . . When our shot was finished at 11:30, the assistant directors called 'lunch.' It was like God passed his healing hand over the wounded, for 1,500 soldiers leaped to their feet and ran for the lunch wagons."

With Fleming back, Selznick was eager to speed up the picture, anticipating as many as five units working simultaneously. Fleming was "more than agreeable" to having Sam Wood set up a unit "for shooting nights or Sundays or any other time," with Vivien Leigh splitting her time between the two. "I think that Hal Kern should spend practically his entire time on the set," Selznick said, "figuring out ways and means of cooking up suggestions and of gathering them from Menzies and myself, etc., to substitute simple angles that do not take [the] time [needed] for elaborate angles, where these elaborate angles are not materially helpful to the scene. . . . I think also that it is important that Vic be more precise about setting the exact first setup for the next morning. On this, too, I think he might feel better if Hal were with him and if Hal could send for Menzies—but only when and where he thought this would be an advantage. To me there is no reason for changing setups in the morning except on the rarest occasions."

Selznick, writing deep into the night, was himself often responsible for last-minute shifts in scheduling. "There were days when we didn't even know what we were doing tomorrow," Ray Klune said. "It was not at all uncommon for David to call me at three in the morning and ask me what we were shooting tomorrow. I'd say, 'David, you've got the schedule right there on your desk, so I know that you know.' He'd say, 'Can we change it?' I'd say, 'At this time of the morning?' This happened time and time again."

On May 23, the company decamped to Lasky Mesa in Agoura, an hour's drive northwest of Culver City, where, between dawn and sunrise, they would attempt, once again, Scarlett's famous vow to "never be hungry again." The setting was the vegetable garden at postwar Tara, but clouds had hidden the rising sun on at least four previous occasions. "We made ten attempts before we shot that scene as Mr. Selznick had visualized it," Menzies recalled. "We always had to gamble with the weather. It was necessary to be on location by 2:30 o'clock in the morning. Nine times we were thrown into despair. Waiting for just the right moment, we would be greeted by fog, mist, rain, or a cold blank sky. On our tenth try, the sun rose as Scarlett kneeled on the ground. The clouds formed about her in one of the most beautiful compositions I have ever seen. It was as though a kind Providence looked down to give us suddenly and generously this remarkable moment."

As Fleming continued to work with the principals, Menzies directed stunt doubles and Cosgrove shots. He made portions of Scarlett and Rhett's escape from Atlanta, filming evenings and weekends, and was seemingly on twenty-four-hour call to Selznick, whose Benzedrine habit kept him going eighteen hours a day. "Mother used to say, 'When you're going to school, he's coming home from work,'" Suzanne Menzies remembered. "So he'd come home early in the morning because he'd been working all night. I never saw him. Once in a while he'd come home for dinner. Or he'd come home, and at two in the morning he'd get a phone call from Selznick to come up to the house. That happened a lot."

Reggie Callow could recall a time when Selznick called Menzies to a seven o'clock meeting in his office and then showed up at nine. "Then," said Callow, "his butler brought his dinner at nine or nine-fifteen. Menzies said, 'I'm going across to the Coral Isle,' which is a Chinese restaurant opposite the studio, and we all went over there. At eight-thirty the phone rang and a secretary said that Mr. Selznick was

With Yankee artillery approaching, Scarlett leads the horse and wagon bearing her charges into a ravine . . .

waiting for us, so we made him wait another half hour while we finished our dinner, and then we went over." On Sunday, May 28, Susan Myrick wrote in a confidential letter to Margaret Mitchell: "The whole company is so damn tired of the picture they are ready to cut each other's throats at any moment."

Sam Wood returned on May 29, directing an exterior with Olivia de Havilland while Fleming completed Clark Gable's drunken monologue on Stage 11. Reggie Callow broke off, going with Wood and Menzies, while Eric Stacey remained with Fleming. "We now had three units working," wrote Clarence Slifer. "Bill Menzies had these sequences so well laid out that when the scenes were cut together there were no differences in visual effects or continuity between them." Wood, who lacked Fleming's compositional eye, was enchanted with Menzies' color drawings—especially his little continuity sketches (which Menzies himself likened to those of Constantin

. . . where they hide in the shadows until the danger has passed. Menzies' gifts as an illustrator invest these moments with a sense of drama few art directors could have achieved. (DAVID O. SELZNICK COLLECTION, HARRY RANSOM CENTER)

Guys, a French watercolorist and illustrator whose work he admired). Never before had Wood encountered the technique of pre-visualizing a sequence, shot for shot, and was grateful for the help. As Callow suggested, "I think [Bill] felt that Sam Wood needed him more than Fleming. Menzies was a big help to everybody; he was great for morale. Everybody loved Bill and I think he loved everybody, too. Really, he did, because he'd come around and be fun and laughing all the time."

Menzies was still doing second unit work of his own when he turned his attentions to packaging matters such as the opening titles, which he felt should presage the gathering winds of war. In a memo to Selznick, he described what they were developing in sketch form: "The Main Titles will be a series of southern landscapes with skies which should by their continued darkening give an increasingly threatening aspect to the scene. . . . The last sky is shattered by an explosion disclosing Sumter with an equally dramatic sky. Dissolve from this to an American flag being pulled down through the smoke and the Southern flag being raised. . . . After the cut of the Southern flag we could dissolve back to a long shot of Sumter burning and in the smoke an indication of the clash of arms and the Yankee horde, but so dim that no actual forms are visible." He proposed scrubbing the troublesome opening with Scarlett and the Tarleton Twins, beginning instead with the "quittin' bell" and Gerald's ride toward Tara, the small figure of Scarlett approaching to meet him, Mammy, in close-up, leaning out the window and imploring her to come back for her shawl.

Nearly six months into production, even Selznick was forced to acknowledge the toll *Gone With the Wind* had taken on practically everyone. "Quite apart from the cost factor," he admitted, "everybody's nerves are getting on the ragged edge and God only knows what will happen if we don't get this damn thing finished." On the morning of June 27, 1939, Menzies returned to Lasky Mesa and directed the pullback on doubles for Gerald and Scarlett that would provide the silhouetted figures for the revised "love of the land" shot. Then Scarlett's double, Joan Rodgers, changed into another dress for the film's climactic shot, another pullback, in which Scarlett, having watched Rhett walk out of her life, returns home to Tara to think of "some way to get him back," refusing to be defeated, declaring, "After all, tomorrow is another day!"

And back in Culver City, Fleming was finishing with Vivien Leigh, her last scene being Gable's departure into the night, her tearful pleading, "If you go, where shall I go, what shall I do?" bringing the immortal response, "Frankly, my dear, I don't give a damn."

# 14

# Something Quite Bold

On June 22, 1939, as *Gone With the Wind* was in its final days of principal photography, David Selznick dispatched a cable to Alexander Korda:

```
WE HAVE SPENT SEVERAL MILLION DOLLARS EDUCATING MENZIES
IN TECHNICOLOR SO I DO NOT BLAME YOU FOR WANTING HIM
STOP PLEASE CABLE IMMEDIATELY LATEST DATE YOU COULD USE
HIM AND WILL TRY TO WORK IT OUT STOP BELIEVE THERE IS
EXCELLENT CHANCE CAN ACCOMMODATE YOU FOR THIS ONE PICTURE
```

Having lost control of London Film, Korda had gained the approval of his partners at United Artists to form a new company, Alexander Korda Film Productions, with initial financing of $1.8 million. The "one picture" to which Selznick referred was a new *Thief of Bagdad* that would bring to bear all the technical advances that had come to the screen in the sixteen years since the Fairbanks original. Korda envisioned a fantasy informed—if not necessarily inspired—by original music, and had hired the Russian-born composer Mischa Spoliansky to create themes and songs for the film. Then, in Korda's whimsical way, Spoliansky was supplanted by Miklós Rózsa, who had memorably scored the producer's last London Film production, *The Four Feathers*. Similarly, Korda engaged Ludwig Berger to direct the picture. Berger, whose stage credits included collaborations with Max Reinhardt, had the notion that music should drive the action in *The Thief of Bagdad*, and in place of

Rózsa insisted upon Oscar Straus, whose *Les Trois Valses* he had filmed in France the previous year.*

Straus, more than twice Rózsa's age, proved unacceptable, delivering, in Rózsa's judgment, "turn-of-the-century Viennese candy-floss" wholly inappropriate to the tone of an Arabian Nights adventure. Rózsa was reinstated as the film's composer, but Berger could never master the spirit of Lajos Bíró's adaptation. Filming began on June 9, 1939, with Berger having the actors play their scenes in time with an audio playback. It was, observed Rózsa, as if they were expected to move like dancers in a pantomime. "They just couldn't get it right, and after a week's work we had practically nothing to show."

Korda stepped in, working alongside Berger, and soon Michael Powell, the thirty-three-year-old director of *The Spy in Black,* was off shooting footage in Cornwall with the film's fifteen-year-old star, the Indian-born actor Sabu Dastagir. "Listen," Korda said to Powell, "Ludwig Berger is going to do the directing but I'm convinced that we will not have finished this summer before the war breaks out; do you want to join the team and produce the sequences that I ask of you?" Known for his quota quickies, Powell was apparently an interim choice, for when Selznick agreed to loan Bill Menzies to the man who held Vivien Leigh's contract, it was not merely to design the picture but to actually direct it—an announcement that got headline play in *The New York Times.* That same day, Louella Parsons led her column with the words: "History repeats itself in the case of William Cameron Menzies . . ."

Selznick fixed a release date of July 5, affording himself ten more days of Menzies' time if Sundays and Independence Day were observed, and as many as thirteen days were he to be worked constantly. Early on, Menzies had urged that they "go as far as possible with the blood and suffering, even to the point of having the doctor blood-spattered and operating on or tending a wound which is just out of the scene." Now Selznick worried that Menzies would "shoot battlefield shots that will be so gruesome as to be censurable." He arranged for story editor Val Lewton to go out on location with him so as to suggest alternate takes where appropriate. "For instance, there should be one shot in which the pool is not colored red with the blood of dead men. On the other hand, to repeat, I want to be sure Menzies makes at least one take as he thinks it should be."

* Berger had delved into fantasy with a well-regarded version of *Cinderella* and was experienced in color filmmaking. He also worked in Hollywood, under contract to Paramount, at the same time that Korda was directing for First National.

Menzies' final week on *GWTW* was filled mostly with the shooting of inserts—the red earth in Scarlett's hand, the pulling of a radish from the ground, the twin graves of Ellen and Gerald O'Hara. There were shots of letters, posters, a bank draft for $300. In early July, a rough cut of the film, still missing certain effects and lacking its opening credits, was shown, quite possibly for the first time ever, at an approximate length of four and a half hours. "It was very spooky," Suzanne Menzies remembered. "We went to the back gate at Selznick, they unlocked it, and there were only a few lights around. We were taken into a screening room, and Hal Kern, the cutter, was there with another man. Daddy was sitting, talking to them through the whole thing, giving his input, because Daddy was going to go to England in a couple of days and they wanted him to see the movie. It was basically finished. It didn't have a score, and it had big scenes missing, but it had a continuity of sorts. We were told not to tell anybody that we had seen it; I think we saw it before even Selznick saw it. Of course, the next day it was: 'Guess what *I* saw last night!'"

There were still a lot of rough edges to the picture, but for being so long, *Gone With the Wind* had a symphonic unity born of graphic integrity. The golden patina of its opening minutes and their idyllic views of the Old South gave way to the pastel clarity of the scenes at Twelve Oaks. With news of the Gettysburg battle casualties—"hushed and grim"—came the cold dominance of blues and grays. Sherman's shelling of Atlanta stirred the red dust in the streets, casting, as Menzies saw it, a "more effective pall" than had it been yellow or buff. The siege brought a quickening of the tempo and, with Butler's arrival at Miss Pittypat's, a suggestion of the rail yard fire that reduced the palette to great masses of red and black. Outside town, the glare was accentuated with orange filters and cool highlights, and, at the ruins of Twelve Oaks, the sky was a liver color with magenta overlays that followed through to Tara and the break for intermission.

Menzies, his younger daughter recalled, liked the first half, up to where Scarlett vowed never to be hungry again. "That's where he said they should have ended it. He *hated* the second half. He thought it was unnecessary." The completed film represented a total of 137 shooting days for the first unit, 93 of which could be credited to Victor Fleming, 24 to Sam Wood, and 18 to George Cukor. Retakes and added scenes amounted to 24 days, and second unit work—much of which could be credited to Menzies—accounted for another 33 days. By the time the film was completely finished, total footage used on *Gone With the Wind* would approach half a million feet of film.

On July 5, his final day on the picture, Menzies took five-year-old Cammie King to M-G-M to film the beginning of Bonnie Blue Butler's fatal pony ride, doubles, their backs to the camera, appearing as Rhett and Scarlett. The next day, July 6, he left for New York via rail as papers around the country carried the news of his new assignment. Six days later, on July 12, 1939, he sailed for England and his third tour of duty with Alexander Korda.

When Menzies arrived at Denham, he found there were already three units at work on *The Thief of Bagdad:* The original Berger unit, now effectively being run by Korda himself, Michael Powell's unit, responsible, in Powell's words, for "a certain number of very visual and decorative scenes like the arrival of a boat, all those wide-eyed shots," and a special effects unit headed by his pal Larry Butler, who was shooting the flying horse sequences on a blue ramp erected in West Hyde. To make matters worse, Menzies found England much closer to war than he had originally thought. "Already the rattling of arms was getting louder and sandbags were appearing all over the place," he said. "One of the first unpleasant things to appear in the studio was a directional sign which read: WALKING CASUALTIES THIS WAY."

Apologetically, Korda explained his predicament and grandly offered Menzies the title of associate producer. Vincent Korda had already designed all the sets; although the film owed much to the Fairbanks version, there was little of the towering majesty that had distinguished the original. "When he first saw Vincent's huge set," Michael Korda wrote of his uncle Alex, "he turned away in disgust and said, 'Tear it down, build it twice the size and paint it red.'* Now there was some doubt it could be built at all, despite the fact that a great deal of money had been invested in the film."

Instead of involving him with the sets or the overall design of the movie, Korda asked Menzies to direct the film's many trick photography sequences, which, he pointed out, were bound to be seen as highlights. Menzies, of course, had been present at the creation of a great many Technicolor effects for *Gone With the Wind,* but here he would be working with Butler's "traveling matte" technique of combining two color images into one composite shot. Given that there were multiple film elements to register, the results were bound to be imperfect, and a blue outline could often be seen surrounding the figures inserted into the action.

"The machine shops at Denham were swell," Butler said. "These chaps were fine craftsmen and wonderful machinists. In converting optical printers used for black and white work to color we had to develop a lot of gadgets and many problems had to be overcome." The people from Technicolor advised against it, at one point

---

* The exterior sets representing Basra had been built on Denham's "City Square" lot, so named because the land had been inaugurated with the Everytown set for *Things to Come.*

Menzies' contributions to *The Thief of Bagdad* (1940) were limited chiefly to directing the special effects shots featuring Rex Ingram and Sabu. He had no influence on the overall look of the film, which was designed by Vincent Korda. (AUTHOR'S COLLECTION)

threatening to have Butler taken off the picture. But the advantage of fluid movement outweighed the technical drawbacks, and the effects accomplished for the first time in *The Thief of Bagdad* would set the standard for blue screen composites for decades to come.

The new *Thief* would contain modern interpretations of memorable events from the silent version, such as where the thief, Abu, must steal the all-seeing eye from the Goddess of Light. "The fantastic scene of Sabu trying to climb the huge idol and filch the magic eye was all double-printing," Menzies noted, "as the idol was a miniature, not much larger than Sabu. So the idol was shot first, and the figure of Sabu, in attitudes of climbing, printed over the scenes." The giant face of the idol was fabricated for shots of Sabu at the summit, some of which were angled downward to emphasize the peril, the rest of the statue being a matte painting executed by Denham's Percy Day. The effect on-screen was extraordinary, indeed one of the highlights of the picture.

On August 18, one month into Menzies' tenure on the film, Ludwig Berger was tactfully dismissed after nearly sixty days of production. Korda replaced him with Tim Whelan, an American who had just finished directing Laurence Olivier and Ralph Richardson in a spy melodrama called *Q Planes.* "Tim Whelan especially specialized in action sequences," Michael Powell explained. "I don't know for sure who filmed what." With four directors on the project—three officially—Korda seemed to be taking a page from the Selznick playbook. "Korda was technically the producer," said actor John Justin, who was making his film debut as the dashing Ahmad, "but he controlled the film totally and, effectively, directed it."

In March, Britain had declared its support for Poland in the aftermath of Germany's invasion of Czechoslovakia, and now that reckoning was at hand. On September 1, Germany attacked Poland on its western, southern, and northern borders, drawing a joint ultimatum from the United Kingdom and France to withdraw its troops. Concurrently, there was a general mobilization of British armed forces. Remembered Menzies: "On Saturday, September 2, 1939, I was working with 300 Hindu extras. On the fatal Sunday [when war was declared] I was sleeping in when my assistant came over (I was living opposite the studio) and said that Korda wanted us to shoot as the weather was good. As I walked through the gate, which was thoroughly sandbagged and a First Aid station, the air raid siren went off about five feet from my head. The War was on—and I turned bright gray. The Hindus all got in the air raid shelters, so I went back home and stood in the front door waiting for the pyrotechnics."

The air assault never materialized, but Korda, at the request of Winston Churchill, commandeered many of those working on *Thief of Bagdad* and turned their talents and resources to the making of a low-budget morale booster that was in cinemas scarcely eight weeks later. "The Sunday when the war broke out, we were still in the middle of filming," said Michael Powell. "And the next day, a Monday, I was already in a bomber filming *The Lion Has Wings,* the first movie about the war." Menzies remained with *Thief,* but managed to get a cable off to Mignon in California:

```
AWAITING DEVELOPMENTS EVERYTHING STILL OKAY
DON'T WORRY LOVE=
```

An item in *The Hollywood Reporter* had the cast and crew working in gas masks, which the actors removed when making a shot. By the end of the month, Menzies was on location in Wales, filming the initial scenes between Abu and Djinn—played by the distinguished black actor Rex Ingram—on a mile-long stretch of yellow sand at Tenby, Pembrokeshire, remaking material Powell had earlier attempted under the cramped conditions of Sennen Cove.

"The conversation Sabu has with the giant djinni, who towers over him on the sands of the beach, presented a problem in close-ups which we had not anticipated," Menzies said. "In going from one to the other in close-up, it was impossible to tell that the djinni was a giant and Sabu just a lad, as both faces were the same size on the screen. We solved the problem by showing Sabu's head at the bottom of the screen, leaving plenty of head room, thus giving the impression that he was small, while the giant's face filled the screen. Simple suggestion you may say, but not so simple when you encounter the problem for the first time." Menzies later told his daughter Suzie that they were stuck in Wales a good long time. "Evidently," said Suzie, "very few people had ever seen a black man in that part of the world in that era. He was beautiful and had that booming voice. Little kids would follow Rex down the village streets and point at him, and he thought it was very funny and marvelous. They called him a Blackamoor."

Menzies stuck it out until the picture was finished, sending occasional wires home assuring his family that he was well and okay. On October 9, it appeared he would be leaving in ten to fourteen days. "At that time there were very few Americans left," he said, "and it looked as if it was going to be pretty tough to get out." Finally, on October 23, he set sail for New York aboard the Dutch liner *Statendam*, which was blacked out and crawling with "mostly amusing and fairly unscrupulous" adventurers. "It was still scary," said Suzie. "It was full of diamond merchants from Antwerp."


In Menzies' absence, Selznick had pared *Gone With the Wind* to a running time of three hours and forty minutes, a reduction of nearly fifty minutes off the version screened for Menzies in July. To bridge the gaps, he commissioned seven titles from Ben Hecht, and when Menzies arrived back in New York on October 27, the picture was in the process of being scored by Max Steiner. Selznick's mind, however, was as much on *Rebecca* as it was on *GWTW,* that film, based on Daphne du Maurier's best-selling novel, having gone before the cameras the previous month.

"I question that we are ever going to get as good an effect for the opening and closing of *Rebecca*—the scenes involving Manderley—as we might have had if Bill Menzies had worked on them," he wrote Ray Klune on October 23. "Since Bill will be back in town shortly, if you can get him in for a few days, or even a week, to work on these two scenes I think it would be more than worthwhile, and I urge that you do so." Menzies consulted on *Rebecca* over a period of three months, directing shots of Manderley in ruins and, in one instance, planning out a crucial sequence.

Working very much on a piecemeal basis, his efforts would go uncredited on the finished film.

Far more important to Menzies' professional future, given that things "looked a bit dreary," was the film version of Thornton Wilder's Pulitzer Prize–winning play *Our Town,* the rights to which had been acquired for $75,000 by independent producer Sol Lesser. Initially, Lesser had wanted to make the picture in color with Ernst Lubitsch directing. Then William Wyler was supposedly borrowed from Goldwyn for the job, an arrangement that lasted exactly one week. Finally, in November 1939, Sam Wood was engaged, a curious choice at first, given the play's minimalist staging, which proved far too integral to ignore. Whether or not Wood was instrumental in bringing Menzies onto the project is uncertain; in a letter to Laurence Irving, Menzies implied he had sought the assignment out on his own, knowing that adapting the play to film would be an interesting challenge. Happily, Lesser was committed to doing a proper job of it and had enlisted the close cooperation of the playwright.

The staging conventions for the play dated from *The Happy Journey to Trenton and Camden,* an earlier one-act that established some of the themes Wilder would explore more fully in *Our Town.* Four kitchen chairs were used to represent an automobile, carrying a family of four some seventy miles. When *Our Town* made its first appearance in 1937, there was no curtain, no scenery. The Stage Manager entered, placing a table and three chairs downstage left, and a like grouping downstage right. Eventually, ladders and a small bench were added, nothing more. The film would need to be similarly stylized for the material to play properly. Yet, shooting the movie on a bare stage would be off-putting to a mass audience, likely dooming it to the art circuit normally reserved to foreign language pictures.

"The play, when I saw it, impressed and delighted me," wrote Lesser. "I was determined to make the film as faithful as I could. But if I had not taken the precaution of asking Thornton Wilder to assist with the script and accept the powers of veto on the production, I am sure that, in spite of all my good intentions, *Our Town* would not have proved half so successful, either as a transcription of a play or as a motion picture."

Lesser retained a stage designer named Harry Horner to consider the problem, only to conclude that Horner knew nothing of film technique. Yet when Menzies came aboard, he reviewed Horner's work and thought he had some very practicable ideas. A Czech immigrant, Horner was related by marriage to Lesser's daughter, Marjorie. "I found this accent on props without the use of scenery such an interesting device," Horner said, "and such an interesting elimination of all that crap that is called scenery, that I thought we should do that in the film. . . . I thought it would be interesting to have only these props, let us say the soda fountain, in focus and the two people close to it, but the rest out of focus." Horner's concept would permit the realistic settings demanded of commercial motion pictures while minimizing their significance. "[Menzies] thought that the idea was marvelous, etc., etc., and though he was now engaged, this famous man insisted that he would share his credit with me, which was an extremely kind thing." Horner would soon return to Broadway, where *Reunion in New York* and *Lady in the Dark* awaited him.

Lesser's draft screenplay was the product of a collaboration between the producer and actor-playwright Frank Craven, who had created the role of the Stage Manager in Jed Harris' landmark production. Lesser, who carried on a lively correspondence with Thornton Wilder, had already considered—and rejected—a number of stylistic devices, including Wilder's own suggestion of opening the film on a jigsaw puzzle "setting the background against the whole United States, that constant allusion to larger dimensions of time and place, which is one of the principal elements of the play." Lesser's own opening, with Craven's Mr. Morgan appearing at the door of his drugstore and saying, "Well, folks, we're in Grover's Corners, New Hampshire . . ." seemed, in Wilder's judgment, "far less persuasive and useful" and was similarly nixed.

Menzies crafted a layout for an entirely different opening. Contained in the final shooting script of January 9, 1940, it drew its inspiration from the play, where the Stage Manager speaks the names of the author, the producer, the director, and the various cast members up front. He proposed no opening titles, just the lone image of Craven approaching the camera:

EXT. HILLTOP (NIGHT)
SILHOUETTE
On top of hill, in silhouette against the star-studded sky, are two parallel split-rail fences, the area between the fences forming what is presumably a cow-run. Over the scene is heard:

SOUND
(MAN WHISTLING)
After a moment a man's head, also in silhouette, appears over the brow of hill directly beyond the far fence of cow-run. The man (MR. MORGAN—FRANK CRAVEN) comes fully into view as he reaches far fence.

 Lots of detail—comes upon scarecrow, adjusts hat, breaks off a small bough and trims it to use as a walking stick, passes behind tree, illumination of struck match, lights pipe, comes to a rustic bridge, replaces broken rail in fence, tastes a nut, leans on the top rail of a pasture gate where, from a side angle, the 1940 town can be seen.

There was concern over the introduction of Simon Stimson, the troubled church organist of *Our Town* (1940). In this conceptual drawing, Stimson is discovered during choir practice, the action framed by a circular church window that places all emphasis on the little man in the foreground. (MENZIES FAMILY COLLECTION)

Craven says his opening lines ("same names as around here today"), then says, "Oh, yes, now for the benefit of those that feel they should have titles . . ." He fumbles in his inside pocket for six sheets of paper, on which he has lettered the credits in Spenserian script. He comments on each sheet. ("These are the people that are going to take part in the picture. Guess you know pretty near all of 'em.") On the sheet that would include Menzies' credit, he says, "Whew! Takes a lot of people to make a picture." On the director's credit he says, "You all know who he is."

Prior to Menzies' arrival, Wilder had expressed concern that some scenes, if more realistically portrayed than onstage, would lose their novelty. In the play, for

When fabricated, Menzies had the hub of the window enlarged so that actor Philip Wood would be contained within it, the vectors pointing in at him from all sides. A focus of town gossips, Stimson is a marked man who will drink himself into an early grave. (AUTHOR'S COLLECTION)

example, the wedding scene was followed through normally, a rarity in pictures. In the theatre, its novelty came from the economy of its settings, the Stage Manager assuming the role of the minister, and the "thinking aloud" passages afforded the characters—all qualities lost in the screenplay. "This treatment seems to me to be in danger of dwindling to the conventional," the author said in reaction to an early draft. "And for a story that is so generalized that's a great danger. The play interested because every few minutes there was a new bold effect in presentation methods. For the movie, it may be an audience-risk to be bold (thinking of the 40 millions) but I think with this story it's still a greater risk to be conventional."

Considering the problem, Menzies decided the idea of throwing the backgrounds out of focus would work for a few individual scenes—the soda fountain exchange between George and Emily, for instance, which was played with a plank and two chairs onstage—but would get monotonous if overused. Stylistically, his natural bent was to resort to close-ups and two-shots—which were typically used sparingly in American films—to give the characters prominence while deemphasizing the backgrounds. Virginia Wright, drama editor of the *Los Angeles Daily News,* followed the preproduction phase in her column "Cinematters," eager to know how Lesser would meet the challenge of making Wilder's poetic little drama into "something more than just a series of episodes in small town life." He solved the problem, Wright concluded, by engaging Menzies as production designer.

> The day we called on Menzies, who, incidentally, is one of the most articulate men in Hollywood, he was just beginning the graveyard sequence and was as excited as a dramatist on the brink of his play's big scene. He has a host of ideas, using gauzes to diffuse the backgrounds and concentrate the eye on the umbrellas and figures in the foreground. All this has to be worked out with Sam Wood, the director. . . . Once they've agreed on the sketches, Menzies turns them over to Mac Johnson, his renderer, and to art director Lewis Rachmil, who in turn passes [these] out to Bert Glennon, the cameraman, and to the head electrician. On the basis of what he's already done, *Our Town* is destined to be something extraordinary on the screen.

In a letter to Wilder, Lesser described their overall approach, offering some specific examples:

> The picture itself will be treated in an unconventional manner with regard to camera set-ups, following our original idea of introducing properties intended to accentuate the moods and visualize something deeper than just the mere dialogue. For instance, in the [drunken church organist] Simon Stimson episodes, with the scenes played in moonlight, the photography will accentuate the black and white shadows. The little white New England houses, which look so lovely in other shots, will look naked and almost ghostly in relation to Simon Stimson, to whom they did not offer nice lovely homes but a cold world that ruined him.
>
> As a further example, when we come to Mrs. Gibbs on the morning of the wedding, we will see her through the kitchen window grinding the coffee, but in the foreground the flower pots will be dripping in the rain to accentuate the general mood, so that Mrs. Gibbs is almost a secondary element in this scene. And just as another example: When [George's sister] Rebecca is crying in her room the morning of the wedding, we see her little

The ladies of the choir gossip after practice. In composing even this simple scene, Menzies deliberately broke the rules of conventional staging. The camera is placed lower in the frame, cutting into Mrs. Soames' hat. Occupying the center of the shot, actress Doro Merande speaks her lines with her back to the camera. Fay Bainter, Merande, and Beulah Bondi work in close, their nighttime surroundings vanishing in the intimacy of their exchange. (AUTHOR'S COLLECTION)

pig bank tied by a ribbon to a corner of the bed, which will remind the audience of what Rebecca likes most in the world. I think this little effect will give as much to an audience as if we had a whole scene about her.

In sending Wilder a copy of the final shooting script, Lesser, who was used to producing westerns, Bobby Breen musicals, and an occasional Tarzan picture, could scarcely contain himself. "I can't commence to tell you my enthusiasm for the sketches that have so far been prepared. They are indeed artistic, and I think we will get a very unusual result." Filming began at the Goldwyn studios on January 17, 1940. Forming the principal cast was a splendid array of character people: Fay Bainter, Beulah Bondi, Thomas Mitchell, Guy Kibbee, Stu Erwin. Playing George Gibbs, a role filled in New York by Frank Craven's son, was twenty-one-year-old William Holden, fresh from his success as Joe Bonaparte in *Golden Boy.* From the original

Emily's graveyard exchange with Mother Gibbs, played with actress
Fay Bainter in the foreground and Martha Scott in the middle distance. "In the play, the dead mother and friends sat on chairs and
talked to her," Menzies said, pondering the problem before the start
of filming, "but I have to have them in graves, and having graves talk
is very dangerous. A laugh at the wrong time would ruin the picture."

Broadway production came Doro Merande, Arthur Allen, Craven, of course, and
actress Martha Scott, who created the role of Emily Webb in the Jed Harris production and had originally come to Los Angeles to test for the part of Melanie in *Gone
With the Wind.* (She was told at the time that she wasn't photogenic.) With the
beginning of the picture not yet settled, Lesser and Wood chose to open production
with the cemetery scene, which was played in New York against the bare wall of the
stage with twelve chairs representing the graves of the townspeople.

Menzies had designed the entire sequence, closing in on the characters to
the point of cutting off an actor's head in one particularly tight grouping. Wood
objected, as such a composition would violate every principle of staging he had
come to embrace. "Mr. Wood wanted the whole head," Lesser recalled. "[Mr. Men-
zies] maintained that this would ruin the shot. I settled that one by suggesting it
be done the way the art director* wanted—if necessary, it was a very easy scene to

* Sol Lesser always identified Menzies as the art director on the picture, but that title officially belonged to
Lewis J. Rachmil, whose credits were primarily Hopalong Cassidy westerns.

do over again. Wood agreed reluctantly. After he saw it, he was convinced that they were getting a style which was completely Bill Menzies' and he never set up again without calling for Menzies to approve."

At the end of that first day, Lesser wrote Wilder yet again:

You are going to get a real thrill, Thornton, when you see on the screen the production of the graveyard sequence as designed by Mr. Menzies. There is great inspiration from the time the mourners under their umbrellas come into the graveyard. We never show the ground—every shot is just above the ground—never a coffin nor an open grave—it is all done by attitudes, poses, and movements—and in long shots. The utter dejection of Dr. Gibbs—we have his clothes weighted down with lead weights so they sag—the composition of Dr. Gibbs at the tombstone is most artistic—and as Dr. Gibbs leaves the cemetery the cloud in the sky gradually lifts, revealing stars against the horizon—and as the cemetery itself darkens, a reflection from the stars strikes a corner of the tombstone which is still wet from the recent rain, and the reflection (halation) seems to give a star-like quality—and the scene gradually goes to complete darkness. We get a vast expanse of what seems to be sky and stars. When this dissolves to the dead people this same reflection of halation appears to touch the brows of the dead. It is lovely—something quite bold!

Menzies liked to employ a wide angle lens for deep focus shots, saying that doing so amounted to a long shot and a close-up at the same time. For Emily's graveyard exchange with Mother Gibbs, actress Fay Bainter's head and shoulders were to fill the immediate foreground, while Martha Scott would stand full figure in the background. No lens was fast enough to hold both characters in focus under such subdued lighting conditions, so it fell to Bert Glennon to achieve the composition with a split screen. In tackling the scenes of Emily in death, revisiting the morning of her sixteenth birthday, Menzies eschewed the common device of the apparition, a double exposure yielding a transparent figure on screen. Instead, the shot was made as normal, then Scott was filmed against a black velvet background, clad in a white dress and flooded with light. A traveling matte was made, enabling the two images to be married in the lab. The result was more in keeping with the play, an Emily more substantial than ghostlike.

Sam Wood told Martha Scott that if she was in films for fifty years, she'd never have anything more difficult to do than those scenes corresponding to the last act of the play. "I had no one to talk with," Scott said. "I had to be by myself with little black markers as people and then they put that on the film." Wood, she added, seemed "uncertain" about a play that was at times so impressionistic. "He had the production stage manager, Ed Goodnow, with whom I worked and who was Jed's man, there to help him. He said to the company, 'Listen, Ed is our man. He knows the workings of this play, he knows the timing, he can help me with cutting it and making it into something as wonderful as the play.' So that helped Sam tremendously. He was a wonderful man."

The West Coast premiere of *Gone With the Wind* took place on December 28, 1939, at L.A.'s Carthay Circle, following gala openings in Atlanta and New York City. Ten thousand spectators lined the streets, all straining to catch glimpses of Clark Gable, Carole Lombard, and "an audience of Hollywood celebrities that surpassed any other that has ever gathered together for a premiere." Searchlights were stationed along San Vicente Boulevard for a block on either side of the theater. Menzies, now deep into preparations for *Our Town,* attended with Mignon, occupying a pair of orchestra seats valued at $11. It was the first time either had seen the completed film with score and titles, yet all the eliminations and polish did nothing to alter Menzies' initial assessment of the picture: it still should have ended at the break.

There was, of course, talk of a sweep at the Academy Awards, the picture having garnered outstanding reviews, and therein lay a particular challenge to the winner of the first Oscar for Art Direction—William Cameron Menzies was no longer an art director. Having pioneered the concept of production design, and being virtually its only practitioner, Menzies had no category into which he could neatly fit. As matters stood, Lyle Wheeler, with whom Selznick had grown increasingly frustrated, was a sure bet for a nomination and an odds-on favorite to win. Selznick sensed this injustice as acutely as anyone, and while he worked to get Menzies nominated for a special award for *GWTW,* he feared that such efforts "would probably increase interest in him, and may boomerang on us in our desire to sign him." This would be doubly true, he acknowledged, should Menzies actually get such an award. "I have made up my mind that when I start producing again there is one man I definitely want and that is Bill," he said in a January memo to Daniel O'Shea, "so I am counting definitely on your working out a deal, and as soon as possible, along the lines we discussed."

Selznick touched on the subject of Menzies in a lengthy letter to Frank Capra, first vice president of the Academy and president of the Screen Directors Guild. "Bill Menzies," he wrote, "spent perhaps a year of his life in laying out camera angles, lighting effects, and other important directorial contributions to *Gone With the Wind,* a large number of which are in the picture just as he designed them a year before Vic Fleming came on the film. In addition, there are a large number of scenes which he personally directed, including a most important part of the spectacle. Day and night, Sundays and holidays, Menzies devoted himself to devising effects in this picture for which he will never be adequately credited."

When the nominations came down on February 11, 1940, Wheeler was indeed in the running, one of a record thirteen nominations accorded the film. Menzies, on the other hand, wasn't mentioned at all. Not that he had been completely ignored by the Academy in the years following his historic 1929 win for *The Dove* and *Tempest;* in 1930, Academy records show that he was under consideration for his work on *Alibi* and *The Awakening,* and in 1931 for his design of *Bulldog Drummond.* The committee that nominated and voted the award was comprised of art directors and alternates from all the major studios—men who knew and, in many cases, revered Menzies' work. So when the awards were bestowed at the Ambassador Hotel on the night of February 29, 1940, *GWTW*'s eight wins were augmented by a special plaque that bore the following words:

TO WILLIAM CAMERON MENZIES
FOR OUTSTANDING ACHIEVEMENT IN THE USE OF COLOR
FOR THE ENHANCEMENT OF DRAMATIC MOOD
IN THE PRODUCTION OF "GONE WITH THE WIND."

As the filming of *Our Town* progressed, the matter of a proper opening for the picture remained a vexing issue. Thornton Wilder hadn't liked Menzies' idea of hand-lettered credits, and as production got under way, they still hadn't found what Sol Lesser referred to as an "emotional reason" for beginning the story back in 1901. "Everyone seems to feel that the opening should have a feeling of air, broadness, and scope," Lesser said, "rather than being confined in a set or in front of a store, but we can't put our fingers on it." In the end, they had it all along, as what they settled on was essentially Menzies' opening with the titles superimposed over Frank Craven's leisurely approach.

In his notes for *Gone With the Wind,* Menzies wrote of painting fences "dead black for dramatic pattern." Now, he opened on the weathered patterns formed by a pair of split rail fences, allowing them to cross the top third of the screen in silhouette as the film's title occupies the morning darkness beneath. While the credits flash, the distant figure of Mr. Morgan approaches, negotiating a loosened plank and then ambling along the pathway, the camera following as he pauses to adjust the hat on

In considering the opening of *Our Town,* Menzies opted for strong diagonal pattern in the form of the split rail fence that leads Mr. Morgan, the narrator, to a Grover's Corners of an earlier time. (ACADEMY OF MOTION PICTURE ARTS AND SCIENCES)

a forgotten scarecrow. An old oak tree passes into view as he lights a pipe and proceeds along the pathway to a wooden bridge, where he hammers a railing back into place with a river stone. At the other side of the bank, the path juts sharply toward the camera, the figure coming into detail as Sam Wood's name fills the screen. He nods a greeting. "The name of our town is Grover's Corners, New Hampshire," he begins. "It's just across the line from Massachusetts. Latitude is forty-two degrees, forty minutes. Longitude is seventy degrees, thirty-seven minutes."

In one eloquently stylized two-minute shot, Menzies was able to establish the time of day, a sense of place for the town known as Grover's Corners, and tell the audience everything it needed to know about Mr. Morgan, the narrator—all while dispensing with the credits, and all without benefit of dialogue. ("The new open-

On film, the artificiality of the opening was mitigated by the easy authority of Frank Craven, whom Brooks Atkinson called "the best pipe and pants-pocket actor in the business." (AUTHOR'S COLLECTION)

ing's fine," Thornton Wilder acknowledged, with obvious relief, in a letter to Sol Lesser. "I shudder at the way you spare no expense, fences, bridges, nut-trees, distant villages, scarecrows—! It's fine.") It was, everyone seemed to agree, the screen equivalent to the look of the play, a gloriously artificial panorama, exquisite in its selective detail, the sort of visual economy necessary to distill a beloved three-act play into a running time of about ninety minutes. Displaying the distant image of the modern-day Grover's Corners on a rear projection screen, Morgan says, "First we'll show you a day in our town—not as it is today in the year nineteen-hundred and forty, but as it used to be in the year nineteen-hundred and one." He signals the operator, and a quick shift of images returns the scene to an earlier day. The story is off and running in little more than three minutes.

Menzies was considered so essential to the making of *Our Town* that his drinking became a source of tension, especially for Sam Wood, who depended on him so thoroughly. "I was the assistant director on the show," said Lee Sholem, "but my biggest job was to keep him off the booze, or, to keep him off it at least long enough for him to get the job done, and then let him go out and have his drinks."

By the third week in February, the company was finishing up with various

The credited art director, Lewis Rachmil, consults a continuity board during
the filming of *Our Town*. Director Sam Wood and Menzies look on. (MEN-
ZIES FAMILY COLLECTION)

cast members and looking toward a close of production sometime in early March.
"Everyone—not only the 'Yes Men'—yes, everyone is most enthusiastic," Lesser said
at the time, "and I think we have something quite different in novelty, both from the
photographic and storytelling standpoint. Now if the motion picture public wants
this kind of a story—all is well."

In the year 1963, Alfred Hitchcock was questioned by an earnest young interviewer
who said that he presumed that all of Hitchcock's films were "pre-designed by an art
director." Did he, in fact, do all the drawings himself?

"Well," said Hitchcock, "art director is not a correct term.

You see, an art director, as we know it in the studios, is a man who designs
a set. The art director seems to leave the set before it's dressed and a new
man comes on the set called the set dresser. Now, there is another function
which goes a little further beyond the art director and is almost in a different realm. That is the production designer. Now, a production designer is a

man *usually* who designs angles and sometimes production ideas. Treatment of action. There used to be a man . . . is he still alive? William Cameron Menzies. No, he's not. Well, I had William Cameron Menzies on a picture called *Foreign Correspondent* and he would take a sequence, you see, and by a series of sketches indicate camera setups. Now this is, in a way, nothing to do with art direction. The art director is set designing. Production design is definitely taking a sequence and laying it out in sketches.

With the completion of *Rebecca,* Selznick closed his studio for an extended period, ultimately liquidating Selznick International in order to draw down the substantial profits generated by *Gone With the Wind.* He began selling off the properties he owned—*The Keys of the Kingdom* and *Claudia,* among others—and loaning his contract talent to other producers. Vivien Leigh and Ingrid Bergman were sent to M-G-M while his one director, Hitchcock, was lent to producer Walter Wanger. The deal with Wanger was concluded on October 2, 1939, establishing Hitchcock as the director of Vincent Sheean's memoir *Personal History,* a property that had been under development since 1935.

Considering the book dated and unsuited to his particular strengths as a storyteller, Hitchcock, in collaboration with his wife, Alma Reville, and his secretary, Joan Harrison, devised an entirely new plotline which carried Sheean's title from the book and little else. Eventually, the title, too, would be dropped, the film instead drawing its name from Sheean's longtime profession—*Foreign Correspondent.* By the time Menzies came aboard in March, reportedly at Hitchcock's behest, a total of twenty-two writers had contributed to the script, including John Howard Lawson, Budd Schulberg, John Meehan, James Hilton, Ben Hecht, and Robert Benchley. Indeed, Selznick may have had a hand in putting the two men together, as Hitchcock had never before tackled a picture as big or as complex. Selznick was also keen to establish a demand for his British import, whose last released picture in the United States was *Jamaica Inn*—a dud.

Menzies found that Hitchcock, himself a former art director, was in the habit of making rough pencil sketches on his copy of the script. Menzies, in turn, worked out more than a hundred oversized drawings of sets and action for the start of production, as well as models of a dozen sets. When shooting began on March 18, 1940, the film was already four months behind schedule and progress was, at times, agonizingly slow. Menzies later recalled "a rather unpleasant association with Hitch" that nevertheless yielded "some pretty good results." Among the principal sequences was a plane crash staged in the same manner as the dirigible crash in *The Lottery Bride.* "I hardly used any miniatures at all," said Menzies, "but did the whole thing

For Emily's funeral procession, Menzies took the convention of the black umbrellas from the landmark stage production of *Our Town* and arranged the shot so as to obscure the faces and forms of the individual mourners, the composition conveying its emotional impact in the stark commonality of grief. (MENZIES FAMILY COLLECTION)

objectively, that is from a point of view always inside the cabin. I also had a very interesting sequence in a windmill where we really got some good photographic effects, and an assassination sequence in Amsterdam in the rain, which I rather borrowed from *Our Town*."

The huddle of black umbrellas to represent Emily's funeral cortege was a memorable feature of Jed Harris' original stage production, and Menzies had elaborated on it, gathering the canopies, glistening in the rainfall, in the foreground of the shot and allowing the night sky to fully occupy the upper half of the frame. There had never been a more spiritual composition for the talking screen, and now Menzies took the same basic elements, expanded their numbers exponentially to fill a public

Menzies freely admitted appropriating the umbrellas for the assassination scene in *Foreign Correspondent* (1940), the jostling of the black canopies effectively tracking the killer's path of escape. (AUTHOR'S COLLECTION)

square, and clustered them to emphasize the particularly brazen murder of a Dutch diplomat, an event that sends John Jones in pursuit of the killer, an adventure similar in substance and pacing to the director's earlier *39 Steps*.*

The windmill scenes were shot during the first days of production and afforded a kinetic maze of hazards and hiding places, the actors confined to a claustrophobic tangle of stairways and gears, the protagonist (Joel McCrea) eluding Nazi agents while attempting to rescue the drugged and disoriented Van Meer, whose memory holds the critical clause of an allied peace treaty. Menzies estimated he made "about 200 drawings" for *Foreign Correspondent*, roughly a quarter of the number he typically did for a feature, implying he worked primarily on the film's complex set pieces.

---

* The principal screenwriter on *Foreign Correspondent* was Charles Bennett, who worked on six of Hitchcock's British films, including *The 39 Steps*.

Menzies' work on the windmill sequence, the core of which he described as a "spiraling dis-closure of a light-knifed stairway," represents a seamless collaboration with supervising art director Alexander Golitzen and his associate Richard "Dick" Irvine, who were charged with the progressive refinement of the set as the continuity evolved. (AUTHOR'S COLLECTION)

"It was my observation," said actress Laraine Day, "that Mr. Hitchcock and Mr. Menzies conferred on every shot that had been drawn by Mr. Menzies. Whether or not there was a storyboard for the entire production, I don't really know, but it would seem reasonable to believe that if every scene was drawn before it was filmed, there must have been a storyboard from which these individual scene depictions were taken for them to discuss. Their working relationship during *Foreign Correspondent* seemed very close."*

The crash, much more elaborate in design and execution than its 1930 predecessor, formed the basis for the climax of the picture. And unlike the dirigible crash in *Lottery Bride,* which took place in frozen environs of the Arctic Circle, the downing of the clipper in *Foreign Correspondent* takes place over the ocean. "The whole thing was done in a *single shot* without a cut!" marveled Hitchcock in his marathon 1962 interview with François Truffaut. "I had a transparency screen made of paper, and behind that screen, a water tank. The plane dived, and as soon as the water got close to it, I pressed the button and the water burst through, tearing the screen away. The volume was so great that you never saw the screen."

The teaming of Alfred Hitchcock and William Cameron Menzies proved an inspired melding of two vastly different artistic sensibilities, Hitchcock being interested in the conveyance of visual information, Menzies in the deepening of the film's graphic impact. Together, they produced one of the grand thrillers of the sound era. When production closed on May 29, 1940, after sixty-five days of shooting and eleven days of retakes, the negative cost of *Foreign Correspondent* stood at $1,484,167—by far the most expensive picture Hitchcock had ever made.

While *Foreign Correspondent* was in production, *Our Town* was being readied for release. To score the movie, Lesser selected Aaron Copland, whose only prior experience in feature films was with John Steinbeck's *Of Mice and Men.* "This was not an ordinary motion picture," Copland wrote. "The camera itself seemed to become animate, and the characters spoke directly to it. Once the narrator actually placed his hand before the camera lens to stop a sequence and introduce the next. . . . Percussion instruments and all but a few brass were omitted. I relied on strings, woodwinds, and the combination of flutes and clarinets for lyric effects. Since *Our Town* was devoid of violence, dissonance and jazz rhythms were avoided. In the open countryside scenes, I tried for clean and clear sounds and in general used straightfor-

* When it came time for Hitchcock to make his traditional cameo appearance in *Foreign Correspondent,* he asked Menzies to direct the shot.

ward harmonies and rhythms that would project the serenity and sense of security of the play."

There was considerable discussion as to whether Emily should be allowed to live, her character having perished in the play. Menzies managed the design of the film so adroitly that the ending could go either way without sacrificing the underlying theme of the material. The decision, therefore, became a matter of retaining a few shots and discarding George Gibbs' poignant moment at the grave of his young wife. Douglas Churchill, who would be reviewing the picture for *Redbook,* advised Lesser to use the happy ending, and Thornton Wilder, in the end, agreed. "In a movie," Wilder reasoned, "you see the people so <u>close to</u> that a different relation is established. In the theatre they are halfway abstractions in an allegory; in the movie they are very concrete. So, insofar as the play is a generalized allegory, she dies—we die—they die; insofar as it's a concrete happening it's not important that she die; it's even disproportionately cruel that she die." To Martha Scott, who found the decision "deeply disturbing," the playwright was even more direct: "Martha, it didn't matter because my message in that play is to see life through the eyes of death."

In a bylined article for *The New York Times,* Menzies described the challenge of *Our Town* as a problem of intimacy: "A story of ordinary people in throes of living and dying, the audience had to move along with the characters. To solve this, we filled the picture with small, intimate sets, practically put the characters in the audience's lap with photography, and violated perspective throughout to heighten the moments of intimate drama."

A press preview took place on the evening of May 9 at Grauman's Chinese Theatre. Sol Lesser cabled Wilder after what he termed "a most unusual and successful" screening:

```
THE VERDICT WAS ONE HUNDRED PER CENT UNANIMOUS VERY
FAVORABLE FROM BOTH PRESS AND LAY AUDIENCE. . . .
I FEEL IT IS SAFE TO SAY THAT PICTURE WILL NOT
DISAPPOINT ANYONE.
```

In a critical sense, Lesser was right. The film's release on May 24 brought a wave of favorable notices, many outright raves. Bosley Crowther praised the filmmakers for utilizing "the fullest prerogatives of the camera" in making it a "recognized witness to a simple dramatic account of people's lives, not just to spy on someone's fictitious emotions." *Time* hailed the picture's simplicity and its fidelity to the spirit of the play. "Thornton Wilder wrote it in the only poetic idiom which Americans always understand—simple U.S. speech in which emotion supercharges the common forms. He wrote it out of the poetic materials to which Americans always respond—the casual routine of their lives amid the sights, sounds, smells of the American earth. Because Sam Wood, who directed *Goodbye, Mr. Chips,* and a splendid cast have transferred *Our Town,* the play, to film without disturbing this basic poetry, *Our Town,* the picture, is a cinema event."

# 15

# The Best Spot in Town

Bill Menzies thought his staging of *Our Town* "probably more important" to his career than *Gone With the Wind*. "Of course, <u>GWTW</u> helped me tremendously, as there was a strong 'grapevine' rumor about town that I had controlled the show," he wrote. "But *Our Town* really did me more good as the picture was a very frail and delicate thing, and although the end got a bit 'arty' I think the first part is interesting inasmuch as its design is with faces and figures rather than moldings and architecture."

On the strength of such an extraordinary pair of assignments, a flood of new opportunities came his way. In January, while he was shooting *Our Town,* writer-director Rowland Brown announced that Menzies would design Brown's independent production *Young Man of Manhattan,* which was being set up at Paramount. In February, he was mentioned for the direction of Ben Hecht's *Angels Over Broadway.* David Selznick contemplated a similar arrangement, proposing a deal for one picture a year but with yearly options for two. Then in March, Sol Lesser trumped Selznick by giving Menzies the plum assignment of directing a London-based production of *The History of Tom Jones, a Foundling.* Menzies wasn't keen on returning to wartime England, but he was even less keen on working for Selznick again.

At the completion of *Foreign Correspondent,* Menzies spent a month working with director Frank Capra, who was mounting his first independent production, *The Life of John Doe.* "At first he bridled a bit and thought I was showing him how to direct, which of course is the danger of this system," Menzies commented. "I ended up in a blaze of glory, though, because I took one sequence that was worrying him to death and took all the 'eggs' out of it.* I think they are as good drawings as I've ever done."

While in the midst of working for Capra, Menzies signed on to another independent production. Producers David L. Loew and Albert Lewin had teamed to produce features for United Artists, Loew handling all the business affairs while Lewin, who had worked under the late Irving Thalberg at M-G-M, saw to the creative end of their productions. "David," said Lewin, "felt strongly about the Nazi problem and wanted to make a contribution if he could, so he decided to make this book, although we were doubtful about its success in the United States." The book, serialized in *Collier's*, was Erich Maria Remarque's *Flotsam*, a novel about "those unfortunate people compelled to escape Germany because of race or political opinion, who find themselves in foreign lands without passports, and who lack the legal right to live anywhere and are therefore shuttled back and forth over all the borders of Europe."

The nomadic theme of *Flotsam* made the film more an exercise in mood and pattern than *Our Town*. Coming onto the project a month prior to shooting, Menzies, in Lewin's estimation, made "upwards of one-thousand sketches" in consultation with director John Cromwell. "Photostats were made of these sketches and they were sent to the set to guide the director and cameraman in camera set-ups and compositions." Assigned his own crew, Menzies worked ahead of Cromwell with a second camera and stand-ins, setting lights, arranging props, and achieving the angles called for in the photostats. "This second unit was responsible for savings in time in eliminating hit-and-miss production methods, and in creating a better-designed picture," said Lewin. "The second crew also filmed many pickup and insert shots."

Made at Universal, *Flotsam* drew on the talents of Jack Otterson, the head of the studio's art department, who, like Menzies, was educated at Yale and the Art Students League. The most elaborate set for the picture—which soon became known as *So Ends Our Night*—was a carnival set depicting the Prater, known as the "Coney Island of Vienna" in pre-Nazi days. A brilliantly colored merry-go-round had animals of every description—giraffes, lions, tigers, elephants, zebras, ostriches. There was a flea circus and an animal show with prancing dogs, seals balancing balls, and a ballyhoo for the fleas. Across a narrow tree-shaded street was a sausage and beer stand. "I'm afraid it's a little untimely, as it's about the passport difficulties in Central Europe in 1937," Menzies said of the story, "but for me it's a field day."

His charcoal sketches for the film, each of which took thirty to sixty minutes to compose, underscored the severity of the world in which the characters moved, their

* According to Menzies' daughter Suzanne, this was the convention sequence, populated with scores of black umbrellas, shot at Hollywood's Gilmore Field. The film was released as *Meet John Doe* (1941).

figures cold and isolated, their surroundings closing in on them. The picture, Menzies wrote at the time, had Fredric March and Margaret Sullavan "seeking throughout" to escape oppression in various Old World locales.

> Therefore, melodramatic escapes keynote the picture. Here, again, violation of perspective becomes of importance. If it heightened the drama to shoot a tree from the viewpoint of an astigmatic worm sitting on a leaf of that tree, or even from that of the tree looking at itself, we did so insofar as the new 28 millimeter lens and our imaginations would permit. Jails, frontier offices, star chambers are exact replicas of such European interiors. There are 138 sets in *So Ends Our Night,* a new record, but they are not elaborate, and each one is vital. We tried to make each speak in visual terms the one word, "Oppression!" Therefore, the efforts of the actors to escape become more necessitous to the audience, heightening suspense and melodrama.

One Sunday while *So Ends Our Night* was in production, Menzies sat in his garden, his pad in his lap, and responded to a lengthy letter of war-related news from Laurence Irving. "I have had a very good year," he wrote, dispensing with talk of the war,

> and I have developed the job that I have always tried to put over so that it has put me in about the best spot in town. Please don't think this smug. I am bringing it up principally to let you know that I really have developed the opportunity for application of our talents to the point where dozens of important people realize its importance, not only in added flavor and appearance but in the economic side, too. I have really proven that good composition is cheaper than bad and it is becoming a definite slogan around town. I am making between 500 to 800 drawings for each production, and working on twelve week guarantees I can do four pictures a year. It's terribly applied, and every once in a while I am tempted to try and find an easier way of making a living, but it really is interesting and absolutely controls the whole staging of the picture. On the set the other day, I overheard the script girl say "we have six sketches to go" instead of saying "six more setups." Of course, some pictures demand it more than others, but I try and get the "nuggets" so that I can display <u>the</u> technique of the thing strongest.

.   .   .

With the completion of his work on *Our Town*, Sam Wood went to Paramount to direct the unremarkable *Rangers of Fortune* and then to RKO, where his *Kitty Foyle* would bring Ginger Rogers an Oscar for Best Actress. Neither film, however, would be greeted with anywhere near the affection or respect accorded *Our Town*. When Wood agreed to make a comedy for producers Frank Ross and Norman Krasna, he insisted upon Menzies as part of the package. Krasna's original screenplay, *The Devil and Miss Jones*, was designed to star Ross' wife, the squeaky-voiced comedienne Jean Arthur. Appearing in the role of the billionaire real estate magnate John P. Merrick—the undercover owner of Neeley's department store and the aforementioned Devil of the story's title—would be Charles Coburn.

Krasna thought Sam Wood "a fabulous technician who knew nothing about the word" and therefore shot the script exactly as written. Menzies quickly grew to dislike the famously difficult Jean Arthur—he said that she had "legs like Indian clubs"—but rejoiced in the rare opportunity to design a comedy. "I think composition to punctuate ridiculous situations was used more and in better taste than is usual," he said, reflecting on the project in 1947. "We also broke the rule that comedy should always be played in high key staging which, of course, has been adopted a great deal since. In other words, when melodrama and comedy were combined, we played it in lighting, staging, etc., as straight melodrama, although we didn't lose the faces as much in lighting as we might in the more morbid type of melodrama."

Lighting was almost an afterthought for the film's sweltering afternoon at Coney Island, a sky cyclorama surrounding a ring of beach jammed with extras of all conceivable shapes and sizes, the detail on a scale worthy of *Gone With the Wind*. "The scene was as grotesque as a caricature by Reginald Marsh," observed Philip K. Scheuer, a visitor to the set. "Men, women, children, papers, boxes, bottles, cups, blankets, campstools, underwear, medicine balls, scraps of food, and sand, sand, sand—in, under, and around them all, getting into everything. You wondered why flesh in gross tonnage lots was always so ugly. . . . The camera got down on its haunches, too, and ferreted out a group consisting of Jean Arthur, Robert Cummings, Spring Byington, and Charles Coburn at lunch. They, at least, appeared happy."

The week production closed on *The Devil and Miss Jones*, nominations for the 13th Academy Awards were released to the press. Of the thirteen black-and-white features up for art direction, Menzies had worked on three—*Rebecca, Foreign Correspondent*, and *Our Town*. And the eventual winner in the new color category was also

Composition in service of the ridiculous: Thomas Higgins (Charles Coburn) and Miss Jones (Jean Arthur) look on as the officious Mr. Hooper (Edmund Gwenn), dubious of Higgins' ability to sell slippers, carefully files away his new employee's disappointing score on an intelligence test. "Don't feel badly—he'll get his just deserts one of these days," she soothes. "I'd like to be as certain of the hereafter, Miss Jones," replies Higgins, actually Merrick—the undercover owner of Neeley's Department Store. (AUTHOR'S COLLECTION)

a Menzies-related project, *The Thief of Bagdad.* That he had greatly influenced the look and visual impact of two of those films is beyond question. It is doubtful, in fact, that Lew Rachmil could ever have mustered a nomination for *Our Town* without Menzies' involvement in the conceptual layout of the film and its overall design. Yet there was no talk of a special award that year, and Menzies' name went missing in all the coverage that surrounded the event on February 27, 1941.

Menzies' name on a picture invariably drew critical comment, even when such well-meaning recognition was misplaced. "Suspenseful and highly exciting plot has been placed in a William Cameron Menzies production that lends authenticity and dignity to the story," *Variety* noted vaguely in its review of *Foreign Correspondent.* "The sets are equal in their size and scope to the extent of the international spy story being unfolded." So many critics assumed Menzies' credit on *The Thief of Bagdad* was for design and art direction that he felt compelled to take out a full-page

Menzies was always at hand when Sam Wood was directing. Here, on the set of *The Devil and Miss Jones* (1941), he watched as Charles Coburn rehearsed a scene in which he attempted to fit a belligerent young girl with a pair of high-topped shoes. "Suppose you wire that kid's pigtail," Menzies suggested. "When Coburn is trying to shoe her like you would a horse, and her pigtail stands out in fright, it ought to be a laugh." Wood embraced the idea and held production until the effect could be rigged. (ACADEMY OF MOTION PICTURE ARTS AND SCIENCES)

ad in *Daily Variety* and *The Hollywood Reporter* to deflect such notions: "Vincent Korda—and Vincent Korda alone—deserves all the credit for the imaginative sets and the designing of *The Thief of Bagdad,* a truly great job."

"I am a Hollywood anomaly," Menzies wrote in a bylined piece for *The New York Times.*

In a town where the spotlight is the goal of most, my work is the less noticeable the better it becomes. As a production designer, it is my job to dramatize the mood of a picture and to keep it "in character." This is done simply by coordinating every phase of the production not covered by dialogue and action of the players. Camerawork, settings, decorations, costumes, must all be carefully planned in advance, so that each contributes in its own way to the desired effect of the whole. Prior to the application of this theory of motion picture production, which, I believe I originated in Hollywood (although it is an old principle of stage presentation), the making of a motion picture was the work of too many cooks, each a chef in his own right, with the result that each department worked for its own aggrandizement rather than for unity. . . . It is but the principle of architectural engineering, which I studied at Yale University in my youth. I have applied it to the making of motion pictures, for the better, I think. And I remain a Hollywood anomaly.

On February 4, 1941, Daniel T. O'Shea advised David Selznick that Menzies had entered into a deal with Sam Wood, although it wasn't yet in writing. "Bill gave me certain promises," O'Shea, now general manager of David O. Selznick Productions, contended, "which he just ignored when it came to making a deal. I think the secret of it is that he just has an easier time of it with Sam Wood. He says his wife doesn't want him going through long hours with us and that, frankly, he's not able to take it anymore." Menzies had laid it on Mignon, but it's unlikely she ever mentioned the subject, much less delivered an ultimatum. She never pried into Bill's work at the studios, nor, for that matter, ever expressed much interest in it, choosing instead to keep his home life as he wanted it. "Everything was there exactly the way he left it," said their daughter Suzie, "because that was the way things were. Tommie Carter, our cook, was in the kitchen, Mother was with her bridge club, Jean and I were at school, the dogs were there. He came back to exactly the same thing he left, which I think he appreciated."

Jean Menzies graduated from the Westlake School for Girls in 1937. "She was very shy, very studious," said her younger sister. "A great student. She got accepted into Stanford when she was sixteen. Then I think she just got cold feet." Jean wanted to be an artist, but she wasn't as naturally talented as her parents. She attended Otis Art Institute for a while, then, at her father's insistence, went back to school in 1940 to take "a good stiff course in life drawing" which she seemed to enjoy. Suzie, at age fifteen, was still at Westlake and usually present for nightly dinners, sometimes to find that her father had been drinking.

"There was always that tension," she remembered. "Was he going to come home drunk? How was Daddy going to be when he came through that front door? We didn't know what we were going to have. His eyes would get very big and very blue and he'd sit there and glower at us like this big toad. Then the next day he'd be wonderful and all apologies to Mother—typical drunk behavior." Mignon would sigh and try not to set him off. "It was an odd marriage. It'd be hard to imagine two people more unalike. Mother had this prissy side to her, which Daddy certainly did not. She didn't drink, she didn't smoke, she went to church. And she had no spirit of adventure whatsoever. But she was like a rock to him. She was something that he could always come home to. She took care of everything. She paid all the bills. She took care of us. Everything she took care of to make his life more comfortable. She carried his breakfast up. We were all trained that when somebody called on the phone to say he was not at home. We were very well trained to take care of Daddy—especially Mother. Grandmother was trained to keep out of his way. And he adored Tommie, who was the best cook in Beverly Hills."

Nanon Toby, who tried to scuttle the "horrid match" between her daughter and Bill Menzies, had come to live with them on North Linden Drive, where she would generally stay in her bedroom and sip cheap wine. "She was a typical Southern lady; she was Blanche DuBois," Suzie said. "Only she wasn't crazy, she was just a drunk. But she always looked nice. She was very sort of chic. Even in these old clothes that she had for years she always managed to put a little scarf on or earrings. She was of another era, yet she was the first woman I ever knew who wore pants. To the beach. She'd wear these sort of pajama-like things. And these big hats, and these flowing scarves. She'd look like Isadora Duncan. She was very intelligent, but we never got along."

Nan was always in the background, a constant, lingering presence in a household that seemed all too often to be dominated by women. She and her son-in-law rarely spoke, and he took to referring to her as "Creeping Jesus."

The "deal" with Sam Wood meant that Menzies would be associated with Wood on a succession of important pictures, Sam typically commanding a fee of $75,000 and Menzies drawing his established rate of $1,000 a week from Wood's employer of the moment. Together, they constituted one outstanding director, capable of working to the industry's highest artistic standards. Their partnership officially began in January 1941 when Wood was engaged to direct *Kings Row* for Warner Bros. As part of the deal, Jack Warner agreed that Menzies would join Wood as production designer, but that they would use him "only five weeks top." Wood's commitment, on the other hand, would be for fifteen weeks.

A long, overwritten novel by the onetime dean of the Curtis Institute of Music, *Kings Row* displayed the rancid underside of *Our Town,* a story bereft of Thornton Wilder's poetic sensibilities but long on fascination, the book being, as *The New*

*York Times* put it, "a choice combination of murderous melodrama and psychopathic horrors." Warners jumped on the screen rights when the book was published by Simon and Schuster in April 1940, paying $35,000 to trump a bid from 20th Century-Fox. Clearly someone at the studio thought it suitable for motion pictures, but just exactly how to get it past the Breen Office was a matter of considerable discussion. Wolfgang Reinhardt, an associate producer on the lot, resisted the assignment: "As far as plot is concerned, the material in *Kings Row* is for the most part either censurable or too gruesome and depressing to be used. The hero finding out that his girl has been carrying on incestuous relations with her father, a sadistic doctor who amputates legs and disfigures people willfully, a host of moronic or otherwise mentally diseased characters, the background of a lunatic asylum, people dying from cancer, suicides—these are the principal elements of the story."

Another Warner producer, David Lewis, had an entirely different take on the book. "It was long and contained enough material for five movies," he said, "but the main story was a very powerful one of two boys who grow up in a small town as inseparable comrades. Parris Mitchell, brought up by his gentle European grandmother, wants to be a doctor, while Drake McHugh is a fun-loving young man with little thought for the future." On July 11, 1940, a week after Reinhardt's demurral, Lewis received a "pink note" from executive producer Hal Wallis: "In view of your interest and enthusiasm for the book *Kings Row,* I am assigning this subject to you."

In developing the script, Lewis turned to a frequent collaborator, screenwriter Casey Robinson. "He happened to be leaving on a vacation to the Far East," Lewis recalled, "so I gave him the book and he promised to read it on the trip. When he returned, I asked him about it. He told me he had gotten as far as the incest between Dr. Tower and his daughter and, certain the book was completely unfilmable, had thrown it into the Indian Ocean." It was the first 200 pages of *Kings Row* that interested Lewis: "The Breen Office had already frowned on our purchase of the book, but by then I already had the reason for Dr. Tower's killing of his daughter Cassandra and himself. Instead of incest, which, of course, was not allowable, I reasoned it would be equally believable that he would keep from Parris, his promising pupil, the one thing that had ruined his own life—an insane wife."

Sam Wood wanted Ginger Rogers for the part of Randy Monaghan, a beautiful Irish girl from the wrong side of the tracks, but Lewis held firm for Warner contract player Ann Sheridan, convinced—correctly, as it turned out—the role would make her a star. Early on, Ronald Reagan was set for the role of Drake, which would turn out to be his best and most memorable part. The casting of Parris proved problematic: Lewis wanted Tyrone Power, but Fox's Darryl Zanuck demanded too much for him, including two Errol Flynn commitments. With time running short, Wood settled on Robert Cummings, who had played the earnest Joe O'Brien in *The Devil and Miss Jones.* Cummings, under contract to Universal, could be had for $1,000 a week, but was in the middle of filming a Deanna Durbin picture, forcing a delay in the start of *Kings Row.*

When Menzies checked onto the Warner lot, he had as his starting point a temporary screenplay dated February 7, 1941. Work was progressing, but there was enough to start visualizing the early portions of the film, including the material establishing insanity in the Tower family. The script began with the title: KINGS ROW 1890 "A good town, everyone says. A good clean town. A good town to live in and a good place to raise your children." Cut to a horse and buggy approaching the camera. "While we discussed the script and the content (and agreed on it so we weren't two people thinking of a picture but one person thinking of a picture), Bill Menzies sketched every scene, every camera angle, every set-up," said Casey Robinson. "He numbered them so that, when Sam finally went onto the set, all he would have to say to James Wong Howe was, 'Jimmie, this is scene number ten,' and Jimmie would go to work lighting the set while Sam worked with the people."

The shooting final, dated April 13, brought a sharp letter of protest from Joseph I. Breen, who questioned the wisdom of making any picture—even one rewritten to conform to the provisions of the Production Code—from a novel so vividly identified in the public mind as "a definitely repellent story, the telling of which is certain to give pause to seriously thinking persons everywhere." It fell to Menzies to stage the picture in a way that would be faithful to the moods and rhythms of the original story while complying in all respects with the demands of the Code. He began by visualizing the individual characters and the costumes they might wear. "I draw the figure in connection with the ground—he grows out of the ground as much as a tree does," he said. His initial sketches, which took the form of thumbnails in the margins of the script, were studied by Howe with an eye toward managing the visual transitions between scenes, achieving a "continuity of movement" with complementary compositions at the end of one scene and the beginning of the next. "It is," said Menzies, "the liquid quality of movement which is the unique asset of motion pictures."

From the revised thumbnails, art director Carl Weyl was able to design some seventy sets for the picture, rendering many as scale models. Working from those models, Menzies made his detailed continuity sketches on illustration board with Paillard and Siberian Pit charcoal, indicating highlights and tonal values with black and casein, an opaque white. When it came time to build the sets, only those portions to be seen by the camera were actually fabricated. As Howe said of Menzies, "He'd tell you how high the camera should be. He'd even specify the kind of lens he wanted for a particular shot; the set was designed for one specific shot only, and if you varied your angle by an inch you'd shoot over the top. Everything, even the apple orchard, was done in the studio. The orchard was such a low set that it was very, very hard not to show the banks of lights. I had to hang shreds of imitation sky over it, blending one with another to hide all that equipment. Menzies created the whole look of the film; I simply followed his orders."

Bob Cummings' absence afforded the director an unanticipated opportunity. "Sam Wood was absolutely wonderful," Ann Sheridan said. "And for the first time in any picture we rehearsed three weeks before one single shot was made. The sets were up and we knew where we were going, what was going to happen." When filming finally did begin on July 14, the scenes between Sheridan and Reagan were the first to be made, Cummings joining in only when he wasn't needed at Universal.

On the set of *Kings Row* (1942), Menzies shows how he captures his first impressions of a script by making "shorthand sketches" in the margins. (AUTHOR'S COLLECTION)

Wood quickly came into conflict with the Warner way of doing things. Two days into production, he declared that he wanted two takes printed for every shot he made. When it was explained they permitted only one print of a given scene, Wood said that he wanted two takes so he could use parts of each, thus enabling him to cut down on the total number of takes he made. Noting that Wood and Menzies made very few setups but that they were "very thorough and complete," unit manager Frank Mattison thought it advisable to let Wood have his way. "Working with Menzies makes you really think," Wood told a visiting journalist. "You play the scene over mentally and get the action—then, if the scene happens to be in a living room, you don't get the doors or the furniture in the wrong place and spoil the scene

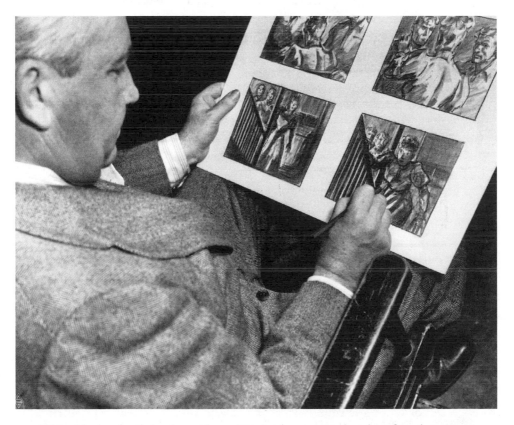

Taking his thumbnail sketches up large, Menzies demonstrates how he refines them into a continuity board. When the Breen Office cautioned the studio over this scene in which Drake (Ronald Reagan) discovers his legs have been amputated, Menzies threw the visual emphasis to Randy (Ann Sheridan) by reflecting in her anguished reaction shots the depth of Drake's horror. (AUTHOR'S COLLECTION)

because you've spoiled the action. We've gone over everything, there's no other way to see it. Makes for faster shooting—and saves film." Added Menzies: "We're two halves of the same thing. Sam likes me to stay on the set. We work everything out together."

David Lewis, another veteran of the celebrated Thalberg unit, had never before observed a director quite like Wood: "He knew nothing about the camera, nothing about script, and little about casting. Not only was Menzies on the set for everything, Sam rarely let me out of his sight either. Before shooting he would say to me, 'What is this scene about?' I would tell him and he would whisper in an actor's ear the magic words that brought forth a fine performance. In spite of his unorthodox method of working, I thought him worth his money."

Wood proved his worth beyond all doubt on the matter of Drake's accident and the subsequent amputation of his legs by Dr. Gordon. The doctor's sadism could only be implied, the nature of Drake's injuries suggested but not shown. Forced to work the rail yards, Drake is thrown into the path of an oncoming train when a stack of pallets collapses. Menzies worked out the continuity of shots so that an exterior dialogue between Drake and Randy ended on the image of an untended coffeepot. Dissolve to a shot of Drake clinging to the outside of a slow-moving train, dropping off as the engine picks up speed. The engineer turns to wave, then reacts in horror as he sees the hazard of the unstable cargo. He shouts a warning just as the pallets begin to tumble and Drake vanishes from the bottom of the frame. End on a shot of the coffeepot crushed under the wheel of a boxcar.

When he awakens, Drake is under the care of Randy and her family. Wood at first resisted the idea of a hole in the bed for Reagan's legs, so that when he turned to the wall, his whole body wouldn't turn with him. Said Lewis, who was called to the set, "The answer was fairly obvious. . . . That would make turning to the wall both difficult and heartbreaking. He tried it and it worked. Menzies, meanwhile, was standing there. As I turned from Sam he whispered, 'I've been trying to get him to do that all day.' I believed him; Menzies was not one to miss a trick."

As Reagan eased into the bed, he could sense its impact on-screen and chose to remain in place as Howe and his crew arranged the lights. "I had experienced a shock at seeing myself with only about two feet of body," he wrote in his autobiography, "and I just stayed there looking at where my body ended. The horror didn't ease up. When the camera crew announced they were ready, I whispered to Sam Wood . . . 'No rehearsal—just shoot it.' I guess he understood. When he said, 'Action,' I screamed, 'Randy, where's the rest of me?' while I reached with my hands, feeling the covers where my legs should have been. There was no retake. Sam quietly said, 'Print it.' I realized I had passed one of the biggest milestones of my career."

The beginning of *Kings Row* was inspired by the opening of *Our Town,* where Frank Craven approached the camera as the titles appeared. Casey Robinson had a similar idea, the camera panning through town, but it lacked the focus of a single figure the eye could follow, and Menzies solved the problem with a hay wagon that appeared in the far distance and grew closer as the credits progressed. The effect was lyrical, the pan continuing past the sign KINGS ROW 1890 and on to the schoolyard, where the main characters are introduced as children and the close relationship between Parris and Cassie is established in the apple orchard that gave Jimmie Howe such fits. "It is possible," Menzies observed, "to set the mood, deliver your credits, and open up on the first scene of the picture with the same footage."

For *Kings Row,* Menzies wanted sharp tonal contrasts that worked against the genteel pretensions of the town. The period costumes were either very black or very white, while the walls of the sets were often white. As with *Our Town,* he chose to work in close, his angles low and clean, building his compositions with the faces rather than the sets. "When Parris arrived home," said Casey Robinson, "you just saw a little scene between two cars and you saw a boy's face, worried. That's what the story was about. It wasn't about a train coming into a station." As with *Our Town,* Menzies established a recurring pattern of horizon fencing, adding a stile where the characters could cross over and transitions could symbolically take place. When it comes time for Parris' passage from adolescence into adulthood, it is accomplished with young Scotty Beckett, in short pants, stepping over the fence, the camera holding on his feet as he disappears from view. A dissolve indicates a change of season and the passage of years, and then two adult feet step back over the fence, the camera holding on them until tilting up to reveal a grown Parris in the person of Robert Cummings.

Said Menzies,

There's a series of dramatic narrative sketches which, while they presented the possibility of a direct attack, called for all the ingenuity we could muster. Six sequences in a doctor's dusty study—and you have to sustain interest and dramatic action. Drab, rundown-at-the-heels place. We used the doctor's books for composition. Jimmie [Howe] caught the atmosphere beautifully; Jimmie's one of the best cameramen I ever worked with, has a great sense of how to light a set. In this truly American, musty 1900 doctor's office we used every device to emphasize the atmosphere and sustain drama. Fuller's earth on books to give dusty effects, diffused effects through old lace curtains, dust in the crevices and sheen on the highlights of the tufted leather chair; and the lighted edge of an old tome—in one sequence we caught this highlight, held it a split second, then moved the man across it. Just chinning yourself on nothing—six sequences in that one study.

One of the more controversial aspects of the novel was a scene in which Parris administered a fatal dose of morphine to his beloved grandmother, stricken with cancer. The Code expressly forbade mercy killing when "made to seem right or permissible" and the filmmakers, at an April 23 meeting with Breen and deputy Geoffrey Shurlock, had agreed to remove any suggestion of it. There was, however, a feeling the episode carried weight only when expressed in terms of the difficult moral choices faced by a young doctor, and the decision was made to shoot the scene regardless, with the hope the staging would be subtle and artistic enough to gain the reluctant approval of the PCA. James Wong Howe described the design of the scene and how it was photographed:

Although the Production Code forbade "the suggestion of a mercy killing of the grandmother by Parris," Menzies was able to stage the scene at her deathbed so that a hypodermic needle loomed large, a pitcher and basin completing the composition and firmly drawing the eye to the foreground. Parris' discovery of his grandmother's grave condition is played with the needle in hand, suggesting the option of euthanasia.

We had a shot with a hypodermic needle in the foreground, about 18 inches from the lens. From behind we saw a bed with the grandmother of this boy, and we saw . . . Bob Cummings about twenty-five or thirty feet in the background. The camera is stationary until he comes into the foreground and picks up this needle. As he walks out of the camera and starts to cry, we know what has happened. . . . This was all done in one shot with the camera in one place. It was a difficult shot for me. I had to carry the focus, to make this hypodermic needle very sharp and also the background sharp. That was accomplished by using a wide angle lens; I think I used a 25mm or half-inch lens to carry the focus. I had to stop down, oh, around f.8 to keep it sharp. By stopping down to f.8, I had to use much more light than I would photographing normally at f.2.3 or 2.8. But it worked out.

On August 20, snowy scenes of Kings Row at wintertime were being shot on Stage 1. Ann Sheridan was making *The Man Who Came to Dinner,* alternating between it and *Kings Row,* often on split days that scarcely left her time for lunch. Bob Cummings was still over at Universal, romancing Deanna Durbin, and the company was eleven and a half days behind on a forty-eight-day schedule. "We must get one thing settled in the next few days and stop all this nonsense," Jack Warner thundered in a memo to David Lewis, "as we have never done business this way and I am not going to permit it to start."

Warner was upset that the part of Cassandra Tower was yet to be filled. Bette Davis wanted the role, but it was considered too small for a star of her magnitude. Olivia de Havilland had turned it down, as would Ida Lupino. Warner suggested either Joan Leslie, Susan Peters, or Priscilla Lane as "the best we can get" but Sam Wood would have none of them. In September, with the film nearly ten weeks into production, Wood went to Paramount to shoot five days of tests for his next collaboration with Menzies, *For Whom the Bell Tolls.* One of the actresses he saw was Betty Field, who was trained at the American Academy of Dramatic Arts and known primarily for her work on the stage. Wood thought her ideal casting for a troubled girl driven to the edge of madness by heredity and parental abuse, and he arranged to have her borrowed by Warners on a three-week guarantee.

"He was wonderful in giving confidence to actors and trusting them and recognizing when they played a scene well," Field said of Wood.

For the part I played in that [picture] they tried out hundreds of girls. They couldn't find any. They finally auditioned me—they were so particular to get this part just right, because it was such an odd part. She was insane, and yet you couldn't say she was insane. Due to censorship you couldn't say there was incest there, you had to imply it by looks between the father and daughter. Only if you'd read the book would you know why they were staring at each other. But I auditioned—actually they gave me a screen test, and he worked so hard on the screen test that actually it took a whole day to do a screen test of a scene. Then they put it into the picture. They didn't bother doing that scene again. He perfected it and perfected it and decided it was just what they wanted for Cassie.

To give Cassandra a ghostlike quality, Menzies specified a No. 1 makeup, which was almost pure white and seldom used. Her frantic encounter with Parris in the empty Tower house, a thunderous storm raging outside, was one of the last scenes shot, the implied justification for the doctor's murder of his own daughter. Menzies staged the scene against a backdrop of lightning, the screen going from intense blackness to flashes of brilliant illumination, the characters growing closer and more passionate with each desperate glimpse. His handling of the material was well within the dictates of the Code, yet with the implication clear and the imagery unmistakable—no rawer sex scene was to be found in any mainstream American film of the decade, a dazzling example of how mood and subtext could trump the work of gifted actors and render a scene's dialogue inconsequential.

When *Kings Row* finished on October 7, 1941, it was twenty-three days over schedule and nearly $300,000 over budget. Most of the delays and overages could be attributed to switching the schedule around, which resulted in carrying some actors for longer terms than anticipated, as well as many sets, which had to be lighted and relighted. "Considering the broken manner in which this show has been shot as regarding sets, cast etc., I only hope it fits together right," said Frank Mattison in a memo to his boss, production manager T. C. "Tenny" Wright. "I have never seen a picture shot in such a hurried manner as this picture has been made. Most of the circumstances were beyond our control and the insistence of Mr. Wood that we have Robert Cummings play the lead in this picture."

For producer David Lewis, one of the most memorable aspects of *Kings Row* was the opportunity to work with William Cameron Menzies, whom he described as "probably the most brilliant man I have ever known in his field." For Lewis, the picture constituted a catalog of fine visual touches, some of which he noted in the pages of his autobiography: "Among Menzies' contributions, apart from the entire tone of the film, were the magnificent opening shot in the schoolyard . . . Parris stepping over the stile into adulthood . . . the staging of the accident in the railroad yard . . . the sight of the crushed coffee pot to indicate Drake's legs . . . the lighting in the bedroom at the grandmother's death . . . the long telegraphic montage between Kings Row and Vienna . . . and many others."

It was, Lewis would say, economical filmmaking with a grandeur unusual in even the priciest of Hollywood epics, abetted as it was by Erich Wolfgang Korngold's majestic score, far from the astringency of Aaron Copland yet no less effective. Years later, in 1951, Menzies himself weighed in on the subject, telling his colleague Leo Kuter that he considered his "very best effort as a production designer" to have been the Warner Bros. production of *Kings Row*.

# 16

# Address Unknown

On May 17, 1941, Sam Wood wrote to Bill Menzies from New York: "I got a phone call at Baltimore which I am not at liberty to disclose, but we have one of the big plums. If you guess what it is, it is very important to treat it confidential at the present time."

The "big plum" was Ernest Hemingway's *For Whom the Bell Tolls,* an assignment Wood effectively inherited from his old boss Cecil B. DeMille. (DeMille thought the novel, when he finally got around to reading it, "really in a communist cause.") Unlike *Kings Row* and *Our Town* before it, both of which were entirely studio affairs, much of the Hemingway picture would be shot in the Sierras. "On location," groused Menzies, "all you have is a series of dialogues with one party shouting to another party on the opposite hillside. On indoor sets we have absolute control. We can avoid crosses in action, and actors are never on the same level when we build sets. I'll have a *lovely* time when we get going on *For Whom the Bell Tolls.*"

Hemingway reportedly modeled the character of Robert Jordan on his pal Gary Cooper, and he had urged DeMille and Paramount to cast Cooper in the film version, a matter that would require the acquiescence of Sam Goldwyn. Meanwhile, columnist Jimmie Fidler declared the latest candidate for the female lead to be Ingrid Bergman, "who'll get it if boss David O. Selznick says yes."

The item was probably a plant, as Selznick was vitally interested in getting Bergman—who had just one American release to her credit—the role of Maria, the young refugee whose parents were murdered by the nationalists during the early days of the Spanish Civil War. Under pressure from Selznick, Hemingway got on board, acknowledging that he, too, would like to see Bergman play the part. But resistance at Paramount was fierce, and the part remained uncast when Wood committed to making the film. There was also the matter of an adaptation, which production head B. G. "Buddy" DeSylva put in the hands of novelist Louis Bromfield. Preparations went forth as Wood and Menzies immersed themselves in the shooting of *Kings Row.*

There was little time between the close of *Kings Row* and the start of *For Whom the Bell Tolls,* the preproduction phase beginning with a convoy of studio cars, trucks, and buses making its way up Route 99 to the California gold rush town of Sonora, 350 miles north of Los Angeles. From there it was some fifty miles east to the Dardanelle, a rustic resort just below the Sonora Pass, where the company would be quartered while Wood, cinematographer Ray Rennahan, and Menzies scouted locations and waited for snow. (As his one hedge against the random compositions of nature, Menzies had some gigantic fake boulders fabricated in Los Angeles and hauled north on a flatbed truck.) Often, Wood would settle on locations that differed for every shot within a given sequence, giving Rennahan's Technicolor cameras the full benefit of their spectacular surroundings while leaving it to Menzies to lend visual continuity to the footage.

"He would select one location for the shot of the bridge when [the old Spanish guide] Anselmo pointed to it, when he and Jordan paused on the trail," recalled Herbert Coleman, Wood's script supervisor on the picture. "The location for the scene between Anselmo and Jordan was picked on the side of a mountain miles away. For the close shot of Jordan in the same scene, another location on another mountain was his choice. For Anselmo's close shot, still another mountainside. To make it seem as if all the scenes were shot in the same location, the same gnarled, twisted limb of a storm-weathered pine tree was placed in each scene."

When the snows came, Wood sent for the rest of the shooting unit, which included technicians, grips, horses, cavalrymen, and a group of players headed by Joseph Calleia, the Maltese actor who would be playing El Sordo, Hemingway's Gypsy renegade. Filming commenced on November 13, 1941, and soon the company was completely snowbound.

"LOCATION CONDITIONS HERE QUITE PRIMITIVE AND VERY COLD," Menzies wired Mignon, "BUT FEEL WELL. STUFF SHOULD BE BEAUTIFUL." A few days later, in a handwritten note, he added: "We are going very slow as we have a three-hour shooting day. I finally had a bath. We have to sleep with fires going or the little plumbing we have freezes. It's been 2 above and 2 below zero."

"We were supposed to meet him for Thanksgiving dinner in Yosemite," recalled

Suzie Menzies, "but he could never get there." Then came December 7 and news of the Japanese attack on Pearl Harbor. Immediately, all planes in California were grounded, including the three bombers that were supposed to take part in a mountaintop assault on the rebels. "Boom!" said Ray Rennahan. "They pulled us back, pulled the whole company back until they could get permission to use the planes." Production on *For Whom the Bell Tolls* was suspended until the following summer, when the aircraft could presumably fly once more and the casting of the leads would be settled.

When Henry Louis Gehrig died on June 2, 1941, a scramble for the rights to his life story was set in motion. The Yankee first baseman's dramatic struggle with amyotrophic lateral sclerosis had been followed by an anxious public to such an extent that ALS became better and more widely known as Lou Gehrig's Disease. Christy Walsh, acting as a friend of Mrs. Eleanor Gehrig, paid a call on Sam Goldwyn and settled the rights with him. To Walsh's mind, Goldwyn had the obvious casting for the Iron Horse in the person of Gary Cooper. The deal seemingly dashed whatever hopes Paramount had in securing Cooper's services on *For Whom the Bell Tolls,* as a timely film version of Gehrig's life would have to be ready for the coming baseball season. Concurrently, there were reports that actor Sterling Hayden would likely be tapped to play Robert Jordan, a bit of news that gained little traction in the press, where items insistently touting Cooper's eventual participation continued to appear.

As messy as the casting of *Kings Row* became, the casting of *For Whom the Bell Tolls* threatened to get even messier. When filming began, neither of the leads had been set, and the search for Maria seemed to be taking on the same monumental proportions as Selznick's search for Scarlett O'Hara. In October, Goldwyn engaged Howard Hawks to direct the Gehrig story, but having done *Sergeant York* and *Ball of Fire* back-to-back, Hawks was physically spent and, in the words of his agent, "didn't care whether he did the picture or not if he was going to be rushed into it." Eventually, a complicated deal took shape, wherein Paramount agreed to loan comedian Bob Hope to Goldwyn for two pictures in exchange for Cooper's participation in *For Whom the Bell Tolls.* What evidently sealed the bargain was Sam Wood's willingness to direct the Gehrig story once *Bell Tolls* was in the can.

Now, with the Hemingway picture on hold, Menzies went straight to work on the Gehrig project, which existed in the form of a draft screenplay by novelist Paul Gallico, the onetime sports editor of the New York *Daily News.* The story, much of which took place in the looming environs of various baseball stadiums, suggested much in the way of dramatic patterns and interesting compositions, but the script

A low angle contains the figures of Teresa Wright and Gary Cooper, enclosing them with texture and shadow. Menzies frequently took in ceilings in the films he designed for Sam Wood, sometimes for pattern, often for intimacy and containment. (AUTHOR'S COLLECTION)

was far from finished, and Goldwyn was wary of a film in which baseball was the dominant factor and not the love story that framed the personal tragedy of Lou and Eleanor Gehrig. There was also another, more practical consideration, which had been noted by Jimmie Fidler as far back as September: "UNHAPPY: Baseball fans and writers are protesting Gary Cooper as Lou Gehrig on the screen because Lou was left-handed and Gary isn't."

Cooper, as it developed, wasn't much of a player, even when using his right hand. "I discovered, to my private horror, that I couldn't throw a ball," he said. "The countless falls I had taken as a trick rider had so ruined my right shoulder that I couldn't raise my arm above my head. Lefty O'Doul, later manager of the Oakland ball club, came down to help me out. 'You throw a ball,' he told me after studying my unique style, 'like an old woman tossing a hot biscuit.' But we went to work, and after some painful weeks he got my arm to working in a reasonable duplication of

Gehrig's throw. There remained one outstanding difference. Gehrig was a southpaw, and I threw right-handed."

Lou Gehrig hit and did most other things from the port side, but he wrote with his right hand. Cooper could indeed act him if his playing could be faked, but Menzies wouldn't abide the old fraud of a double, shot from the rear and matched with finish shots of the lead actor. His compositions, for one, would suffer, and Wood, who had once played semipro ball (and had three broken fingers on his left hand to prove it) wouldn't hold for it either. Like most of his fixes, Menzies' solution to the problem was absurdly simple: Cooper would swing and catch right-handed, then they would flip the film in the lab. For such shots as these, Cooper and the other players would be dressed in uniforms on which the names and numbers were reversed, as in a mirror image.

L.A.'s Wrigley Field was where much of the outdoor filming took place, but the minor league ballpark faced northeast, making the position of the sun a big problem. One day they needed a shot of Gehrig running to first base when the baseline was in deep shadow. Forced to improvise, Menzies staged the shot on the third base line, with Cooper running from home to third, then had the film flipped. For the shot to work, the numbers on the backs of the visible uniforms had to be ones, elevens, or eights. The opposing team, Washington, reversed well because of the Ws. Another problem was the wartime shortage of male extras for shots that took in the bleachers, prompting the Screen Actors Guild to grant a waiver that permitted the company to include nonunion personnel in its $5.50-a-day calls for atmosphere players. Augmented with stills and stereos of Comiskey Park and Wrigley Field in Chicago, and stock shots made at New York's Yankee Stadium, the movie's fleeting ballpark scenes were thoroughly convincing, owing, in no small part, to the presence of Gehrig's real-life colleagues on the team's famed Murderers' Row—Bob Meusel, Mark Koenig, and Babe Ruth, who drew a $25,000 payday and third billing behind Gary Cooper and Goldwyn contract player Teresa Wright.

Work on *For Whom the Bell Tolls* was grueling, by far the roughest location shoot for Menzies since *The Son of the Sheik*. "We climb about all day like Alpinists," Sam Wood said at the time. "The real heroes are the grip men. They pack heavy lamps and the dead weight of cameras and sound equipment. They string cable from cliff to cliff, mount precipices, and set up block and tackle." When the company returned to Sonora Pass to complete the bomber footage, there was still snow on the ground. Both Menzies and Wood wore visored caps and, after the first day, covered their noses and lips with camera tape. Still, their faces were raw and peeling when

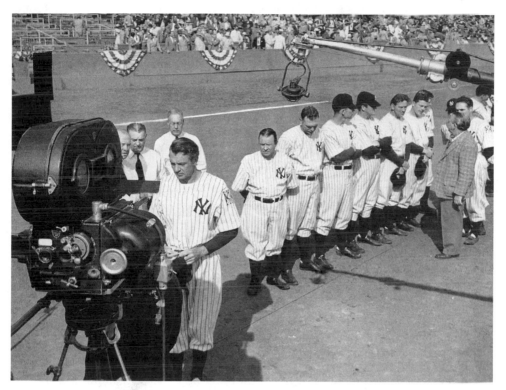

Menzies lines up a shot at L.A.'s Wrigley Field for the Lou Gehrig Appreciation Day sequence in *The Pride of the Yankees* (1943). Eighteen hundred extras were used for the shots that took in the stands, Gary Cooper in the extreme foreground, the Yankees extending in a diagonal line through the middle distance. "I've seen the episode in the newsreels," Sam Wood said of the event, "and think it is the most dramatic scene I've ever witnessed." (AUTHOR'S COLLECTION)

they got back to Los Angeles, and Menzies was so close to snow blindness he had to spend two days in a darkened room. ("With the ointment on," Wood commented, "we look like Amos and Andy.") The snow would be gone in July, when they would start making scenes with the principals, but then Wood had a more pressing problem with Sam Goldwyn over the matter of credits on *The Pride of the Yankees*.

Goldwyn had balked at giving Menzies a card to himself, saying he had agreed to no such thing and that Menzies could share a card with cinematographer Rudolph Maté. There was, however, an understanding between Menzies and Wood that Menzies would have his own card on each of their pictures together, a matter revisited after *Kings Row* had been previewed while they were shooting in Sonora and Menzies' name had been lumped in with four others. "I have been concerned about Menzies' credit," Wood wrote in a letter to Goldwyn, "because I have a certain obligation to give him a full card with 'Production Designed by William Cameron Menzies' on it. I may not have taken this up with you at the beginning of the picture. Rather than have Menzies disappointed, you may put him on half of my card."

And so when *The Pride of the Yankees* had its gala opening the following month, premiering at the Astor Theatre on Broadway and simultaneously playing one-night stands at forty RKO houses in metropolitan New York, the final credit read:

Directed by
## SAM WOOD
Production Designed by
## WILLIAM CAMERON MENZIES

A stand-up guy, Wood was also acutely conscious of how much he needed Bill Menzies—particularly on a production as vast and as unwieldy as *For Whom the Bell Tolls.* "Sam leaned on him one hundred percent," said Ray Rennahan. "Bill designed the costumes, the locations, the compositions. He drew it all out before we ever saw the sets. Of course, we would readjust everything to fit the camera when we could get on them, but Bill designed that picture one hundred percent. All interiors and exteriors and everything else." Menzies readily acknowledged the fact that his continuity sketches, as thoughtful and as thorough as they were, could express only entrances, first groupings, and finishes, and that it was impossible to plan everything on paper. To keep the action from looking wooden or long scenes from seeming static, there was much to be worked out on the set. "Anytime there was any kind of a question about some particular angle or setup," said Rennahan, "Bill could take a piece of paper and sketch that off so fast and say, 'Well, that's what I had in mind. Can you do that?' Well, sure I could."

With Gary Cooper now on board, *For Whom the Bell Tolls* resumed production on July 2, 1942. A few days later, and under protest from Sam Wood, dancer-actress Vera Zorina, her hair somewhat carelessly cropped to a length of just two inches, arrived at Sonora to assume the role of Maria, a part for which she had vigorously lobbied. "Sam refused to acknowledge her presence," said Herbert Coleman. "Most of us liked her. She was a lonely figure. She'd come to the location every day but never near the set. We'd see her wandering around in the distance." After a week of shooting around her, wind and rain hampering his progress, Wood made a single scene in which Zorina exchanged a short greeting with Cooper, sent the film down to Hollywood for processing, then got on the phone and threatened to resign if Ingrid Bergman was not immediately given a test.

Initially, Wood had dismissed Bergman as a "big horse." He came around after some spirited advocacy on the part of his daughter Jeane, who had read—and loved—the Hemingway book. The matter of Zorina's haircut had been botched, and Bergman's own trimming, once given the part, was done under Selznick's personal supervision. When she arrived on the set, Cooper came down the mountainside toward her. "Hallo Maria?" he said. And at once Menzies gained the most exquisite female face he would ever place before a camera. "He once said that he had always wanted to fill the screen with a woman's face," his daughter Suzie remembered, "but until Ingrid Bergman came along, he had never found one that could stand up to such magnification." Menzies' close-ups of Bergman—who, incidentally, wore no makeup—were so tight that Ray Rennahan was once heard to suggest, only half jokingly, "Let's pull back to a long shot now and show the chin and hair."

They were eleven long weeks on location. In a July letter penciled to his wife, Menzies described his daily routine:

Don't think I'm complaining too much, honey, but it's hard to write when your day consists of a little guy calling you out to breakfast at 6:30. Leave at 8. Climb a mountain at 8:30, shoot til 12:30. Climb down the mountain to lunch & I really mean a mountain. Climb back after lunch. Shoot til 6:00 then climb another mountain to pick out the shooting for the next day, to the cabin by seven or 8 or 9. Bath and shave (sometimes) & you have never seen so many rings around a bathtub in your life & so to bed. . . . Everyone in the troupe except Sam is swell. He is really a pain in the ass. We have yokels who tore up the hill to see the movies & Sam really gets up on top of a mountain & hams all over the place.

There was also the matter of color design for a picture that relied much more heavily on exteriors than had *Gone With the Wind*. Everyone agreed the location was wonderfully like the Sierra de Guadarrama, the Spanish mountain range where Hemingway's story was set, except that the California version was considerably greener than the tawny original. Rennahan had filters to knock out the colors Menzies didn't want, but yellow was difficult and the result on-screen was bilious. Instead, a squad of painters was sent roaming over ten acres, spraying out hot spots on trees and rocks and dusting the landscape with lampblack to bring it more in line with the grim mood of the action. "[The] hillside is bare of green, with fire-blackened pines and harsh rocks," Sam Wood said of the palette. "If flowers spring up overnight, we pull up stakes and go where it's bare. Painters spray paint to kill the colors in boulders and trees. *For Whom the Bell Tolls* has to be in a monotone. Everything looks earth-colored. The only hues are Pilar's dress, which is dull purple, and Maria's shirt,

Menzies' sketches of the bombing of the bridge in *For Whom the Bell Tolls* (1943). A far less dynamic version, staged in miniature, was eventually used in the film. (MENZIES FAMILY COLLECTION)

which is woodland green. The guerrillas and peasantry look as if they hadn't washed in years. The fire in the cave, too, also smoked them up."

It wasn't always easy for Menzies to get the colors he had designed into the film, even after approving the dailies shipped up from Los Angeles. "It's almost impossible not to be scenic," Menzies said, "but we must be powerfully scenic in this film." Karl Struss, who spent three weeks shooting second unit work with him, lamented a complete lack of control over Technicolor's fussy processing: "For instance, there was a scene of some prisoners coming out of a dense fog. Well, to put a little color into it, I put a #62 filter over the lights, so to put some warmth into it. This was a flashback, so it didn't have to be so literal. Well, when I saw the dailies, it looked great; when I saw the finished picture the fog was white. Some guy in the lab with nobody to supervise him thought 'fog doesn't look like that' and did what he wanted. That's discouraging."

Some of the men, including Herbert Coleman and assistant director Joe

Youngerman, brought their families up for the summer and lived in trailers. Others paired off with the starlets routinely sent up by the studio. "They used to ship them in by the carload," Suzie Menzies said.

> Mother heard about that later; I think [sketch artist] Joe St. Armand told her about that. But I think that's something you can dismiss. I mean, Daddy was up there for months. . . . I don't know that Mother believed that, but looking back on it, she should have. I can remember saying to her, "Why don't you divorce him?" But she would never leave him because of that. She knew he was having affairs at Universal. And there was one woman—an old friend of hers—who was kind of a constant during *Gone With the Wind*. . . . But he wasn't a flagrant womanizer like so many were. Daddy had a lot of class, but in the movie business, it happens. And it happens to everybody.

Sam Wood had his eye on Ingrid Bergman, but according to Wood's daughter Jeane, Gary Cooper got there first. "Every woman who knew him fell in love with Gary," Bergman said. Wood's younger daughter, Gloria, visited the set and discovered her father had settled on another girl, who remained his mistress for the rest of his life. "It was so primitive and romantic up there among the stars and the high peaks before the winter snows cut off the whole region," Bergman wrote in her autobiography. "The climate was incredible. We chilled in the morning, sweated in the afternoon sun, and froze at night." At the end of all that location work, there was another six weeks of interiors to be made at Paramount's Hollywood studios. Gloria Wood later quoted Gary Cooper on the subject of his luminous costar: "I have never felt so loved in my life—for a short time—then after the picture was over, she wouldn't even answer the phone."

Though anticipation for the picture was on a par with that for *Gone With the Wind*, wartime restrictions on new construction would have made the set-heavy Selznick production impossible in the days following Pearl Harbor. Menzies managed to hold aside enough of the budget to pay for the fabrication of a cave back at the studio. The commodious set, constructed of plaster and chicken wire and roomy enough for a crew of fifty, would permit shots impossible to make on location, where the real cave selected for exteriors proved too small to accommodate two Technicolor cameras, sound equipment, lamps and reflectors, Menzies, Wood, Rennahan, and the company's four principal players—a group that included Akim Tamiroff and the renowned Greek tragedienne Katina Paxinou.

*For Whom the Bell Tolls* finished in Los Angeles on October 31, 1942, almost a year after the first shots were made in the snows east of Sonora. As Ingrid Bergman wrote in a letter to Irene Selznick: "I am stunned at the patience, the preparation, and perfection Wood spends on the story."

Without a break, Menzies went around the corner to RKO, where he would design a Cary Grant vehicle for producer David Hempstead. *Mr. Lucky* would be Grant's first picture as a solo attraction after years of being paired with the likes of Katharine Hepburn, Irene Dunne, and Rosalind Russell. Hempstead, who had been Sam Wood's producer on *Kitty Foyle,* brought Menzies onto the project with an eye toward mitigating the government conservation order that imposed a $5,000 maximum for new set materials on any one production. With old sets being pulled out and repurposed, he reasoned, how they looked was less important than how they were shot.

New conventions were already in place. Where wallpaper was formerly applied directly to wood surfaces, a layer of cheesecloth now went between the two, making the paper removable and the wall section reusable. Where the average height of a set used to be twelve feet, now they were generally only eight. A section to be burned in a given scene was now made of asbestos instead of wood, the flames supplied by strategically placed gas jets. Even nails were being straightened and used again, cutting the industry's consumption of new ones by as much as 95 percent. In such an era, Menzies' bold images, his dialogues staged in silhouette, his tricks with color and lighting made even better sense. His continuities, coupled with more thorough rehearsals, saved much more than the 25 percent reduction in film usage mandated to cover the extra stock needed for training films and other governmental purposes. "I'm a romanticist," Menzies said at the time. "I was born one and educated as one. But in this motion picture business it's also essential that I be as practical as a plumber."

Mindful of all this, Sam Goldwyn signed Menzies to a one-picture contract in January 1943. The project at hand had long been referred to around town as the Lillian Hellman Soviet story. About the time of Menzies' engagement, it acquired a title—*The North Star.* The idea of a Soviet documentary was supposedly the brainchild of Harry Hopkins, one of the president's closest advisors, who favored Lend Lease for the Soviet Union and wanted a film to help soften up the American public. "No matter the different system; that was an internal affair," screenwriter Walter Bernstein wrote. "The enemy of our enemy was our friend."

The core creative team was comprised of Goldwyn contract talent: playwright Hellman, director William Wyler, cinematographer Gregg Toland. Over time, the documentary evolved into a semidocumentary and then, ultimately, a big-budget commercial feature. When Wyler accepted a commission in the U.S. Army Air Force, the Russian-born Lewis Milestone took his place. When Menzies signed on, his job, in part, would be to stretch the film's meager construction budget in the design and fabrication of the Severnaya Zvezda collective, the Ukrainian farming village of the story's title.

As James Vance, then a twenty-three-year-old sketch artist, recalled, "I was over at Columbia working for several art directors, doing sketches, and I got a call from [art director] Perry Ferguson, who I knew from having worked for Vincent Korda when the Kordas were based at Goldwyn. The war had depleted the ranks of experienced artists and draftsmen, and someone fairly inexperienced, as I was, could get in with someone like Ferguson. So I went over, and we talked, and he hired me. He didn't say anything about Menzies, but I was in there one day—first week, I think—and he opened the door and said, 'Jim, I want you to meet Bill Menzies.' And I nearly fainted."

Ferguson would be nominated for an Academy Award for his work on *The Pride of the Yankees* and Sam Wood would draw a nomination in the direction category for *Kings Row.* And although Milestone had a much greater hand in shaping the script, Menzies was officially associate producer on *The North Star,* not the production designer. When he did put pencil to paper, it was to rough in a map of the village for Ferguson, who then had it worked out in detail on an enormous drafting board several yards square. As a scale model took shape, the first of some 1,200 continuity sketches were made by Jimmy Vance.

"What I knew about Bill was that he shot low," said Vance. "So, what did I do? I tried to shoot low. He said, 'I want this narrow road with a wagon at the end of it, almost at the vanishing point. And I want it surrounded by birch trees.' And, of course, I said, 'Where are you going to get birch trees?' He said, 'We'll make 'em.' So he got cypress and he wrapped them with toilet paper. And he burned the holes. So the first sketch I ever made for him was literally like that—the steppes of Russia and this little tiny wagon. And it gets bigger and bigger until finally the horse comes up and goes underneath us and we're on two people going to town in this wagon."

Filming began on March 1, 1943, the face of the Goldwyn backlot having been altered considerably by the removal of the English village square from *Wuthering Heights* and a Washington intersection built for the Bob Hope comedy *They Got Me Covered.* The recovered materials went into new facades representing the relatively modern buildings of the collective—a hospital, the radio station, a school—their governmental simplicity contrasting with the thatched-roof peasant cottages in which lived the principal characters. The South Sea lagoon from John Ford's *The*

*Hurricane* was leveled and reconfigured into a tributary of the Volga river, and a rail spur—dubbed "the Goldwyn shortline"—was dressed with freight cars similarly hewn from salvaged junk and scrap lumber.

Menzies took an immediate dislike to Lillian Hellman. ("She's the kind of woman who looks at your fly when you're introduced to her.") Hellman, in turn, came to regard him as the most reasonable member of the creative team, someone whose ideas invariably improved the picture. Milestone, on the other hand, submitted fifty pages of suggested script revisions, an affront that prompted her to sever her eight-year relationship with Goldwyn and buy out the remainder of her contract. With a number of minors in the cast, including seventeen-year-old Farley Granger, the film quickly fell behind schedule, many of its actors limited by law to just four hours of work a day. And the film had tonal issues, its idyllic scenes of life in the collective on its final day of peace joltingly at odds with the German air attacks and atrocities to follow. On the sixth day of shooting they were already two days behind, and on the ninth day they were four days behind. By April 1, Menzies was directing a second unit with actors Dean Jagger, Ruth Nelson, and Esther Dale. Augmenting the human players was a menagerie of farm animals—fifty sheep, six horses, six colts, ten head of cattle, two pigs, and the wranglers to keep them in line, dog and bird trainers as well. It soon seemed as if a lot of time went into checking on pigs and dogs.

In July, after a rough cut of the picture had been assembled, Goldwyn decided a critical scene needed rewriting and appealed to Hellman to return to California. Forty minutes into a screening of the assembled footage, Hellman began to cry, softly at first, then hysterically. "You let Milestone turn this into a piece of junk!" she screamed at her longtime employer. "It will be a huge flop, which it deserves to be."

*The North Star* finished in October, long after the cast had been dismissed, thirty-five days over schedule and well over its $1.5 million budget. When it was released the following month, critic James Agee judged it "one long orgy of meeching, sugaring, propitiation, which, as a matter of fact, enlists, develops, and infallibly corrupts a good deal of intelligence, taste, courage, and disinterestedness." As its author so vigorously predicted, it was indeed a huge flop.

As Menzies saw to the filming of *The North Star,* Sam Wood was making *Saratoga Trunk,* another picture that starred Gary Cooper and Ingrid Bergman, this time for Warner Bros. Although the movie—at least superficially—looked as if it had been staged by Menzies, the production design was officially the work of protégé Joseph St. Armand. The difference was plain to Eric Stacey, the first assistant on *Gone With*

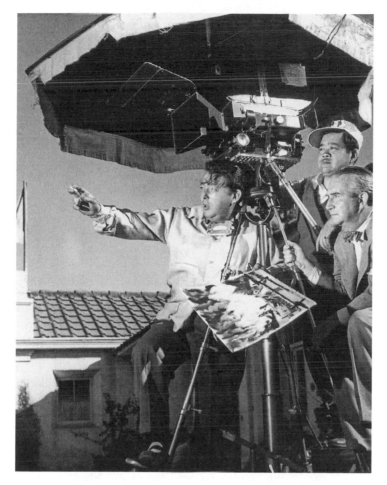

Lewis Milestone, James Wong Howe, and Menzies on the set of
*The North Star* (1943). The artwork in the director's hand was likely
rendered by Jimmy Vance, Menzies' illustrator on the picture.
(ACADEMY OF MOTION PICTURE ARTS AND SCIENCES)

*the Wind,* who was now a unit manager under Warner production manager Tenny
Wright. Wood, Stacey advised Wright in a memo, was "very vague about how he
is going to stage scenes, and after he has done a scene, goes home and sleeps on
it, gets another idea and does it again the next day." Wood was also terribly for-
getful, sometimes having to return to a set to pick up a shot he had neglected to
make earlier. Said Stacey: "This bears out what I told you at the beginning of the
picture—how much he misses someone like Bill Menzies to make up his mind and

tell him things." Under Wood's direction, *Saratoga Trunk* finished more than forty days over schedule.

Sam Wood's daughters both became actresses. Jeane Wood did her work primarily onstage and seemed largely content to be the wife of radio announcer and producer John Hiestand. Gloria, the younger, was more ambitious and decamped to New York, where she changed her name to get out from under her father's shadow. An admirer of Katharine Hepburn, Gloria appeared in two early film roles as Katherine Stevens. In 1941, she proposed to legally change her name to Katie, then decided a more distinctive moniker would come from simply taking the initials K.T. and forgoing a first name altogether. "It's just that there are so many Marys, Kates, Joans, Junes, Anitas, Bettys, Helens, Barbaras, and such that I thought I would get me something no one else has used." Later that same year, K.T. Stevens, twenty-two, made her Broadway debut in George S. Kaufman and Edna Ferber's oddly pitched saga of generational excess, *The Land Is Bright*. A few months after the show's closing, Sam Wood acquired the film rights and entered into a contract with Columbia Pictures to produce and direct it.

Columbia was one of the smaller studios, and its prestige product was usually the result of Harry Cohn, the company's famously explosive president, affording top-rank directors such as George Stevens and Howard Hawks an unusual degree of latitude. Thus, Sam Wood could cut a deal with Cohn and cast his own daughter in a series of pictures, something he likely would be unable to do at M-G-M or Warners. The understanding called for one picture a year with Wood producing and directing. In May 1943, while *Saratoga Trunk* was in production, Wood acquired a second property with his daughter in mind, an epistolary novella from 1938 called *Address Unknown*, a book *The New York Times* hailed as "the most effective indictment of Nazism to appear in fiction."

As might be expected, it wasn't long before Wood invited Bill Menzies into the new venture, handing him a picture to direct for the first time in seven years. "As far as I'm concerned, William Cameron Menzies is entitled to credit as associate producer on *For Whom the Bell Tolls, Our Town, Kings Row,* and every other movie that we have made together," Wood told Louella Parsons. Within days, the two men had screenwriter Lester Cole at work on a script, Cole having just written *None Shall Escape* for Columbia, a prophetic film portraying the trial of a Nazi officer for war crimes. By the end of the month, veteran actor Paul Lukas, who was garnering terrific notices as the idealistic antifascist in Warners' *Watch on the Rhine,* had been announced for the lead, and news of K.T. Stevens' casting had been the top item in one of Hedda Hopper's columns.

The adding of *Address Unknown* to Columbia's program for the 1943–44 season caused *Hollywood Reporter* columnist Irving Hoffman to ponder the reluctance of producers—many Jewish—to make films depicting the plight of the Jews in Europe. "The answer, of course, is that Hollywood is afraid to. It is afraid to make pictures about Jews, about Negroes, and about other minorities because it might cause a kickback at the box office." It was not lost on Hoffman that one studio, scrappy little Columbia, was now in the process of making two such films—*None Shall Escape* and *Address Unknown*. "From the time *Address Unknown* first appeared in *Story* magazine, we have looked forward to its cinemadaptation. *Address Unknown* has the authority and sincerity of its convictions, and is being produced by a man who possesses those same qualities. He is William Cameron Menzies, whose name wouldn't cause a ripple among the screen's cash customers, but he is certainly one of the most important creative figures in Hollywood. We believe *Address Unknown* has been delivered into the right hands. It is another laborious forward step in the development of that gigantic plaything known as the screen."

Lester Cole made some essential changes to Kressmann Taylor's original story,

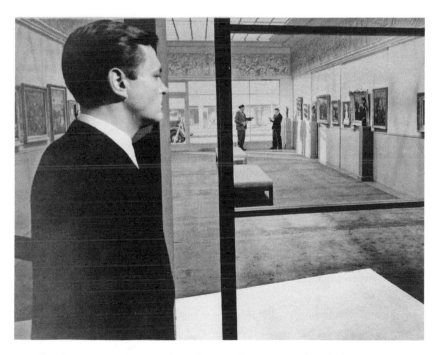

Depth creates opportunities for isolation and emptiness in the Schulz-Eisenstein Gallery, the San Francisco location for *Address Unknown* (1944). (AUTHOR'S COLLECTION)

tailoring the part of the doomed Griselle to young K.T. Stevens by making her the daughter of the Jewish art dealer Max Eisenstein instead of his sister. He also added the character of Heinrich Schulz, the son of Eisenstein's business partner, a gentile, to create a love interest for a tale that otherwise chronicled the relationship of two middle-aged men. The final script came from an unlikely collaboration between Menzies and a freelancer named Herbert Dalmas, whose métier at the time was westerns and serials. As Menzies would later acknowledge, the picture was essentially made on the drawing board. "The whole secret of motion picture making is in preparation," he said. "What comes after that is hard work." When production began on November 22, most of the creative effort had already been expended.

Sam Wood came onto the set to pose for pictures with his daughter and actor Peter van Eyck. ("We understand one another perfectly," Stevens once said of her father.) The first sequence to be shot was Griselle's Berlin stage debut, where she recites the Beatitudes in defiance of state censorship and is exposed as a Jew to the belligerent audience. She manages to escape, only to have the police catch up with her on the steps of Martin Schulz's gated house. When he refuses her entry, fearful for his own life and newfound standing with the influential Baron von Friesche, Griselle is brutally murdered by the Gestapo as Schulz listens in a dead panic from the other side of the door, his eyes fixed on a bloody handprint she has left behind.

In staging the pursuit, Menzies vowed he would not highlight the swastika armbands—an overdone device, he felt. He solved the problem by simply giving each man a lantern that could be shined into the lens of the camera, the resulting glare obliterating the familiar symbol of the fascist state whenever it came into view. Though the part of Griselle wasn't terribly big, it was a meaty one and K.T. Stevens reveled in it. "It was worth waiting five years for," she said.

Menzies used a sort of conspiratorial shorthand with cinematographer Rudolph Maté, the man with whom he had shot *Foreign Correspondent* and *The Pride of the Yankees.* Together they achieved a stark, unsettling look for the picture, with solid blacks and desperate, unforgiving whites, Griselle's costume glowing like a flame in the dark alleyways of Berlin, the angry mob stalking her only yards away, the graphic tension accentuated by forced, violent perspectives that gave the picture a nightmare quality. "He knew so much about black and white and the use of mass," said Jimmy Vance. "If something needed to be dark, he would have the decorator bring in a big black case."

Armed with some eight hundred continuity sketches, Menzies moved the film along at an admirable pace, keeping the entire enterprise on schedule and under budget. "He was a very professional man," said Richard Kline, the movie's seventeen-year-old camera assistant. "I know that he and Rudy Maté had a very

The spatial distances between characters inform the compositions in *Address Unknown*. At Munich, Martin Schulz (Paul Lukas) urgently seeks the approval and friendship of Baron von Friesche (Carl Esmond), a well-connected nobleman who disapproves of the Jewish girl engaged to Martin's son. "You are going to have to choose, Herr Schulz," the baron tells him. "You cannot sit on two stools at once—at least not here in Germany." (AUTHOR'S COLLECTION)

close relationship. It was really a film that went off very smoothly, with no interference. . . . I don't recall any problems at all with the film, other than it being a smooth operation."

*Address Unknown* wrapped on January 13, 1944. After putting it before a preview audience, Menzies rewrote some scenes to expand the role of actor Carl Esmond, who had been borrowed from Paramount to play the sinister Baron von Friesche. With retakes done by the end of January, the picture was ready for its New York opening on April 16, scarcely a month after Paul Lukas scored a surprise win as Best Actor for *Watch on the Rhine*. The critical reaction was terrifically positive, with both *The Hollywood Reporter* and *Daily Variety* posting rave reviews.

"William Cameron Menzies," led the *Reporter*, "offers in *Address Unknown* a beautifully-made picture which fairly glitters with brilliant performances, led by Paul Lukas in an unforgettable portrayal and lovely K.T. Stevens, whose delicately sensitive interpretation of her first important role marks her for stardom." *Daily Variety* declared the feature a "notable success" for Menzies after years as Wood's associate. "He builds up his situations shrewdly and handles them with an appreciation of highest dramatic values, the result being *Address* is a carefully contrived production of distinction."

In New York, the *Times'* Thomas M. Pryor affirmed that *Address Unknown,* given its only minor liberties, lacked "none of the punch" of the original story. "The tragic atmosphere of the picture has been heightened through the brilliant use of low key lighting effects by William Cameron Menzies, the director, who is better known as Hollywood's leading production designer. Mr. Menzies, cloaking the greater part of the story in deep, brooding, shadowy photography, methodically builds the tension into one of the most spine-chilling climaxes you'll encounter in many weeks of moviegoing."

Columbia set a May 6 opening for *Address Unknown* in fifty-one cities, and after a decidedly checkered career as a director spanning fifteen years, Menzies finally found himself the author of an unqualified critical success. ("Apparently," wrote Philip K. Scheuer, "he is one of the few pictorial craftsmen left in Hollywood—and not ashamed of it.") Yet after striving for the very position in which he now found himself, Menzies was ambivalent and unsure if he really wanted to continue on the course that was now finally open to him. He talked wistfully of returning to England after the war and opening a pub on the outskirts of London, something he had been saying since before the attack on Pearl Harbor. "To tell the truth," he said in an interview with the magazine *U.S. Camera,* "I'm not overly fond of directing. In the first place, I'm inclined to be lazy. I don't like getting up at dawn in order to be on the set well ahead of everyone else and getting the day's work lined up. . . . I imagine I get just as much pleasure out of my work as does any painter or sculptor, but I just don't know how to take this business of being a director."

# 17

# Ivy

Sam Wood had several properties in the queue to follow *Address Unknown*. In addition to *The Land Is Bright*, which was still earmarked for his daughter, there was *Jubal Troop*, a western from the novel by Paul Wellman, and *Tatiana*, an original by *Mayerling* author Irmgard von Cube. Wood thought the Wellman book a good fit for Gary Cooper, and Menzies was making plans to produce and stage the film as Wood went off to direct Cooper in *Casanova Brown*. In February, the annual Academy Awards ritual brought a particularly egregious slight in the nominations of Hans Dreier and Haldane Douglas for color art direction on *For Whom the Bell Tolls*, their principal contribution to the picture being the cave interior that enabled the company to return from Sonora.

With the New York opening of *Address Unknown*, hopes ran high that the new Wood-Menzies partnership would deliver a hit. The reviews were gratifying, but the film faced a moviegoing public sated with stories of wartime Europe and eager for escapism. Where only two months earlier *None Shall Escape* had done more than $1 million in domestic rentals, *Address Unknown* managed scarcely half that amount—despite sterling notices and the Academy Award–winning presence of Paul Lukas. Wood's relationship with Harry Cohn cooled, and *Jubal Troop* was put on ice. Eight months after the finish of *Casanova Brown*, Wood signed on as director of *Guest Wife*, a romantic comedy for producer Jack H. Skirball. The following month, after almost a year of inactivity, Menzies, at the behest of David Hempstead, accepted the offer of a one-year contract at RKO.

· · ·

Throughout the 1940s, David O. Selznick made repeated entreaties in his drive to lure Bill Menzies back into the fold. As early as January 1940, a one-picture deal had been worked out, a guarantee of six weeks with options, but Selznick's quarry eluded him, unwilling to submit to the 24/7 bombardment to which DOS subjected all of his charges. In March 1941, Sam Goldwyn was eager to borrow Menzies if only Selznick could sign him to a contract. In May of that year, Selznick anxiously inquired about Menzies when he heard *Kings Row* had been delayed. In November, he was told Menzies was "simply dying" to do *The Keys of the Kingdom,* which he had set up for Gregory Peck at Fox. Nothing worked out, and in October of 1943 Reeves Espy of the Myron Selznick office assured the producer they would be "delighted" to talk about Menzies whenever he was available, but that he had nearly a year to run on his existing contract. "Please bear in mind," cautioned Espy, "that Bill contemplates freelancing and is not interested in a term deal."

With Wood having committed to *Casanova Brown,* Selznick told Daniel O'Shea he doubted that Wood would take Menzies with him to International Pictures. "The difference in our operation working without Menzies is so tremendous that I wonder if we shouldn't make another stab at getting him." Then came the commercial failure of *Address Unknown,* and Selznick's ardor momentarily cooled. Over the summer, he immersed himself in the shooting of *Spellbound,* a psychological thriller under the direction of Alfred Hitchcock. As with most Selznick productions, the film was subjected to a lot of second-guessing, and in October the producer expressed dissatisfaction with its stylistic centerpiece, a dream sequence as set forth in the screenplay by Ben Hecht.

Impressed by a birthday portrait Salvador Dalí painted of Jack Warner's wife, Hitchcock had asked that the artist be commissioned to create four gray-tone paintings, each to serve as a Surrealist dreamscape for the repressed experiences of one John Ballyntine, who has come to Green Manors in the persona of Dr. Anthony Edwardes, a distinguished psychologist—and may, in fact, be guilty of the real Dr. Edwardes' murder. Said Hitchcock, "What I was after was . . . the vividness of dreams. . . . All Dalí's work is very solid and very sharp, with very long perspectives and black shadows. . . . All dreams in the movies are blurred. It isn't true. Dalí was the best man for me to do the dreams because that is what dreams should be."

The material was filmed, but Selznick was never completely satisfied with the results. "The more I look at the dream sequence in *Spellbound,*" he wrote, "the worse I feel it to be. It is not Dalí's fault, for his work is much finer and much better for the purpose than I ever thought it would be. It is the photography, setups, lighting, et cetera, all of which are completely lacking in imagination and all of which are about what you would expect from Monogram. I think we need a whole new shake on this sequence, and I would like to get Bill Menzies to come over and lay it out and shoot it."

Dalí, by then in New York, expressed the desire that his work in American pictures be accessible to all. "Il y a three," he said of the number of settings. "And every people understand dese dream." Menzies considered Dalí a bit of a crackpot. Although under contract to RKO, he came to the studio at Selznick's urgent request, and the two men had a conversation Selznick described as "very exciting." Menzies ran the picture, then spent two days in discussions with art director James Basevi. The overall intent was to honor Dalí's unsettling atmosphere while providing a clearer progression of the dreamed events. Mac Johnson was put to work on the drawings, photographic copies of which were shipped east for Dalí's approval. "We are not changing anything on any of his paintings," an accompanying note stressed. "We are introducing transitional elements to relate one painting to another painting in relation to [Gregory] Peck's dialogue. . . . Throughout the entire dialogue, the camera is moving forward."

Menzies then directed four days of retakes, specifically a gambling room sequence with actor Norman Lloyd, a rooftop miniature, and some smoke effects. Now officially on loan, there were days, Selznick observed, "on which he just comes over for an hour or two, and has to rush back to his other job." Work on the sequence was completed in March 1945, but the finished picture, scored by Miklós Rózsa, wasn't released until December of that year. Menzies declined credit for his work on *Spellbound,* which, according to studio records, amounted to a total of thirteen days.

The new picture on Menzies' schedule was *The Greatest Gift,* a story by Philip Van Doren Stern that had come to Cary Grant by way of a twenty-four-page pamphlet serving as the author's 1943 Christmas card. Grant took the story to RKO, the studio for which he was about to make *None but the Lonely Heart.* The purchase was finalized in March 1944, and soon playwright Marc Connelly was at work on the story of one George Pratt, suicidal, stuck in a "mudhole for life, doing the same dull work day after day" and wishing he'd never been born. Connelly expanded it, making it the Jekyll-and-Hyde tale of a bad George allowed to exist in the absence of the good George—the one who had never been born. By year's end, when Menzies came onto the project, Connelly was gone, Clifford Odets (Grant's director on *None but the Lonely Heart*) was drafting his own version of the seemingly unlickable screenplay, and George Pratt had become George Bailey.

*The Greatest Gift* got as far as continuity sketches for its arresting opening, in which little Zuzu Bailey encounters her dead grandfather in a "music conservatory" that turns out to be heaven. Eschewing the Hollywood cliché of clouds and choirs, Odets' first shot called for "a pleasant, neat street, lined with old-fashioned trees and several comfortable residence houses about." As the four-year-old approaches the camera, Menzies illustrated a world eerily disproportionate to conventional reality, the trees oversized, the girl tiny in comparison, the conservatory gigantic, its doors and stairs dwarfing the solitary figure of the child who, back on earth, is lying near death, and whose appearance alerts the grandfather to a "great peril" in the life of his son.

Development of *The Greatest Gift* (known as "Project 1838" in the RKO files) continued into the spring of 1945. According to screenwriter Dalton Trumbo, who did some uncredited work on the script, the film was put on hold after its producer—presumably Hempstead—went on an "alcoholic binge."* In May, Menzies was shifted to *Deadline at Dawn,* working with first-time director Harold Clurman, a founder of New York's famed Group Theatre and a genuine snob when it came to moviemaking.

"Daddy did an awful lot on that," said Suzanne Menzies. "He may have had his name taken off it because he *hated* Harold Clurman." It's easy to see Menzies' compositional hand in the look of the film, starting with its noirish *Kings Row*–style opening that takes place behind the titles. Yet the experience could not have been a happy one. "Just who IS directing RKO's *Deadline at Dawn*—Harold Clurman or William Cameron Menzies?" Reed Porter pointedly asked in his *Hollywood Review* column of June 11. Clurman himself described the picture in his autobiography as "run of the mill" and dismissed it as being of no importance. "My almost casual attitude toward the job met with resentment," he wrote, "perhaps because I finished the film on time and it proved moderately profitable."

When Menzies finished with *Deadline at Dawn,* it was announced he would direct Ferenc Molnár's 1929 comedy *The Lawyer* for producer Val Lewton. It was Lewton's notion to turn the play about an urbane jewel thief and his best friend and attorney into a musical. "It is, to date, the most fascinating job I've attempted," Menzies said at the time. "We are really throwing the book at it. I think it will be a complete departure in musicals and, in a great many ways, in all pictures. I hope and think it will be an important milestone in my long and bumpy career. It is also a very pleasant situation to make my own drawings for myself!"

With *The Lawyer* in active development, Menzies' services were once again

---

* Hempstead later resurfaced as associate producer on *Portrait of Jennie* (1949).

requested by Selznick, this time for the producer's gigantic Technicolor western, *Duel in the Sun*. Frustrated in his efforts to land Menzies as the film's production designer, Selznick had instead engaged Josef von Sternberg to advise on "angles and lighting" but found that von Sternberg lacked the preparatory skills that made Menzies so valuable. "He came in at the very tail-end—that dance, that big dance," director King Vidor said of Menzies' participation. "I guess that's what you call the barbecue scene. Yeah, the big dance in the patio of the house. . . . It was typically Selznick to bring him on for just one scene, bring somebody on."

Menzies spent five days on the picture in early August 1945, designing the only major sequence left to be done. "The crane shot that we did for the last day's shooting was more or less all laid out by Menzies," recalled Lee Garmes (who had replaced Hal Rosson as principal cameraman on the film). "Vidor was there in a supervisory capacity, and Menzies more or less did the scene. . . . It was really Menzies that initiated the whole idea and the whole concept. We followed his sketches, and when we came up [at the end of a long dolly shot], we ended up with the kids in the tree." Menzies' traveling camera opened on a fire pit, a side of beef turning on an open spit, the cooks at work, then trundled through the smoke, past the carvers, catching casual snatches of dialogue, past the revelers, the solitary guest wiping his mouth on a tablecloth, Butterfly McQueen, in fancy serving dress and lace apron ("when I'm married I'm going to have lots and lots of parties . . . "), then moving up to an overlooking tree branch, coming to rest on a black boy and a white boy lazily trading fishing stories against a background of celebratory chaos.

Lewton protégé Nathaniel Curtis had been put to work on the script for *The Lawyer*, and in September Lewton and Menzies were far enough along to consider casting in a memo to production executive William Dozier. At the time, they favored Angela Lansbury, Virginia Mayo ("we are rather enthusiastic about this girl"), and Laraine Day, whose singing voice, it was noted, they were prepared to dub. Eventually, contract starlet Marian Carr was selected to star opposite Bob Cummings, with filming set to begin in December. Late in November, however, the start date was pushed back. A few weeks later, an item in *Variety* indicated the picture had been called off altogether due to litigation over the rights to the play. A separate item noted that Menzies had checked off the RKO lot, having, with the cancellation of *The Lawyer*, nothing left to do. "Understood RKO is looking for another vehicle to call him back to produce and direct it," the paper added.

Meanwhile, *The Greatest Gift* had been resurrected as the first project in four years for Frank Capra, who had spent the war in uniform. Acquired by Capra's new production partnership, Liberty Films, the property was passed to the husband-wife writing team of Frances Goodrich and Albert Hackett, who were charged with devel-

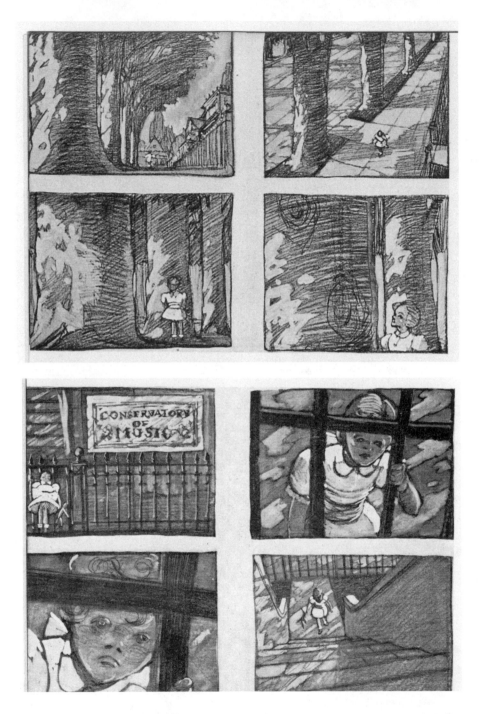

Little Zuzu Bailey is dwarfed by her heavenly surroundings in the opening moments of RKO's *The Greatest Gift*. Menzies stayed with the project when it was acquired by Liberty Films and director Frank Capra, sketching at least one alternate opening in which Benjamin Franklin was portrayed as the head angel, flying his trademark kite while considering the earthly trials of George Bailey. Recast with James Stewart in the lead and released as *It's a Wonderful Life* (1946), the film's actual opening wasn't nearly as cinematic.

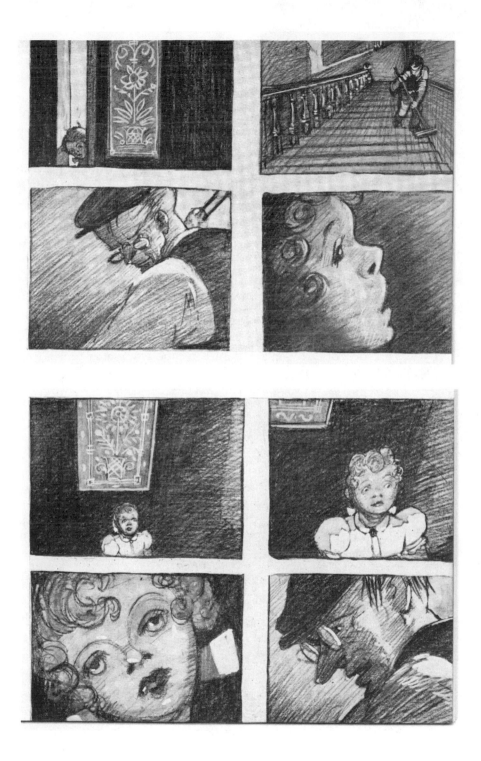

oping a screenplay that paid off the title *It's a Wonderful Life.* Since the completion of *Meet John Doe,* Capra had made just one commercial feature, the compact *Arsenic and Old Lace,* filmed at Warner Bros. in 1941 but held from release until 1944. *It's a Wonderful Life,* despite its small town setting, promised greater scope, and again Capra, as with *Meet John Doe* before it, engaged Menzies to take all the "eggs" out of the heaven sequence and the events leading up to the moment on the iron bridge when George Bailey stares morosely into the icy black water and contemplates ending it all. Jimmy Vance had relocated to Kansas City when he received a call from Menzies to come back to work: "We started right on it. My first memory is that we did some studies for Heaven. He asked me, 'What's Heaven look like?' And we tried to figure out without being corny. I remember the bridge. I don't remember doing anything inside the house or the bank—anything like that. He took me out to the RKO ranch once, and there was a huge snow scene."

When the picture went into production in April 1946, Menzies was on the set, primarily to hold the veteran director's hand. By his own admission, Capra was nervous at the prospect of directing a $1.5 million production after such a lengthy hiatus. "It's frightening to go back to Hollywood after four years," he told Thomas Pryor of *The New York Times,* "wondering whether you've gone rusty or lost your touch. I keep telling myself how wonderful it would be just to sneak out somewhere and make a couple of quickie Westerns—just to get the feel of things again." Suzie Menzies could remember her father going over to Beverly Hills High School at night to shoot the ballroom scene, the first major sequence to be filmed. "And I remember his drawings. The scene turned out pretty much as I remembered it. He worked on a lot of that movie." Yet Menzies' name appears on none of the surviving production records, nor does the work he did on the movie appear to have been budgeted—raising the possibility his weekly salary was covered out of Capra's own pocket.

Menzies appears to have stayed with *It's a Wonderful Life* through the completion of winter exteriors, for Vance recalled starting work on *Arch of Triumph* almost immediately upon finishing with Capra. "The studios were so busy then that I had to work in the washroom of our house in Beverly Hills. Bill would come by every day, sometimes in the morning but always at night. I did both those movies in my house." Based on a book by Erich Maria Remarque and starring Ingrid Bergman, Charles Boyer, and Charles Laughton, *Arch of Triumph* would be a major production for Enterprise Studios, a new entity formed by David Loew (who, in partnership with Albert Lewin, had made *So Ends Our Night*) and former Warner Bros. publicity chief Charles Einfeld. Its producer, David Lewis, had previously worked with Menzies on *Kings Row.* The film would also mark Menzies' fifth and final pairing with Lewis Milestone.

To Jimmy Vance, Menzies during this period was an avuncular, almost fatherly figure, wryly showing him the ropes in a profession still largely undefined. Once, his mentor took him to a revival theater on Vine Street to see *Our Town,* pointing out the ideas he thought worked well in the film and the reasoning behind them. "He was always so nice and trying to offer advice," said Vance. "One time he said, 'Jim, someday you'll be an art director, and when you are, sometimes you'll get stuck and won't know what to do. If I were you, I'd start on the smallest object I could think of and then expand.' I said, 'Well, what do you mean?' He said, 'Maybe it's an ashtray. Or a lamp or something. Then work out from it, instead of trying to put everything in a box. Do it in reverse.' I also remember talking to Bill one time about color. He said, 'I'd like to do a scene that's all black-and-white with just one patch of color somewhere.'"

A ponderous tale of love and revenge, *Arch of Triumph* offered few opportunities to break new ground. Overwritten and miscast, it lumbered through four months of principal photography. Yet during its making a long-anticipated reunion between Menzies and Sam Wood took shape, its basis a tentative agreement between the two men to film a specific property should Menzies secure an option. *The Story of Ivy* was by the prolific English novelist Marie Belloc Lowndes, whose 1913 thriller *The Lodger* had been the basis of Alfred Hitchcock's first great movie success. With a deal to make pictures for International, Wood set up a company, Inter-Wood Productions, Inc., and acquired the rights to *Ivy* for $25,000. In June, the property was placed in the hands of screenwriter Charles Bennett, whose work with Hitchcock during the latter's prime British period made him an ideal choice to adapt to the screen a minor classic of betrayal and murder.

Inter-Wood established offices on the Universal lot, and in September signed Menzies to a five-year contract, effectively picking up the partnership where it had left off at Columbia two years earlier. As before, Menzies' deal called for him to produce the films Wood directed and vice versa. *The Story of Ivy* would be Wood's picture, leaving Menzies to direct the company's next production, a thriller titled *Purgatory Street.* Late in July, as Universal and International announced their plans to merge, Olivia de Havilland tentatively agreed to star in *Ivy,* giving the project momentum and a year-end start date. Other cast members added in the run-up to filming: Richard Ney, Sir Cedric Hardwicke, Patric Knowles (borrowed from Paramount), and on December 11, 1946—the day filming commenced—Herbert Marshall.

Ultimately, de Havilland spurned the title role when she discovered her agent had a financial interest in the new company, and a last-minute switch landed de Havilland's younger sister, Joan Fontaine, in the part. Extravagantly budgeted at $1,759,500 and comfortably scheduled for seventy-two camera days, *Ivy* moved smoothly through the production process, even as Fontaine struggled with Wood's technique as a director. "Wood had . . . Menzies draw every set-up," said Charles Bennett. "There was nothing for Sam Wood to do. He was an allegedly great director, but I remember Fontaine coming up to me on the set and saying, 'Charles, I don't understand what Sam wants me to do. He can't explain what he wants. He talks and I don't understand what he's saying.' That was his problem. There was nothing you could do about Sam. He was completely unverbal."

Menzies found himself in almost total control of the picture, while not having to deal with the actors in any significant way. ("Actors were on one side of the camera," said Joan Fontaine, "while the filmmakers were on the other. They seldom met.") He invested *Ivy* with a morbid elegance, suggestively ornate, while keeping the principal sets small and evocative. The approach required the thoughtful use of props—what he liked to call his "inanimate actors"—and kept two full-time set dressers busy. The most expensive interior in a film that required just fourteen interiors was the Lextons' four-room apartment, which covered roughly five hundred square feet of stage space. Menzies kept the camera in close, even for scenes that were not essentially close-ups, maintaining that close work amplified slight emotions and sustained a greater overall effect on the audience. "The audience," he said, "is so close to the action that it virtually breathes the same air as the actors."

Menzies began the picture with Ivy's visit to a fortune-teller, but then worried the film's first minutes were too soft. "You can afford a little footage at the beginning for exposition," he later said, "but, if possible, I would handle it as melodramatically as possible. A violent and dynamic shove-off is a great help. In fact, one of the things wrong with *Ivy* is that the first real right hand wallop isn't until the end of the second reel." That wallop was the revelation of Ivy's affair with Dr. Roger Gretorex, the details of their secret assignations, and Gretorex's vow never to give her up. Staged in a pavilion outside the swirl of an elegant dance, the scene gains in intensity as the guests gather to watch a spectacular fireworks display, the furious commotion in the sky paralleling the intimate commotion between Ivy and her lover just out of the crowd's earshot. Given the heat of their exchange, the details are almost of no consequence; the scene generates its own emotional energy entirely apart from the conflict between its characters.

Wanting to devote more time to his painting, Jim Vance declined the opportunity to work on *Ivy,* putting Menzies together instead with production illustrator Ted Haworth. "I knew Ted's work," said Vance, "and knew that he and Menzies would get along great." Having worked principally with art directors, Haworth started the picture with little knowledge of production design. "[Menzies] could take the most ordinary thing in a picture," marveled Haworth, "and make it so cinematically fascinating. He had a way of dividing the motion picture screen, taking big patterns and using those patterns for foreground and background. In the simplest of close-ups, you had the longest of long shots combined. Bill Menzies' philosophy was that if you were going to show a close-up, make it closer than any close-up has ever been. If you are going to make a long shot, make it a longer long shot than anyone else has ever done. Nobody could do what he did, just nobody."

Told there would be a great change in her life—a change for the better—once she breaks with this other man, Ivy determines that she must poison her husband to be free for the attentions of the wealthy—but inconveniently scrupulous—Miles Rushworth. Stressing visual irony, Menzies went for the extreme tonal contrasts he achieved on *Kings Row*, specifying pure white for most of the gowns worn by Joan Fontaine and framing her against violent patterns of light and dark. When it came time to design the opening titles, Menzies employed for the background a garden urn entwined with what was called "painted" or variegated ivy. As the lettering clears and Sam Wood's credit fades from the screen, the urn and the ivy begin to darken. About two feet into a four-foot dissolve, the urn changes into the stark image of a death's head, the ivy surrounding it having turned completely to black. The image then fades into the complementary composition of the first shot, in which Ivy, in white, approaches the shadowy house where the old woman, Mrs. Thrawn, will look into her future and see "Misfortune . . . terrible misfortune."

As happy as he was with *Ivy,* and as faithful as it was to his vision, Menzies still spoke of the "worries of production" and the demands placed upon him as both producer and production designer. "Life is so tediously violent," he rued. Required, along with the crew, to be on the set at 8:30 each morning, Menzies typically worked an eleven- or twelve-hour day, arriving home no earlier than nine at night. "He didn't always drive," his daughter Suzie remembered, "and I was picking him up one day at Universal. He disappeared for about half an hour, and he came back just bombed to the eyeballs. And I had to practically carry him across to the car. Sam Wood came along and said, 'Can I help?' and I said, very tightly, 'No . . . thank you . . .' He didn't say a word on the way home, but boy was I mad. 'How dare you do this to me, your daughter?' That sort of thing. I didn't say anything, but I was furious. It was so humiliating. Everybody on the set was looking. 'There goes Bill again.' It was terribly embarrassing."

Menzies wound up *Ivy* with a terrific shock, sending the title character plummeting down an elevator shaft as the police close in on her. Charles Bennett thought Wood a "strange director" and didn't think his work on the movie very good. "I will never forget the horrible ending to *Ivy*—where the girl falls down the thing and boom!" he said some forty years after the film's release. "I remember my son watching it one day on the telly and saying, 'Oh, that's a sudden end.' I said, 'That's not the way I wrote it.' The ending, as far as I was concerned at least, was Sir Cedric Hardwicke, as the detective, giving some sort of reasoning for what had happened. But no, not a bit of it. Boom! Desperately sudden."

*Ivy* closed on February 18, 1947, fourteen days ahead of schedule and $97,000 under budget. In many ways, it was Menzies' purest work of design since *Kings Row,* a picture in which, in the words of Richard Sylbert, there wasn't one frame you couldn't see him drawing. "We had a very good preview with *Ivy* at Pomona, which is a mixed audience—farmers and college students," Menzies reported in an April letter to Laurence Irving. "It's a good show, I think, of its type, quite morbid but with what I've always tried to do, get box office and art on the same film, because art is no good unless there is someone in there to see it."

As he oversaw the cutting, dubbing, and scoring of *Ivy,* Menzies was also on the lookout for new properties to be made under the Inter-Wood arrangement with Universal-International. A bid was reportedly made for *The Emperor's Physician,* a story of Christ's early years by Reverend J. R. Perkins, and in late January the trades carried news of Menzies' purchase of *The Marble Arch,* an unpublished mystery yarn in which he proposed to cast actress Jane Wyatt and *Ivy's* Richard Ney. Most of his time, though, was given over to *Purgatory Street,* a novel published as part of Simon and Schuster's Inner Sanctum series by the American mystery writer Roman McDougald. Menzies put Howard Emmett Rogers to work on a screenplay, the two men plumbing for graphic opportunities in the story of a combat pilot so altered by plastic surgery his own wife thinks him an imposter. Sam Wood proposed casting Robert Donat in the lead, having directed the actor in *Goodbye, Mr. Chips,* and Menzies suggested Joan Fontaine for the wife. Then in June, *Ivy* opened to mixed reviews and pallid box office, and Wood's relationship with the studio soured, just as it had with Columbia following the release of *Address Unknown.*

The picture was previewed for the trades and the general press on Friday, June 6, at the Academy theater in Beverly Hills. *"Ivy,"* wrote James Agee in *The Nation,* "is an unusually ornate melodrama about an Edwardian murderess; it stars Joan Fontaine, who pops her eyes, coarsens her jaw, and wears her elegant clothes very effectively. The real star is whoever was chiefly responsible for the dressing, setting, lighting, and shooting, and that, I infer from past performance, is the producer, William Cameron Menzies." The film got a lot of promotional breaks; *Ivy* was *Life* magazine's Movie of the Week and Menzies himself appeared on an ABC interview show called *Bride and Groom* to hype the picture. It opened at five theaters in greater Los Angeles, but was bettered by a number of recent U-I releases—*The Egg and I, The Dark Mirror, The Killers, Canyon Passage, Song of Scheherazade.* Even *Smash Up,* which was considered a weak performer, did marginally better.

Then, as if to compound Menzies' battered commercial reputation, *The Green Cockatoo* was given a limited American release in July—a full decade after its completion. The *Film Daily* rated Menzies' work on the film "mediocre" and suggested the picture "shows its age." The *Motion Picture Daily* was only moderately kinder: "Cinemagraphically below par and for the most part slowly paced, the film does have, however, some scattered moments of taut suspense, notably when [John] Mills and another underworld character engage in a knife fight in the recesses of a blitzed tenement." In New York, Jesse Zunser of *Cue* dismissed it in just three sentences: "For those who needed it, the Rialto's *Green Cockatoo* is additional proof that the British can make just as bad pictures as anyone else. This third-rate gangster melodrama . . . was filmed six years ago [*sic*] and forgotten until this week. Let's just imagine it never happened."

As the anemic returns for *Ivy* became evident, Menzies' name disappeared from column items concerning *Purgatory Street*. The film's September 1 starting date got set back to December due to "casting difficulties." In early September, Charles Bennett was reported as working on the script, but then Sam Wood told Hedda Hopper he was looking for an unknown for the lead, and interest in the project fell off precipitously.

Nineteen forty-seven, which had started out so hopefully, became a year in which Menzies' drinking began to impact his ability to earn a living. Sam Goldwyn refused to hire him again after the debacle of *The North Star*, and now he had likely damaged his relationship with Sam Wood, who neither smoked nor drank. ("Daddy did some wild things," his daughter Suzie admitted. "He drove home one night from a bar with somebody's car hooked to the back bumper.") In 1942, Menzies' daughter Jean had married Lowell Lauesen, a music major at UCLA, and in December 1944, while Lowell, a navy technician, was stationed in San Diego, she presented her father with a grandchild, Pamela Mignon. Now, in June, a grandson, Barry Cameron, was added to the family. Menzies turned fifty-one on July 29, and seventeen days later, on August 15, 1947, he took the pledge, giving up booze for the sake of his home life as well as his career. Wrote Mignon, "When he finally went on the wagon . . . he became a soapbox orator on 'the evils of liquor' and wondered why he hadn't come to his senses sooner—and how I wish he had."

Soon, Sam Wood was making more news in politics than in pictures, having founded the anticommunist Motion Picture Alliance for the Preservation of American Ideals in 1944. "If my father had never met William Randolph Hearst," mused Jeane Wood, "I think he might have been a good Democrat." Both Jeane and her sister, Gloria, were loyal Democrats, a fact that eventually drove a wedge between them and their father. "They adored the man," said actor Jack Harris, a close family friend, "but detested his politics. He accused them of being communists, and that made matters worse." In October, as *Purgatory Street* was foundering, Wood traveled east to appear before the House Un-American Activities Committee to testify on communist efforts to gain control of the Screen Directors Guild. "I definitely feel these people should be labeled as agents of a foreign country," he testified. "If you drop their rompers, you'll find the hammer and sickle on their rear end."

According to Suzie, Menzies cringed at Wood's stridency and his growing intolerance of other viewpoints: "The only thing Sam Wood ever said to me was 'Where's Bill?' Daddy bitched about him a lot—I think about politics. Daddy was a little to the left, but he certainly wasn't a communist. . . . He didn't agree with Sam's politics, and I think Sam had sense enough not to talk it up too much in front of Daddy. He didn't want to lose him. Besides, Daddy was the most un-political person I ever knew in my life. I don't think he even voted. He threatened to vote for Henry Wallace if we voted for Dewey, but I don't think he actually voted for anyone." On December 2, Sam Wood announced that he had called off *Purgatory Street* and would instead be dusting off *The Land Is Bright* as his next picture. Eleven days later, he closed down Inter-Wood, indicating it would "cease to function in its association with Universal-International." He did, however, retain the rights to *Purgatory Street* and *Jubal Troop,* and said that he would seek to line up with another studio as a producer-director. "There has been talk that independent activities might abate under economic pressure," Edwin Schallert commented in the *Los Angeles Times,* "and this is one of the first tangible evidences affecting an important film maker." It is said that an amicable ending of their association was reached between William Goetz of U.I. and Wood. "Casting problems," he added, "are many for the independents."

# 18

# Making a Living

When Inter-Wood ceased operations, Sam Wood returned to the relative security of Metro-Goldwyn-Mayer. Menzies, having established his credentials as a producer on an expensive flop, wasn't nearly so fortunate. In January 1948, he entered into an agreement with Walter Wanger to write and produce a film of Rosamond Lehmann's 1945 novel *The Ballad and the Source*. Being a young girl's understanding of an old woman's sometimes scandalous life, it was a story almost impossible to adapt to the screen. Menzies accepted the assignment on spec while Wanger tried setting it up as part of a two-picture deal—first with Selznick, then with Metro (where Menzies was dispatched one day to explain the adaptation to his old directorial colleague, story editor Kenneth MacKenna). Delivered late March, Menzies' screen treatment detailed shots and values as much as dialogue and action, making the document a difficult read.

Around this same time, Menzies formed a partnership with producer Ben Finney, an adventurer and gadabout whose interest in James H. Street's Civil War–era novel *Tap Roots* had resulted in Wanger's feature production of the same title. Blessed with money he inherited from his father, a popular vice chancellor at the University of the South, Finney could afford to bankroll a pair of short films made expressly for the relatively new medium of television. It was Menzies' notion to shoot compact thrillers based on the public domain stories of such famous authors as Wilkie Collins and Edgar Allan Poe. Designing these for the tiny, low-resolution screens of the day would mean telling such stories in close shots and stark patterns of light and shadow, keeping costs low while delivering the spit and polish of feature productions.

Bill and Mignon Menzies, circa 1945
(MENZIES FAMILY COLLECTION)

Their first effort, Poe's "The Tell-Tale Heart," dispensed with twenty-one pages of dialogue in just fifty-five sketches. Opening on actor Richard Hart's sweating face, his breathing labored, the camera pulled back to reveal the "I" of Poe's story as a patient in an insane asylum, explaining in voice-over how he, as the guest of an old man, became obsessed with his host's "evil eye." Eschewing synchronous sound in favor of narration, Menzies finished the picture in the space of one very long day. Its total cost, he later told *Look* magazine, was somewhere south of $9,000. "In those early days of producing films strictly for television," Finney commented, "no one seemed to be certain of the preferred length, fifteen minutes or thirty minutes . . . . It fit in a fifteen-minute time slot and, as it would have been difficult to pad Poe, we let it go at that."

The next Menzies-Finney production, similarly timed, was an adaptation of Collins' "A Terribly Strange Bed." For this one, the producers retained the services of actors Richard Greene and Roman Bohnen, with Greene speaking the narration. Both subjects completed, Menzies and Finney staged a showing on the night of May 7, 1948, at the Hal Roach Studios, where both films had been shot. Menzies

explained to the assembled group of press and TV executives that each subject had
been filmed in a day, and that picture contrast had been considerably boosted by
the use of black, white, and gray costuming exclusively. "For grisly, terrifying effect,
the closeups of agonized faces and devices of destruction will curdle the corpuscles
of viewers," the man from *Variety* concluded, "but the kiddies will have to leave the
room lest they want to grapple with nightmares. It's definitely not family fare for the
hour before retiring." The effect was somewhat muted, the review went on to note,
because the films were projected onto a big screen and not shown on a closed-circuit
arrangement that would more closely have approximated their impact on a home
screen.

One thing that came from the gathering was an affiliation with Charles Longenecker, a talent agent whose company Telepak agreed to distribute the films.
"Unfortunately," said Finney, "we found out too late that thirty-minute films were
being demanded." In association with Telepak, Menzies directed a third film for TV,
an original twenty-one-minute picture titled *The Marionette Mystery*. In contrast to
the earlier productions, *The Marionette Mystery* was rendered in dialogue rather than
narration and featured a solid cast of actors known for their work on radio and in
feature pictures—John Hoyt, Regis Toomey, Lois Moran, Gale Gordon, and Gloria
Holden. Soon, Longenecker and his partners were making plans to market the films,
establishing Telepak offices in Chicago and New York.


When it became apparent that Menzies' 124-page treatment of *The Ballad and the
Source* wasn't going to fly—Bill Dozier, writing on behalf of both himself and Joan
Fontaine, felt the treatment "only adds to the confusion of the original novel rather
than simplifies it"—Menzies began casting about for another picture. Wanger was
still smarting from the colossal failure of *Joan of Arc*, his $4.6 million partnership
with Ingrid Bergman and Victor Fleming, and badly in need of the revenue only a
hit movie could bring. By any measure, *The Ballad and the Source* would be costly,
Wanger having paid $250,000 for the rights alone. According to Norman Lloyd, it
was Menzies' idea to create an inexpensive movie around the standing sets on the
Universal-International lot that had been built for the Bergman spectacle. Exteriors
of fifteenth-century France, he reasoned, could easily be adapted to a story of the
French Revolution. By early April, Wanger had such a property in hand—an original story by Robert F. Kent and Alfred Neumann titled *The Bastille*.

Wanger settled the project with Eagle-Lion, a production entity formed by rail
magnate Robert Young and attorney Arthur Krim, the future head of United Artists. Menzies signed onto the picture for a fee of $10,000 and a separate card as pro-

A continuity board for *A Terribly Strange Bed* (1949). Designed for television, the story was told primarily in close shots, the compositions made up of faces rather than forms. The few long shots were simple and evocative, with deep blacks and stark contrasts. (MENZIES FAMILY COLLECTION)

ducer; Anthony Mann was similarly set as the film's director. As arrangements were being finalized, the script by Aeneas MacKenzie was being revised and sharpened by screenwriter Philip Yordan, who had previously done some uncredited work on *Tap Roots*.

"I read the script," Yordan recalled.

It was nothing but speeches, Robespierre and all this, and I said, "Tony, this is such shit, it doesn't make any sense. You have a good cast, but you can't follow the script unless you're a student of the French Revolution." He says, "Look, what can you do with it so I can shoot it?" I said, "You've got Bob Cummings. You've got Richard Basehart, a fine actor. I'll tell you what, let's make it very simple. Let's set it in the French Revolution, but what happens is there's a black book that's got all the names [of the enemies of the Revolution] in it and if Robespierre gets hold of that book, all of these people are going to go to the guillotine. Bob Cummings is the good guy. He's got to find that book before Robespierre. So the whole picture is about the black book. In the meantime you've [still] got the French Revolution and all the characters making their speeches, all of that."

As with *Ivy*, Menzies was the titular producer, but in reality he was the production designer, working, for a change, with a director who had what Yordan called a "camera" eye. ("He saw things. He understood the camera.") Menzies' job, in collaboration with Mann, cinematographer John Alton, and art director Edward Ilou, would be to squeeze all the production values possible from a picture budgeted at roughly an eighth of what *Ivy* had cost. His strategy would be simple: use the standing sets to give the picture size, then film the interiors on partial sets where imaginative staging and sharp lighting effects could disguise a general lack of period detail.

"They didn't have all the money in the world that Metro had for sets and so on," said Arlene Dahl, the film's leading lady, "but they had Cameron Menzies, who could take two walls and make it look like a great ballroom by hanging a chandelier just right, and John by getting the camera angle just right, they could make twelve people look like millions of people. And also because of the design of the sets, they could make it look really lavish because of the camera angles and the way the set had been designed. I mean, it really looked like a much bigger picture than it was."

Filming began on August 23, 1948, Menzies, Mann, and Alton having worked the entire movie out in advance. Menzies, in particular, enjoyed the process and took to quoting his forty-two-year-old director on the subject of camera placement. Mann, he said, agreed that "no weird or contrived angles may be used without sufficient motivation." Said Mann: "There is only one right setup." The Revolution as served forth in *Reign of Terror* was obsessively dark, claustrophobic, off-kilter as in a madman's dream, the blade of the guillotine ever looming. "I loved the photography in *Reign of Terror*," said Reggie Callow, Mann's assistant director. "It was perfect for that type of picture—stark black-and-white—strong shadows."

The shadows, of course, enabled the filmmakers to build only exactly what was needed to put the shot across. "If an art director was to design a front door of a church," Ted Haworth explained,

they would go to great lengths to make the tallest door you ever saw or do some trick to make it look outstanding, and then hope the cameraman or the director would say, "We love that setup; that's exactly the shot we want." Menzies would do a door that was three inches thick, had a piece of iron on it, and maybe a key sticking out of it, but the door would only be ten feet high because you would want the camera to be reasonably close to the actor coming out of the door. Then to insinuate this was a church, he'd have a

The arrival of Citizen Duval in *Reign of Terror* (1949). Interiors were designed to be played on partial, minimalist sets where flame and shadow could be used to create visual interest. (MENZIES FAMILY COLLECTION)

little platform of stone steps, all of this tailored to the camera, not forty or a hundred feet back, which you would have to jump cut to get into. As the door creaked open, pigeons would fly out. You thought you saw a door a hundred feet high, but you didn't. . . . Bill literally would trim the shot to exactly what he wanted to show and spend the money on.

Menzies' ingenuity wasn't just limited to the shrewd design of sets. "It was only through William Cameron Menzies' ability that we were able to achieve any style, feeling, or period," Anthony Mann acknowledged in a late interview.

For instance, we were faced with the problem of re-creating the Commune, which was supposed to be packed with thousands and thousands of people. And the money we had could only get us 100 people for one day. So Menzies devised a scheme whereby for that day we put all these people on a platform like a football or baseball field, but straight up so it would be square.

And we sat 100 people crowded into this small space, put the camera so they would just fill the frame, and John Alton lit it with some shafts of light at different angles. . . . I shot all the reactions to all the speeches of Robespierre and Danton and so forth. Then we took it and multiplied it twenty times, projecting it on a rear-projecting machine so that we no longer had 100 people, we had 2000. All we had in the foreground was a big, big door with guards standing on duty. As this door opened, Robespierre walked in and the people rose, the 2000 people against this background. And then for all the speeches we just went into a big close-up of Robespierre against this background of people who were screaming and yelling. We were able to achieve this tremendous effect with only 100 people. And this was conceived completely by Cameron Menzies.

With 60 percent of its budget covered by a loan from Bank of America, *Reign of Terror* was completed at a negative cost of $220,000. Wanger pronounced himself "extremely pleased" with the production. "I think it looks very, very good," he assured Menzies. "I think that with careful editing and working out the opening properly we've got a chance for a very effective picture." Wanger talked of working out a deal in New York for *The Ballad and the Source* and proposed involving Menzies in a group of European productions he was contemplating. Nothing was terribly firm though, and as work on *Reign of Terror* wound down, Menzies began teaching a course on film design at USC.

The year 1949 would be a lean one. *The Tell-Tale Heart* was placed into competition for one of the first Emmy Awards and subsequently shown on the ABC series *Actors Studio.* Emboldened, Telepak tried offering a series of thirteen episodes based on James Fenimore Cooper's Leatherstocking tales. Longenecker and partner Merrill Pye made the rounds of the big New York agencies, pointing out that major directors like Raoul Walsh, Frank Capra, and King Vidor were contemplating video projects and that TV sets were selling at the rate of 1,200 units a week. Carrying the title *Yankee Spy,* the Leatherstocking series would be produced and directed by Menzies and sell for approximately $9,000 an episode. Another series, fulfilling the promise of the Poe and Collins films, was also priced at $9,000 an episode. A third series, for which *The Marionette Mystery* would serve as the pilot, was called *Your Witness* and priced out at $10,500 a week. Pye confirmed good interest, but costs were still too high for an industry very much in its infancy.

Menzies taught, took part in forums and roundtables, and told Hal Humphrey

Spectacle on a shoestring: Menzies' depiction of the Commune in *Reign of Terror* relied on the clever use of process work. The edges of the screen in this shot are concealed by a huge doorway in the foreground. In all, Menzies used no more than twenty people to augment the rear projection and complete the sequence. (AUTHOR'S COLLECTION)

of the Los Angeles *Mirror News* he didn't think filmed programs would be seen in large numbers on television until producers had exhausted all the possibilities in live shows. "Most TV viewers are not interested now in the scope which films offer because the gadget or novelty value of video more than makes up for this lack of flexibility in the live shows. When sponsor competition gets keener and producers have exhausted most of the live show possibilities, then the film industry will come into its own in TV." Costs, Menzies suggested, would be going up rather than down, and a good half hour filmed subject would soon run $15,000 to $20,000. ("Under that, it's not worth it for the producer and others involved.") The "finale" to TV, he concluded, would be "the nickel in the slot"—pay television, either in the form of a coin mechanism or as an added item on the phone bill.

*Reign of Terror* was released over the summer of 1949, garnering good reviews and

The opening moments of *Ivy* (1947)
in which the title character consults a fortune teller . . .

Ivy Lexton's white dress starkly contrasts with turn-of-the-century London and the black garb of Mrs. Thrawn, whose dark prognostications set the story in motion. (MENZIES FAMILY COLLECTION)

paying for itself while never really becoming the lucrative hit its makers expected. In June, NBC's *Fireside Theatre* broadcast *A Terribly Strange Bed* in tandem with Strindberg's *The Stronger*, the latter drawing greater attention due to the participation of its star, actress Geraldine Fitzgerald. Then September brought the sudden death of Sam Wood, who suffered a heart attack at the Beverly Drive offices of the Motion Picture Alliance. Though he hadn't seen much of Wood since the dissolution of Inter-Wood, Menzies served as an active pallbearer at his funeral, as did Louis B. Mayer, Clark Gable, Dore Schary, and agent Bert Allenberg. Wood's will, the details of which were made public the same week, required an affidavit of any beneficiary affirming that "such beneficiary is not a member of the Communist party or any other Communist organization, or any organization which has been determined by the United States government to be subversive or connected with any Communist organization." In the will, Wood left his mistress a bequest of $25,000. Said his widow: "I have lost my Rock of Gibraltar."

It continued to be slow into 1950, and Menzies channeled most of his energies into the weekly class he was teaching on the USC campus. Titled "The General Technique of Pictures," it was a survey of the working tools of the production designer and—as Menzies put it—the "smart" director.

"We had a number of Indian students at the time," recalled photographer and USC alum Robert Willoughby, "and I felt they must have gone back to India [having] learned a lot [from] being there. Menzies created imagery for all of us, and we applied it in different ways. He would say, 'You see a car in an empty field, and one of the car doors is open. And you feel something's wrong.' He was showing us how he translated his ideas for directors, how he visualized. He could tell any story through his imagery by putting things in or eliminating them. . . . He told us how two images can combine to create a different image. A gestalt. And I've used that my entire career. You can take a regular-looking girl, followed by a man looking in horror, and it creates something different in your mind."

Through his lectures, Menzies put forth a number of convictions. As recorded by one of his students, they included admonishments and truisms culled from some thirty years in the movie business:

- A designer usually falls back on scale, distortion, or color contrast.
- A violated perspective gives a forceful, angular effect.
- A reverse angle can snap the audience out of a certain mood created by the original angle being used.

The French countryside as rendered by Menzies for *Reign of Terror.* Exteriors such as these gave the film size. (MENZIES FAMILY COLLECTION)

- Dramatic repetition *is* effective.
- Economy can sometimes make a picture look too arty—beware of trying too hard or you'll achieve a false result.
- If you can alibi anything to yourself it's all right to use it; you are not being too arty.
- Simplicity and restraint are key words to remember in designing a set, for the audience must grasp the whole scene and meaning at a glance.
- You must pre-plan, pre-plan, and pre-plan still more; you must prepare, *in advance,* good composition.
- Production design is, in reality, directorial mechanics.

"Menzies was a great raconteur," said Willoughby. "He knew exactly what he was doing. He not only charmed us, but he told us about *Kings Row* where he put the camera up against the houses or against the people. His visual imagery was unequaled. . . . I remember we got a 16mm print of *Kings Row,* and we could see exactly what he had created in the imagery just by the placement of the camera."

Menzies chats with students at the USC School of Cinema, circa 1951.
(ACADEMY OF MOTION PICTURE ARTS AND SCIENCES)

.   .   .

Menzies was chairing one of the Academy's nomination committees when he was sought out by screenwriter Stanley Rubin, whose production of Guy de Maupassant's *The Necklace* had beat out *The Tell-Tale Heart* for an Emmy. A newly minted producer at RKO, Rubin had a screenplay for Menzies to direct, convinced the veteran designer had the best chance of pulling off a stylish production on what was essentially a two-week schedule. Said Rubin, "I was a great admirer of Mr. Menzies—I thought he was the best production designer in the business—and I felt that this was a picture that needed design to create the mood I wanted. . . . I was thrilled to have him on the picture."

The story was *The Man He Found,* a standard-issue suspense thriller in which the payoff was the discovery of a secret encampment in rural Wisconsin where a clutch of Nazis are hiding the fire-deformed madman known to the world as Adolf Hitler. It was hardly material that demanded subtlety, yet Menzies gave it every compositional advantage, illustrating some five hundred setups prior to the start of production. (Two-hundred setups would have been average for such a picture.) As he sketched, Menzies allowed for technical tricks that would enable him to complete at least thirty setups a day. "He enjoyed this picture because it was experimental,"

Richard Kritzer, one of his students, noted, "because it was done with the prevailing thought that 'television is here, let's watch the budget.'"

As much as 80 percent of *The Man He Found* would be staged in close-ups. Loosely grouped four-shots could be made into tight two-shots on the optical printer, saving precious time at a cost of just $6 per shot. (It was, Menzies pointed out, even cheaper than a chemical dissolve.) Stereopticons would be used instead of process plates, saving time because the camera and the projector didn't have to be synchronized. (This would also enable Menzies to shoot low angles, something he couldn't do were the images moving.) Though much of the script consisted of exterior sequences, only about 4 percent of the film would actually be shot out of doors. He would hold the set budget to $9,000, Menzies explained, by building "only what the camera will *actually* photograph, and this can be seen, in advance, by the sketch of your setup—your production design."

Since it was Rubin's conviction the two leads should be "unfamiliar faces" to movie audiences, the part of magazine writer Matt Corbin was awarded to actor-comedian Elliott Reid. In the female lead would be RKO contract player Carla Balenda (the former Sally Bliss), one of the actresses brought forth by Howard Hughes since his 1948 acquisition of the studio. Neither had done much work in pictures, Reid being principally a radio and stage actor. "I was a movie fan from when I was eight years old," he said, "and I knew the name of William Cameron Menzies when I was a child. I didn't know what he did, but I had seen his name on-screen. Over the course of the movie, we would have these lunches, and they were very, very convivial.

> We did a lot of outdoor stuff up at Lake Tahoe, and they'd set up these picnic lunches. Menzies was a charming, charming man and a good raconteur, and had lived, needless to say, a very, very full life long before most of us were even up and about and working. He had quite a lot of stories about Fairbanks. The picture you got, I must say, was not the most flattering. Apparently, Fairbanks had a rather childish sense of humor, a rather primitive sense of humor. He described one episode: It was late in the afternoon; they had done their work for the day. Menzies wanted to get up on one of those square things that are on wheels. They're very big, with a small platform from which you could address a crowd, maybe ten feet high. Somehow, Menzies ended up standing on this thing, maybe to get a bird's-eye view of some set that was on the studio floor, to check something out. And Fairbanks was down there with two or three other guys. So they were talking, and at some point someone said, "Well, okay, I guess that takes care of

that. We'll just start up again tomorrow." And as they were working their way out the door of the studio, Fairbanks, or someone working for him, pulled the switch that turned all the lights off, leaving Menzies in pitch black up on that platform. That was Fairbanks; he was prankish. Menzies also said that he had quite an eye for young girls. He'd go to Japan—he liked Japan—and he liked the young, *quite young,* girls over there. And while in Japan, he had a kimono made with a ghastly word written on the back of it—I guess the filthiest that is in the Japanese language—and gave it to Menzies as a gift. Of course, with all the Japanese in Los Angeles, there were people falling back in horror at the sight of this thing, and Menzies hadn't the faintest idea as he was walking around in it.

Menzies, Stanley Rubin discovered, was only able to relate to the actors as graphic elements, and his tight compositions left them feeling boxed in. "Very late in the shooting of the picture," Rubin said, "I began to become aware that what I was getting was more design than performance. I brought this up to Menzies, and he didn't disagree with me. I think he was just trapped in his own talent. I never felt he was at ease with the actors, but I didn't know how to say that to him. What I did say to him was: 'Don't be locked in by your own design.' And, of course, he *was* locked in by his own design."*

Elliott Reid grew quite fond of his director and marveled at his attention to detail. "Menzies was meticulous that everything looked right. Up at Lake Tahoe, I remember he said, 'Those tules are too heavily banked over there.' He had—obviously—a terrific eye for how things looked." Between scenes, Menzies would rail against the regimentation of the lawns in Beverly Hills ("It's such a bore! Such a bore!") and express regret that he had married so early. "If I had my time over again," he declared, "I'd be single as a bugger." His use of the word was visibly shocking, as Reid was of British parentage. Hastily, Menzies added: "But, I have to say that Mignon has been so wonderful. She has come and gotten me and taken me

---

* Menzies' problem, Lewis Milestone suggested, was common to all art directors who thought they wanted to direct. "They wanted a beautifully-composed picture," he told Kevin Brownlow. "They're not interested in movement or tempo, just a beautiful picture. Well, that's only good for the first scene. Pretty soon an actor's got to move someplace, and there goes the composition, you see, and I tried to sell him that idea. And sometimes he was buying it and sometimes not. I got a lot from him, and, I daresay, he got a lot from me, but he didn't use it because he was still sold on beautifully-composed pictures. And Bill's trouble when he went to direct, you see, he hated actors. He used to say, 'You build a magnificent set, then you get these Hamlets in and they ruin it for you.' Immediately they come in, there goes the set. Well, that's true of any room, you know. You have a beautiful room, and you give a party. As soon as the guests arrive you no longer see the room—and he could never swallow that."

Elliott Reid and Carla Balenda in *The Whip Hand* (1951)
(AUTHOR'S COLLECTION)

home." Said Reid, "He implied that he had been in the gutter, and that he owed his sobriety to her. He wanted to give her full credit for being such a great wife to him. Perhaps it was just a mood he was in."

*The Man He Found* finished on schedule and cost, as Menzies remembered it, about 20 percent less than *Reign of Terror*. Everyone seemed happy with the picture, a tight and moody suspense drama that likely would have soared with bigger names in the leads. It looked destined for a fall release when Howard Hughes viewed it one night and dictated a reaction. "I got a memo from Mr. Hughes," recounted Stanley Rubin.

He objected to the fact that the heavies—the villains—were Nazis who had stolen into the United States and were hiding—including Hitler. He said the Nazis were no longer in the news, Hitler was no longer in the news. He wanted the last five or six minutes of the film, where you reveal the heavies, changed so that the heavies were revealed to be communists. Well, I was appalled. I was appalled, first of all, because the story was of a piece. You had to reshoot a couple of scenes in the middle of the picture where you saw the heavies at work, as I recall, and what that entailed I hated. But mainly I hated making the heavies communists, because this was the beginning of the anticommunist hysteria and I didn't like contributing to that hysteria by making this film reveal its heavies as so-called communists.

So I said I would not make those changes. And that I would prefer to be removed from the picture and to have my name as writer and producer removed from the picture—if Mr. Hughes wanted to go ahead with that change. Mr. Hughes, it turned out, did want to go ahead with that change, and so I bowed out and, as I recall, Lewis Rachmil took the thing over. Frank Moss was brought in to write the changes that Hughes was intent upon doing. During the war Frank and I were in the Motion Picture unit of the Army Air Corps. The irony is that this is the only film that I've done in all the years which would have paid residuals to me, because I was the writer on it, and instead Moss got the residuals.

Ten days of added scenes were made in November 1950, with editor Stuart Gilmore directing. "I was presented with this script," said Elliott Reid, "and it was just nauseating.

The problem was they couldn't get rid of all these Aryan super-blond Hitler-type young gods, who were like the storm troopers in this town. Some of them even wore black, and you couldn't erase them off the negative, so apparently all the communists were these Wagneresque Aryan, blond young men. Well, it was such a disaster, not to be believed. The early part of the picture is the same, and then, really, I didn't have to do that much different. It was really the denouement where I'm in the canoe with the girl and we paddle closer and closer to this little strange island that's in the middle of this lake. There's a Swiss chalet kind of building on it, and, originally, Bobby Watson came tearing out with half his face burned—all the rubber makeup pasted on him—and he was screaming and yelling, having gone mad. He had gotten out of the bunker and escaped to Wisconsin, of all places, and was living with the few henchmen still faithful to him. Then they inserted this other thing. It's still the same shot when we were supposedly looking at Hitler, and then they cut to this dance of death of these terrible, broken people that the communist hierarchy has decided must be put into a reeducation camp and subjected to surgery. And some of them are hobbling around on crutches. It's the most ghastly, pathetic, stupid thing you ever saw in your life.

Hughes would continue to tinker with the picture until its approval under the Production Code in June 1951. "When we saw what happened to the film," said Carla

Balenda, "we couldn't believe it. It no longer made any sense." Under the title *The Whip Hand,* it was nevertheless a minor sensation when trade-shown at the studio in October. "RKO's *The Whip Hand* emerges as a near masterpiece in suspense," raved *Daily Variety.* "Fascinating in theme, expertly produced and beautifully enacted by a cast of comparative unknowns, film is perhaps the best modestly-produced melodrama of the season. . . . For William Cameron Menzies, who designed the production and directed, pic is a work of art."

Menzies picked up another picture to direct in September 1950, but where *The Man He Found* offered a chance to experiment with new filming economies, *Drums in the Deep South* was simply a bargain-basement *Gone With the Wind* that couldn't overcome the limitations of a minuscule budget. The producers were the King (*née* Kozinsky) Brothers, former slot machine and pinball moguls known for the "cheapies" they ground out for Monogram. "They have a way of surrounding themselves with good people," Philip Yordan observed in 1948, "and it makes working pleasant.

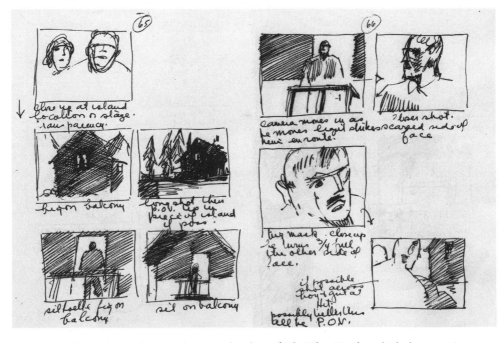

Menzies' thumbnails showing the original ending of *The Whip Hand* in which the mysterious figure on the island is revealed to be Adolf Hitler. (MENZIES FAMILY COLLECTION)

They worship a guy with a name, no matter whether he's a success or a has-been. They have a lot of guys like this on their payroll, guys who hit the skids, and who couldn't get jobs any other place now."

By the Kings' collective reckoning, *Drums in the Deep South* would be a class attraction, their first under a scheme to finance their movies through the public sale of stock. Authorized by the California Division of Corporations to issue a million $1-par shares within the state, they sold $300,000 worth to capitalize the new company and cover the negative cost of the picture, drawing more than seven hundred investors. Menzies signed onto the project for a fee of $5,000 and 2.5 percent of the net profits—never had there been a King film that wasn't profitable—and actor James Craig was borrowed from M-G-M to play the lead. The Kings even sprang for Super Cinecolor, a three-color enhancement of the original two-color bipack process often favored by second-string independents. Yet the whole thing had to be shot on a three-week schedule. "*Drums in the Deep South* was such a piece of junk," Yordan said decades later. "I hadn't known Menzies had sunk that low. He didn't have the right contacts; that happened to a lot of people in that period."

Menzies did the best he could to give the film scope, but unlike *Reign of Terror,* which had the incalculable advantage of the *Joan of Arc* exteriors, there were no standing sets on the Goldwyn lot that could lend production values to a plantation story of the Confederate South. Former actor Arthur Gardner functioned as assistant to the producers, principally Frank King, the slow-moving middle brother. "Frank King was the brains of the whole company," Gardner said. "Without Frank, these other guys couldn't have moved. The youngest one didn't do anything at all; he just showed up in the morning. The oldest one contributed something, but it was Frank who ran the company. And he was a smart, bright guy. Big, heavyset man. I think he weighed 270 pounds. And he learned fast. He had great artistic sense, good story values, and so on. Frank and I worked with the writers on every film."

There was money for a brief trip to Sonora, where second unit footage incorporating one of the Sierra Railroad's antique steam engines was shot by another *GWTW* veteran, B. Reeves "Breezy" Eason. Closer to home, scenes set in a mountain cavern were made in Franklin Canyon. "Bill was in command of the entire picture—the sketches, choosing the locations, directing the actors, and so on," Gardner said. "I think [art director] Frank Sylos was employed, probably, because the union called for it." Production wrapped in mid-November, but it wasn't until May 1951 that Frank King made a deal with RKO to distribute the picture. When, upon its release, the film started to make money, King tried chiseling Menzies' participation in the net profits. An outraged Harold Rose, Menzies' agent of fourteen years, returned the papers unsigned.

"Working for the King Brothers was just a sketch," said Suzanne Menzies. "They had this retinue, and they'd go for a meeting, and there was always this one mysterious guy who'd sit over by the door with his back to a wall, watching everybody come in. Daddy thought they were kind of interesting."


Early in 1951, Menzies was used briefly by David Selznick for "retakes, added scenes, etc." on *Gone to Earth,* a co-production with Alexander Korda for which Selznick controlled all rights in the Western Hemisphere. It was thankless work, good only for the money it brought in at a time when work was scarce. Menzies filled the lean months at home by painting intricate patterns on the walls of the upstairs hallway, incorporating a window seat and four bedroom doors in a colorful mashup of folk designs, a quiltlike transformation of what had previously been a plain vaulted space. "Swedish, Swiss, Hungarian—they were mixed together as in a pattern book," said his daughter Suzie. He traveled to England with producer Sid Rogell, proposing to film Jules Verne's *20,000 Leagues Under the Sea* for J. Arthur Rank in Technicolor. Upon his return, Gabriel Pascal wanted him to design the long-delayed *Androcles and the Lion.* Pascal, the Hungarian-born producer-director who held the film rights to the plays of George Bernard Shaw, had been trying for years to get *Androcles* made, but funding for the project had proven elusive in the wake of the colossal failure of his *Caesar and Cleopatra,* which supplanted *Things to Come* as the most expensive British film ever made.

Casting the title role was a challenge because Howard Hughes had to approve the choice. Both Pascal and the late G.B.S. himself wanted Charlie Chaplin, who by 1950 had become a political liability. Jose Ferrer flirted with the part, which would have required him to leave a Broadway revival of *Twentieth Century.* Eddie Bracken was tested, as was Harpo Marx. "The test he made was fabulous," Valerie Pascal, the producer's wife, said of Harpo, "but the studio said no." Five weeks into the process, film and TV comedian Alan Young was confirmed for Androcles, but Young, it was said, would be unavailable until the middle of May. In June, Menzies was brought aboard to replace Harry Horner, who was going off to direct his first film. In time, the original director, H. C. Potter, left to do a play, and Chester Erskine, having just completed *A Girl in Every Port* for the studio, was tapped as his replacement. Being a writer as well as a director, Erskine insisted on rewriting Noel Langley's adaptation, a move Pascal opposed because Langley's version had gained the blessing of Shaw.

"Gabriel couldn't get the man he wanted as director," wrote Valerie Pascal, "and the studio insisted on Chester Erskine, who had worked on the screenplay with Ken Englund. 'Shaw would have thrown this in the ashcan,' Gabriel said after reading the first scenes of their effort. He tried to work things out with the scenario writers, but time was limited and he had either to call off the film or start shooting. When the cameras began to roll, it became obvious that he and the director did not see eye-to-eye. To overcome the rumors that 'nobody can work with Pascal' Gabriel tried not to blow up, but he came home every day more and more disgusted. 'I should get rid of my director or quit,' he would say. 'He has the typical Hollywood conception of the thing and I should not compromise.'"

Alan Young remembered *Androcles* as a confused affair because Hughes envisioned something along the lines of *Quo Vadis*, a Technicolor spectacle being filmed in Rome by Metro-Goldwyn-Mayer. It became Menzies' job to impose size on an otherwise intimate satire. "He took me around," said Young, "to show me one little gimmick he had. He had painted people in the arena and then added little bits of cloth so when the wind blew there'd be little bits of movement.* I thought that was ingenious."

Pascal was eruptive and difficult to understand. Erskine promptly had him banned from the set, leaving him to communicate via the hastily scribbled notes he slipped to Alan Young. Menzies, meanwhile, worked mainly with cinematographer Harry Stradling, who had photographed *The Devil and Miss Jones.* Yet Menzies would not permit himself to be credited as production designer. (According to Harold Rose, the credit meant "nothing today because every art director gets that type of credit.") Being neither producer nor director on the film, Menzies left the on-screen credit to Horner, his one-time protégé. Within a month of finishing with *Androcles,* he took on the montage sequences for the multipart 20th Century-Fox comedy *We're Not Married!* His fee was a flat $6,000 for four weeks' work, a job he finished on schedule and budget. Again, at his insistence, there was to be no credit nor publicity of any sort regarding his involvement with the film.

As 1951 drew to a close, Menzies' spirits were lifted by the prospect of quick money at Fox and the death of his mother-in-law, Nanon Toby. Suzanne Menzies, who had married former Trojan center Russell Antles the previous year, could remember driving up from Oceanside (where her husband, a Marine captain, was stationed) and being greeted by a wide grin at the door of 602 North Linden. "The old lady died!" her father cheerfully announced.

"Creeping Jesus" had expired at the age of eighty-two, but her spectral presence in the household lingered and proved more indelible than anyone suspected. Within days of her death, there were signs the house was haunted, as the same rapping

---

* Menzies, Young discovered, had included a likeness of Shaw in the crowd.

noises she made on the wall in life could sometimes be heard at night. "Her room and Grandma/Grandpa's bedroom were separated by a bathroom," Pamela Lauesen remembered. "Evidently, everybody heard it after she was gone. I don't remember hearing it, and surely no one in the house would have pointed it out to the children at the time. We would have freaked. Anyway, Grandma called the rat people, the plumber, etc., to see if the sound was coming from any explainable source. It kept up until Grandpa died, then stopped."

With the completion of his work on *We're Not Married!*, Menzies made plans to travel to New York to direct another film for television, this one the pilot for a proposed series based on the exploits of master criminal Fu Manchu. Funding the project was Herbert Bayard Swope, Jr., an NBC production executive who hoped to land a network commitment for thirteen half hour episodes. Sir Cedric Hardwicke would star as Nayland Smith due to his great personal friendship with author Sax Rohmer. John Carradine would play Fu Manchu, and the unusually strong support-ing cast would consist of John Newland, Colin Keith-Johnston, Melville Cooper, and actress Rita Gam (the "Hedy Lamarr of TV").

"I don't know whether I like the television business or not," Menzies said in his first letter home. "It's all in such a rush, and nobody seems to care whether it's good or not as long as they get the show on. Swope is a nice guy, but they don't seem to have any regard for the quality at all. Cedric and I ganged up on them and made them rewrite the script. The author is one of those phony baloneys that talks with a prop English accent which drives Cedric crazy. I had some pretty good ideas, and we ended up with a pretty good attack."

Acting as art director on the show was Richard Sylbert, who had designed scores of live video productions and was thrilled to be working with the legendary William Cameron Menzies. "I was," Sylbert recalled, "very well trained—self-trained—because I had done, by that time, a hundred or so live television shows."

And you do your own drawings, your own details. You do your own deco-rating. You do everything yourself. Menzies had never seen anybody quite like that, even though I was just a kid. So I did all the drafting. We would talk about the scene, and he would talk about shots. He would sketch each set on a sheet of hotel stationery to show what he wanted and I would do the rest. It was a black-and-white film, so he wanted the sets to be black, white, and gray to create a strong graphic image. I would draw the setup, elevated, for what the scene was about, the style of it—Fu Manchu's den, somebody's English Georgian apartment. I would do all of that myself, and he would take these plans and set his camera around in his mind, but first he made sketches solving problems. (For instance, we never left the studio, so how would we do the exterior?) I did the decorating as well. I had my own scenic artist—I was the only person who had any crew in New York. We had no history; there was nothing to learn from anybody who knew anything. It was as barren as it must have been in Fort Lee in 1918.

Shooting was delayed until April 1952, affording Menzies extra preparatory time and the opportunity to visit his eighty-seven-year-old mother in New Haven. Rohmer's first story, "The Zayat Kiss," would also be the first episode of the new series. "We seem to be getting straightened out," he reported in a letter to Mignon on April 6, "and we expect to shoot next Monday and Tuesday. I think we finally have a pretty good script. It's corn, of course, but I think the staging and Cedric will doll it up."

Hardwicke opened on Broadway that night in Shaw's *Don Juan in Hell,* somewhat restricting the time he could devote to filming. They erected minimalist sets at the derelict old Biograph studio in the Bronx. "There were pigeons roosting in the grid," said Sylbert, "and there was a large burnt spot in the middle of the stage floor left by the many homeless who had sought comfort there over the years." Everything had to be trucked in—lights, sound equipment, sandbags. There were none of the ready conveniences one took for granted in Hollywood. "This whole trip has been a mess," Menzies said, "but I suppose if the pilot turns out all right everything will seem all right. . . . I have worked like hell with very little enjoyment out of it and haven't even gotten up to New Haven but a couple of times. They seem to understand however. I always seem to get through fiddling around with these birds at about 7:30, which is too late to do anything but go to bed. . . . The only place to make films is in California."

Much was accomplished through suggestion and the careful placement of lamps, doors, and furnishings. Menzies ran most scenes in extended takes, relying on composition rather than movement to create visual interest. Carradine was posed entirely in silhouette, his voice bridging the action. The job was completed on April 23, it having taken four long weeks to produce a single twenty-six-minute film. "I finally finished the damn thing," Menzies reported, "and it's certainly a load off my back. Good or bad, it's the longest thing I've ever tackled. Even the King thing seems like a breath of Spring compared to this one, and the lousy part of it is it may be for nothing, as I'm not at all sure whether I want to go on with it or not, even if they wanted me, which is doubtful."

Having left his USC class in the care of Ted Haworth, there was nothing much—in terms of work—for Menzies to come home to. "Daddy was just groping for anything," said his daughter Suzie. "He didn't really have an easy time. I mean, towards the end, really, he was just taking any job he could get because he had to make a living. . . . He and Mother had rough times; they had to fire Tommie, which just killed them both. It was tough. Goldwyn wouldn't hire him. Even after he had quit drinking for a long time, Goldwyn wouldn't hire 'that drunk.'"

There was talk of a picture with Clare Boothe Luce titled *Pilate's Wife* (with Nicholas Ray directing) but nothing ever came of the idea. A solid job, in fact, wouldn't emerge until late summer, when Menzies began work on a masterful exercise in childhood paranoia called *Invaders from Mars*.

# 19

# Worth Every Penny

On August 10, 1952, Bill Menzies sat down to compose a long, chatty note to Laurence Irving. He had owed his old friend a letter since early spring, when a copy of Irving's hefty biography of his grandfather, the actor Henry Irving, arrived in the mail.

> To pick up since I saw you last, the "20 Thousand Leagues Under the Sea" deal fell through, needless to say, but Disney bought it and for a time it looked as if I might do it for him. He is very changeable, however, and naturally quite opinionated, so I am not exactly banking on it, although I talked to him a few weeks ago and he said he was having a hell of a time with the scenario and would call me. I was supposed to do a ballet for Korda (the Sleeping Beauty) but I understand Alex is pretty tired both physically and financially, so I am discounting that one too.
>
> I had a long run with Gabby, helping him out on "Androcles." You have seen him in the meantime, so no doubt he has told you our troubles. . . . Personally, I think "Androcles" is a pretty lousy picture (don't quote) but they had several very successful previews. I don't know why it hasn't been released yet, but this is typical of everything about Howard Hughes.
>
> After "Androcles" I went on a junket to New York with Cedric to make a "pilot" or sample film for a series of television pictures of "Fu Manchu." Cedric and I had a wonderful time except for making the film. If you think

picture people are crummy you should meet the N.Y. television type. One thing, I did meet Sax Rohmer, who you probably know, and almost ended up owning the series as old Sax went for me in a big way. I am supposed to go back and do some more, but Cedric goes on the road with "Don Juan in Hell" until January.

In the meantime, the picture business is in a bad way with television. I noted of almost 400 pictures a year Hollywood probably won't put out more than 100. Of course, it is as much the fault of bad pictures as it is television, which is indescribably terrible, but the mob seems to go for it and it is becoming one of the big businesses in America. I am supposed to start a series with Bob Cummings in Oct, but the deadlines are so terrible and the casualty lists are frightening. I'm afraid I'm a little too old for that sort of nonsense.

As a hobby I have been trying to resuscitate the paneled room, and I have made a part mock-up and part real section of a room in my garage studio. The permanent panels are on plywood (birch) and the architect can give me the dimensions and openings and I can deliver the complete room on panels. I will send you photos when Mignon gets around to shooting it. It is principally architectural on the Piranesi side and the few architects, etc., who have seen it have been quite enthusiastic. In fact, I may do one for a small hotel in Mexico.

He went on to write about the family—Jean's kids were "growing shockingly"—and touched on the reduced circumstances of Sam Taylor, who hadn't directed a picture in nearly a decade. "Sam seems quite dilapidated but, like myself, goes un-wined. It will be five years the fifteenth of this month since I have knocked off a bumper. Now the doc tells me I have to go easy on cigarettes, fats, and sugars. This is a hell of a thing to wish on the ex-playboy of the western world."

*Invaders from Mars* had been two years in development when producer Edward L. Alperson recruited Menzies to direct it. Alperson had a distribution deal with 20th Century-Fox and was coming off his latest picture under the arrangement, a lively western titled *Rose of Cimarron*. Alperson's formula was to put inexpensive names in clever genre-based stories that could be filmed for a price, preferably in color. A onetime Omaha theater usher, Alperson wasn't a terribly creative man, but he had an exhibitor's zeal for salesmanship and appreciated the value of proven talent.

*The Invaders* (as it was originally called) told the story of a twelve-year-old boy who witnesses the landing of a spacecraft. Nobody will believe him as, one by one, the adults in his life are turned into malevolent zombies, their sole purpose to serve their alien masters. The original screenplay was the work of John Tucker Battle, whose association with Orson Welles stretched back to the days of the Mercury Theatre. Battle and his wife, Rosemary, were ardent science fiction buffs, and the notion of a child whose parents are suddenly no longer his parents came from a nightmare Rosemary had as a little girl. "The mother is the boy's security," she reasoned, "and it was taken away from him. After all, what could be more frightening than to have your own mother turn against you?"

Battle brought his original screenplay to his friend Arthur Gardner, who had formed a partnership with Jules V. Levy. As Allart Pictures, Gardner and Levy optioned the property for $500 and began developing it with the hope of lining up financing. Levy, at the time, was working as an assistant for Eddie Alperson. "Jules," said Gardner, "showed Alperson the script, and he thought it was great, he would finance it, but it needed work. For a year we worked with Alperson as he insisted on changes and more changes until our option expired. Then Alperson went behind our backs and bought the script." Sci-fi movies, major and minor, were flooding the market—*Rocketship X-M, Destination Moon, The Thing from Another World, When Worlds Collide, The Day the Earth Stood Still.* In January 1952, Alperson announced that *Invaders from Mars,* in color, had been set as his next independent production.

Battle, in time, fell away from the project, and Alperson brought in a new writer, a former journalist and sometimes scenarist named Richard Blake. It was Blake who was charged with tightening the original script and rendering it filmable on a $300,000 budget. Having worked at Republic, Blake knew where economies could be taken without compromising the basic integrity of a story. Characters were combined, scenes eliminated, and eventually a new ending was adopted, framing the whole fantastic business as a childhood nightmare. When Menzies took charge in August 1952, the picture was as if formed in the mind of a twelve-year-old.

For the early scenes of relative normalcy, Menzies drew on design conventions he established for earlier pictures, viewing, for instance, the action in young David MacLean's room through the frame of an outdoor window, suggesting an entire house while constructing only a few necessary feet of clapboard exterior, leaving the mood in the foreground implied rather than explicit. Opposite was the scene of a hilltop, a railing disappearing into its horizon, the patterns not unlike those bracketing Frank Craven's approach at the start of *Our Town.* The setting turns ominous with the descent and burrowing in of the Martian ship. "The design of the setting and lighting may become a very important element in the securing of any desired emotional effect," said Menzies, "and therefore, in many cases, authenticity is sac-

This classic composition for *Invaders from Mars* (1953) encapsulates the film's mounting tensions while neatly illustrating how Menzies directed through design. Young David MacLean's parents beckon menacingly in the foreground as David and his protector, Dr. Pat Blake, occupy the middle distance. Behind them, in the far distance, is the alternate authority figure of the desk sergeant, his surroundings a child's idea of what a police station would look like, spare and impersonal. (AUTHOR'S COLLECTION)

rificed and the architectural principles violated, all for the sake of the emotional response that is being sought."

As David learns not to trust the adults he has always relied upon, the environments of traditional authority grow larger and more threatening. A police station is stark and dreamlike, a long corridor leading to an elevated desk sergeant, the threatening figures of the boy's transformed parents dominating the foreground. Where a grown-up might imagine the details of such a setting through the texture of experience, a youngster would lack the firsthand knowledge of such a place. In David's world, a single clock adorns the wall, nothing more. A jail cell becomes a striking pattern of bars and shadows, the perspective violated as he is pressed miserably into a corner, huddled amid strong blacks and isolated from any vestige of trust and security. Diagonals dominated Menzies' compositions—the observatory telescope, the weaponry, large and small, the surgical instrument used to implant the controlling crystal at the base of a victim's brain.

"He'd made quite a few little drawings and sketches of his ideas as he was devel oping them," said veteran art director Boris Leven, "and then I came onto the picture. I knew Bill not terribly long, but we became quite friendly and I tried to carry out his ideas as much as I could." Leven's greatest challenge from the standpoint of design was in depicting the interior of the Martian spacecraft, described in the original script as a circular room approximately fifteen feet high and composed of a "shiny metallic substance" similar to polished aluminum. The look that emerged was simple and uncluttered.

*Invaders from Mars* was set to film at Republic Studios—an advantage in that Republic had one of the best visual effects departments in the industry. The famed Lydecker brothers—Howard and Theodore—were used to working on tight budgets, but Alperson was funding the picture through his own corporation and wanted everything done as inexpensively as possible. Menzies and Leven would submit ideas, the Lydeckers would cost them out, then Alperson and his production manager would kick them back. "They'd see $1,000 for a special effect," said Theodore Lydecker, "then they'd scratch it out because it was too much. Then they'd find out they needed it and try to get it as cheap as they could."

The final script revisions were dated September 17, 1952, and represented Menzies' influence in the restructuring of the third act. A key image in the film would be its solitary Martian, a figure Battle, a devoted reader of the pulps, described as "approximately thirty inches in height, dressed in a singlet that resembles soft chain mail. . . . He is extremely brontocephalic, and his tremendously large skull is completely devoid of hair. His eyes are small and deep-set and peer from their dark sockets with a strange ophidian luster." Menzies made conceptual sketches of the creature, evolving him to the point where the domed head revealed a "tiny ageless face" and the merest indication of a body. "There is the suggestion of a stomach, with the appendages trailing off into vague tentacles."

As the start of production approached, the continuity boards were finalized and Menzies prepared for what amounted to a three-week shoot. The film's fractional sets were clustered on Republic's Stage 2, a 21,000-square-foot studio space dubbed the Mabel Normand Stage for its link to the lot's original tenant, producer-director Mack Sennett. Filming was set to begin on Wednesday, September 24. Script supervisor Mary Yerke asked Menzies where his drawings were, and he told her that he thought *she* had them. They searched everywhere. "They were in the production office the night before," Yerke said, "but now they were all gone. Menzies was heartbroken. He'd planned to direct the picture using the drawings. Without them he had a difficult time."

Once production began, Menzies' mind was typically on the composition of the film, not the actors. He designed *Invaders from Mars* as if it were black-and-white, limiting his palette to the spare and deliberate use of color for dramatic effect. The barren trees and fence railings were darkened, as in *Gone With the Wind,* to a point of near-blackness. Compromised by the invading aliens, the elder MacLeans wear black while Dr. Pat Blake, the sympathetic therapist who seems to be David's only hope, is clad in the white dress of the clinician, its only splash of color coming from a bright red kerchief positioned directly over her heart. When the action moves to the underground caverns where the Martians have lodged themselves, Menzies makes strategic use of green to create an otherworldly effect, the film being virtually devoid of the color otherwise.

"He knew what he wanted," said Jimmy Hunt, the juvenile actor cast in the role of David. "I know there was a little bit of confusion because the storyboards had been stolen. Each day they were making up the storyboards again as they went along. It was the hardest film that I had ever worked on because of the fact that we did it in such a short period of time. I'm not saying that Menzies was a taskmaster, but he did make us work pretty hard."

Though he was in practically every scene, Hunt managed an understated performance in a part that would have been easy to overplay. "It was like a dream you have where you're trying to get away from someone and you can't run, or where you're trying to tell someone something and no one wants to believe you. Menzies would explain the kind of look that he would want. I had never taken any acting lessons. . . . He'd say, 'You need to be scared here. Try to tell this guy . . .' Mostly, though, he'd think in visual terms." Being just twelve years old, Hunt's presence invariably complicated the schedule. "We had to have three hours of school, and they were very strict about that. If the teacher needed ten more minutes to get something in, then they had to wait that ten minutes until she was finished. . . . They had midgets who would come in and do the stand-in stuff for us. They would light the set with them."

Menzies clearly enjoyed *Invaders from Mars*—for the design opportunities it presented and for the people who helped him make it. The cameraman was John F. Seitz, who shot his first picture in 1916 and had six Academy Award nominations to his credit. "We did that film in very nice time," Seitz remembered, "and Edward Alperson, the producer, was very pleased. We hustled to do it, and we brought it in for less money." Menzies would relax and tell stories between takes, leaving the assistant director in an awkward position, reluctant to interrupt him or push him along. He was, however, all business when setting up a shot. "I never got to know him," said actor William Phipps, "but my memory of him is that he was always lost in thought, like he was far away someplace."

"Menzies," said Mary Yerke, "was respected. Everybody kept a kind of dis-tance from him. He was very meticulous. At one point on the interior set of the [MacLeans'] house, he just fussed and fussed over one of the pictures hanging on the wall to get it just right. Nobody ever said anything to him. He just kept adjusting it, and I wondered if we were ever going to be able to finish the picture if he kept going on like this." Throughout, Menzies enjoyed the full support and confidence of Eddie Alperson, who had been a branch manager for Universal the year Fair-banks' *Thief of Bagdad* was hailed as a masterpiece.

*Invaders from Mars* would come to be regarded as a triumph of design and composition in service to the emotional thrust of the story. It worked because Men-zies shot it from the boy's perspective, incorporating strong foreground elements to underscore the peril. When the film wrapped, Menzies packed up and moved on, Alperson being uncommonly interested in the editing of his own pictures. And those who worked on the film were not quite aware just yet that they had witnessed the creation of a minor classic, a movie that would keep Menzies' name alive for generations to come. "He was very businesslike," Jimmy Hunt said in retrospect, "and he treated me more like a grown-up than as a child. As I look back now, I never knew what a genius the man was. I didn't know his history."


Menzies was four months out of work following the completion of *Invaders from Mars,* and it was apparently during that long fallow stretch that he went back to drinking, a lapse he successfully managed to conceal from his wife and family. When he did work again, it was for Sol Lesser, who was assembling a package of shorts to be shot in Stereo-Cine, a color 3-D process for which Lesser held the U.S. rights. The proposed title of the feature, to be distributed through RKO, was *Three-D Follies.*

In February 1953, Menzies briefly returned to the RKO-Pathé studios in Culver City—the former home of Selznick International—to direct "Acrobaticks," a dis-play of aerial gymnastics performed on and above a set representing the rooftops of Paris. He and his crew then decamped to Palm Springs to shoot "Fun in the Sun," a segment designed to showcase tennis star Gussie Moran, Olympic swimmer Pat McCormick, golfer Ben Hogan, and comic diver Harold "Stubby" Kruger. Predict-ably, all did not go smoothly in getting shots from the sports stars that properly exploited the stereoptic effect. ("Ben Hogan," said Menzies' daughter Suzie, "was terribly difficult.") Following the completion of six segments, Lesser killed plans to release them as a feature, reportedly when he was unable to secure the services of comedian Milton Berle as master of ceremonies.

Menzies' name was frequently in the trades as the principal director of *Three-D*

Shooting *Invaders from Mars* on the Mabel Normand Stage at Republic, Menzies, his right arm raised, is about to call action on the military assault on the Martian stronghold.  (PHOTOFEST)

*Follies,* and it may have been that association that inspired producer Walter Mirisch to hire him to direct Allied Artists' first and only venture into 3-D, *The Maze.* "I thought he would be a good choice," said Mirisch. "The background of the picture was a Scottish castle, and Bill had lived a long time in England and had a good feel for that milieu." Based on a book by the Swiss chemist and fantasist Maurice Sandoz, *The Maze* was supposed to somehow utilize the designs of Salvador Dalí, whose twelve black-and-white illustrations had accompanied the book's original edition. But by the time Menzies signed on, Dalí and his conceptions were off the table and he was left with scant time to prepare and none of the first-rate talents who had surrounded him on *Invaders.* The talky script was by Dan Ullman, whose credits were predominantly in the milieu of the cheap western. The sets, by Poverty Row veteran Dave Milton, were plain and unimaginative. Unable to influence the overall look of the film, Menzies was left to thumbnail the visual effects and make an occasional embellishment, such as to specify the silver hair and stark black outfit of the castle's butler. And, according to Mirisch, he was drinking on the picture.

Without an overall design concept, the effects tended to be gimmicks—a beach ball bouncing toward the camera . . . a letter held out . . . bats that fly at the viewer. In an early highlight, an acrobatic number incorporated the sensation of a dancer swung out at the audience by her partners. Shot in two weeks, *The Maze* would be the last feature film directed by William Cameron Menzies. "Unfortunately," said Walter Mirisch, "by the time we finished the movie, the 3-D craze had just about petered out, and the picture was not successful, either artistically or commercially."

Completion of *The Maze* coincided with the general release of *Invaders from Mars.* In Menzies' absence, the movie had been deemed too short to top a double bill and was artificially lengthened to a running time of seventy-eight minutes. Menzies' careful compositions were somewhat diminished by Alperson's liberal use of stock footage showing the army on the roll, but the overall effect was still potent, the imagery memorable. The trade notices, pointing to Menzies' obvious influence, were consistently excellent. "William Cameron Menzies designed and directed the production and certainly much of the film's success can be credited to him," the reviewer for *Daily Variety* wrote. "The settings and his conceptions of space paraphernalia are very imaginative, and his direction too is of the best, especially in the latter minutes when the action moves at a feverish pace."

In Los Angeles, *Invaders from Mars* played a quartet of regional theaters, drawing good crowds and quickly spreading to the neighborhood houses of Orange and Ventura Counties. Fox, in its initial release, reported domestic rentals of $784,000, prompting a full-scale reissue of the picture in 1955. Its true impact on the culture, however, would have to wait for its move to television where, in black-and-white, it

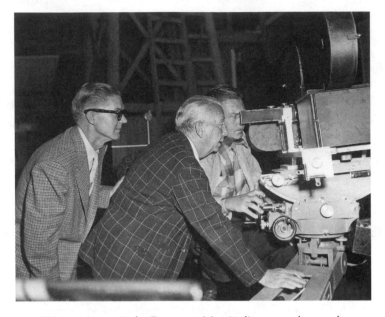

Using an improvised 3-D camera, Menzies lines up a shot on the set of *The Maze* (1953). "The boys who worked on our studio camera crew came to me one day and told me they thought they could rig a 3-D system of our own," producer Walter Mirisch recalled. "I said, 'Well, before we lease another system, let's see what you can do.'" (MENZIES FAMILY COLLECTION)

would infiltrate the dreams of countless baby boomers, some of whom would go on to make sci-fi classics of their own.

Despite an appreciative reception, *Invaders from Mars* was generally regarded as a movie for kids, and its modest success had no impact on its maker's employment options. In five months, the only solid job Menzies could land was another shot at television—albeit a promising one. Ronald Colman, who had refused to make a TV pilot of his radio series *The Halls of Ivy,* somehow agreed to make one for a proposed anthology series based on the writings of W. Somerset Maugham. The celebrated author's short stories had populated three portmanteau features imported from England, and it was reasonably believed their popularity could also power a weekly series. For once there was a generous budget and a top-flight cast that carried more star power than any of Menzies' recent features—Colman, Angela Lansbury, Nigel Bruce, Brenda Forbes, Ron Randell, George Macready, and Sean McClory. *A String of Beads* was shot at Roach in September 1953. Menzies made an elegant job of it, but the series never sold. A few days following its completion, Nigel Bruce died of a heart attack at the age of fifty-eight, making *String of Beads* his final appearance before a camera.

In early 1954, Menzies was recruited by David Selznick to direct a musical "prologue" to accompany the release of *Indiscretion of an American Wife*, a feature Selznick had produced in Italy with Jennifer Jones and director Vittorio De Sica. In the company of DOS and James Wong Howe, Menzies flew to New York in February and asked Dick Sylbert to help him set up the shoot. "I was just this kid," said Sylbert, "but we set it up, went into the city, I think, and we spent the day together. I could see that he was having trouble." Recording star Patti Page was to sing two numbers derived from Alessandro Cicognini's score for the feature, but nothing ever was simple where Selznick was involved. "I am deep in the hassle already," Menzies advised Mignon within a day of his arrival. "When you say 'Selznick' you say trouble. . . . We are finally using a very exciting penthouse at Tudor City on the 23rd floor with enormous windows and the whole of New York around us, and if it wasn't that David is involved, it would probably be interesting. At least it will soon be over and I can come home and settle down to worrying about not having a job again."

The prospect of regular work finally came with Ronald Colman's capitulation and commitment to a *Halls of Ivy* TV series. The rights to the NBC radio show, a literate comedy about a college president and his doting wife, had been acquired by Television Programs of America, whose production chief, former PRC president Leon Fromkess, would be in charge. On March 30, Hedda Hopper reported that Fromkess would be giving Colman "just the greatest directors" for his show—Norman Z. McLeod and William Cameron Menzies. (McLeod, who had no previous experience working with Colman, had directed *The Secret Life of Walter Mitty* during Fromkess' tenure as a production executive at Goldwyn.) The plan was for the two men to alternate, McLeod directing one week, Menzies the next. Colman, it developed, was wary of television and nearly impossible to direct. At age sixty-three, he looked ten years younger but couldn't be convinced of it. "For twenty weeks," writer Barbara Merlin recounted, "we couldn't get a reverse angle because Ronnie would not allow it. . . . On his 'bad' side he had three wrinkles on his neck which bothered him, and then he had more crow's feet on one side than he did on the other and he didn't think he looked as good on that side." Colman employed a TelePrompTer, which left his scenes looking contained and static. He protested changes to the recycled radio scripts they were using, resisting efforts to inject a little movement. There was tension between him and his wife and costar, Benita Hume, and the two divvied up laugh lines as if dividing a jar of cookies. Over time, the grind of producing thirty-nine consecutive episodes took a toll on its aging participants, and when the show's run ended in September 1955, it was due more to fatigue than to sponsor disinterest.

Colman would be dead within three years, Menzies, a younger man, even sooner. At age fifty-nine he looked seventy, beaten down by years of intense work and insecurity, and depleted by the Turkish cigarettes he chain-smoked to quiet his nerves. "I think Ronald Colman was responsible for Daddy's first heart attack," said Suzanne Menzies, "because he was working on *Halls of Ivy* at the time. There was such acrimony between Benita and Ronald. Everybody was fighting. They were not getting along, from what I gather, and Colman was being so difficult. I guess he was nervous about his career, and probably didn't like doing television."

The heart attack was a mild one, but getting Menzies to relax was never easy. "He didn't like movies," said Suzie. "And he'd get restless. He had this little tiny butt, and it was uncomfortable for him to sit still for two hours. He could sit through a football game, but not a movie." Live performances were no better, and he was never at ease. One night, as Mignon squeezed down a crowded row to her seat, she looked back to discover that Bill had caught his fly in the hair of a woman in the next row and was desperately trying to free himself. "For a man who was too embarrassed (according to Mignon) to buy toilet paper at the market," commented Pam Lauesen, "this must have been an excruciating moment." He hated seeing his own pictures in a theater. He got dragged to *Anchors Aweigh,* loathed it, and walked out. Yet he loved the widescreen compositions and the spirited use of color in M-G-M's *Seven Brides for Seven Brothers.* "That's the way they should make musicals!" he said approvingly.

Clearly, Menzies was intrigued by the format and eager to compose a widescreen picture. The opportunity presented itself when impresario Mike Todd engaged him to design *Around the World in 80 Days* in the revolutionary process known as Todd-AO. Originally, Todd had been involved in the production of Cinerama attractions—showy travelogues that married three side-by-side 35mm images to create the all-engulfing effect of super widescreen. But shooting and projecting Cinerama was a cumbersome process, and when Todd quarreled with his partners prior to the release of *This Is Cinerama* (1952) he was persuaded to sell out his interest. Convinced Cinerama could be substantially improved, Todd found an unlikely partner in an optical scientist named Brian O'Brien, a full professor at the University of Rochester. Todd told O'Brien everything he needed to know about Cinerama, its advantages and drawbacks. "Doctor," he said in conclusion, "I want you to get me something where everything comes out one hole."

The result, developed under O'Brien's direction at American Optical, combined the enhanced definition of 65mm film stock with a lens capable of capturing panoramic shots at an angle of 128°. (The lens became informally known as the "bug-eye.") Todd found backers and eventually secured the film rights to the stage musical *Oklahoma!* That movie, which reportedly cost $4.5 million to make, became the shakedown for the Todd-AO process. Then Todd went to Hollywood to hire, as his son Mike Jr. put it, "a couple of old film production hands." One was Percy Guth, formerly Walter Wanger's comptroller, who was given the job of general manager. The other was William Cameron Menzies. "Todd said that all during production of the picture, Guth kept giving him reasons why he couldn't do things, while Menzies helped him devise ways to get them done."

Menzies came aboard on June 14, 1955, when he signed on as associate producer of the picture. Background shots had already been made in Bali and India, and Todd had already selected John Farrow to co-write and direct the picture. To star, he had chosen the Mexican comedian Cantinflas to play Passepartout, valet to Phileas Fogg, and David Niven to enact the fastidious adventurer of Jules Verne's famous novel. Menzies left for England on July 27, where Todd's compressed schedule of sixty-six camera days dictated his every move.

"Everyone here is so worried about time," he wrote, "that I was plunged immediately into very strenuous work and got no chance to recover from that damn flying." London was hot, the traffic terrible, and although he found some excellent locations, he feared they would be difficult to shoot. Within a week, Menzies was commuting between England and Spain. "I got to the Prado and saw the Goyas, Velazquezs, and El Grecos," he reported. "They were badly hung, but I really got one of the biggest emotional thrills of my life. Then I drove to Toledo—and here is [the] real Spain. I thought Edinburgh was old, but in Toledo the rocks, the people, the buildings all sort of blend together. The set in Chinchón is unbelievable. No art director could ever match it. The whole town is a series of balconies hanging over the plaza, which is a bull ring with a 12th century cathedral up high brooding over the whole thing."

Working closely with him was Ken Adam, a German-born designer earning his first credit as art director on a major motion picture. At age thirty-four, Adam knew Menzies' work and quickly came to regard him as a mentor. "I was just breaking away from playing it safe in my own designs," he said. "Bill was the one who encouraged me, if necessary, to treat designs more theatrically. Heightened realities. Stylization over reality. Make more use of color. He was a big influence on me." Menzies, Adam recalled, had the overall design of the film already set in his mind. "We discussed the concept for the English, French, and Spanish locations, studio sets and so forth, when he arrived, but he had a pretty good idea of how the film should look. It was an enormous help for me, and a completely new and exciting experience."

Mike Todd was a powerful personality, a master showman and big-stakes gambler who kept his projects going through sheer force of will. Short and stocky, bristling with energy, he was once characterized by humorist S. J. Perelman as "an ulcer no larger than a man's hand." As with Selznick, he worked around the clock, but where Selznick instinctively knew the mechanics of story and structure, Todd knew only what he liked. "Bill had great problems with Mike Todd," said Ken Adam, "because Mike practically wouldn't move without him. He was at his beck and call twenty-four hours a day. He was completely exhausted, but in the evenings he used to come to an apartment we had in Pont Street, Belgravia, and he used to spend most evenings with us. Which was the only relaxation he had. Then we both got calls from Mike to get to the Dorchester and work with him all night."

Filming began in Chinchón on August 12 with John Farrow setting the stage for Cantinflas' famed bullfight routine, the largest and trickiest sequence in the picture. "Farrow was slowly assembling groups of townspeople and telling them how to react," recalled Mike Todd, Jr. "Dad went crazy—it seemed totally unnecessary to him to have to show people who lived there how to watch a bullfight and drink wine." All 6,500 residents of the town had been engaged as extras, and Farrow needed to finish with them by the end of the day. Itchy and impatient, Todd clashed with his director. As he later recounted the incident: "We started in Spain, it was nine o'clock—and nothing happened. So I said a few words to him, and this guy said, 'I've been making pictures for so and so many years.' And one word led to another, and he said the one thing nobody should ever say to me—'Why don't you do it yourself?'"

Todd turned to cinematographer Lionel "Curly" Lindon, called for camera, and began pointing and shouting, "Get this! Get that!" With Todd "directing" and Menzies backing him up, they had in two days what Todd Jr. described as "about ten minutes of some of the most exciting and colorful action footage in the whole picture." Back in London, Menzies was glad his agent, Harold Rose, was in town on holiday. "I was very upset about it," he said of the rupture between Farrow and Todd, "but two such violent characters are bound to collide. At Harold's advice I am staying on the show, but everything is in a complete state of turmoil. It can only last a few weeks longer, or maybe days, and then I will be home, thank God. You never know what's happening from one day to the next."

Rose urged Menzies to take over as director, as Menzies, it seemed, had "quite a drag" on Mike Todd. "Dad," said Mike Todd, Jr., "wasn't overwhelming in his praise of collaborators and often didn't get along with them. On the surface he got along just to get things done, but he was often scornful of people he worked with. Menzies was one of the people that he had great admiration for." Being the credited director of *Around the World in 80 Days* would certainly have been a career boost for

William Cameron Menzies, but it likely would have come at a terrible price. "This will probably be a great show—an eye-filler at least," he acknowledged in a letter home. "I am looking for a softer spot from now on in. Everyone thought I'd inherit the show, but I'm just as glad I didn't. I don't feel too good anyway, and being completely responsible would probably kill me."

He was, Ken Adam observed, an "almost destroyed human being," a shell of the man he once must have been. "He was literally working himself to a standstill because Todd had no respect for people's private time or private life. I fell for it, and I always fall for these sorts of people. They are monsters, but you can't help admiring them and somehow the danger is that you become their slave. Bill became more and more nervous, and he used to go through a bottle of scotch in my apartment at night. He was not in his best form, you know."

On Noël Coward's recommendation, Todd interviewed Michael Anderson, the thirty-five-year-old director of a tense docudrama called *The Dam Busters*. "He took the cigar out of his mouth," Anderson remembered, "and asked, 'If you were

On the set of *Around the World in 80 Days* (1956) in Durango, Colorado, producer Mike Todd and director Michael Anderson (in hat and sunglasses) consult the script as their associate producer peers over Anderson's shoulder. This is very likely the last photograph ever taken of William Cameron Menzies on a movie set. (ACADEMY OF MOTION PICTURE ARTS AND SCIENCES)

on a penny farthing bicycle, traveling through the streets of Chelsea, where would you put the camera?' I said, 'On the handlebars.' He said, 'You're hired.'" Menzies, Anderson found, had thought the film through as much as was humanly possible under the extraordinary circumstances of working for a "maniac" like Todd. "I never worked with Menzies on the design of the film," he said, "because by the time I came on he had finished all that. . . . He was always ahead of the game, and always attending to details. There was very little that was ever missing. The walls that were floating, the ceilings that moved out—all the technical things that perhaps an art director or production designer who hadn't also directed might not have taken into consideration were all there."

Complicating the shoot was the Todd-AO system, which ran 65mm negative through the camera at 30 frames per second. The nonstandard speed required another camera running at 24 frames per second to create prints that could be shown in theaters that lacked special projection equipment. Takes for *Oklahoma!* had to be made twice—once in 65mm at 30 fps and again in 35mm at 24 fps. For *Around the World in 80 Days,* the process was simplified with side-by-side cameras, but the arrangement was still cumbersome and the project seemed more than what any one person could contain.

"I have completely lost track of the show," Menzies admitted. "Todd is really in the saddle now and running everything. We have these lousy meetings at night to make our day complete. . . . It's his money and his foolishness. I think it will iron out somewhat when we get home. We must do that soon because we might get snowed out in Durango [Colorado] if we are much after the middle of September. . . . I feel twenty years older than when I went away."

Miraculously, the European unit finished within days of its original schedule, and the company was able to commence work in Durango pretty much as planned. "This has been an experience," said Menzies, "and I wish I could have been younger to enjoy it. All it has done has been to keep me dead tired most of the time." Scenes of Phileas Fogg and Passepartout in the American West had to be made without benefit of rear projection, as no equipment could yet accommodate 65mm footage. "There was no process," said Michael Anderson, "so the whole side of the train had to come off. The cameras had to be put on platforms, and the actors had to be put on the open train. You'd get the train up to forty or fifty miles an hour, bring the actors in and start rehearsing with the train going at full speed and the camera crew hanging on for dear life. That all had to be thought out beforehand."

In Los Angeles, the picture was spread all over town—the San Francisco exteriors were made on Forty Acres, the ruins of Tara still standing nearby; the French countryside was a stretch of the Columbia Ranch in Burbank; the Bombay Wharf a standing set on the backlot of 20th Century-Fox. The balloon ascent was filmed at Universal, while most all the film's interiors were shot on the near-deserted RKO lot, soon to be purchased and revitalized by Desilu. Having scouted all these prior to leaving for Europe, Menzies managed to stay one jump ahead of Anderson and his company. "On the overall picture, he was always ahead of any anticipation I might have," the director said. "I remember the day when we did the shot where they run through the [Bombay] temple with the monkeys. I was thinking ahead saying, 'How are we ever going to keep the monkeys in place?' And Bill had already designed in the fact that every monkey would be tethered by a little wire to its collar which was invisible. He had thought of *all* those things."

For scenes on the SS *Henrietta,* a partial set wouldn't do, though Todd, at first, couldn't be convinced of it. Said Anderson:

> I think there was always sort of a barrier between him and Mike in a sense, because Bill Cameron Menzies was so high up on an artistic level that sometimes he would do things that would have Mike say, "What do you want to do that for? You know, I don't need the whole ship built." But Bill would say, "No, but if you're going to shoot this whole sequence as written, you're going to need the whole ship built." So I think there was a feeling that Bill was too extravagant, but in fact, of course, he wasn't. When the ship, for instance, had to be torn apart by the crew to burn the wood, he designed it so that it came apart and then could be put back together again for Take Two. I think Mike was always a little bit shocked by the fact that Bill made it so lavish and, equally, Mike couldn't really complain, because that's what he wanted.
>
> There was one great moment when the ship had docked and they come down the gangplank. It was built in a studio, though it didn't look like it. I put the actors on the camera and moved the camera away as the ship was supposed to leave port, so it gave the impression the ship was moving. Mike had seen the dailies—he hadn't been on the set, because I very rarely saw Mike Todd on the set—and Bill and I were coming down the corridor. Mike stopped, pulled his cigar out of his mouth, and said, "Menzies, god-damnit, I always thought you were spending too much money, but when I saw that ship move . . . You're worth every penny!"

Menzies stayed with the production through the conclusion of miniature work in February 1956, long after Michael Anderson had returned to England. Todd, meanwhile, had taken to regarding New York as his base of operations. Left in Hollywood to finish the picture with Menzies were Percy Guth, Curly Lindon, James Sullivan (the film's U.S.-based art director), and Lee Zavitz. "I think he was very proud of his own ability," Anderson said, recalling Bill Menzies nearly half a century later. "He was a man who knew what he could do, and he was totally capable of doing anything. He had this great pride in his work. You couldn't fault him, either in color, or design, or what was needed in terms of the scene. He always had this great sense of looking at you as if to say, 'Isn't it great?' And I would think: It's really fantastic. And I would relish that side of Bill."


"He was sick," said his daughter Suzie. "I don't know when he knew he was going to have the operation—which was going to destroy him. I mean, they took out his salivary glands and part of his tongue; he couldn't talk, he couldn't eat." Not long after the completion of *Around the World in 80 Days,* Menzies was diagnosed with cancer of the mouth. Just shy of his sixtieth birthday, he submitted to a disfiguring surgery that robbed him of whatever joy was left to him in life. "It was a horrible operation; what they did to him was awful. He had tubes all the time, because he couldn't swallow. He drooled and he couldn't eat. Everything had to be whipped up for him in a blender. He loved to eat and he loved to talk, and he couldn't do either. It was so horrible, I remember thinking: Why didn't he die? He *did* die, in fact, on the operating table, and they brought him back. And I thought: Why did they bring him back?"

In August 1955, as Menzies was traveling to Spain for Mike Todd, a fourth grandchild had been born in California; the baby was six weeks old before his grandfather got his first-ever look at him. Now, in his convalescence, Menzies doted on his grandchildren and reveled in their company. Pam, the eldest, was eleven, her brother, Barry, was eight, her cousin Toby, Suzie's daughter, was two. "Daddy used to drive down a lot," said Suzie. "Lowell, who was my brother-in-law, got him a white Buick with red leather upholstery, a convertible. It was dreadful, it looked like a pimp's car. He liked the car, though. He had always driven Fords, and he always had to have a convertible. I lived in the Palisades; it was a pretty good drive down Sunset. He'd come down to see Rusty in particular, because he loved the boy baby. Rusty was this huge, huge baby. And he loved Toby, too. She was so cute. He had always wanted a boy, but got stuck with two girls. But he ended up with two grandsons."

Occasionally there was news in the paper of Mike Todd, who was undertaking new projects and still fiddling with *Around the World in 80 Days.* When he saw a rough cut of the picture, Todd expressed dissatisfaction with the miniature of the *Henrietta* used for the final leg of Fogg's epic journey: "Everybody said it was marvelous, it was great, and to do it the Hollywood way, it was okay. But it's late in the picture, and everything else we've done is for real. When I say late in the picture, it's the last big production number before we wind up the story." Todd bought a schooner from the Scripps Institute, made a side-wheeler of it, and personally supervised its partial demolition in the waters off Newport Beach. "I've considered it carefully, and while it may sound expensive, it is something that is absolutely necessary." Although he claimed the picture cost "close to $6,500,000," when Todd sought an injunction in Superior Court to prevent the city of Los Angeles from seizing negatives and prints for nonpayment of property tax, the film's production cost was given as $4,367,255.

The picture had its world premiere in New York on October 17, 1956, and Todd's faith in the venture was thoroughly and gloriously vindicated. *Daily Variety* assessed its box office potential and labeled it the "surefire hit of the year." Bosley Crowther touted it as "a sprawling conglomeration of refined English comedy, giant screen travel panoramics, and slam-bang Keystone burlesque." The other critics piled on, throwing around adjectives like titanic, thrilling, dazzling, breathtaking. "You can," said Rose Pelwick in the *Journal-American,* "roll out every glowing adjective in the book for Michael Todd's production of *Around the World in 80 Days.* . . . For Todd's come up with a fabulous entertainment that'll have you laughing and gasping and applauding. . . . It's big. It's beautiful. It's hugely amusing."

The Los Angeles opening at the Carthay Circle didn't come until December 22, and Todd cleared the theater the following afternoon for a special holiday showing for everyone who had worked on the film. Menzies sat with his son-in-law, Russ Antles, while Suzie, Mignon, Jean and Lowell and their kids sat elsewhere in the 1,500-seat house. For Menzies and those who knew him, the picture struck a valedictory note, its size and flamboyance harking back to the Fairbanks *Thief of Bagdad,* its opening scene in the Reform Club recalling the Senior Conservative Club and the clattering spoon at the beginning of *Bulldog Drummond,* its temple interior remindful of the one Anton Grot created in forced perspective for the first picture Menzies ever worked on, *The Naulahka.* He thought Shirley MacLaine, a blue-eyed Scottish girl, horribly miscast as a Kali Princess. The nature of David Niven's character meant he wasn't called upon to do much emoting, and that threw the picture to Cantinflas, whose wide-eyed reaction shots and set pieces were scattered throughout the film. In all, Menzies liked and admired *Around the World in 80 Days,* which Todd always correctly viewed as a show rather than a movie. As a stabilizing force throughout an expensive, chaotic shoot, moving the project along and figuring out how to get things done when the money ran low, Bill Menzies was as responsible for getting it made as any one person other than Mike Todd himself.

About this time there was an offer of work from Hecht-Lancaster, who wanted Menzies to design a picture (possibly *The Sweet Smell of Success*). Mignon was grateful for him to have something in the offing. "It made him feel pretty good that he was still wanted," Suzie said. But Menzies knew *Around the World in 80 Days* would be his final picture, that he no longer had the stamina for a feature assignment, and that going on a set in his condition would be unthinkable. "I vaguely remember that he wore ascots and/or scarves to cover up his jaw," Pam Lauesen wrote. "It must have been horrible for someone so verbal to not be understood. He had one of those gray plastic slates kids draw on, then pull up to erase. He would use it in disgust when he couldn't be understood. He lost weight, which made his mouth and jaw look even more pronounced." And, recalled Barry Lauesen, his eldest grandson, he still managed to smoke.

"I stopped by to see him one night on the way home from work," said Jimmy Vance. "Not the best time to visit someone, but I felt I should go see him for Christmas. . . . I was surprised Mignon let me see him. She said, 'Oh, Bill would be glad to see you.' She took me in, and Bill came down the stairs. He looked tired, he looked ill. He was drooling, and he couldn't control it. He said, 'Isn't this awful?' I felt glad I saw him. I think I left him a tie; I was always sending him ties."

On February 18, 1957, nominations for the 29th annual Academy Awards were announced, and for one final time, a picture designed by William Cameron Menzies drew a nomination for Art Direction. (Its seven other nods included those for Cinematography, Costume Design, Direction, and Best Picture.) If he took note, there is no memory of it within the family. "He was so miserable," Suzie said, "and my mother was just wasting away. Actually, though, he didn't die of cancer. He died of a heart attack. I think he died because he wanted to die." To the last, Mignon remained hopeful that Billy was getting better. He was, she reported in a letter to his brother, John, going into the UCLA Medical Center for another operation and was "beside himself with worry."

He died on the morning of March 5, 1957. "When he was dying," wrote his granddaughter Pam, "he was sitting in a chair in his bedroom, which was most probably where it usually was in the center of the room. He kept talking to someone in the corner, but Grandma couldn't understand what he was saying. We always suspected that it was Nan (or 'Gigi' as we called her—for great-grandmother). . . . The history of Mignon and Nanon's relationship showed a big-time jealousy on the part of Gigi toward her daughter. Plus she was a force to be reckoned with in life, and I always thought it was Nan's last 'gotcha' from the grave."

"Mother was with him," said Suzie, "sitting and holding his hand, together till the very end. It was like Falstaff: he started to get cold from the feet up. And just sat in that chair and died. This was all about three in the morning, and Mother waited until about six to call us. And she told Russ; he answered. Russ was devastated; he adored Daddy. All my friends loved him." In New Haven, John Menzies said to his son, "Uncle Bill died and I've got to go out and tell Mother." Ellen Menzies was under constant care, her mind lost, at ninety-two, in the fog of advanced age. "He said she cried," his son John remembered, "but I don't know that she knew *why* she was crying. The last five years of her life, at least, she was *non compos.*"

The obituaries led with his work on Todd's epic picture, which was still playing to packed houses and advanced prices, and would go on to earn more than $25 million in rentals. Also mentioned were *Gone With the Wind, Things to Come,* and *Our Town.* The private funeral service at Forest Lawn on March 7 was followed by cremation and placement in a niche alongside Nanon Toby—an irony not lost on the members of his family. The will, drawn in 1929, left his entire estate, valued at $70,000, to Mignon.


With work as scarce as it was for the last decade of his life, it's possible Bill Menzies went to his grave convinced he had been forgotten. The press obituaries were free of testimonials, and there were no appreciations in film journals or magazines. The sole exception was a tribute from his friend and colleague Laurence Irving, which ran in *The Times* of London on March 11, 1957. In part, it read:

> All those who have studied or contributed to the development of films as a graphic art will have learnt with very deep regret of the death of William Cameron Menzies. For to him, more than to anybody, Hollywood and later England owe their understanding of the designer's power to enhance the visual impact of an image on the screen by employing the ancient art of composition with its dramatic relation of the human figure to its surroundings. . . . If style is an ingredient of an artist's enduring reputation, the films designed by Menzies will always attract the admiration of connoisseurs.

In August 1958, *Invaders from Mars* was released to television, where it was typically programmed for kids on Saturday afternoons. Even in black-and-white, Menzies' bold compositions had their unsettling impact, the film's imagery entrancing young viewers who prompted frequent repeat showings. In time, there was a quiet stirring of interest in the man whose name came last on the credits, a director whose name was so distinctive it stayed with young minds long after the names of even the actors were forgotten. Poor prints of *Things to Come* also made it to the airwaves, the film suffering from having fallen into the public domain in the United States.

After her Billy died, Mignon Menzies found herself alone after having been surrounded by friends and family all her adult life. "An incessant photographer of all of us," recalled her granddaughter Pam, "she began taking photos off the TV, starting with Peggy, a girl on *American Bandstand* who reminded her of herself at that age—not a beauty, but a great dancer and popular. Mignon carried on a lively correspondence and sent photos to Peggy, Dick Clark, Jack Paar, Johnny Carson, Gypsy Rose Lee (who wanted her to come on her show, but Mignon responded that she'd sooner die), to name a few—and she and her photos were mentioned on air by all her TV 'friends.'"

In October 1967, Mignon welcomed a local newspaper columnist to the house on Linden Drive, eager to talk about Billy and his work on *Gone With the Wind*, which was being reissued for the fourth time. "We had quite a social time the day Mr. Lloyd—the writer—and a lady from M-G-M Studio came in for the interview," she wrote Pam, who was away at college. "Your mother and Suzie were here too—and could give so many details—as they went to the studio a lot during the shooting of 'Gone With the Wind.' They were both awfully nice and we served coffee and goodies and making it all very friendly and cozy. They went up to see the hall and were <u>impressed</u>. Thought I'd tell you so that you'd get the paper." In the end, the columnist couldn't really have a lot to say, as the reformatting of *GWTW* for 70mm and widescreen effectively destroyed Menzies' compositions. It would be another three decades before the film would again be commercially released in its original aspect ratio.

Nineteen seventy brought publication of the late Léon Barsacq's landmark history of movie design, *Le Décor de Film,* which contained a number of references to Menzies' work as a designer. The same year, John Baxter included a full chapter on Menzies and *Things to Come* in his *Science Fiction in the Cinema,* a book that quickly became a standard reference in the field. Two years later, for an entry in *The International Encyclopedia of Film,* associate editor John Gillett celebrated Menzies as "probably the most influential designer in the Anglo-American cinema (and virtually an auteur in his own right)."

Nineteen seventy-two also brought a tribute from Orson Welles, who took the opportunity to highlight Menzies' work in the introduction to a public television screening of *The Thief of Bagdad.* "It stars Douglas Fairbanks, Sr.," Welles told the viewing audience, "and the art director is William Cameron Menzies. Now we never talk enough about art directors in films. Critics have finally got around to talking about the authors of the script, but I haven't noticed any big movement in favor of the art director. He's an unsung hero. Underpaid, undervalued, and in the case of William Cameron Menzies, a man impossible to over-praise. Since here's a movie which has been conceived, from beginning to end, pictorially within its own style with perception and an elegance really unmatched in its own field."

The Barsacq book, with the addition of a two-page filmography and biographical sketch of Menzies by Elliott Stein, was published for the first time in English by the New York Graphic Society in 1976. The late 1970s then saw the mounting of two major exhibitions: "Designed for Film: The Hollywood Art Director" at New York's Museum of Modern Art, and "The Art of Hollywood" at the Victoria and Albert Museum in London. Sponsored by Thames Television, the exhibition catalog for "The Art of Hollywood" spotlighted the work of eight major art directors, including Menzies, who was accorded his own chapter. Since the selection included Cedric Gibbons and Van Nest Polglase, Orson Welles declined an invitation from producer John Hambley to write a foreword, noting that "Menzies is the only name on your list that I could enthuse over."

Mignon died in 1982 at the age of eighty-seven. The house on Linden had to be sold to pay the estate taxes. Prior to its demolition, a family friend who was a professional photographer arrived to shoot the vaulted hallway Menzies had painted for his own amusement over the spring of 1951, feeling that it should be preserved. (One of the shots made that day appeared in the 1994 "Hollywood at Home" issue of *Architectural Digest*.) Fortunately, a thorough search of the house yielded a wealth of original artwork—finished drawings, continuities, and preliminary sketches, including Menzies' earliest visualizations of *Gone With the Wind*.

In 1990, a five-week exhibition devoted exclusively to the work of William Cameron Menzies was organized by the Museum of the Moving Image in New York. Films shown included *Our Town, For Whom the Bell Tolls*, and *Gone With the Wind*, along with such rarities as *Tempest, Zampa*, and *A Terribly Strange Bed*. Richard Sylbert, and production designers George Jenkins and Kristi Zea delivered lectures, and a small installation of artwork accompanied the programs.

Today, the title of production designer is commonly taken on a film by the lead art director, who shares the responsibilities with the director and cinematographer that Menzies once shouldered alone. If Menzies has a legacy in the process of modern filmmaking, it is in the storyboards now routinely developed for all major films. On a more visceral level, however, it was Menzies who first showed Hollywood it was possible to bring unity and purpose to the look of a film, conveying unspoken information in a way that broadened and deepened the emotional impact of the drama.

"He had a prodigious capacity for work," Laurence Irving wrote, "and to this was added the humility and integrity which is the mark of the true artist. Newcomers to Hollywood, whom lesser men might have regarded as rivals and interlopers, he greeted with unselfish kindness; he gave eagerly the benefit of his experience to those who, catching his enthusiasm, became his disciples."

On March 13, 2014, George Lucas endowed three faculty chairs at the USC School of Cinematic Arts. Fittingly, he named the endowed chair in Cinematic Design for the great Russian director Sergei Eisenstein, the chair in Visual Effects for the master magician Georges Méliès, and the chair in Production Design for William Cameron Menzies. Installed as the first holder of the Menzies chair was Alex McDowell, whose credits include *Fear and Loathing in Las Vegas, Fight Club, Minority Report,* and *Man of Steel.* "Menzies," he said at the dedication, "led a revolution in the visualization, spectacle, and immersion of the audience in the medium of film at the time of its last great upheaval: The transition from silent film to sound and color. In the process, he single-handedly transformed the craft of art direction into the art of production design, and in doing so cemented the central triumvirate of film creation—director, cinematographer, and production designer—in the film industry."

Lucas himself was more plainspoken, freely acknowledging that he was pursuing his own agenda about the school and what he thought it should teach. The naming of the chairs after Eisenstein, Méliès, and Menzies, he added, was a way of saying "don't forget the basics. Don't get enamored with new technology . . . it doesn't change anything. The art of what we do is exactly the same. The goal that we have is exactly the same as Sergei Eisenstein, Georges Méliès, and William Cameron Menzies. It's beyond technology. It's the art of movies."

# ACKNOWLEDGMENTS

This is a book I've always felt should be written. Why it never was is still something of a mystery to me, but I'm happy to have been afforded the opportunity to write it myself. The process began with a phone call placed to the home of Jean Menzies Lauesen, whom I knew to be the elder daughter of William Cameron Menzies, early in 1999. Happily, she was listed in the phone book. Unhappily, she had died only a few months earlier. It was my great fortune, however, that her daughter Pamela happened to be at the phone that day. Pam put me in touch with her aunt, Suzanne Menzies Antles, and thus the job began.

Suzie, as it turned out, had a tremendous collection of materials—drawings, sketchbooks, paintings, stills, scripts, letters, scrapbooks—relating to her father's career that nobody had ever had the time to organize. I spent the following year sifting, filing, and inventorying everything there, delighting in what I found and lamenting what I had hoped to find that wasn't there. I also recorded some thirteen hours of conversations with Suzie, whose memory was astonishing and whose wonderfully dry sense of humor made every minute a pleasure. Work progressed slowly, and the book was only two-thirds finished when I had to put it aside to research and write my biography of Spencer Tracy. It was still unfinished when Suzie died of cancer in 2007.

If there is one person ultimately responsible for enabling this project to come to fruition, it is Pam Lauesen. She has taken up the mantle of archivist and family historian, and has done the job beautifully. Without her help, I don't know where this book would have ended up. Also providing essential help and moral support were Suzie's daughter, Toby Antles, and Pam's husband, George Goad. In New Haven, a talk with John Cameron Menzies, Jr., and his family was very kindly facilitated by his son, Donald R. Menzies. In Scotland, Nana MacKenzie and her daughter, Helen, were the perfect tour guides in taking Pam and George to various family landmarks, including Castle Menzies and the house where William Cameron Menzies' grandparents lived, and where Menzies himself stayed as a child. Family lore was contributed as well by Stephen MacKenzie and his wife, Anna, and by Kenneth MacKenzie.

In London, Kevin Brownlow provided valuable data on Menzies from his personal files, while Nick Cooper, proprietor of a terrific website devoted to the film *Things to Come* (at www.625.org.uk), was a prime source of information as well as consultation. While in England, my friends Andrew and Melanie Kelly generously provided a place to stay. It was through Andrew that I had the pleasure of meeting Sir Christopher Frayling, author of the British Film Institute's excellent monograph on *Things to Come*.

Seeing some of Menzies' rarer films proved a challenge at times, and I'm grateful to Robert Gitt, senior preservation officer at the UCLA Film Archive, for running *Always Goodbye* and *Almost Married* for Pam Lauesen and me at the archive's Hollywood facilities. I also want to thank Jere Guldin, senior archivist at UCLA, for arranging for us to see *Drums of Love* and *Lady of the Pavements*. In Fullerton, Ronnie James supplied examples of Menzies' TV work from his vast archive of original video.

As usual, Ned Comstock unearthed a wealth of material at USC's Cinematic Arts Library, including original drafts from the library's 20th Century-Fox script collection and a complete set of the drawings Menzies made for *So Ends Our Night*. Hardly any book of this nature gets done without Ned's enthusiastic participation, and I wouldn't be the first to suggest that, among those of us who do this sort of work, Ned is a national treasure. Karl Thiede once again provided information from his amazing research library, including reliable profit and loss data I could never have found anywhere else.

Karen Jacobsen, special projects director for the Art Directors Guild, helped me contact some of the senior members of the guild who knew and worked with Menzies. Sportscaster Chris Marlowe shared memories of his mother, K.T. Stevens, and put me in touch with Jack Harris, with whom I spent a very pleasant afternoon discussing Chris' grandfather, Sam Wood. Master photographer James Kohatsu did a wonderful job capturing Menzies' oversized art boards as digital images. Tom Weaver and Michael Blake put me in touch with Richard Kline, who remembered his work on *Address Unknown* when still a teenager. In London, Catherine Surowiec reviewed an early proof of this book and offered many helpful comments and corrections. For various assists and suggestions I am also grateful to Cari Beauchamp, Patricia King Hanson, the late Charles Higham, Miles Kreuger, Leonard Maltin, and Anthony Slide.

A number of libraries and institutions were consulted in the course of researching this book, and I am grateful to the librarians and administrators who made that aspect of my work so rewarding.

Margaret Herrick Library, Academy of Motion Picture Arts and Sciences: Stacey Behlmer, Barbara Hall, Matt Severson, Faye Thompson. British Film Institute: Claire Thomas. David O. Selznick Collection, Harry Ransom Center: Steve Wilson. Motion Picture and Television Reading Room, Library of Congress, Washington, D.C.: Zoran Sinobad. Film Study Center, Museum of Modern Art, New York: Charles Silver.

20th Century-Fox Archive, Arts Library, University of California, Los Angeles: Lauren Buisson (with thanks as well to David F. Miller of the 20th Century-Fox Legal Department). UCLA Film and Television Archive: Mark Quigley. Cinematic Arts Library, University of Southern California: Steve Hanson. Regional History Collection, University of Southern California: Dace Taube. Warner Bros. Archive: Haden Guest.

I am particularly grateful to those select few who knew and worked with William Cameron Menzies, and who took time to talk with me about him: Ken Adam, Michael Anderson, Hilyard Brown, June Caldwell, Laraine Day, Andre De Toth, Joan Fontaine, Charles French, Arthur Gardner, Jack Harris, Jimmy Hunt, Richard Kline, Julian "Bud" Lesser, Norman Lloyd, Elliott Reid, Stanley Rubin, Martha Scott, Herbert B. Swope, Richard Sylbert, James Vance, and Alan Young.

Scott Eyman has been an invaluable sounding board, as well as an indispensable source of wisdom, encouragement, and gratuitous insults. My agent, Neil Olson, saw the value in this project, and has trained a sharp eye on all aspects of its development, much to my appreciation.

Victoria Wilson, senior editor and associate publisher, is the reason this book exists in its present form, having embraced such an unlikely subject with enthusiasm and dedication. I shall always be grateful for her support and guidance.

My wife, Kim Geary, makes all of this possible, not only through her interest in subjects such as Menzies, but also through her conviction that all American history is relevant. She keeps me on an even keel, a considerable feat at times.

James Curtis
Brea, California
May 2015

# NOTES

ABBREVIATIONS

AMPAS: Margaret Herrick Library, Academy of Motion Picture Arts and Sciences, Los Angeles

DOS: David O. Selznick Collection, Harry Ransom Center, University of Texas, Austin

FOX: 20th Century-Fox Collection, Theatre Arts Library, Special Collections, University of California, Los Angeles

FXSC: 20th Century-Fox Script Collection, Cinema-TV Library, University of Southern California, Los Angeles

IAM: Institute of the American Musical, Los Angeles

MGM: Metro-Goldwyn-Mayer script collection at the Cinema-TV Library, University of Southern California, Los Angeles

MPAA: Motion Picture Association of America. Production Code Administration Records, Margaret Herrick Library, Academy of Motion Picture Arts and Sciences, Los Angeles

UCLA: Film and Television Archives, University of California, Los Angeles

USC: Universal Pictures Collection, Cinema-TV Library, University of Southern California, Los Angeles

WB: Warner Bros. Collection, University of Southern California, Los Angeles

WCM: William Cameron Menzies Family Collection, Los Angeles

WW: Walter Wanger Collection, Wisconsin Historical Society, Madison

INTRODUCTION

ix  "Hotel Westbury": Richard Sylbert to the author, via telephone, 1/23/01.

x   "Korda got a nomination": Vincent Korda actually won the Oscar for *Thief of Bagdad* in 1941. Lyle Wheeler won for *Gone With the Wind* the previous year.

x   "stupid little plaque": Anthony Slide points out that the Academy gave plaques in many categories in the early years of the awards, and that winners were later invited to exchange their plaques for genuine Oscars. "I would assume some of Cedric Gibbons' 'Oscars' were actually 'stupid little plaques,'" he says.

x   "Gibbons had a heart attack": Between the years 1949 and 1956, Cedric Gibbons garnered another nineteen nominations and five statuettes. In one year alone he was nominated for four M-G-M features.

xi  "Grot": Anton Grot (1884–1974) never won an Academy Award for Art Direction, but he was nominated five times in the 1930s, most significantly for *Svengali* and *The Sea Hawk*. In 1940, he and the Warner Bros. Art Department shared a certificate of honorable mention from the Academy for the design and perfection of a water ripple and wave machine.

xi    "I won an Academy Award": Richard Sylbert received his first Oscar for *Who's Afraid of Virginia Woolf?* (1966).

xii    "those pirate movies": Sylbert is referring to Grot's work on *Captain Blood* (1935) and *The Sea Hawk* (1940), both of which starred Errol Flynn.

xii    "the old Gold Medal Studio": In 1952, it still would have been the old Biograph Studio, which was built in 1911 and had been inactive for nearly twenty years. It was renamed Gold Medal following a renovation that was completed in 1956.

## 1. ATLANTA BURNING

3    inferno: For details of the burning of the Atlanta rail yard, I relied on the accounts of Wilbur G. Kurtz contained in Richard B. Harwell, ed., "Technical Advisor: The Making of 'Gone With the Wind': The Hollywood Journals of Wilbur G. Kurtz," *Atlanta Historical Journal*, Summer 1978; in an undated letter from Kurtz to C. F. Palmer (AMPAS); and in undated manuscript pages (AMPAS). Also useful was "'Gone With the Wind': Survey of Technical Treatment," *Kinematograph Weekly*, 4/25/40.

4    "We planned": Ronald Haver, *David O. Selznick's Hollywood* (New York: Alfred A. Knopf, 1980), p. 254.

4    "For all scenes": WCM to David O. Selznick, 11/9/38 (AMPAS).

5    "increase the feeling": Ibid.

5    "with particular emphasis": Alan David Vertrees, *Selznick's Vision* (Austin: University of Texas Press, 1997), p. 74.

5    "We'd move the camera": Haver, *David O. Selznick's Hollywood*, p. 254.

6    "Heavy ground fog": Will McCune to Ray Klune, 12/9/38 (DOS).

7    "This smoke": Harwell, ed., "Technical Advisor: The Making of 'Gone With the Wind': The Hollywood Journals of Wilbur G. Kurtz," p. 97.

7    "suddenly the holocaust": Haver, *David O. Selznick's Hollywood*, p. 257.

9    scores of cars: Some accounts of the night of December 10 suggest homeowners surrounding the Pathé lot panicked at the sight of the sky-high flames and started throwing kids, pets, clothing into their cars and jamming the streets, but there are no specific recollections or newspaper stories to support this. "It was common knowledge in Culver City that this was happening," said June Caldwell, a longtime resident, "so we drove up on Jefferson Boulevard, which is on the other side of Ballona Creek, to where you could see the back of the Selznick studio. We sat there in our cars, fascinated with the fact that this was going on in our little town."

9    "When our counter": Clarence Slifer, "Creating Visual Effects for G.W.T.W.," *American Cinematographer*, August 1982.

9    "her tests": Rudy Behlmer, ed., *Memo from David O. Selznick* (New York: Viking, 1972), p. 180.

10    "biggest thrills": David O. Selznick to Irene Selznick, 12/12/38, as quoted in Behlmer, ed., *Memo from David O. Selznick*, p. 180.

11    "The older people": William Cameron Menzies, autobiographical essay, 8/16/45 (WCM).

11    "The child": William Cameron Menzies, "Let the Pixies Get You," *Hollywood Reporter*, 10/23/44.

13   "slightest clue": Suzanne Antles to the author, Thousand Oaks, 8/15/00.

13   "no compulsory attendance": Menzies, autobiographical essay.

14   "He taught": Robert F. Karolevitz, *The Prairie is My Garden* (Aberdeen, SD: North Plains Press, 1969), p. 47.

14   "two or three days": Ibid., p. 81.

14   "the greatest painter": Menzies, autobiographical essay.

16   "The first part": Fred J. Balshofer and Arthur C. Miller, *One Reel a Week* (Berkeley: University of California Press, 1967), p. 133.

17   "Palm trees": Dudley Early, "Man on Olympus," *The Family Circle*, 9/13/40.

18   "I made a date": Menzies, autobiographical essay.

18   "[The] sets": *Variety*, 1/18/18.

## 2. AN ARTIST OF THE MODERN SCHOOL

20   "We were offered": Mignon T. Menzies to Pamela Lauesen, 1/1/73 (WCM).

20   "I got through": Menzies, autobiographical essay, 8/16/45 (WCM).

22   "For some reason": Menzies, autobiographical essay.

22   "Right in the middle": Early, "Man on Olympus."

23   "rapidly advancing": *Motion Picture Classic*, December 1919.

23   "an early designer": William Cameron Menzies, "Pictorial Beauty in the Photoplay," in *Introduction to the Photoplay* (Los Angeles: University of Southern California, 1929), p. 87.

24   "miserable winter": Menzies, autobiographical essay.

24   "more or less of a job": WCM to Mignon Menzies, 11/3/19 (WCM).

24   "Mayflower": Miriam Cooper, *Dark Lady of the Silents* (Indianapolis: Bobbs-Merrill, 1973), p. 162.

25   "fineness of light": *Variety*, 3/11/21.

26   "Los Angeles": Menzies, autobiographical essay.

26   "simplicity and beauty": Radio interview, 1936, as quoted in Donald Deschner, "Anton Grot: Warners' Art Director, 1927–1948," *Velvet Light Trap*, Fall 1975.

26   "dreaded": Cooper, *Dark Lady of the Silents*, p. 170.

26   "The director": *Variety*, 1/27/22.

26   "no businessman": Cooper, *Dark Lady of the Silents*, p. 186.

28   "This will introduce": Letter, Raoul Walsh to Douglas Fairbanks, undated (WCM).

30   "Madison Square Garden": Menzies, "Pictorial Beauty in the Photoplay," p. 89.

## 3. THE THIEF OF BAGDAD

34   "He worked and worked": John Hambley and Patrick Downing, *The Art of Hollywood* (London: Thames Television, 1979), p. 91.

35   "make the story": "Tale of Bagdad for Fairbanks," unsourced Los Angeles newspaper clipping (WCM).

36   "defeat that thing": Ralph Hancock and Letitia Fairbanks, *Douglas Fairbanks: The Fourth Musketeer* (New York: Henry Holt, 1953), p. 203.

36   "designed the costumes": David Chierichetti, *Hollywood Director* (New York: Curtis Books, 1973), p. 36.

36    "night and day": Edward Knoblock, *Round the Room* (London: Chapman & Hall, 1939), p. 323.

37    "Those things are anchored": Hancock and Fairbanks, *Douglas Fairbanks: The Fourth Muske-teer,* p. 204.

38    "played with shadows": Ibid.

38    "took me out back": Raoul Walsh, *Each Man in His Time* (New York: Farrar, Straus & Giroux, 1974), p. 163.

39    "the size of it": Cooper, *Dark Lady of the Silents,* p. 202.

40    "trace them on glass": Leo Kuter, "Production Designer," *Society of Motion Picture Art Directors Bulletin,* March 1951.

42    "smells food": Ryan, "Fantasy Arrives on the Screen."

42    "The rival princes": Walsh, *Each Man in His Time,* p. 166.

42    "cut seaweeds": Menzies, "Pictorial Beauty in the Photoplay," p. 90. This technique was used again in Fairbanks' *The Black Pirate* (1926).

43    "The steelworkers": Walsh, *Each Man in His Time,* p. 168.

43    "Llewellyn Crane": Ibid.

44    "Poetry in motion": "Tuesday Night," CBC Radio, 1974, as quoted in Eileen Whitfield, *Pick-ford: The Woman Who Made Hollywood* (Lexington: University Press of Kentucky, 1997), p. 211.

45    "the spell": *Los Angeles Times,* 7/11/24.

45    "I saw it": Orson Welles, introduction to *The Thief of Bagdad, The Silent Years,* 1972.

## 4. THE HOODED FALCON

46    "like a dream": Don Ryan, "Fantasy Arrives on the Screen," *Picture Play,* May 1924.

46    "the realm": Ibid.

47    "a heap": Knoblock, *Round the Room,* p. 323.

47    "GREAT STORIES": George Fitzmaurice to WCM, 1/10/24 (WCM).

48    "letting the actor": Michael Morris, *Madam Valentino* (New York: Abbeville Press, 1991), p. 125.

48    "I was conceited": Natasha Rambova, *Rudy: An Intimate Portrait of Rudolph Valentino* (London: Hutchinson, 1926), p. 134.

48    "cleverest": Ibid, p. 130.

49    "ARE YOU AVAILABLE": George Ullman to WCM, 4/18/24 (WCM).

49    "magician": Proof, Ritz-Carlton full-page ad (WCM).

49    "a big picture": Joseph E. Henabery, *Before, In and After Hollywood* (Lanham, MD: Scarecrow Press, 1997), p. 250.

50    "series of comedies": Anita Loos, *A Girl Like I* (New York: Viking, 1966), p. 187.

50    "tell you something": Henabery, *Before, In and After Hollywood,* p. 250.

51    "The Valentinos": Ibid., p. 252.

51    "ARRIVING HOLLYWOOD": George Ullman to WCM, 11/13/24 (WCM).

51    "Much could be said": "Menzies Calls Films Art," 10/5/24 (WCM).

52    "tough problem": Henabery, *Before, In and After Hollywood,* p. 251.

52    "how sorry I was": *Los Angeles Times,* 12/21/24.

53    "Mrs. Valentino": Henabery, *Before, In and After Hollywood,* p. 256.

53    "He didn't like it": Jack Scagnetti, *The Intimate Life of Rudolph Valentino* (Middle Village, NY: Jonathan David, 1975), p. 79.

53   "The female lead": Henabery, *Before, In and After Hollywood,* p. 329.

53   "the Valentinos got word": Ibid.

54   "a glimpse": Rambova, *Rudy: An Intimate Portrait of Rudolph Valentino,* p. 131.

54   "As we chatted": Frank Daugherty, "Is Art Direction Art?," *The Film Spectator,* 7/19/30.

55   "contracts were ready": S. George Ullman, *Valentino As I Knew Him* (New York: A. L. Burt, 1926), p. 102.

55   "That contract": Michael Morris, *Madam Valentino* (New York: Abbeville, 1991), p. 164.

56   "so much color": *Los Angeles Times,* 5/24/25.

56   "long talk": Ullman, *Valentino As I Knew Him,* p. 106.

57   "We did everything": Scagnetti, *The Intimate Life of Rudolph Valentino,* p. 89.

58   " 'intellectual type' ": Myrna Loy, with James Kotsilibas Davis, *Being and Becoming* (New York: Alfred A. Knopf, 1987), p. 42.

58   "wrong with his stomach": Scott Eyman, "Clarence Brown: Garbo and Beyond," *Velvet Light Trap,* Spring 1978.


5. MATURING PERIOD

60   "the coup": *Los Angeles Times,* 9/13/25.

60   "greatest pantomimist": Kevin Brownlow, *The Parade's Gone By* (New York: Alfred A. Knopf, 1968), p. 145.

63   "maturing period": Richard Kritzer, "An Analysis of the Technique of Production Design in Cinema as Employed by William Cameron Menzies" (graduate thesis, University of Southern California, June 1952), p. 22.

63   "never saw him": Charles French to the author, via telephone, 1/23/01.

65   "lay out a set": Menzies, "Pictorial Beauty in the Photoplay," p. 88.

66   "pine trees": *Beverly Hills Post,* 4/1/54.

67   "France in 1451": *Exhibitors Herald,* 10/30/26.

69   "Daddy was so proud": Suzanne Antles to the author, Thousand Oaks, 11/1/00.

70   "Together": Anita Loos, *A Girl Like I* (New York: Viking, 1966), p. 188.

73   "The art director": Menzies, "Pictorial Beauty in the Photoplay," p. 89.

73   "receptive": Charles Higham, *Hollywood Cameramen* (Bloomington: Indiana University Press, 1970), p. 127.

73   "the first place": Menzies, "Pictorial Beauty in the Photoplay," p. 90.

74   wasn't as costly: According to the research library of Karl Thiede, *Two Arabian Knights* cost $488,968 to produce and had domestic rentals of $743,886.

75   "a laugh": Menzies, "Pictorial Beauty in the Photoplay," p. 89.

75   "covered the floor": Ibid., p. 90.

75   "Texture": Menzies, "Pictorial Beauty in the Photoplay," p. 90.

78   "Tourjansky was a perfect delight": Brownlow, *The Parade's Gone By,* p. 233.

78   "don't know anything": *Los Angeles Times,* 1/1/28.

78   "You get your perspective": Ibid.

78   "My own policy": Menzies, "Pictorial Beauty in the Photoplay," p. 89.

80   final cost: According to Karl Thiede, the domestic gross for *Tempest* was $971,889. With foreign rentals worked in, the film may have broken even.

80 "the one thing": *New York Times,* 5/6/28.

80 "books on architecture": John Barrymore to WCM, 1928 (WCM).


### 6. I COULD SEE THE FUTURE CLEARLY

81 "triumph": Untitled clipping (WCM).

81 "real atmosphere": *New York Times,* 1/3/28.

82 "just an assignment": Ted Perry and David Shepard, *Henry King, Director: From Silents to Scope* (Los Angeles: Directors Guild of America, 1995), p. 71.

82 "almost continual changes": *Los Angeles Times,* 1/22/28.

87 "We became friends": Laurence Irving, *Designing for the Movies* (Lanham, MD: Scarecrow Press, 2005), p. 34.

88 "When I had left": *New York Sun,* 1/14/30.

88 "stage was wired": Irving, *Designing for the Movies,* p. 40.

88 "Taylor and the sound men": Kevin Brownlow, *The Parade's Gone By* (New York: Alfred A. Knopf, 1968), p. 234.

90 "average set": Daugherty, "Is Art Direction Art?," *The Film Spectator,* 7/19/30.

90 "acoustical demands": Menzies, "Pictorial Beauty in the Photoplay," p. 92.

91 "added handicap": *Los Angeles Times,* 9/1/29.

91 "big idea": *New York Times,* 12/1/40.

91 "fascinatingly interesting": Sidney Howard to Helen Howard, as quoted in Arthur Gewirtz, *Sidney Howard and Claire Eames: American Theater's Perfect Couple of the 1920s* (Jefferson, NC: McFarland, 2004), p. 249.

91 "picture was a melodrama": *New York Times,* 12/1/40.

92 "Precision": Irving, *Designing for the Movies,* p. 44.

93 "the company worked": Joan Bennett and Lois Kibbee, *The Bennett Playbill* (New York: Holt, Rinehart & Winston, 1970), p. 202.

94 "lousy film": Irving, *Designing for the Movies,* p. 44.

96 "As an art director": Menzies, "Pictorial Beauty in the Photoplay," p. 86.

98 awards banquet: Details of the first Academy Awards ceremony are from *Academy Bulletin* No. 22, 6/3/29; *Variety,* 5/22/29; *Los Angeles Times,* 2/18 and 5/17/29; and *Hollywood Daily Citizen,* 5/17/29. Mignon Menzies remembered Fairbanks' comment to her husband in a conversation with George Goad. "Of course, they were both drunk!" she added.


### 7. PROFOUND UNREST

100 "the best": *New York Times,* 4/9/29.

100 "skillful": *Los Angeles Times,* 5/24/29.

100 "Talking pictures": *Los Angeles Times,* 5/26/29.

101 "learned urban dwellers": Daugherty, "Is Art Direction Art?"

102 "a lot of pains": *Photoplay,* July 1929.

102 "quiet persistence": Irving, *Designing for the Movies,* p. 43.

102 "very hard": Elizabeth Goldbeck, "The Woman That Was Mary," *Motion Picture,* September 1929.

102   "emphasize": Sam Taylor to Laurence Irving, 3/9/29, as quoted in Scott Eyman, *Mary Pickford: America's Sweetheart* (New York: Donald I. Fine, 1990), p. 192.

102   "working together": Irving, *Designing for the Movies*, p. 69.

103   "sound equipment": Scott Eyman, *Five American Cinematographers* (Metuchen, NJ: Scarecrow Press, 1987), p. 13.

103   "The sets": Edward Bernds, *Mr. Bernds Goes to Hollywood* (Lanham, MD: Scarecrow Press, 1999), pp. 85–86.

104   "chief assets": *New York Sun*, 8/14/29.

105   "realistic form": WCM to John Huchins, 5/22/29 (WCM).

106   "Music": *Los Angeles Times*, 8/18/29.

106   "We showed Napoleon": Higham, *Hollywood Cameramen*, p. 127.

106   "Riesenfeld . . . has not fully": *Los Angeles Times*, 7/28/29.

107   "bit of a nuisance": *New York Evening Telegram*, 1/20/30.

107   "The picture": *New York Evening Telegram*, 1/10/30.

107   "wanted to direct": Menzies, autobiographical essay (WCM).

109   "ten minutes": *Motion Picture News*, 1/25/30.

109   "He was lacking": Lillian Gish, *The Movies, Mr. Griffith, and Me* (Englewood Cliffs, NJ: Prentice Hall, 1969), p. 306.

111   "The memory": Mary Ellin Barrett, *Irving Berlin: A Daughter's Memoir* (New York: Simon & Schuster, 1994), pp. 81–82.

111   "walked through": Harry Richman (with Richard Gehman), *A Hell of a Life* (New York: Duell, Sloan & Pearce, 1966), p. 154.

112   "best staged": *The Film Mercury*, 3/21/30.

113   "cinema designer": William Cameron Menzies, "Cinema Design," *Theatre Arts Monthly*, September 1929.

113   "enjoying myself": *Los Angeles Times*, 7/20/30.

114   "too fast": A. Scott Berg, *Goldwyn* (New York: Alfred A. Knopf, 1989), p. 192.

114   "one of the peculiarities": Menzies, "Cinema Design."

115   "the painter": Daugherty, "Is Art Direction Art?"


8. A FEW FAINTLY REPRESSED BRONX CHEERS

116   "artistic triumphs": New York *Daily News*, 7/6/30.

117   "musical pantomimes": *Judge*, n.d. (WCM).

117   "copyright": New York *Daily News*, 7/6/30.

117   "greatest genius": Ibid.

118   "Lincoln's immortality": Ibid.

118   "straightforwardly shot": Higham, *Hollywood Cameramen*, p. 127.

119   "a genius": Barrett, *Irving Berlin: A Daughter's Memoir*, p. 87.

119   "era of revues": *Los Angeles Times*, 9/7/30.

120   "great job": Barrett, *Irving Berlin: A Daughter's Memoir*, p. 143.

120   money-loser: According to the Research Library of Karl Thiede, *Reaching for the Moon* had a respectable domestic gross of $855,568. At a cost of $1,127,969, however, it would have needed to bring in more than twice that amount to break even.

120    one picture: Details of Menzies' employment at Fox come from records in the 20th Century-Fox Collection, Theatre Arts Library, Special Collections, University of California, Los Angeles.

120    "plenty of time": Unidentified clipping (WCM).

121    "Wise boy": *Los Angeles Examiner,* 12/22/30.

122    "Give them a hand": New York *Daily News,* 5/23/31.

122    "*The Spider . . .* was novel": Menzies, autobiographical essay (WCM).

123    "fool the camera": *Los Angeles Daily News,* 6/3/38.

123    "'corking' good": Winfield Sheehan to WCM, 7/28/31 (WCM).

123    "sustained sequences": *Hollywood Spectator,* n.d. (WCM).

124    "entertaining, amusing": *Judge,* n.d. (WCM).

124    At a cost: Figures on *Always Goodbye* and *The Spider* are from the Research Library of Karl Thiede.

125    "nothing contrary": James B. M. Fisher, résumé, 12/4/31 (MPAA).

126    "first in a series": *Hollywood Reporter,* 12/5/31.

127    "A number of changes": Résumé, 4/21/32 (MPAA).

128    "much more rewarding": Higham, *Hollywood Cameramen,* p. 85.

129    "building a beam": "Methods of Executing Tricks, Stunts, and Process Shots," 6/23/32 (James Wong Howe Collection, AMPAS).

131    "paucity of screen names": *Variety,* 7/26/32.

131    Worldwide revenues: Figures on *Almost Married* are from the Research Library of Karl Thiede.

131    "several million kids": *Hollywood Reporter,* 9/3/32.

132    "skillfully handled": *New York Times,* 9/18/32.

132    "cameraman's nightmare": *Los Angeles Times,* 9/17/32.

133    "bunch of turbans": *Rob Wagner's Script,* 10/22/32.

133    "Worldwide rentals": Figures on *Chandu the Magician* are from the Research Library of Karl Thiede.

## 9. WONDERLAND

134    "piece of impressionism": Reginald Berkeley, *Cavalcade,* Final Shooting Script, 9/19/32.

138    "own them both": Kenneth L. Geist, *Pictures Will Talk* (New York: Scribners, 1978), p. 59.

138    "[The] idea": *Variety,* 8/1/33.

138    "The story": *New York Times,* 9/11/32.

142    "The costumes": Geist, *Pictures Will Talk,* p. 59.

142    "The only part": Jeanne Stein, "Fusspot and Fortune's Fool: Edward Everett Horton," *Focus on Film,* No. 1, January/February, 1970.

142    "I guess": Suzanne Antles to the author, Thousand Oaks, 9/29/99.

143    "music, screaming": Joseph L. Mankiewicz and William Cameron Menzies, *Alice in Wonderland,* illustrated shooting script, September 1933.

143    "We trust": James Wingate to A. M. Botsford, 12/9/33 (MPAA).

144    "did wonders": Paul Perez to WCM, 12/13/33 (WCM).

145    "Nothing grows": *Variety,* 12/26/33.

145    "worst flops": *Rob Wagner's Script,* 12/23/33.

145    "disappointing": *New York Times,* 1/7/34.

145   topped $50,000: Figures on *Alice in Wonderland* are from *Variety,* 12/26/33 and 1/2/34, and from the Research Library of Karl Thiede.

146   "Miss Dell": *Daily Variety,* 2/26/34.

146   "capital reproduction": *Los Angeles Times,* 3/23/34.

146   "short story": *New York Times,* 4/21/34.

148   "rather poisonous": WCM to Ellen Menzies, 12/10/28 (Courtesy John Menzies and family).

148   "such a responsibility": Mignon Menzies to Pamela Lauesen, 4/3/72 (WCM).

149   "twelve years": Cecil B. DeMille, 6/19/34 (WCM).


10. THE SHAPE OF THINGS TO COME

150   "Newton": WCM to Mignon Menzies, 8/14/34 (WCM).

151   "at worst": WCM to Mignon Menzies, 8/29/34 (WCM).

151   "terribly slowly": WCM to Mignon Menzies, 10/9/34 (WCM).

151   "an H G Wells film": H. G. Wells to WCM, 10/9/34 (WCM).

151   "still running": WCM to Mignon Menzies, 11/3/34 (WCM).

152   "After dining": Irving, *Designing for the Movies* (Lanham, MD: Scarecrow Press, 2005), p. 107.

152   "greatly excited": H. G. Wells, *Things to Come* (London: Cresset Press, 1935), p. 11.

152   "ransacking": Michael Korda, *Charmed Lives* (New York: Random House, 1979), p. 123.

153   "Vincent Korda": Orlton West, "How *Things to Come* Was Made," *Home Movies and Home Talkies,* October 1936.

153   "most unassuming": André de Toth to the author, Burbank, 11/10/99.

153   "great friends": WCM to Mignon Menzies, 2/15/35 (WCM).

153   mistress: According to scuttlebutt of the period, Menzies was involved with costume designer Elizabeth Haffenden, later a well-known lesbian.

153   "trick English clothes": WCM to Mignon Menzies, 2/19/35 (WCM).

153   "miss you terribly": WCM to Mignon Menzies, 3/1/35 (WCM).

154   "old Hollywood strain": WCM to Mignon Menzies, 3/14/35 (WCM).

154   "one big thing": WCM to Mignon Menzies, 4/15/35 (WCM).

154   "Wells' novel": Raymond Massey, *A Hundred Different Lives* (New York: McClelland & Stewart, 1979), p. 191.

154   "West End": *The Scotsman,* 4/16/35.

155   "Menzies and Korda": Brian McFarlane, ed., *Sixty Voices* (London: British Film Institute, 1992), p. 195.

155   "funny collection": WCM to Mignon Menzies, 12/1/35 (WCM).

155   "unbelievably jake": WCM to Mignon Menzies, 6/21/35 (WCM).

155   "Alex": WCM to Mignon Menzies, 7/23/35 (WCM).

155   "final scenes": H. G. Wells to WCM, n.d. (WCM).

156   "fantastically difficult": Massey, *A Hundred Different Lives,* p. 192.

157   "peppery wire": *New York Sun,* 9/3/35.

157   "in shape at last": David C. Smith, *The Correspondence of H. G. Wells* (London: Pickering & Chatto, 1996), p. 31.

158   "difficult job": Massey, *A Hundred Different Lives,* p. 192.

159   "glad he has left": WCM to Mignon Menzies, 11/13/35 (WCM).

159    "another Monday": WCM to Mignon Menzies, 11/18/35 (WCM).

160    "Fortunately": WCM to Mignon Menzies, 12/1/35 (WCM).

160    "lights came on": Francis D. "Pete" Lyon, *Twists of Fate* (Evanston, IL: Evanston Publishing, 1993), p. 68.

160    "the jitters": WCM to Mignon Menzies, 1/21/36 (WCM).

161    "My work": Sir Cedric Hardwicke, *A Victorian in Orbit* (Garden City: Doubleday, 1961), p. 232.

161    "This Bliss music": Wells, *Things to Come,* p. 12.

162    "high-flung City Ways": Ibid., p. 103.

162    "lower part": West, "How *Things to Come* Was Made."

163    "huge disillusionment": Nick Cooper, *The Shaping of Things to Come* (London: Network DVD, 2007), p. 14.

166    "America sees this film": *Motion Picture Herald,* 3/7/36.

166    "lavishness of treatment": *Variety,* 3/4/36.

166    "leviathan": *The Times* (London), 2/23/36.

167    "death of a nation": *The Listener,* 3/18/36.

168    "easy to nag": *The Observer,* 2/23/36.

169    "We ran the show": WCM to Mignon Menzies, 3/4/36 (WCM).

## 11. WHAT I'VE WANTED TO DO ALL MY LIFE

170    "Picture has been cut": *Variety,* 4/22/36.

170    "pessimistic": *New York Times,* 4/18/36.

171    "mechanically brilliant": *Los Angeles Times,* 4/19/36.

171    "I don't think Mother wanted to go": Suzanne Antles to the author.

171    "put out or not": WCM to Mignon Menzies, 5/21/36 (WCM).

172    "His manner": Garry O'Connor, *Ralph Richardson: An Actor's Life* (New York: Applause, 2000), p. 87.

172    "practically suicidal": WCM to Mignon Menzies, 6/23/36 (WCM).

172    early performance: Figures on *Things to Come* are from the Research Library of Karl Thiede.

173    "Pommer is so involved": WCM to Mignon Menzies, 7/7/36 (WCM).

173    "very wobbly": WCM to Mignon Menzies, 7/16/36 (WCM).

173    "a lot better": WCM to Mignon Menzies, 8/17/36 (WCM).

173    "not altogether qualified": *The Epic That Never Was,* BBC, 1965.

174    "The Fascisti thing": WCM to Mignon Menzies, 9/2/36 (WCM).

175    "He was amazed": WCM to Mignon Menzies, 11/12/36 (WCM).

176    "fairly realistic": Richard Greene, ed., *Graham Greene: A Life in Letters* (New York: W. W. Norton, 2008), p. 81.

176    "the other one": WCM to Mignon Menzies, 12/9/36 (WCM).

176    "thick in scenario": Greene, ed., *Graham Greene: A Life in Letters,* p. 82.

176    "an English gangster": Menzies, autobiographical essay.

177    "experience with Korda": Irving, *Designing for the Movies,* p. 107.

177    "hitting the bottle": John Mills, *Up in the Clouds, Gentlemen, Please* (London: Gollancz, 2001), p. 202.

178    "I need a man": Joseph J. Cohn Oral History with Rudy Behlmer, August–November, 1987 (AMPAS).

179   "haven't settled": David O. Selznick to Daniel O'Shea, 1/16/37 (DOS).

179   "will supervise": *Los Angeles Times*, 6/7/37.

180   "Daddy was on that plane": Suzanne Antles to the author, Thousand Oaks, 2/7/01.

180   "New York is terribly warm": WCM to Suzanne Menzies, n.d. (WCM).

181   "actively take charge": Aljean Harmetz, *On the Road to Tara* (New York: Abrams, 1996), p. 99.

182   "invaluable": David O. Selznick to Henry Ginsburg, 8/12/37 (DOS).

182   "we need a man": Behlmer, ed., *Memo from David O. Selznick*, pp. 151–52.

## 12. PRODUCTION DESIGNED BY . . .

183   "gloomy books": "Daddy read two or three books a day," Suzanne Menzies recalled. "He always had stacks of books beside his bed. He'd go down to Marian Hunter and select all these gloomy books."

184   "finally reached": David O. Selznick to Henry Ginsberg and Daniel O'Shea, 12/15/37 (DOS).

185   "these conferences": Harwell, ed., "Technical Advisor: The Making of 'Gone With the Wind': The Hollywood Journals of Wilbur G. Kurtz."

186   "in the backyard": Suzanne Antles to the author.

186   "four-hour picture": Harwell, "Technical Advisor: The Making of 'Gone With the Wind': The Hollywood Journals of Wilbur G. Kurtz," p. 31.

186   "Menzies' sketch": Harwell, Ibid., p. 33.

187   "ash-hopper": Ibid., p. 41.

187   "more enthusiastic": Behlmer, ed., *Memo from David O. Selznick*, p. 155.

190   "the word 'drafting' ": David O. Selznick to Russell Birdwell, 2/14/38 (George Cukor Collection, AMPAS).

191   "Production Designed": It should be noted that William Cameron Menzies was not the first individual to be credited with production design on an American motion picture. Kevin Brownlow points out that Rudyard Kipling received such a credit on *Without Benefit of Clergy* (1921) for sketching the scenes and properties used in the film. Later, in the year prior to the release of *The Young in Heart*, Broadway costume designer John W. Harkrider (1899–1982) was credited as production designer on the Universal musical *Top of the Town*. Apparently it was felt that Harkrider merited the credit for handling the design of sets as well as costumes on the picture. There is, however, no indication he did any continuity work on the film, an essential element of Menzies' approach to the job. Subsequently, Harkrider received the credit on eight other Universal releases, including the Deanna Durbin musical *One Hundred Men and a Girl*. I am grateful to Patricia King Hanson, executive editor of the *American Film Institute Catalog*, for making me aware of this.

191   "in conversation": William Burnside to David O. Selznick, 7/13/38 (DOS).

192   "entire effect": David O. Selznick to Barbara Keon, 9/27/38 (DOS).

193   "the montage": David O. Selznick to WCM et al., 10/15/38 (DOS).

194   "Mr. Cukor working": David O. Selznick to WCM et al., 10/13/38 (Ronald Haver Collection, AMPAS).

194   "I am hopeful": David O. Selznick to WCM et al., 10/17/38 (George Cukor Collection, AMPAS).

194   "detailed drawing continuity": WCM to David O. Selznick, 11/9/38 (Ronald Haver Collection, AMPAS).

194   "in any case": David O. Selznick to WCM, 11/16/38 (Ronald Haver Collection, AMPAS).

195   "translucent screen": Harwell, "Technical Advisor: The Making of 'Gone With the Wind': The Hollywood Journals of Wilbur G. Kurtz," p. 84.

195   "studio interest": Ibid., p. 90.

196   "big argument": Raymond Klune, UCLA Oral History with John Door, 1969.

196   "KEY FIRE SCENES": Behlmer, ed., *Memo from David O. Selznick,* p. 179.


13. GWTW

197   "dream house": Harwell, ed., "Technical Advisor: The Making of 'Gone With the Wind': The Hollywood Journals of Wilbur G. Kurtz."

198   "first final scenes": David O. Selznick to WCM et al., 1/6/39 (DOS).

198   "starting a sketch": *Los Angeles Daily News, 6/3/38.*

199   "The only thing": Behlmer, ed., *Memo from David O. Selznick,* pp. 188–89.

200   "running all over the place": *New York Times, 2/5/39.*

200   "conflicting opinions": David O. Selznick to WCM, 1/28/39 (Ronald Haver Collection, AMPAS).

201   "No attempt": William Cameron Menzies, handwritten notes, n.d. (DOS).

201   "can't get artistry": Behlmer, *Memo from David O. Selznick,* p. 194.

201   "really effective stuff": Ibid., p. 195.

202   "in silhouette": Slifer, "Creating Visual Effects for G.W.T.W."

202   "imperceptible darkening": Menzies, handwritten notes.

202   "walking sequence": Early, "Man on Olympus."

202   "bazaar sequence": Ibid.

203   "no moaning": Susan Myrick, *White Columns in Hollywood* (Macon: Mercer University Press, 1982), p. 89.

203   "hot color": Early, "Man on Olympus."

203   "two or three hundred thousand feet": Vertrees, *Selznick's Vision*, pp. 66–67. This book contains a detailed analysis of the fire sequence and its evolution, including a breakdown of who directed each individual shot.

204   seven days of shooting: Gavin Lambert, *GWTW: The Making of* Gone With the Wind (Boston: Little, Brown, 1973), p. 84.

204   "very good script": Higham, *Hollywood Cameramen,* p. 46.

204   "first ten days": *The Making of a Legend:* Gone With the Wind, Turner Entertainment/Selznick Properties, 1988.

204   "When Cukor left": Higham, *Hollywood Cameramen,* p. 46.

205   "did not like Mr. Selznick": Marcella Rabwin in *The Making of a Legend:* Gone With the Wind.

206   "Blue is a cold": Early, "Man on Olympus."

206   "light blue filter": Menzies, handwritten notes.

206   "Rolling country": WCM to Will Price, 3/9/39 (Ronald Haver Collection, AMPAS).

207   "OUTSIDE WINDOWS": WCM to David O. Selznick, 3/31/39 (Ronald Haver Collection, AMPAS).

207   "I shall be finished": Myrick, *White Columns in Hollywood,* p. 240.

208   "I was nervous": James Curtis, *Spencer Tracy: A Biography* (New York: Alfred A. Knopf, 2011), p. 383.

208    "one of the few geniuses": Ridgeway Callow, American Film Institute Oral History with Rudy Behlmer, 1976.

208    "everything in the world": Myrick, *White Columns in Hollywood*, p. 135.

208    "many happy evenings": Irving, *Designing for the Movies*, pp. 107–8.

209    "rather poisonous blue": Menzies, handwritten notes.

209    "hot summer day": Gladys Hall, "*Gone With the Wind:* On the Set with Gladys Hall," *Screen Romances,* January 1940.

210    "feeling very ill": Patrick McGilligan, *Backstory* (Berkeley: University of California Press, 1986), pp. 256–57.

210    went to a dance: For details of Sam Wood's early life, I am grateful to actor-director Jack Harris, who was close to Wood's elder daughter, Jeane, from 1954 until her death in 1996. Harris discussed his knowledge of the Wood family in an interview at his Hollywood home on February 18, 2000.

212    "freezing cold": Haver, *David O. Selznick's Hollywood*, p. 279.

212    "I liked that scene": Gavin Lambert, *GWTW*, p. 109.

214    "the shot": David O. Selznick to Jack Cosgrove, 3/13/39 (Ronald Haver Collection, AMPAS).

214    "devised and created": Ridgeway Callow Oral History.

214    "concrete ramp": Haver, *David O. Selznick's Hollywood*, p. 286.

214    "diesel engine": Myrick, *White Columns in Hollywood*, p. 269.

215    "all of the extras": Slifer, "Creating Visual Effects for G.W.T.W."

215    "I think that Hal Kern": Behlmer, *Memo from David O. Selznick,* p. 206.

215    "There were days": Haver, *David O. Selznick's Hollywood,* p. 276.

215    "ten attempts": *New Haven Register,* 1/21/40.

216    "Mother used to say": Suzanne Antles to the author, Thousand Oaks, 11/1/00.

216    "his butler": Ridgeway Callow Oral History.

217    "The whole company": Myrick, *White Columns in Hollywood,* p. 22.

217    "three units": Slifer, "Creating Visual Effects for G.W.T.W."

218    "Wood needed him": Ridgeway Callow Oral History.

218    "Main Titles": WCM to David O. Selznick, 5/29/39 (Ronald Haver Collection, AMPAS).

218    "apart from the cost": Haver, *David O. Selznick's Hollywood,* p. 292.

## 14. SOMETHING QUITE BOLD

219    "SEVERAL MILLION": David O. Selznick to Alexander Korda, 6/22/39 (DOS).

220    "get it right": Miklós Rózsa, *A Double Life* (Tunbridge Wells, Kent: Midas Books, 1982), p. 83.

220    "Listen": David Lazar, ed., *Michael Powell: Interviews* (Jackson: University Press of Mississippi, 2003), p. 34.

220    "as far as possible": WCM to David O. Selznick, 1/17/38 (DOS).

220    "one shot": David O. Selznick to Raymond Klune, 6/27/39 (DOS).

221    "very spooky": Suzanne Antles to the author.

222    "certain number": Lazar, *Michael Powell: Interviews,* p. 35.

222    "rattling of arms": Menzies, autobiographical essay (WCM).

222    "Vincent's huge set": Michael Korda, *Charmed Lives* (New York: Random House, 1979), p. 136.

222    "The machine shops": "Cooperative Research Laboratory Needed," *International Photographer,* January, 1941.

223 "fantastic scene": *New York Times,* 12/1/40.

224 "Tim Whelan especially specialized": Lazar, *Michael Powell: Interviews,* p. 35.

224 "technically the producer": McFarlane, ed., *Sixty Voices,* p. 144.

224 "On Saturday": Menzies, autobiographical essay.

224 "The Sunday": Lazar, *Michael Powell: Interviews,* p. 34.

225 "The conversation": *New York Times,* 12/1/40.

225 "Evidently": Scot Holton and Robert Skotak, "William Cameron Menzies: A Career Profile," *Fantascene* 4, 1978.

225 "At that time": Menzies, autobiographical essay.

225 set sail for New York: Alexander Korda eventually took the unfinished *Thief of Bagdad* to America, where exteriors were completed in the Mojave Desert and at the Grand Canyon by his brother Zoltan. The film was released to great acclaim in December 1940.

225 "I question": David O. Selznick to Raymond Klune, 10/23/39 (DOS).

226 "The play, when I saw it": *New York Times,* 6/9/40.

226 "accent on props": Harry Horner, "Producing the Film," transcript, American Film Institute, 10/11/76.

227 "setting the background": "'Our Town' from Stage to Screen," *Theatre Arts Monthly,* November 1940.

229 "This treatment": Ibid.

230 "something more than just": *Los Angeles Daily News,* 1/3/40.

230 "unconventional manner": "'Our Town' from Stage to Screen," *Theatre Arts Monthly.*

231 "can't commence to tell you": Ibid.

232 "the dead mother": *Los Angeles Daily News,* 1/3/40.

232 "Mr. Wood wanted": Bernard Rosenberg and Harry Silverstein, *The Real Tinsel* (New York: Macmillan, 1970), p. 44.

233 "real thrill": "'Our Town' from Stage to Screen," *Theatre Arts Monthly.*

233 "no one to talk with": Ray Nielsen, "Martha Scott in 'Our Town,'" *Classic Images,* September 1985.

234 "production stage manager": Martha Scott, Southern Methodist University Oral History with Ronald L. Davis, 6/18/88.

234 "increase interest": David O. Selznick to Daniel O'Shea, 1/23/40 (DOS).

234 "Bill Menzies": Behlmer, ed., *Memo from David O. Selznick,* p. 240.

235 "Everyone seems to feel": "'Our Town' from Stage to Screen," *Theatre Arts Monthly.*

237 "I was the assistant director": Tom Weaver, *Interviews with B Science Fiction and Horror Movie-Makers* (Jefferson, NC: McFarland, 1988), p. 289.

238 "everyone is most enthusiastic": "'Our Town' from Stage to Screen."

238 "not a correct term": "On Style," *Cinema,* August/September, 1963.

239 "rather unpleasant association": WCM to Laurence Irving, 9/30/40 (Courtesy of John H. B. Irving).

242 "spiraling disclosure": Will Connell, "William Cameron Menzies," *U.S. Camera,* March 1942.

243 "my observation": Laraine Day to the author, via email, 9/25/00.

243 *"single shot":* François Truffaut, *Hitchcock/Truffaut* (New York: Simon & Schuster, 1967), p. 97.

243 When production closed: Schedule and financial data on *Foreign Correspondent* are from the Walter Wanger Collection (WW).

243   "not an ordinary motion picture": Aaron Copland and Vivian Perlis, *Copland/1900 Through 1942* (New York: St. Martin's/Marek, 1984), p. 303.

244   "In a movie": "'Our Town' from Stage to Screen," *Theatre Arts Monthly.*

244   "didn't matter": Nielsen, "Martha Scott in 'Our Town.'"

244   "ordinary people": *New York Times*, 12/1/40.

244   "VERDICT": "'Our Town' from Stage to Screen," *Theatre Arts Monthly.*

244   "the fullest prerogatives": *New York Times*, 6/14/40.

244   "Wilder wrote it": *Time*, 6/3/40.

## 15. THE BEST SPOT IN TOWN

246   "more important": WCM to Laurence Irving, 9/30/40 (Courtesy of John H. B. Irving).

246   "he bridled": Ibid.

247   "felt strongly": Rosenberg and Silverstein, *The Real Tinsel*, p. 115.

247   "Photostats": Albert Lewin, "'Peccavi!,'" *Theatre Arts Monthly*, September 1941.

247   "little untimely": WCM to Laurence Irving, 9/30/40 (Courtesy of John H. B. Irving).

248   "melodramatic escapes": *New York Times*, 12/1/40.

248   "very good year": WCM to Laurence Irving, 9/30/40 (Courtesy of John H. B. Irving).

249   "fabulous technician": McGilligan, *Backstory*, p. 231.

249   "composition to punctuate": WCM to Laurence Irving, 4/21/47 (Courtesy of John H. B. Irving).

249   "grotesque": *Los Angeles Times*, 1/26/41.

250   Lew Rachmil: Rachmil returned to B-Westerns after *Our Town* and became a producer in 1941.

251   "Hollywood anomaly": *New York Times*, 12/1/40.

252   "certain promises": Daniel O'Shea to David O. Selznick, 2/4/41 (DOS).

252   "Everything was there": Suzanne Antles to the author, Thousand Oaks, 2/7/01.

253   "only five weeks top": J. L. Warner, memo for record, 1/11/41. Warner also permitted Wood to bring his own script clerk, who would also double as his personal secretary, at $100 a week (WB).

254   "plot is concerned": Rudy Behlmer, *Inside Warner Bros.* (New York: Viking, 1985), p. 135.

254   "It was long": David Lewis, *The Creative Producer* (Metuchen, NJ: Scarecrow Press, 1993), pp. 180–81.

254   "happened to be leaving": Ibid.

255   "discussed the script": McGilligan, *Backstory*, p. 305.

255   "definitely repellent story": Gerald Gardner, *The Censorship Papers* (New York: Dodd, Mead & Company, 1987), p. 184.

255   "draw the figure": Will Connell, "William Cameron Menzies," *U.S. Camera*, March 1942.

255   "liquid quality": *What's Happening in Hollywood*, 12/11/43.

255   "tell you how high": Higham, *Hollywood Cameramen*, p. 88.

256   "absolutely wonderful": Ray Hagen and Laura Wagner, *Killer Tomatoes* (Jefferson, NC: McFarland, 2004), p. 181.

257   "Working with Menzies": Connell, "William Cameron Menzies."

258   "He knew nothing": Lewis, *The Creative Producer*, p. 184.

258   "The answer": Ibid.

258   "experienced a shock": Ronald Reagan, *An American Life* (New York: Simon & Schuster, 1990), pp. 95–96.

259 "It is possible": Richard Kritzer, "An Analysis of the Technique of Production Design in Cinema" as Employed by William Cameron Menzies (graduate thesis, University of Southern California, June 1952), p. 67.

259 "When Parris arrived home": McGilligan, *Backstory,* p. 306.

259 "dramatic narrative sketches": Connell, "William Cameron Menzies."

261 "hypodermic needle": James Wong Howe, UCLA Oral History with Alain Silver, 1969.

261 "one thing settled": Behlmer, *Inside Warner Bros.,* p. 139.

261 "He was wonderful": Betty Field, Columbia University Oral History, March 1959.

262 "broken manner": Frank Mattison to T. C. Wright, 10/7/41 (WB).

262 "Menzies' contributions": Lewis, *The Creative Producer,* p. 185.

263 "very best effort": Kuter, "Production Designer," March 1951.


16. ADDRESS UNKNOWN

264 "communist cause": Scott Eyman, *Empire of Dreams* (New York: Simon & Schuster, 2010), p. 338.

264 "On location": Will Connell, "William Cameron Menzies," *U.S. Camera,* March 1942.

265 "select one location": Herbert Coleman, *The Man Who Knew Hitchcock* (Lanham, MD: Scarecrow Press, 2007), p. 93.

266 "Boom!": Ray Rennahan, American Film Institute Oral History with Charles Higham, June 1970.

266 "didn't care": Todd McCarthy, *Howard Hawks* (New York: Grove, 1997), p. 333.

267 "Baseball fans": *Los Angeles Mirror,* 9/1/41.

267 "I discovered": Maria Cooper Janis, *Gary Cooper Off Camera* (New York: Abrams, 1999), p. 149.

268 "We climb about": "Director Sam Wood's Location Diary," souvenir program, *For Whom the Bell Tolls.*

269 "I have been concerned": Sam Wood to Samuel Goldwyn, 6/16/42 (Samuel Goldwyn Collection, AMPAS).

270 "Sam leaned on him": Ray Rennahan, UCLA Oral History with James Ursini, 1969.

270 "any kind of a question": Ray Rennahan, American Film Institute Oral History.

270 "refused to acknowledge": Coleman, *The Man Who Knew Hitchcock,* p. 100.

271 "fill the screen": Suzanne Antles to the author.

271 "Let's pull back": Ezra Goodman, "Production Designing," *American Cinematographer,* March 1945.

271 "Don't think I'm complaining": WCM to Mignon Menzies, 7/29/42 (WCM).

271 "hillside is bare": "Director Sam Wood's Location Diary."

272 "scene of some prisoners": Eyman, *Five American Cinematographers,* p. 17.

273 "ship them in": Suzanne Antles to the author, Thousand Oaks, 2/7/01.

273 "Every woman": Larry Swindell, *The Last Hero* (Garden City: Doubleday, 1980), p. 246.

273 "so primitive": Ingrid Bergman and Alan Burgess, *My Story* (New York: Delacorte, 1980), p. 114.

273 "never felt so loved": K.T. Stevens, as quoted by Jack Harris.

274 "stunned": Laurence Leamer, *As Time Goes By* (New York: HarperCollins, 1986), p. 96.

274 "No matter": Walter Bernstein, *Inside Out* (New York: Alfred A. Knopf, 1996), p. 126.

275 "over at Columbia": James Vance to the author, Carmel, 3/24/00.

276   sixth day of shooting: I am grateful to Andrew Kelly for sharing notes taken by him from the production files of *The North Star* at AMPAS.

276   "piece of junk": A. Scott Berg, *Goldwyn* (New York: Alfred A. Knopf, 1989), p. 376.

276   "one long orgy": *The Nation,* 10/30/43.

277   "very vague": Rudy Behlmer, ed., *Inside Warner Bros.* (New York: Viking, 1985), p. 226.

278   "so many Marys": *Los Angeles Times,* 4/28/41.

278   "entitled to credit": *Los Angeles Examiner,* 9/10/43.

279   "The answer": *Hollywood Reporter,* 11/16/43.

280   "The whole secret": Goodman, "Production Designing."

280   "very professional": Richard Kline to the author, via telephone, 12/3/07.

281   "beautifully-made": *Hollywood Reporter,* 4/17/44.

282   "notable success": *Daily Variety,* 4/17/44.

282   "tragic atmosphere": *New York Times,* 4/17/44.

282   "Apparently": *Los Angeles Times,* 5/17/44.

282   "To tell the truth": "William Cameron Menzies," *U.S. Camera,* August 1944.

## 17. IVY

283   two months earlier: According to the research library of Karl Thiede, *Address Unknown* posted domestic rentals of $585,000, while *None Shall Escape* showed rentals of $1,078,000.

284   "bear in mind": Reeves Espy to David O. Selznick, 10/13/43 (DOS).

284   "The difference": David O. Selznick to Daniel O'Shea, 1/24/44 (DOS).

284   "What I was after": Matthew Gale, ed., *Dalí and Film* (London: Tate, 2007), p. 178.

284   "dream sequence": Behlmer, ed., *Memo from David O. Selznick,* p. 342.

285   "Il y a three": *Los Angeles Times,* 9/10/44.

285   "not changing": Notes on Dalí Paintings, n.d. (DOS).

285   "an hour or two": David O. Selznick to Richard L. Johnston, 11/21/44 (DOS).

286   "an awful lot": Suzanne Antles to the author.

286   "casual attitude": Harold Clurman, *All People Are Famous* (New York: Harcourt, Brace & Jovanovich, 1974), p. 153.

286   "most fascinating": Menzies, autobiographical essay (WCM).

287   "tail-end": King Vidor, UCLA Oral History with James Ursini, 1969.

287   "crane shot": Lee Garmes, UCLA Oral History with James Ursini, 1969.

287   "RKO is looking": *Variety,* 12/19/45.

290   "started right on it": James Vance to the author.

290   "frightening": *New York Times,* 1/26/47.

292   "every set-up": Ronald L. Davis, *Words into Images* (Jackson: University Press of Mississippi, 2007), p. 13.

292   "Actors": Joan Fontaine, in a note to the author, 9/22/00.

292   "The audience": Richard Kritzer, "An Analysis of the Technique of Production Design in Cinema as Employed by William Cameron Menzies," p. 65.

292   "afford a little footage": WCM to Laurence Irving, 4/21/47.

292   "the most ordinary thing": Vincent LoBrutto, *By Design* (Westport, CT: Praeger, 1992), p. 21.

293   "He didn't always drive": Suzanne Antles to the author.

293 "horrible ending": McGilligan, *Backstory,* pp. 43–44.

294 *Ivy* closed: Production details and figures on *Ivy* are from the Universal Studios Collection (USC).

294 "very good preview": WCM to Laurence Irving, 4/21/47.

294 "unusually ornate": *The Nation,* 8/16/47.

295 "mediocre": *Film Daily,* 8/1/47.

295 "Cinemagraphically": *Motion Picture Daily,* 7/22/47.

295 "For those who needed it": *Cue,* 7/26/47.

295 "went on the wagon": Mignon Menzies to Pamela Lauesen, 4/3/72 (WCM).

295 "never met": Jack Harris to the author.

296 "people should be labeled": *Los Angeles Times,* 10/21/47.

296 "independent activities": *Los Angeles Times,* 12/15/47.

## 18. MAKING A LIVING

298 "those early days": Ben Finney, *Once a Marine—Always a Marine* (New York: Crown, 1977), p. 112.

299 "terrifying effect": *Daily Variety,* 5/10/48.

300 "I read the script": Patrick McGilligan, *Backstory 2* (Berkeley: University of California Press, 1991), p. 357.

301 "all the money": Arlene Dahl, SMU Oral History interview with Ronald L. Davis, 9/24/75.

301 "loved the photography": Ridgeway Callow, American Film Institute Oral History.

301 "front door of a church": Vincent LoBrutto, *By Design* (Westport, CT: Praeger, 1992), p. 21.

302 "style, feeling, or period": Christopher Wicking and Barrie Patterson, "An Interview with Anthony Mann," *Screen,* July–October, 1969.

303 "very, very good": Walter Wanger to WCM, 10/1/48 (WW).

304 "Most TV viewers": *Los Angeles Mirror,* 7/5/49.

305 "Indian students": Robert Willoughby to Scott Eyman, 11/20/03 (Courtesy of Scott Eyman).

307 "great admirer": Stanley Rubin to the author, via telephone, 8/29/06.

307 "He enjoyed this picture": Kritzer, "An Analysis of the Technique of Production Design in Cinema," p. 75.

308 "*actually* photograph": Ibid., p. 76.

308 "movie fan": Elliott Reid to the author, Hollywood, 2/21/01.

309 Menzies' problem: Lewis Milestone to Kevin Brownlow, Los Angeles, 1969 (Courtesy of Kevin Brownlow).

310 "I got a memo": Stanley Rubin to the author.

311 "what happened": Peter Harry Brown and Pat H. Broeske, *Howard Hughes: The Untold Story* (New York: Dutton, 1996), p. 282.

312 "near masterpiece": *Daily Variety,* 10/19/51.

312 "They have a way": Robert Lewin, "The King Brothers," *Life,* 11/22/48.

313 "piece of junk": Philip Yordan to Scott Eyman, 2/29/00 (Courtesy of Scott Eyman).

313 "Frank King was the brains": Arthur Gardner to the author, via telephone, 7/7/00.

314 "just a sketch": Suzanne Antles to the author, 8/17/01.

314 "The test he made": Valerie Pascal, *The Disciple and His Devil* (New York: McGraw Hill, 1970), p. 225.

314  "couldn't get the man": Ibid.

315  "took me around": Alan Young to the author, via telephone, 5/8/00.

315  "every art director": Harold Rose to WCM, 3/31/52 (WCM).

316  "Her room": Pamela Lauesen to the author, via email, 3/2/11.

316  "the television business": WCM to Mignon Menzies, 3/17/52 (WCM).

316  "very well trained": Richard Sylbert to the author.

317  "pigeons roosting": Richard Sylbert and Sylvia Townsend, *Designing Movies* (Westport, CT: Praeger, 2006), p. 33.

317  "This whole trip": WCM to Mignon Menzies, 4/9/52 (WCM).

317  "finally finished": WCM to Mignon Menzies, 4/23/52 (WCM).

317  "groping": Suzanne Antles to the author.


19. WORTH EVERY PENNY

319  "pick up": WCM to Laurence Irving, 8/10/52 (Courtesy of John H. B. Irving).

321  "The mother": Robert Skotak and Scot Holton, "Invaders from Mars," *Fantascene* 4, 1978.

321  "Jules": Arthur Gardner, *The Badger Kid* (Victoria, BC: Trafford, 2008), p. 37.

321  "design of the setting": Kritzer, "An Analysis of the Technique of Production Design in Cinema as Employed by William Cameron Menzies," p. 65.

322  "quite a few little drawings": Boris Leven, American Film Institute seminar, n.d.

322  "They'd see $1,000": Skotak and Holton, "Invaders from Mars."

323  "in the production office": Ibid.

323  "He knew what he wanted": Jimmy Hunt to the author, via telephone, 3/14/01.

324  "very nice time": John F. Seitz, American Film Institute Oral History with James Ursini, May 1971–May 1972.

324  "I never got to know him": Tom Weaver, *Attack of the Monster Movie Makers* (Jefferson, NC: McFarland, 1994), p. 256.

325  "Menzies . . . was respected": Skotak and Holton, "Invaders From Mars."

326  "very businesslike": Jimmy Hunt to the author.

327  "a good choice": Walter Mirisch, *I Thought We Were Making Movies, Not History* (Madison: University of Wisconsin Press, 2008), p. 59.

327  drinking on the picture: In separate conversations, Walter Mirisch told both Anthony Slide and Scott Eyman that Menzies was drinking during production of *The Maze*.

327  "Unfortunately": Mirisch, *I Thought We Were Making Movies, Not History*, p. 59.

327  "designed and directed": *Daily Variety*, 4/8/53.

327  domestic rentals: Figures on *Invaders from Mars* are from the research library of Karl Thiede.

329  "I was just this kid": Richard Sylbert to the author.

329  "deep in the hassle": WCM to Mignon Menzies, 2/13/54 (WCM).

329  "twenty weeks": Juliet Benita Colman, *Ronald Colman: A Very Private Person* (New York: William Morrow, 1975), p. 264.

330  "Colman was responsible": Suzanne Antles to the author.

330  "get me something": Joel Sayer, "Mike Todd and His Big Bug-Eye," *Life*, 3/7/55.

331  "all during production": Michael Todd, Jr., and Susan McCarthy Todd, *A Valuable Property* (New York: Arbor House, 1983), p. 278.

331  "worried about time": WCM to Mignon Menzies, 7/29/55 (WCM).

331  "I got to the Prado": WCM to Mignon Menzies, 8/9/55 (WCM).

331  "just breaking away": Ken Adam to the author, via telephone, 8/2/00.

332  "slowly assembling": Roy Frumkes, "An Interview with Mike Todd, Jr." (1995), posted at www.in70mm.com.

332  "We started in Spain": Todd and Todd, *A Valuable Property,* p. 282.

332  "very upset": WCM to Mignon Menzies, 8/18/55 (WCM).

332  "wasn't overwhelming": Frumkes, "An Interview with Mike Todd, Jr."

333  "great show": WCM to Mignon Menzies, n.d. (WCM).

333  "almost destroyed": Ken Adam to the author.

333  "took the cigar out": Todd, Jr., and Todd, *A Valuable Property,* p. 282.

334  "the design of the film": Michael Anderson to the author, via telephone, 10/23/01.

334  "lost track": WCM to Mignon Menzies, 8/17/55 (WCM).

334  "an experience": WCM to Mignon Menzies, 9/7/55 (WCM).

334  "There was no process": Michael Anderson to the author.

335  "he was always ahead": Michael Anderson to the author.

336  "He was sick": Suzanne Antles to the author.

336  "Daddy used to drive": Suzanne Antles to the author.

336  "Everybody said": Todd, Jr., and Todd, *A Valuable Property,* p. 303.

337  "considered it carefully": *New York Times,* 2/5/56.

337  "surefire": *Daily Variety,* 10/18/56.

337  "sprawling": *New York Times,* 10/18/56.

337  "every glowing adjective": *New York Journal-American,* 10/18/56.

338  "I vaguely remember": Pamela Lauesen to the author, via email, 3/2/11.

338  "stopped by": James Vance to the author.

338  "He was so miserable": Suzanne Antles to the author.

338  "When he was dying": Pamela Lauesen to the author, via email, 3/2/11.

338  "Mother was with him": Suzanne Antles to the author.

339  "Uncle Bill died": John Cameron Menzies, Jr., to the author, New Haven, 3/23/03. Ellen Menzies lived to be ninety-seven, and died in New Haven on December 24, 1962.

340  "An incessant photographer": Pamela Lauesen to the author via email, 8/17/11.

340  "quite a social time": Mignon Menzies to Pamela Lauesen, 10/3/67.

341  "a prodigious capacity": *Times* (London), 3/11/57.

# APPENDIX I

### The Lullaby

Written by Edward Knoblock (Knickerbocker, October 8, 1923). Scenery designed by William Cameron Menzies. Produced by Charles Dillingham. Directed by Fred G. Latham. Cast: Florence Reed, Frank Morgan, Rose Hobart, Leonard Mudie, Alice Fleming, Mary Robson, Rupert Lumley, Grace Perkins, Henry Plimmer.

### The Ambulance Chaser

Written by Sam and Bella Spewack (Hollywood Playhouse, January 21, 1931). Scenery designed by William Cameron Menzies. Cast: Harry Green, Thomas Jackson, Willette Morris, Don Gallaher.

### Grand Guignol

Written by H. P. Maltby, Andre De Lorde, Reginald Berkeley, Eliot Crawshay-Williams (Hollywood Music Box, December 28, 1932). Scenery designed by William Cameron Menzies. Produced by George K. Arthur. Directed by Robert Vignola, Donald Crisp, Reginald Berkeley. Cast: Mitchell Lewis, Doris Lloyd, Grace Stafford, Eric Snowdon, Edward Cooper, Raymond Lawrence, Ethel Griddies, Adda Gleason, May Beatty, Elspeth Dudgeon, Donald Murray, Boyd Irvin, Henry Mowbray.

### Anna Christie

Written by Eugene O'Neill (Lobero, Santa Barbara, July 30, 1941). Scenery designed by Kate Drain Lawson from sketches by William Cameron Menzies. Presented by The Selznick Company. Managing Director: Alfred de Liagre. Directed by John Houseman. Cast: Ingrid Bergman, J. Edward Bromberg, Damian O'Flynn, Jessie Busley, John Miller, Peter Bronte, Edmond Glover, Walter Brooke, William Alland.

NOTE: This production moved to San Francisco for a two-week engagement at the Curran Theatre beginning August 4, 1941.

# APPENDIX II

### The Naulahka

Director: George Fitzmaurice. Based upon the novel by Rudyard Kipling and Charles Wolcott Balestier. Scenario: George B. Seitz. Photography: Arthur C. Miller. Settings: Anton Grot. Associate: William Cameron Menzies. Production: Astra Film Corp. Distribution: Pathé. Release Date: February 24, 1918. Length: 6 reels. Cast: Antonio Moreno, Doraldina, Helene Chadwick, J. H. Gilmour, Warner Oland, Mary Alden, Edna Hunter.

### The Mark of Cain

Director: George Fitzmaurice. Story: Carolyn Wells. Scenario: Philip Bartholomae. Photography: Arthur C. Miller. Settings: Anton Grot. Associate: William Cameron Menzies. Production: Astra Film Corp. Distribution: Pathé. Release Date: November 4, 1917. Length: 5 reels. Cast: Mrs. Vernon Castle, Antonio Moreno, J. H. Gilmour, Elinor Black, John Sainpolis.

### Innocent

Director: George Fitzmaurice. Based upon the play by George Broadhurst. Scenario: Ouida Bergére. Photography: Percy Hilburn. Settings: Anton Grot. Associate: William Cameron Menzies. Production: Astra Film Corp. Distribution: Pathé. Release Date: January 27, 1918. Length: 5 reels. Cast: Fannie Ward, John Miltern, Armand Kaliz, Frederick Perry, Nathaniel Sack.

NOTE: Menzies likely entered the Navy before work on this film was completed.

### The Test of Honor

Director: John S. Robertson. Based upon the novel *The Malefactor* by E. Phillips Oppenheim. Scenario: Eve Unsell. Photography: J. Monteran. Settings: R. Ellis Wales. Associate: William Cameron Menzies. Production: Famous Players-Lasky. Distribution: Paramount. Release Date: April 6, 1919. Length: 5 reels. Cast: John Barrymore, Constance Binney, Marcia Manon, Robert Schable, J. W. Johnson, Bigelow Cooper.

NOTE: Although Menzies apparently received no credit on this film, he included it on a handwritten list (as *The Malefactor*) under the heading "Movies I have staged."

## Redhead

Director: Charles Maigne. Story: Henry Payson Dowst. Scenario: Charles Maigne. Photography: Al Liguori. Production and Distribution: Select Pictures Corp. Release Date: April 27, 1919. Length: 5 reels. Cast: Alice Brady, Conrad Nagel, Robert Schable, Charles A. Stevenson, Charles Eldridge, May Brettone.

NOTE: No art direction credit could be determined for this film, but Menzies included it on a hand-written list under the heading "Movies I have staged."

## Come Out of the Kitchen

Director: John S. Robertson. Based upon the novel by Alice Duer Miller. Scenario: Clara Beranger. Photography: Jacques Monteran, Hal Young. Production: Famous Players-Lasky. Distribution: Paramount. Release Date: May 11, 1919. Length: 5 reels. Cast: Marguerite Clark, Frances Kaye, Bradley Barker, Albert M. Hackett, George Stevens, May Kitson, Eugene O'Brien, Frederick Esmelton, Craufurd Kent.

NOTE: No art direction credit could be determined for this film, but Menzies included it on a hand-written list under the heading "Movies I have staged."

## The Avalanche

Director: George Fitzmaurice. Based upon the novel by Gertrude Atherton. Scenario: Ouida Bergére. Photography: Arthur C. Miller. Settings: George Fitzmaurice. Associate: William Cameron Menzies. Production: Famous Players-Lasky. Distribution: Artcraft. Release Date: June 22, 1919. Length: 5 reels. Cast: Elsie Ferguson, Lumsden Hare, Zeffie Tilbury, Fred Esmelton, William Roselle, Grace Field, Warner Oland.

NOTE: In contemporary publicity, it was noted that George Fitzmaurice designed most of the sets. Menzies apparently received no credit, but he included the film on a handwritten list under the heading "Movies I have staged."

## The Firing Line

Director: Charles Maigne. Based upon the novel by Robert W. Chambers. Scenario: Clara Beranger. Photography: Al Liguori. Production: Famous Players-Lasky. Distribution: Paramount-Artcraft. Release Date: July 6, 1919. Length: 6 reels. Cast: Irene Castle, Isabelle West, May Kitson, Anne Cornwall, Gladys Coburn, R. Vernon Steele, David Powell, J. H. Gilmour, Frank Losee.

NOTE: No art direction credit could be determined for this film, but Menzies included it on a hand-written list under the heading "Movies I have staged."

## His Bridal Night

Director: Kenneth Webb. Based upon the play by Lawrence Irving Rising. Scenario: Kathryne Stuart. Photography: Jacques Monteran, George Folsey. Production and Distribution: Select Pictures Corp. Release Date: July 14, 1919. Length: 5 reels. Cast: Alice Brady, James L. Crane, Edward Earle, Daniel Pennell, Daisy Belmore, Mrs. Stuart Robson.

NOTE: No art direction credit could be determined for this film, but Menzies included it on a hand-written list under the heading "Movies I have staged."

### A Society Exile

Director: George Fitzmaurice. Based upon the play *We Can't Be as Bad as All That* by Henry Arthur Jones. Scenario: Ouida Bergére. Photography: Arthur C. Miller. Production: Famous Players-Lasky. Distribution: Artcraft. Release Date: August 17, 1919. Length: 5 reels. Cast: Elsie Ferguson, William P. Carleton, Warburton Gamble, Julia Dean, Henry Stephenson, Zeffie Tilbury, Bijou Fernandez, Alexander Kyle.

NOTE: No art direction credit could be determined for this film, but Menzies included it on a handwritten list under the heading "Movies I have staged."

### The Misleading Widow

Director: John S. Robertson. Based upon the play *Billeted* by F. Tennyson Jesse, H. M. Harwood. Scenario: Frances Marion. Photography: Roy Overbaugh. Production: Famous Players-Lasky. Distribution: Paramount-Artcraft. Release Date: September 7, 1919. Length: 5 reels. Cast: Billie Burke, James L. Crane, Frank Mills, Madeline Clare, Fred Hearn, Mrs. Priestley Morrison, Frederick Esmelton, Dorothy Waters.

NOTE: No art direction credit could be determined for this film, but Menzies included it (as *Billeted*) on a handwritten list under the heading "Movies I have staged."

### The Witness for the Defense

Director: George Fitzmaurice. Based upon the play by A. E. W. Mason. Scenario: Ouida Bergére. Photography: Hal Young. Settings: William Cameron Menzies. Production: Famous Players-Lasky. Distribution: Paramount-Artcraft. Release Date: September 14, 1919. Length: 5 reels. Cast: Elsie Ferguson, Vernon Steel, Warner Oland, Wyndham Standing, George Fitzgerald, J. H. Gilmour, Amelia Summerville, Cora Williams, Blanche Standing.

### The Teeth of the Tiger

Director: Chet Withey. Based upon the novel by Maurice Leblanc. Scenario: Roy Somerville. Photography: Al Ligouri. Settings: William Cameron Menzies. Production: Famous Players-Lasky. Distribution: Paramount-Artcraft. Release Date: November 2, 1919. Length: 6 reels. Cast: David Powell, Marguerite Courtot, Templar Saxe, Myrtle Stedman, Joseph Herbert, Charles L. MacDonald, William Riley Hatch, Charles Gerard.

### His Wife's Friend

Producer: Thomas H. Ince. Director: Joseph De Grasse. Based upon the novel *The White Rook* by John Burland. Scenario: R. Cecil Smith. Photography: John S. Stumar. Production: Thomas H. Ince. Distribution: Paramount-Artcraft. Release Date: December 21, 1919. Length: 6 reels. Cast: Dorothy Dalton, Warren Cook, Henry Mortimer, Richard Neil, Paul Cazeneuve, Tom Cameron, William Williams.

NOTE: No art direction credit could be determined for this film, but Menzies included it (as *The White Rook*) on a handwritten list under the heading "Movies I have staged."

### Sinners

Director: Kenneth Webb. Based upon the play by Owen Davis. Scenario: Eve Unsell. Photography: George Folsey. Production and Distribution: Realart Pictures Corp. Release Date: March 15, 1920.

Length: 5 reels. Cast: Alice Brady, Agnes Everett, Augusta Anderson, Lorraine Frost, Nora Reed, James L. Crane, W. P. Carleton, Frank Losee, Craufurd Kent, Robert Schable.

NOTE: No art direction credit could be determined for this film, but Menzies included it on a hand-written list under the heading "Movies I have staged."

### Dr. Jekyll and Mr. Hyde

Director: John S. Robertson. Based upon the novelette *The Strange Case of Dr. Jekyll and Mr. Hyde* by Robert Louis Stevenson. Scenario: Clara S. Beranger. Photography: Roy Overbaugh. Settings: Robert M. Haas, Clark Robinson. Production: Famous Players-Lasky. Distribution: Paramount-Artcraft. Release Date: April 1920. Length: 7 reels. Cast: John Barrymore, Martha Mansfield, Brandon Hurst, Charles Lane, J. Malcolm Dunn, Cecil Clovelly, Nita Naldi, George Stevens, Louis Wolheim.

NOTE: Although Menzies received no credit on this film, he included it in a draft summary, circa 1941, of titles to which he contributed.

### The Deep Purple

Director: Raoul Walsh. Based upon the play by Paul Armstrong, Wilson Mizner. Scenario: Earle Browne. Photography: Jacques Bizeul. Settings: William Cameron Menzies. Production: Mayflower Photoplay Corp. Distribution: Realart Pictures Corp. Release Date: May 2, 1920. Length: 7 reels. Cast: Miriam Cooper, Helen Ware, Vincent Serrano, W. J. Ferguson, Stuart Sage, William B. Mack, Lincoln Plumer, Ethel Hallor, Harold Horne, Lorraine Frost, Louis Mackintosh.

### Scrambled Wives

Producer: Adolph Klauber. Director: Edward H. Griffith. Scenario: Gardner Hunting. Photography: William McCoy, Ray June. Production: Marguerite Clark Productions. Distribution: Associated First National. Release Date: March 1921. Length: 7 reels. Cast: Marguerite Clark, Leon P. Gendron, Ralph Bunker, Florence Martin, Virginia Lee, Alice Mann, Frank Badgley, America Chedister, John Mayer, John Washburn.

NOTE: No art direction credit could be found for this film, but Menzies included it on a handwritten list under the heading "Movies I have staged."

### The Oath

Director: Raoul Walsh. Based upon the novel *Idols* by William John Locke. Scenario: Ralph Spence. Photography: Dal Clawson. Settings: William Cameron Menzies. Production: Mayflower Photoplay Corp. Distribution: Associated First National. Release Date: April 1921. Length: 8 reels. Cast: Miriam Cooper, Robert Fischer, Conway Tearle, Henry Clive, Ricca Allen, Anna Q. Nilsson.

### Serenade

Producer-Director: Raoul Walsh. Scenario: James T. O'Donohoe. Photography: George Peters. Settings: William Cameron Menzies. Production: R. A. Walsh Productions. Distribution: Associated First National. Release Date: August 1921. Length: 7 reels. Cast: Miriam Cooper, George Walsh, Rosita Marstini, James A. Marcus, Josef Swickard, Bertram Grassby, Noble Johnson, Adelbert Knott, Tom Kennedy.

*Kindred of the Dust*

Producer-Director: Raoul Walsh. Based upon the novel by Peter Bernard Kyne. Scenario: James T. O'Donohoe. Photography: Charles Van Enger, Lyman Broening. Settings: William Cameron Menzies. Production: R. A. Walsh Co. Distribution: Associated First National. Release Date: February 27, 1922. Length: 8 reels. Cast: Miriam Cooper, Ralph Graves, Lionel Belmore, Eugenie Besserer, W. J. Ferguson, Caroline Rankin, Pat Rooney, John Herdman.

*Rosita*

Director: Ernst Lubitsch. Based upon the play *Don César de Bazan* by Adolphe Philippe Dennery and Philippe François Pinel. Story: Norbert Falk, Hans Kraly. Adaptation: Edward Knoblock. Photography: Charles Rosher. Art Director: William Cameron Menzies. Settings: Sven Gade. Production: Mary Pickford Co. Distribution: United Artists. Release Date: September 3, 1923. Length: 9 reels. Cast: Mary Pickford, Holbrook Blinn, Irene Rich, George Walsh, Charles Belcher, Frank Leigh, Mathilde Comont, George Periolat, Bert Sprotte, Snitz Edwards.

NOTE: A completely unrelated feature derived from the same source material was released by Paramount on November 4, 1923. Titled *The Spanish Dancer,* the film starred Pola Negri, Antonio Moreno, and Wallace Beery.

*The Thief of Bagdad*

Director: Raoul Walsh. Story: Elton Thomas. Scenario Editor: Lotta Woods. Consultant: Edward Knoblock. Titles: George Sterling. Photography: Arthur Edeson. Associates: Richard Holahan, P. H. Whitman, Kenneth MacLean. Art Director: William Cameron Menzies. Consulting Art Director: Irvin J. Martin. Associate Artists: Anton Grot, Paul Youngblood, H. R. Hopps, Harold Grieve, Park French, William Utwich, Edward M. Langley. Editor: William Nolan. Production: Douglas Fairbanks Pictures. Distribution: United Artists. Release Date: March 18, 1924. Length: 12 reels. Cast: Douglas Fairbanks, Snitz Edwards, Charles Belcher, Julanne Johnston, Anna May Wong, Winter-Blossom, Etta Lee, Brandon Hurst, Tote Du Crow.

*The Only Woman*

Director: Sidney Olcott. Story: C. Gardner Sullivan. Photography: Antonio Gaudio. Settings: William Cameron Menzies. Editor: Hal C. Kern. Production: Joseph M. Schenck Productions. Distribution: First National. Release Date: October 26, 1924. Length: 7 reels. Cast: Norma Talmadge, Eugene O'Brien, Edward Davis, Winter Hall, Matthew Betz, E. H. Calvert, Stella di Lanti, Murdock MacQuarry, Rev. Neal Dodd, Brooks Benedict, Charles O'Malley.

*Her Night of Romance*

Director: Sidney Franklin. Story: Hans Kraly. Photography: Ray Binger, Victor Milner. Art Direction: William Cameron Menzies, Park French. Editor: Hal C. Kern. Production: Talmadge Producing Corporation. Distribution: First National. Release Date: October 27, 1924. Length: 8 reels. Cast: Constance Talmadge, Ronald Colman, Albert Gran, Jean Hersholt, Robert Rendel, James O. Barrows.

*The Lady*

Director: Frank Borzage. Based upon the play by Martin Brown. Continuity: Frances Marion. Photography: Antonio Gaudio. Settings: William Cameron Menzies. Editor: Hal C. Kern. Production:

Joseph M. Schenck Productions. Distribution: First National. Release Date: February 8, 1925. Length: 8 reels. Cast: Norma Talmadge; Wallace MacDonald; Brandon Hurst; Alf Goulding; Doris Lloyd; John Fox, Jr.; Paulette Duval; Emily Fitzroy; Margaret Seddon; Miles McCarthy; Marc MacDermott; George Hackathone; Walter Long.

### Learning to Love

Producer: Joseph M. Schenck. Director: Sidney Franklin. Story and Adaptation: John Emerson, Anita Loos. Photography: Victor Milner. Settings: William Cameron Menzies. Production: Talmadge Producing Corporation. Distribution: First National. Release Date: January 25, 1925. Length: 7 reels. Cast: Constance Talmadge, Antonio Moreno, Emily Fitzroy, Edythe Chapman, Johnny Harron, Ray Hallor, Wallace MacDonald, Alf Goulding, Byron Munson, Edgar Norton.

### Her Sister from Paris

Producer: Joseph M. Schenck. Director: Sidney Franklin. Based upon the play *The Twin Sister* by Ludwig Fulda. Adaptation: Hans Kraly. Photography: Arthur Edeson. Art Director: William Cameron Menzies. Editor: Hal C. Kern. Production: Talmadge Producing Corporation. Distribution: First National. Release Date: August 2, 1925. Length: 7 reels. Cast: Constance Talmadge, Ronald Colman, George K. Arthur, Gertrude Claire.

### Graustark

Producer: Joseph M. Schenck. Director: Dimitri Buchowetzki. Based upon the novel by George Barr. Adaptation: Frances Marion. Photography: Gaetano Gaudio. Settings: William Cameron Menzies. Production: Joseph M. Schenck Productions. Distribution: First National. Release Date: August 30, 1925. Length: 7 reels. Cast: Norma Talmadge, Eugene O'Brien, Marc MacDermott, Roy D'Arcy, Albert Gran, Lillian Lawrence, Michael Vavitch, Frank Currier, Winter Hall, Wanda Hawley.

### The Dark Angel

Director: George Fitzmaurice. Based upon the play by H. B. Trevelyan. Adaptation: Frances Marion. Photography: George Barnes. Settings: William Cameron Menzies. Production: Samuel Goldwyn. Distribution: First National. Release Date: September 4, 1925. Length: 8 reels. Cast: Ronald Colman, Vilma Banky, Wyndham Standing, Frank Elliott, Charles Lane, Helen Jerome Eddy, Florence Turner.

### The Eagle

Producer: John W. Considine, Jr. Director: Clarence Brown. Based upon the story "Dubrowsky" by Alexander Pushkin. Adaptation: Hans Kraly. Titles: George Marion, Jr. Photography: George Barnes, Dev Jennings. Settings: William Cameron Menzies. Editor: Hal Kern. Production: Art Finance Corporation. Distribution: United Artists. Release Date: November 8, 1925. Length: 7 reels. Cast: Rudolph Valentino, Vilma Banky, Louise Dresser, Albert Conti, James Marcus, George Nichols, Carie Clark Ward, Michael Pleschkoff, Spottiswoode Aitken, Gustav von Seyffertitz.

### Cobra

Director: Joseph Henabery. Based upon the play by Martin Brown. Adaptation: Anthony Coldewey. Photography: J. D. Jennings, Harry Fishbeck. Settings: William Cameron Menzies. Editor: John H. Bonn. Production: Ritz-Carlton Pictures. Distribution: Paramount. Release Date: November 30, 1925.

Length: 7 reels. Cast: Rudolph Valentino, Nita Naldi, Casson Ferguson, Gertrude Olmstead, Hector V. Sarno, Claire De Lorez, Eileen Percy, Lillian Langdon, Henry Barrows, Rosa Rosanova.

### The Wanderer

Producer-Director: Raoul Walsh. Based upon the play by Maurice V. Samuels. Screenplay: James T. O'Donohoe. Photography: Victor Milner. Settings: William Cameron Menzies. Production: Famous Players-Lasky. Distribution: Paramount. Release Date: February 1, 1926. Length: 9 reels. Cast: Greta Nissen; William Collier, Jr.; Ernest Torrence; Wallace Beery; Tyrone Power; Kathryn Hill; Kathlyn Williams; George Rigas; Holmes Herbert; Snitz Edwards.

### The Bat

Producer-Director: Roland West. Based upon the play by Mary Roberts Rinehart and Avery Hopwood. Adaptation: Roland West. Continuity: Julien Josephson. Titles: George Marion, Jr. Photography: Arthur Edeson. Settings: William Cameron Menzies. Editor: Hal C. Kern. Production: Feature Productions. Distribution: United Artists. Release Date: March 14, 1926. Length: 9 reels. Cast: Andre de Beranger, Charles Herzinger, Emily Fitzroy, Louise Fazenda, Arthur Houseman, Robert McKim, Jack Pickford, Jewel Carmen, Sojin Kamiyama, Tullio Carminati, Eddie Gribbon, Lee Shumway.

### Kiki

Producer: Joseph M. Schenck. Director: Clarence Brown. Based upon the play by Andre Picard and David Belasco. Adaptation: Hans Kraly. Titles: George Marion, Jr. Photography: Oliver Marsh. Settings: William Cameron Menzies. Editor: Hal C. Kern. Production: Joseph M. Schenck Productions. Distribution: First National. Release Date: April 4, 1926. Length: 9 reels. Cast: Norma Talmadge, Ronald Colman, Gertrude Astor, Marc McDermott, George K. Arthur, Irwin Connelly, William Orlamond, Catherine Bennett, Frankie Darro.

### The Son of the Sheik

Producer: John W. Considine, Jr. Director: George Fitzmaurice. Based upon the novel *The Son of the Sheik* by E. M. Hull. Adaptation: Frances Marion, Fred De Gresac. Titles: George Marion, Jr. Photography: George Barnes. Settings: William Cameron Menzies. Production: Feature Productions. Distribution: United Artists. Release Date: July 9, 1926. Length: 7 reels. Cast: Rudolph Valentino, Vilma Banky, George Fawcett, Montagu Love, Karl Dane, Bull Montana, Binunsky Hyman, Agnes Ayres.

### Fig Leaves

Director: Howard Hawks. Story: Howard Hawks. Screenplay: Hope Loring, Louis D. Lighton. Photography: Joseph August. (Technicolor sequence.) Settings: William Cameron Menzies, William Darling. Editor: Rose Smith. Production and Distribution: Fox. Release Date: August 22, 1926. Length: 7 reels. Cast: George O'Brien, Olive Borden, Phyllis Haver, Andre de Beranger, William Austin, Heinie Conklin, Eulalie Jensen.

NOTE: Menzies' work was confined to the Garden of Eden sequence at the beginning of the film.

### The Duchess of Buffalo

Producer: Joseph M. Schenck. Director: Sidney Franklin. Based upon the play *Sybil* by Max Bordy, Franz Martos. Adaptation: Hans Kraly. Titles: George Marion, Jr. Photography: Oliver Marsh. Art

Director: William Cameron Menzies. Editor: Hal C. Kern. Production: Constance Talmadge Productions. Distribution: First National. Release Date: September 5, 1926. Length: 7 reels. Cast: Constance Talmadge, Tullio Carminati, Edward Martindel, Rose Dione, Chester Conklin, Lawrence Grant, Martha Franklin, Jean De Briac.

### The Beloved Rogue

Producer: John W. Considine, Jr. Director: Alan Crosland. Story and Screenplay: Paul Bern. Titles: George Marion, Jr., William Anthony. Photography: Joseph August. Art Director: William Cameron Menzies. Editor: Hal C. Kern. Production: Feature Productions. Distribution: United Artists. Release Date: March 12, 1927. Length: 10 reels. Cast: John Barrymore, Conrad Veidt, Marceline Day, Lawson Butt, Henry Victor, Slim Summerville, Mack Swain, Angelo Rossitto, Nigel de Brulier, Lucy Beaumont, Otto Matieson, Jane Winton, Rose Dione, Bertram Grassby, Dick Sutherland.

### Venus of Venice

Producer: Joseph M. Schenck. Director: Marshall Neilan. Story and Screenplay: Wallace Smith. Titles: George Marion, Jr. Photography: George Barnes. Art Director: William Cameron Menzies. Editor: Hal C. Kern. Production: Constance Talmadge Productions. Distribution: First National. Release Date: March 20, 1927. Length: 7 reels. Cast: Constance Talmadge, Antonio Moreno, Julanne Johnston, Edward Martindel, Michael Vavitch, Arthur Thalasso, André Lanoy, Carmelita Geraghty, Mario Carillo, Tom Ricketts, Hedda Hopper.

### Camille

Producer-Director: Fred Niblo. Based upon the novel by Alexandre Dumas, *fils*. Screen Story: Fred De Gresac. Adaptation and Screenplay: Olga Printzlau, Chandler Sprague. Titles: George Marion, Jr. Photography: Oliver Marsh. Art Director: William Cameron Menzies. Production: Joseph M. Schenck Productions. Distribution: First National. Release Date: April 21, 1927. Length: 9 reels. Cast: Norma Talmadge, Gilbert Roland, Lilyan Tashman, Rose Dione, Oscar Beregi, Harvey Clark, Helen Jerome Eddy, Alec B. Francis, Albert Conti, Michael Visaroff, Evelyn Selbie, Etta Lee, Maurice Costello.

### Topsy and Eva

Supervisor: Myron Selznick. Director: Del Lord. (Uncredited: D. W. Griffith.) Based upon the play by Catherine Chisholm Cushing. Adaptation: Lois Weber. Continuity: Scott Darling. Titles: Dudley Early. Photography: John W. Boyle. Art Director: William Cameron Menzies. Production: Feature Productions. Distribution: United Artists. Release Date: June 16, 1927. Length: 8 reels. Cast: Rosetta Duncan, Vivian Duncan, Gibson Gowland, Noble Johnson, Marjorie Daw, Myrtle Ferguson, Nils Asther, Henry Victor.

### Two Arabian Knights

Producer: John W. Considine, Jr. Director: Lewis Milestone. Based upon the story by Donald McGibney. Screen Story: Wallace Smith, Cyril Gardner. Continuity: James O'Donohue. Titles: George Marion, Jr. Photography: Antonio Gaudio. (Uncredited: Joseph August.) Art Director: William Cameron Menzies. Editor: Douglas Biggs. Production: The Caddo Company. Distribution: United Artists. Release Date: September 23, 1927. Length: 9 reels. Cast: William Boyd, Mary Astor, Louis Wolheim,

Ian Keith, Michael Vavitch, M. Visaroff, Boris Karloff, De Witt Jennings, Nicholas Dunaew, Joan Vachon, Denis D'Auburn.

### *Sorrell and Son*

Producer-Director: Herbert Brenon. Based upon the novel by Warwick Deeping. Adaptation: Elizabeth Meehan. Screenplay: Herbert Brenon. Photography: James Wong Howe. Art Director: William Cameron Menzies. Associate: Julian Boone Fleming. Editor: Marie Halvey. Production: Feature Productions. Distribution: United Artists. Release Date: November 12, 1927. Length: 10 reels. Cast: H. B. Warner, Anna Q. Nilsson, Mickey McBan, Carmel Myers, Lionel Belmore, Norman Trevor, Betsy Ann Hisle, Louis Wolheim, Paul McAllister, Alice Joyce, Nils Asther, Mary Nolan.

### *Quality Street*

Director: Sidney Franklin. Based upon the play by James M. Barrie. Adaptation and Scenario: Hans Kraly, Albert Lewin. Titles: Marian Ainslee, Ruth Cummings. Photography: Hendrik Sartov. Settings: Cedric Gibbons, Allen Ruoff. (Uncredited: William Cameron Menzies.) Editor: Ben Lewis. Production and Distribution: Metro-Goldwyn-Mayer. Release Date: December 31, 1927. Length: 8 reels. Cast: Marion Davies, Conrad Nagel, Helen Jerome Eddy, Flora Finch, Margaret Seddon, Marcelle Corday, Kate Price.

NOTE: In his unpublished autobiography, director Sidney Franklin recalled being loaned to M-G-M for two films by Joseph Schenck. As a condition of the arrangement, Franklin wanted Menzies, with whom he had worked on four previous pictures, to design Green Willow Village, the first major set to be built on Lot Two. Known as Quality Street, the exterior stood, in increasingly dilapidated condition, until 1978.

### *The Dove*

Producer-Director: Roland West. Based upon the play by Willard Mack. Continuity: Wallace Smith, Paul Bern. Titles: Wallace Smith. Photography: Oliver Marsh. Settings: William Cameron Menzies. Executed by Paul Crawley. Editor: Hal C. Kern. Production: Joseph M. Schenck Productions. Distribution: United Artists. Release Date: December 31, 1927. Length: 9 reels. Cast: Norma Talmadge, Noah Beery, Gilbert Roland, Eddie Borden, Harry Myers, Michael Vavitch, Brinsley Shaw, Kalla Pasha, Charles Darvas, Michael Dark, Walter Daniels.

### *Sadie Thompson*

Director: Raoul Walsh. Based upon the story "Miss Thompson" by W. Somerset Maugham. Adaptation: Raoul Walsh. Titles: C. Gardner Sullivan. Photography: Oliver Marsh, George Barnes, Robert Kurrle. Art Director: William Cameron Menzies. Production: Gloria Swanson Productions, Inc. Distribution: United Artists. Release Date: January 7, 1928. Length: 9 reels. Cast: Gloria Swanson, Lionel Barrymore, Raoul Walsh, Blanche Friderici, Charles Lane, Florence Midgley, James A. Marcus, Sophia Artega, Will Stanton.

### *What Price Beauty*

Director: Tom Buckingham. (Uncredited: Alan Hale.) Story and Scenario: Natacha Rambova. Titles: Malcolm Stuart Boylan. Photography: J. D. Jennings. Art Director: William Cameron Menzies. Production: S. George Ulman. Distribution: Pathe. Release Date: January 22, 1928. Length: 5 reels. Cast: Nita Naldi, Pierre Gendron, Virginia Pearson, Dolores Johnson, Myrna Loy, Sally Winters, La Supervia, Marilyn Newkirk, Victor Potel, Spike Rankin, Templar Saxe.

### Drums of Love

Producer-Director: D. W. Griffith. Adaptation: Gerrit Lloyd. Photography: Karl Struss, G. W. Bitzer, Harry Jackson. Settings: William Cameron Menzies, Park French. Editor: James Smith. Production: Feature Productions. Distribution: United Artists. Release Date: January 24, 1928. Length: 9 reels. Cast: Mary Philbin, Lionel Barrymore, Don Alvarado, Tully Marshall, William Austin, Eugenie Besserer, Charles Hill, Rosemary Cooper, Joyce Coad.

### The Garden of Eden

Producer: John W. Considine, Jr. Director: Lewis Milestone. Based upon the play by Rudolf Bernnauer, Rudolph Oesterreicher. Adaptation: Avery Hopwood. Scenario: Hans Kraly. Titles: George Marion, Jr. Photography: John Arnold. (Technicolor sequence.) Art Director: William Cameron Menzies. Editor: John Orlando. Production: Feature Productions. Distribution: United Artists. Release Date: February 4, 1928. Length: 8 reels. Cast: Corinne Griffith, Louise Dresser, Lowell Sherman, Maude George, Charles Ray, Edward Martindel.

### The Love of Zero

Director: Robert Florey. Photography: Edward Fitzgerald. Staging: William Cameron Menzies. Production: Florey-Menzies Productions. First Los Angeles Showing: May 9, 1928. Length: 2 reels. Cast: Joseph Mari, Tamara Shavrova, Anielka Elter.

### Tempest

Producer: John W. Considine, Jr. Director: Sam Taylor. (Uncredited: Viktor Tourjansky, Lewis Milestone.) Story and Adaptation: C. Gardner Sullivan. (Uncredited: Vladimir Nemirovich-Danchenko.) Titles: George Marion, Jr. Photography: Charles Rosher. Art Director: William Cameron Menzies. Editor: Allen McNeil. Music: Hugo Riesenfeld. Production: Feature Productions. Distribution: United Artists. Release Date: July 8, 1928. Length: 10 reels. Cast: John Barrymore, Camilla Horn, Louis Wolheim, Boris de Fas, George Fawcett, Ullrich Haupt, Michael Visaroff.

### The Woman Disputed

Directors: Henry King, Sam Taylor. Based upon the play by Denison Clift. Adaptation: C. Gardner Sullivan. Photography: Oliver Marsh. Art Director: William Cameron Menzies. Editor: Hal C. Kern. Music: Hugo Riesenfeld. Production: Joseph M. Schenck Productions. Distribution: United Artists. Release Date: August 11, 1928. Running Time: 87 minutes. Cast: Norma Talmadge, Gilbert Roland, Arnold Kent, Boris de Fas, Michael Vavitch, Gustav von Seyffertitz, Gladys Brockwell, Nicholas Soussanin.

### Battle of the Sexes

Director: D. W. Griffith. Based upon the story "The Single Standard" by Daniel Carson Goodman. Adaptation: Gerrit Lloyd. Photography: Karl Struss, Billy Bitzer. Settings: William Cameron Menzies, Park French. Editor: James Smith. Music: R. Schildkret, Hugo Riesenfeld. Production: Art Cinema Corporation. Distribution: United Artists. Release Date: October 12, 1928. Running Time: 88 minutes. Cast: Jean Hersholt, Phyllis Haver, Belle Bennett, Sally O'Neil, Don Alverado, William Bakewell, John Batten.

## *Revenge*

Producer-Director: Edwin Carewe. Based upon the story "The Bear Tamer's Daughter" by Konrad Bercovici. Screenplay: Finis Fox. Photography: Robert Kurrie, Al. M. Greene. Art Director: William Cameron Menzies. Editor: Jeanne Spencer. Music: Hugo Riesenfeld. Production: Edwin Carewe Productions. Distribution: United Artists. Release Date: November 3, 1928. Running Time: 70 minutes. Cast: Dolores Del Rio, James Marcus, Sophia Ortiga, LeRoy Mason, Rita Carewe, Jose Crespo, Sam Appel, Marta Golden, Jess Cavin.

## *The Awakening*

Producer-Director: Victor Fleming. Story: Frances Marion. Screenplay: Carey Wilson. Titles: Elizabeth Hilliker, H. H. Caldwell. Photography: George Barnes. Art Director: William Cameron Menzies. Editor: Viola Lawrence. Music: Hugo Riesenfeld. Production: Samuel Goldwyn. Distribution: United Artists. Release Date: November 17, 1928. Running Time: 90 minutes. Cast: Vilma Banky, Walter Byron, Louis Wolheim, George Davis, William H. Orlamond, Carl von Hartmann.

## *The Rescue*

Producer-Director: Herbert Brenon. Based upon the novel by Joseph Conrad. Screenplay: Elizabeth Meehan. Titles: Elizabeth Hilliker, H. H. Caldwell. Photography: George Barnes, Joseph F. Biroc, James Wong Howe. Art Director: William Cameron Menzies. Editor: Marie Halvey. Music: Hugo Riesenfeld. Production: Samuel Goldwyn. Distribution: United Artists. Release Date: January 12, 1929. Running Time: 96 minutes. Cast: Ronald Colman, Lily Damita, Alfred Hickman, Theodore von Eltz, John Davidson, Philip Strange, Bernard Siegel, Sojin, Harry Cording, Luska Winters, Duke Kahanamoku, George Rigas.

## *Lady of the Pavements*

Director: D. W. Griffith. Based upon the story "La Paiva" by Karl Vollmoeller. Adaptation and Scenario: Sam Taylor, Garrit Lloyd. (Uncredited: Hans Kraly.) Dialogue: George Scarborough. Titles: Gerrit Lloyd. Photography: Karl Struss, G. W. Bitzer. Settings: William Cameron Menzies, Park French. Editor: James Smith. Music: Hugo Riesenfeld. Production: Art Cinema Corporation. Distribution: United Artists. Release Date: February 16, 1929. Running Time: 85 minutes. Cast: William Boyd, Jetta Goudal, Lupe Velez, Albert Conti, George Fawcett, Henry Armetta, William Bakewell, Franklin Pangborn.

NOTE: This film was also released in an 8-reel silent version.

## *Coquette*

Director: Sam Taylor. Based upon the play by George Abbott, Ann P. Bridgers. Adaptation: John Grey, Allen McNeil. Dialogue: Sam Taylor. Photography: Karl Struss. Settings: William Cameron Menzies. Production: Pickford Corporation. Distribution: United Artists. Release Date: March 30, 1929. Running Time: 76 minutes. Cast: Mary Pickford, John Mack Brown, Matt Moore, John Sainpolis, William Janney, Henry Kolker, George Irving, Louise Beavers.

NOTE: A silent version of this film was planned, but Mary Pickford decided there was no need for one after openings in Los Angeles and New York. "The talking version seems to have taken hold tremendously at the United Artists Theater," she said in a statement, "and there are enough theaters wired for talking now to take care of all moviegoers."

### Alibi

Producer-Director: Roland West. Based upon the play *Nightstick* by John Griffith Wray, J. C. Nugent, Elaine S. Carrington. Screenplay: Roland West, C. Gardner Sullivan. Photography: Ray June. Art Director: William Cameron Menzies. Editor: Hal Kern. Music: Hugo Riesenfeld. Production: Feature Productions. Distribution: United Artists. Release Date: April 20, 1929. Running Time: 90 minutes. Cast: Chester Morris, Harry Stubbs, Mae Busch, Eleanor Griffith, Regis Toomey, Purnell B. Pratt, Irma Harrison.

NOTE: This film was also released in an 8-reel silent version.

### This Is Heaven

Producer-Director: Alfred Santell. Story: Arthur Mantell. Screenplay: Hope Loring. Dialogue and Titles: George Marion, Jr. Photography: George Barnes, Gregg Toland. Art Director: William Cameron Menzies. Editor: Viola Lawrence. Music: Hugo Riesenfeld. Production: Samuel Goldwyn. Distribution: United Artists. Release Date: March 1929. Running Time: 90 minutes. Cast: Vilma Banky, James Hall, Fritzi Ridgeway, Lucien Littlefield, Richard Tucker.

NOTE: This film was also released in an 8-reel silent version.

### Bulldog Drummond

Producer: Samuel Goldwyn. Director: F. Richard Jones. Associate Director: A. Leslie Pearce. Based upon the play by "Sapper" and Gerald Du Maurier. Adaptation: Sidney Howard. Continuity: Wallace Smith. Photography: George Barnes, Gregg Toland. Settings: William Cameron Menzies. Editors: Frank Lawrence, Viola Lawrence. Production: Samuel Goldwyn. Distribution: United Artists. Release Date: August 3, 1929. Running Time: 90 minutes. Cast: Ronald Colman, Claude Allister, Lawrence Grant, Montagu Love, Wilson Benge, Joan Bennett, Lilyan Tashman, Charles Sellon, Adolph Milar, Tetsu Komai, Gertrude Short, Donald Novis.

NOTE: This film was also released in a 7-reel silent version.

### Three Live Ghosts

Producer: Max Marcin. Director: Thornton Freeland. Based upon the play by Frederick Stewart Isham and Max Marcin. Adaptation: Max Marcin. Screenplay: Helen Hallett. Photography: Robert Planck. Art Director: William Cameron Menzies. Editor: Robert Kern. Production: Feature Productions. Distribution: United Artists. Release Date: September 15, 1929. Running Time: 87 minutes. Cast: Beryl Mercer, Hilda Vaughn, Harry Stubbs, Joan Bennett, Nancy Price, Charles McNaughton, Robert Montgomery, Claud Allister, Arthur Clayton, Tenen Holtz.

### Impressions of Tschaikowsky's Overture 1812

Producer: Hugo Riesenfeld. Pictorial Effects: William Cameron Menzies. Photography: Karl Struss. Production: Feature Productions. Distribution: United Artists. Release Date: October 5, 1929. Running Time: 10 minutes.

### The Taming of the Shrew

Director: Sam Taylor. Based upon the play by William Shakespeare. Adaptation: Sam Taylor. Photography: Karl Struss. Art Directors: William Cameron Menzies, Laurence Irving. Editor: Allen McNeil. Production: Pickford Corporation/Elton Corporation. Distribution: United Artists. Release Date: October 26, 1929. Running Time: 76 minutes. Cast: Mary Pickford, Douglas Fairbanks, Edwin Maxwell, Joseph Cawthorn, Clyde Cook, Geoffrey Wardwell, Dorothy Jordan.

### The Locked Door

Producer-Director: George Fitzmaurice. Assistant Dramatic Director: Earle Browne. Based upon the play *The Sign on the Door* by Channing Pollock. Adaptation: C. Gardner Sullivan. Dialogue: George Scarborough. Photography: Ray June. Settings: William Cameron Menzies. Editor: Hal Kern. Production: Feature Productions. Distribution: United Artists. Release Date: November 16, 1929. Running Time: 74 minutes. Cast: Rod La Rocque, Barbara Stanwyck, William Boyd, Betty Bronson, Harry Stubbs, Harry Mestayer, Mack Swain, ZaSu Pitts, George Bunny.

### Condemned

Director: Wesley Ruggles. Dialogue Director: Dudley Digges. Based upon the novel *Condemned to Devil's Island* by Blair Niles. Screenplay: Sidney Howard. Photography: George Barnes, Gregg Toland. Settings: William Cameron Menzies. Editor: Stuart Heisler. Production: Samuel Goldwyn. Distribution: United Artists. Release Date: December 7, 1929. Running Time: 86 minutes. Cast: Ronald Colman, Ann Harding, Louis Wolheim, Dudley Digges, William Elmer, Albert Kingsley, William Vaughn.

NOTE: This film was also released in an 8-reel silent version.

### Irish Fantasy

Producers: Hugo Riesenfeld, William Cameron Menzies. Director: O. O. Dull. Continuity: Sidney Lazarus. Photography: Paul Perry. Editor: D. Marion Staines. Production: Feature Productions. Distribution: United Artists. Release Date: December 14, 1929. Running Time: 10 minutes. Cast: Donald Novis, Helen Foster, Nick Cogley, Harry Watson.

### New York Nights

Producer: John W. Considine, Jr. Director: Lewis Milestone. Based upon the play *Tin Pan Alley* by Hugh Stanislaws Stange. Adaptation: Jules Furthman. Photography: Ray June. Settings: William Cameron Menzies. Editor: Hal Kern. Production: Joseph M. Schenck Productions. Distribution: United Artists. Release Date: December 28, 1929. Running Time: 82 minutes. Cast: Norma Talmadge, Gilbert Roland, John Wray, Lilyan Tashman, Roscoe Karns, Mary Doran.

### Lummox

Producer-Director: Herbert Brenon. Based upon the novel by Fannie Hurst. Adaptation: Elizabeth Meehan. Dialogue: Fannie Hurst. Photography: Karl Struss. Settings: William Cameron Menzies. Executed by Park French. Editor: Marie Halvey. Music: Hugo Riesenfeld, Jack Danielson. Production: Feature Productions. Distribution: United Artists. Release Date: January 18, 1930. Running Time: 88 minutes. Cast: Winifred Westover, Dorothy Janis, Lydia Yeamans Titus, Ida Darling, Ben Lyon, Myrta Bonillas, Cosmo Kyrle Bellew, Anita Bellew, Robert Ullman, Clara Langsner, William Collier, Jr., Edna Murphy, Torben Meyer.

## Glorious Vamps

Producers: Hugo Riesenfeld, William Cameron Menzies. Director: O. O. Dull. Continuity: Sidney Lazarus. Photography: Robert Planck. Editor: D. Marion Staines. Production: Feature Productions. Distribution: United Artists. Release Date: January 25, 1930. Running Time: 11 minutes. Cast: Bobby Watson, Christine Maple.

## Be Yourself!

Supervising Producer: John W. Considine, Jr. Associate Producer: William Cameron Menzies. Director: Thornton Freeland. Based upon the story "The Champ" by Joseph Jackson. Adaptation: Max Marcin, Thornton Freeland. Photography: Karl Struss, Robert H. Planck. Settings: William Cameron Menzies. Executed by Park French. Editor: Robert J. Kern. Music: Hugo Riesenfeld. Production: Joseph M. Schenck Productions. Distribution: United Artists. Release Date: February 8, 1930. Running Time: 77 minutes. Cast: Fannie Brice, Robert Armstrong, Harry Green, G. Pat Collins, Gertrude Astor, Budd Fine, Marjorie "Babe" Kane, Rita Flynn.

## Puttin' on the Ritz

Supervising Producer: John W. Considine, Jr. Associate Producer: William Cameron Menzies. Director: Edward Sloman. Dance Director: Maurice Kusell. Story: John W. Considine, Jr. Dialogue: William K. Wells, James Gleason. Music: Hugo Riesenfeld. Songs: "Puttin' on the Ritz," "Alice in Wonderland," "With You" Music and Lyrics: Irving Berlin. Photography: Ray June. (Technicolor sequence.) Settings: William Cameron Menzies. Executed by Park French. Editor: Hal Kern. Music and Lyrics: Irving Berlin. Production: Joseph M. Schenck Productions. Distribution: United Artists. Release Date: March 1, 1930. Running Time: 88 minutes. Cast: Harry Richman, Joan Bennett, James Gleason, Aileen Pringle, Lilyan Tashman, Purnell Prat, Richard Tucker, Eddie Kane, George Irving, Sidney Franklin.

## The Wizard's Apprentice

Producers: Hugo Riesenfeld, William Cameron Menzies. Director: Sidney Levee. Photography: Alfred Schmid. Editor: D. Marion Staines. Production: Feature Productions. Distribution: United Artists. Release Date: April 1, 1930. Running Time: 9 minutes. Cast: Fritz Feld, Greta Granstedt, Josef Swickard, Bernard Seigel.

## One Romantic Night

Producer: John W. Considine, Jr. Director: Paul L. Stein. Based upon the play The Swan by Ferenc Molnár and Melville Baker. Screenplay: Melville Baker. Photography: Karl Struss. Settings: William Cameron Menzies. Executed by Park French. Editor: James Smith. Music: Hugo Riesenfeld. Production: Joseph M. Schenck Productions. Distribution: United Artists. Release Date: April 12, 1930. Running Time: 73 minutes. Cast: Lillian Gish, Rod La Rocque, Conrad Nagel, Marie Dressler, O. P. Heggie, Albert Conti, Edgar Norton, Billie Bennett, Philippe De Lacy, Byron Sage, Barbara Leonard.

## The Bad One

Supervising Producer: John W. Considine, Jr. Producer-Director: George Fitzmaurice. Assistant Dramatic Director: Earle Browne. Story: John Farrow. Adaptation and Dialogue: Carey Wilson, Howard Emmett Rogers. Photography: Karl Struss. Art and Technical Director: William Cameron Menzies.

Settings Executed by Park French. Editor: Donn Hays. Music: Hugo Riesenfeld. Production: Joseph M. Schenck Productions. Distribution: United Artists. Release Date: May 3, 1930. Running Time: 70 minutes. Cast: Dolores Del Rio, Edmund Lowe, Don Alverado, Blanche Frederici, Adrienne D'Ambricourt, Ullrich Haupt, Mitchell Lewis, Ralph Lewis, Charles McNaughton, Yola D'Avril, John St. Pous, Henry Kolker, George Fawcett, Victor Potel, Harry Stubbs, Tommy Dugan.

### Hungarian Rhapsody

Producers: Hugo Riesenfeld, William Cameron Menzies. Director: Eugene Forde. Continuity: Eugene Forde. Photography: Robert Planck. Editor: D. Marion Staines. Production: Feature Productions. Distribution: United Artists. Release Date: May 15, 1930. Running Time: 10 minutes. Cast: Dorothy Janis, Paul Fix, Michael Visaroff, Joseph Melville.

### Raffles

Producer: Samuel Goldwyn. Directors: Henry D'Abbadie D'Arrast, George Fitzmaurice. Based upon the stories by Ernest William Hornung. Screenplay: Sidney Howard. Photography: George Barnes, Gregg Toland. Art Direction: William Cameron Menzies, Park French. Editor: Stuart Heisler. Production: Samuel Goldwyn. Distribution: United Artists. Release Date: July 26, 1930. Running Time: 72 minutes. Cast: Ronald Colman, Kay Francis, David Torrence, Frederick Kerr, Bramwell Fletcher, John Rogers, Wilson Benge, Alison Skipworth, Frances Dade.

NOTE: This film was also released in an 8-reel silent version.

### Forever Yours

Director: Marshall Neilan. Based upon the play *Secrets* by Rudolph Besier and May Edginton. Screenplay: Benjamin Glazer. Photography: Karl Struss. Art Director: William Cameron Menzies. Production: Pickford Corporation. Filmed: July–August 1930. Cast: Mary Pickford, Kenneth MacKenna, Don Alverado, Nella Walker.

NOTE: Pickford abandoned this film after approximately six weeks of shooting and took an estimated loss of between $200,000 and $300,000. An all-new version was released in 1933 under the title *Secrets*.

### Zampa

Producers: Hugo Riesenfeld, William Cameron Menzies. Supervisor: Sidney Levee. Director: Eugene Forde. Based on the opera by Ferdinand Herold. Photography: Karl Struss. Editor: D. Marion Staines. Production: Feature Productions. Distribution: United Artists. Release Date: September 1, 1930. Running Time: 10 minutes. Cast: Wallace MacDonald, Estelle Bradley, Buddy Roosevelt.

### Du Barry, Woman of Passion

Producer-Director: Sam Taylor. Based upon the play *Du Barry* by David Belasco. Adaptation: Sam Taylor. Photography: Oliver Marsh. Settings: William Cameron Menzies. Executed by Park French. Editor: Allen McNeil. Production: Joseph M. Schenck Productions. Distribution: United Artists. Release Date: October 11, 1930. Running Time: 90 minutes. Cast: Norma Talmadge, William Farnum, Conrad Nagel, Hobart Bosworth, Ullrich Haupt, Alison Skipworth, E. Alyn Waren, Edgar Norton, Edwin Maxwell, Henry Kolker.

## The Lottery Bride

Producer: Arthur Hammerstein. Director: Paul L. Stein. Story: Herbert Stothart. Adaptation: Horace Jackson. Continuity and Dialogue: Howard Emmett Rogers. Photography: Ray June. (Technicolor sequence.) Settings and Effects: William Cameron Menzies. Sets Executed by Park French. Editor: Robert Kern. Music: Rudolph Friml. Lyrics: J. Kiern Brennan. Production: Joseph M. Schenck Productions. Distribution: United Artists. Release Date: October 25, 1930. Running Time: 80 minutes. Cast: Jeanette MacDonald, John Garrick, Joe E. Brown, ZaSu Pitts, Robert Chisholm, Joseph Macaulay, Harry Gribbon, Carroll Nye.

## Abraham Lincoln

Producer: John W. Considine, Jr. Director: D. W. Griffith. Associate Dialogue Director: Harry Stubbs. Story: John W. Considine, Jr. Adaptation: Stephen Vincent Benét. Continuity and Dialogue: Stephen Vincent Benét, Gerrit Lloyd. Photography: Karl Struss. Settings: William Cameron Menzies. Executed by Park French. Editorial Advisor: Hal Kern. Editor: James Smith. Music: Hugo Riesenfeld. Production: Feature Productions. Distribution: United Artists. Release Date: November 8, 1930. Running Time: 96 minutes. Cast: Walter Huston; Una Merkel; Kay Hammond; Lucille LaVerne; Edgar Deering; Otto Hoffman; Charles Crockett; Hobart Bosworth; Russell Simpson; Ian Keith; Henry B. Walthall; Oscar Apfel; W. L. Thorne; Helen Freeman; Helen Ware; E. Alyn Warren; Jason Robards; Gordon Thorpe; Cameron Prudhomme; James Bradbury, Sr.; Jimmie Eagle; Frank Campeau.

## Reaching for the Moon

Producer: Irving Berlin. Director: Edmund Goulding. Story with Music: Irving Berlin. Screenplay: Edmund Goulding. (Uncredited: William Anthony McGuire.) Additional Dialogue: Elsie Janis. Photography: Ray June, Robert Planck. Settings: William Cameron Menzies. Editor: Lloyd Nosler, Hal Kern. Production: Feature Productions. Distribution: United Artists. Release Date: February 21, 1931. Running Time: 92 minutes. Cast: Douglas Fairbanks, Bebe Daniels, Edward Everett Horton, Claud Allister, Jack Mulhall, Walter Walker, June MacCloy, Helen Jerome Eddy, Bing Crosby.

## Kiki

Director: Sam Taylor. Assistant Dramatic Director: Earle Browne. Based upon the play by Andre Picard and David Belasco. Adaptation: Sam Taylor. Photography: Karl Struss. Settings: William Cameron Menzies. Editor: Allen McNeil. Music: Alfred Newman. Production: Feature Productions. Distribution: United Artists. Release Date: March 14, 1931. Running Time: 89 minutes. Cast: Mary Pickford, Reginald Denny, Joseph Cawthorn, Margaret Livingston, Phil Tead, Fred Walton, Edwin Maxwell.

## Always Goodbye

Associate Producer: John W. Considine, Jr. Directors: William C. Menzies, Kenneth MacKenna. Story: Kate McLaurin. Continuity and Dialogue: Lynn Starling. Photography: Arthur Edeson. Art Direction: William Darling. Editor: Harold Schuster. Production and Distribution: Fox. Release Date: May 24, 1931. Running Time: 62 minutes. Cast: Elissa Landi, Lewis Stone, Paul Cavanagh, John Garrick, Frederick Kerr, Lumsden Hare, Herbert Bunston, Beryl Mercer.

### The Spider

Associate Producer: William Sistrom. Directors: William C. Menzies, Kenneth MacKenna. Based upon the play by Fulton Oursler and Lowell Brentano. Continuity and Dialogue: Barry Conners, Philip Klein. (Uncredited: Leon Gordon.) Photography: James Wong Howe. Art Direction: Gordon Wiles. Editor: Al De Gaetano. Music: Carli Elinor. Production and Distribution: Fox. Release Date: September 27, 1931. Running Time: 65 minutes. Cast: Edmund Lowe, Lois Moran, El Brendel, John Arledge, George E. Stone, Earle Foxe, Manya Roberti, Howard Phillips, Purnell Pratt, Jesse De Vorska, Kendall McComas, Ruth Donnelly.

### Almost Married

Associate Producer: William Sistrom. Directors: William Cameron Menzies, Marcel Varnel. Based upon the novel *The Devil's Triangle* by Andrew Soutar. Screenplay: Wallace Smith, Guy Bolton. Photography: John Mescall, George Schneiderman. Art Direction: Gordon Wiles. Editors: Ralph Dietrich, Harold Schuster. Music: George Lipschultz. Production and Distribution: Fox. Release Date: July 17, 1932. Running Time: 51 minutes. Cast: Violet Heming, Ralph Bellamy, Alexander Kirkland, Allan Dinehart, Herbert Mundin, Maria Alba, Gustav von Seyffertitz, Tempe Pigott.

### Chandu the Magician

Associate Producer: Robert North. Directors: Marcel Varnel, William C. Menzies. Based upon the radio drama by Harry A. Earnshaw, Vera M. Oldham, and R. R. Morgan. Screenplay: Barry Conners, Philip Klein. (Uncredited: Guy Bolton.) Photography: James Wong Howe. Art Direction: Max Parker. Editor: Harold Schuster. Music: Louis De Francesco. Production and Distribution: Fox. Release Date: September 18, 1932. Running Time: 75 minutes. Cast: Edmund Lowe, Irene Ware, Bela Lugosi, Herbert Mundin, Henry B. Walthall, Weldon Heyburn, June Vlasek, Nestor Aber, Virginia Hammond.

### Cavalcade

Producer: Winfield Sheehan. Director: Frank Lloyd. War Scenes: William C. Menzies. Based upon the play by Noel Coward. Continuity: Sonya Levien. Screenplay: Reginald Berkeley. Photography: Ernest Plamer. Art Direction: William Darling. Editor: Margaret Clancey. Music: Louis De Francesco. Production and Distribution: Fox. Release Date: April 15, 1933. Running Time: 110 minutes. Cast: Diana Wynyard, Clive Brook, Una O'Connor, Herbert Mundin, Beryl Mercer, Irene Browne, Tempe Pigott, Merle Tottenham, Frank Lawton, Ursula Jeans, Margaret Lindsay, John Warburton, Billy Bevan, Desmond Roberts.

### Trick for Trick

Director: Hamilton MacFadden. Technical Effects: William C. Menzies. Based upon the play by Vivian Cosby, Shirley Warde, and Harry Wagstaff Gribble. Screenplay: Howard J. Green. (Uncredited: Thomas Dugan.) Photography: L. W. O'Connell. Art Direction: Duncan Cramer. Editor: Robert Bischoff. Music: Samuel Kaylin. Production and Distribution: Fox. Release Date: April 21, 1933. Running Time: 69 minutes. Cast: Ralph Morgan, Victor Jory, Sally Blane, Tom Dugan, Luis Alberni, Edward Van Sloan, Willard Robertson, Dorothy Appleby, Boothe Howard, Clifford Jones.

### I Loved You Wednesday

Directors: Henry King, William Cameron Menzies. Ballet and Dances: Sammy Lee. Based upon the play by Molly Ricardel and William Du Bois. Screenplay: Philip Klein, Horace Jackson. Photography: Hal Mohr. Art Direction: Joseph Wright. Editor: Frank Hull. Music: Louis De Francesco. Production and Distribution: Fox. Release Date: June 16, 1933. Running Time: 75 minutes. Cast: Warner Baxter, Elissa Landi, Victor Jory, Miriam Jordan, Laura Hope Crews, June Vlasek.

### Alice in Wonderland

Associate Producer: Louis D. Lighton. Director: Norman Z. McLeod. (Uncredited: William Cameron Menzies.) Based upon the books *Alice's Adventures in Wonderland* and *Through the Looking-Glass* by Lewis Carroll. Screenplay: Joseph L. Mankiewicz, William Cameron Menzies. Music: Dimitri Tiomkin. Photography: Harry Sharp, Bert Glennon. Technical Effects: Gordon Jennings, Farciot Edouart. Masks and Costumes: Wally Westmore, Newt Jones. Settings: Robert Odell. Editor: Ellsworth Hoagland. Production and Distribution: Paramount. Release Date: December 22, 1933. Running Time: 76 minutes. Cast: Leon Erroll, Louise Fazenda, Ford Sterling, Skeets Gallagher, Raymond Hatton, Polly Moran, Ned Sparks, Sterling Holloway, Roscoe Ates, Alison Skipworth, Lillian Harmer, Richard Arlen, Edward Everett Horton, Jackie Searl, Charlie Ruggles, Baby LeRoy, May Robson, Alec B. Francis, William Austin, Cary Grant, Edna May Oliver, Jack Oakie, Roscoe Karns, Mae Marsh, W. C. Fields, Gary Cooper, Charlotte Henry.

### Wharf Angel

Associate Producer: Albert Lewis. Directors: William Cameron Menzies, George Somnes. Based upon the play *The Man Who Broke His Heart* by Frederick Schlick. Screenplay: Samuel Hoffenstein, Frank Partos. Dialogue: Stephen Morehouse Avery. Photography: Victor Milner. Art Directors: Hans Dreier, John Goodman. Production and Distribution: Paramount. Release Date: March 16, 1934. Running Time: 65 minutes. Cast: Victor McLaglen, Dorothy Dell, Preston Foster, Alison Skipworth, David Landau, John Rogers, Mischa Auer.

### The Notorious Sophie Lang

Producer: Bayard Veiller. Director: Ralph Murphy. (Uncredited: William Cameron Menzies.) Based upon the stories by Frederick Irving Anderson. Screenplay: Anthony Veiller. Photography: Alfred Gilks. Art Directors: Hans Dreier, Robert Odell. Production and Distribution: Paramount. Release Date: July 20, 1934. Running Time: 64 minutes. Cast: Gertrude Michael, Paul Cavanagh, Arthur Byron, Alison Skipworth, Leon Errol, Ben Taggart, Ferdinand Gottschalk, Del Henderson, Jack Mulhall, Lucio Villegas, Adrian Rosley.

### Cleopatra

Producer-Director: Cecil B. DeMille. (Montage: William Cameron Menzies.) Adaptation: Bartlett Cormack. Screenplay: Waldemar Young, Vincent Lawrence. Music: Rudolph Kopp. Photography: Victor Milner. Art Directors: Hans Dreier, Roland Anderson. Editor: Anne Bauchens. Production and Distribution: Paramount. Release Date: October 5, 1934. Running Time: 102 minutes. Cast: Claudette Colbert, Warren William, Henry Wilcoxon, Gertrude Michael, Joseph Schildkraut, Ian Keith, C. Aubrey Smith.

### Things to Come

Producer: Alexander Korda. Director: William Cameron Menzies. Based upon the novel *The Shape of Things to Come* by H. G. Wells. Screenplay: H. G. Wells. (Uncredited: Lajos Bíró.) Music: Arthur Bliss. Photography: Georges Perinal, Edward Cohen. Special Effects: Ned Mann. Settings: Vincent Korda. Supervising Editor: William Hornbeck. Editors: Charles Crichton, Francis Lyon. Production: London Film Productions. Distribution: United Artists. Release Date: February 20, 1936 (England), April 24, 1936 (United States). Running Time: 108 minutes (England), 96 minutes (United States). Cast: Raymond Massey, Edward Chapman, Ralph Richardson, Margaretta Scott, Cedric Hardwicke, Maurice Braddell, Sophie Stewart, Derrick De Marney, Ann Todd, Pearl Argyle, Kenneth Villiers, Ivan Brandt, Anne McLaren, Patricia Hilliard, Charles Carson.

### Conquest of the Air

Menzies is sometimes credited with having worked on this troubled Korda production. He is mentioned in passing in "The Conquest of the Air: A First View" in the March 1938 issue of *World Film News,* but it appears his involvement was brief.

### The Green Cockatoo

Producer: William K. Howard. (Uncredited: William Cameron Menzies, Alexander Korda, Robert T. Kane.) Director: William Cameron Menzies. (Uncredited: William K. Howard.) Story and Scenario: Graham Greene. Screenplay and Dialogue: Edward O. Berkman. Music: Miklós Rózsa. Song: "Smoky Joe" Music and Lyrics by William Kernell. Photography: Mutz Greenbaum. Art Director: A. Cornwall. Editor: Russell Lloyd. Production: New World Pictures. Distribution: 20th Century-Fox Film Corporation. Release Date: March 1940. Rereleased as *Race Gang,* 1953 (Greenspan & Seligman). Running Time: 64 minutes. Cast: John Mills, Rene Ray, Robert Newton, Allan Jeayes, Charles Oliver, Bruce Seton, Julien Vedey, Frank Atkinson.

NOTE: This film was originally submitted to the British Board of Film Classification in July 1939 under the title *Four Dark Hours.* It was released in the United States in July 1947 by Devonshire Films. For its British rerelease under the title *Race Gang,* it was trimmed to a running time of 56 minutes.

### Nothing Sacred

Producer: David O. Selznick. Assistant to the Producer: William Cameron Menzies. Director: William Wellman. Based upon the story "Letter to the Editor" by James H. Street. Screenplay: Ben Hecht. Music: Oscar Levant. Photography: W. Howard Greene (Technicolor). Special Effects: Jack Cosgrove. Art Director: Lyle Wheeler. Editor: James E. Newcom. Production: Selznick International. Distribution: United Artists. Release Date: November 26, 1937. Running Time: 75 minutes. Cast: Carole Lombard, Fredric March, Charles Winninger, Walter Connolly, Sig Rumann, Frank Fay, Troy Brown, Maxie Rosenbloom, Margaret Hamilton, Olin Howland, Raymond Scott and his Quintette.

### The Adventures of Tom Sawyer

Producer: David O. Selznick. Assistant to the Producer: William H. Wright. Director: Norman Taurog. (Uncredited: George Cukor.) Based upon the novel by Mark Twain. Screenplay: John V. A. Weaver. (Uncredited: Ben Hecht.) Music: Lou Forbes. Photography: James Wong Howe (Technicolor). Special Effects: Jack Cosgrove. Art Director: Lyle Wheeler. Cave Sequence Designed by William Cameron Menzies. Editor: Margaret Clancey. Production: Selznick International. Distribution: United Artists. Release Date: February 11, 1938. Running Time: 93 minutes. Cast: Tommy Kelly, Jackie Moran, Ann Gillis, May Robson, Walter Brennan, Victor Jory, David Holt, Victor Kilian, Nana Bryant, Olin Howland, Donald Meek, Charles Richman, Margaret Hamilton, Marcia May Jones, Mickey Rentschler, Cora Sue Collins, Philip Hurlic.

### The Young in Heart

Producer: David O. Selznick. Assistant to the Producer: William H. Wright. Director: Richard Wallace. (Uncredited: Lewis Milestone.) Based upon the novella *The Gay Banditti* by I. A. R. Wylie. Adaptation: Charles Bennett. Screenplay: Paul Osborn. Music: Franz Waxman. Photography: Leon Shamroy. Special Effects: Jack Cosgrove. Production Designer: William Cameron Menzies. Art Director: Lyle Wheeler. Editor: Hal C. Kern. Production: Selznick International. Distribution: United Artists. Release Date: October 27, 1938. Running Time: 90 minutes. Cast: Janet Gaynor; Douglas Fairbanks, Jr.; Paulette Goddard; Roland Young; Billie Burke; Minnie Dupree; Henry Stephenson; Richard Carlson; Lawrence Grant; Walter Kingsford; Irwin S. Cobb; Lucile Watson.

### Made for Each Other

Producer: David O. Selznick. Director: John Cromwell. Based upon the novel *Of Great Riches* by Rose Franken. Screenplay: Jo Swerling. Music: Lou Forbes. Photography: Leon Shamroy. Special Effects: Jack Cosgrove. Production Designer: William Cameron Menzies. Art Director: Lyle Wheeler. Editor: James E. Newcom. Production: Selznick International. Distribution: United Artists. Release Date: February 10, 1939. Running Time: 85 minutes. Cast: Carole Lombard, James Stewart, Charles Coburn, Lucile Watson, Eddie Quillan, Alma Kruger.

### Gone With the Wind

Producer: David O. Selznick. Director: Victor Fleming. (Uncredited: George Cukor, Sam Wood, William Cameron Menzies.) Based upon the novel by Margaret Mitchell. Screenplay: Sidney Howard. (Uncredited: Ben Hecht, Oliver H. P. Garrett, Jo Swerling.) Music: Max Steiner. Photography: Ernest Haller, Lee Garmes (Technicolor). Special Effects: Jack Cosgrove. Production Designer: William Cameron Menzies. Art Director: Lyle Wheeler. Supervising Editor: Hal C. Kern. Editors: James Newcom, Richard Van Enger, Ernest Leadly. Production: Selznick International. Distribution: Metro-Goldwyn-Mayer. World Premiere: December 15, 1939. Running Time: 220 minutes. Cast: Clark Gable, Vivien Leigh, Leslie Howard, Olivia de Havilland, Thomas Mitchell, Barbara O'Neil, Evelyn Keyes, Ann Rutherford, George Reeves, Fred Crane, Oscar Polk, Butterfly McQueen, Victor Jory, Everett Brown, Howard Hickman, Alicia Rhett, Rand Brooks, Carroll Nye, Laura Hope Crews, Eddie Anderson, Harry Davenport, Leona Roberts, Jane Darwell, Ona Munson.

### Cavalcade of the Academy Awards

Supervisor: Frank Capra. Commentator: Carey Wilson. Other Contributors: Gordon Hollingshead, Jack Chertok, Ira Genet, Owen Crump, Charles Rosher, DeLeon Anthony. Production: Academy of Motion Picture Arts & Sciences. Distribution: Warner Bros. Release Date: April 1940. Running Time: 17 minutes.

NOTE: Menzies is briefly seen accepting his special award for *Gone With the Wind*.

## Rebecca

Producer: David O. Selznick. Director: Alfred Hitchcock. Based upon the novel by Daphne du Maurier. Adaptation: Philip MacDonald, Michael Hogan. Screenplay: Robert E. Sherwood, Joan Harrison. Music: Franz Waxman. Photography: George Barnes. Special Effects: Jack Cosgrove. Art Director: Lyle Wheeler. Supervising Editor: Hal C. Kern. Editor: James Newcom. Production: Selznick International. Distribution: United Artists. Release Date: April 12, 1940. Running Time: 127 minutes. Cast: Laurence Olivier, Joan Fontaine, George Sanders, Judith Anderson, Nigel Bruce, Reginald Denny, C. Aubrey Smith, Gladys Cooper, Florence Bates, Melville Cooper, Leo G. Carroll.

NOTE: Menzies directed the shots of Manderley at the beginning and end of this film and designed the brief sequence in which "I" follows Rebecca's dog, Jasper, into the beach cottage at the edge of the estate.

## Our Town

Producer: Sol Lesser. Director: Sam Wood. Based upon the play by Thornton Wilder. Screenplay: Thornton Wilder, Frank Craven, Harry Chandlee. Music: Aaron Copland. Photography: Bert Glennon. Special Effects: Jack Cosgrove. Production Designer: William Cameron Menzies. Associate: Harry Horner. Art Director: Lewis J. Rachmil. Editor: Sherman Todd. Production: Principal Artists. Distribution: United Artists. Release Date: May 24, 1940. Running Time: 90 minutes. Cast: William Holden, Martha Scott, Fay Bainter, Beulah Bondi, Thomas Mitchell, Guy Kibbee, Stuart Erwin, Frank Craven, Doro Merande, Ruth Toby, Douglas Gardner, Arthur Allen, Charles Trowbridge, Spencer Charters, Dix Davis, Tim Davis.

## Foreign Correspondent

Producer: Walter Wanger. Director: Alfred Hitchcock. Screenplay: Charles Bennett, Joan Harrison. Dialogue: James Hilton, Robert Benchley. Music: Alfred Newman. Photography: Rudolph Maté. Special Photographic Effects: Paul Eagler. Special Production Effects: William Cameron Menzies. Art Director: Alexander Golitzen. Associate: Richard Irvine. Supervising Editor: Otho Lovering. Editor: Dorothy Spencer. Production: Walter Wanger Productions. Distribution: United Artists. Release Date: August 16, 1940. Running Time: 111 minutes. Cast: Joel McCrea, Laraine Day, Herbert Marshall, George Sanders, Albert Basserman, Robert Benchley, Edmund Gwenn, Eduardo Ciannelli, Harry Davenport, Martin Kosleck, Frances Carson, Ian Wolfe, Charles Wagenheim, Edward Conrad, Charles Halton, Barbara Pepper, Emory Parnell, Roy Gordon, Gertrude Hoffman, Martin Lamont, Barry Bernard, Holmes Herbert, Leonard Mudie, John Burton.

## The Thief of Bagdad

Producer: Alexander Korda. Associate Producers: Zoltan Korda, William Cameron Menzies. Directors: Ludwig Berger, Michael Powell, Tim Whelan. (Uncredited: William Cameron Menzies, Zoltan Korda, Alexander Korda.) Scenario: Lajos Bíró. Screenplay and Dialogue: Miles Malleson, Music: Miklós Rózsa. Photography: Georges Périnal (Technicolor). Special Effects: Lawrence Butler. Art Director: Vincent Korda. Supervising Editor: William Hornbeck. Editor: Charles Crichton. Production: Alexander Korda. Distribution: United Artists. Release Date: December 25, 1940. Running Time: 105 minutes. Cast: Conrad Veidt, Sabu, June Duprez, John Justin, Rex Ingram, Miles Malleson, Morton Selten, Mary Morris, Bruce Winston, Hay Petrie, Adelaide Hall, Roy Emerton, Allan Jeayes.

## Meet John Doe

Producers: Frank Capra, Robert Riskin. Director: Frank Capra. Story: Richard Connell, Robert Presnell. Screenplay: Robert Riskin. (Uncredited: Myles Connolly.) Music: Dimitri Tiomkin. Photography: George Barnes. Special Effects: Jack Cosgrove. Art Director: Stephen Goosson. Editor: Daniel Mandell. Studio: Warner Bros. Production: Frank Capra Productions. Distribution: Vitagraph. Release Date: February 14, 1941. Running Time: 120 minutes. Cast: Gary Cooper, Barbara Stanwyck, Edward Arnold, Walter Brennan, Spring Byington, James Gleason, Gene Lockhart, Rod La Rocque, Irving Bacon, Regis Toomey, J. Farrell MacDonald, Warren Hymer, Harry Holman, Andrew Tombes, Pierre Watkin.

NOTE: According to Menzies, he spent a month on this project during the summer of 1940. Some publicity materials indicated that he had designed the production, but he received no screen credit.

## So Ends Our Night

Producers: David L. Loew, Albert Lewin. Director: John Cromwell. Based upon the novel *Flotsam* by Erich Maria Remarque. Screenplay: Talbot Jennings. Music: Louis Gruenberg. Photography: William Daniels. Special Effects: Jack Cosgrove. Production Designer: William Cameron Menzies. Art Director: Jack Otterson. Editor: William Reynolds. Production: David L. Loew-Albert Lewin, Inc. Distribution: United Artists. Release Date: February 14, 1941. Running Time: 120 minutes. Cast: Fredric March, Margaret Sullavan, Frances Dee, Glenn Ford, Anna Sten, Erich von Stroheim, Allan Brett, Joseph Cawthorn, Leonid Kinskey, Alexander Granach, Roman Bohnen, Sig Rumann, William Stack, Lionel Royce, Ernst Deutsch, Spencer Charters, Hans Schumm, Walter Stahl, Philip Van Zandt, Fredrik Vogeding, Joe Marks, Gerta Rozan, James Bush, Emory Parnell, Kate MacKenna, Edith Angold, Edward Fielding, William von Brincken, Gisela Werbezirk, Lisa Golm, Adolf Milar.

## The Devil and Miss Jones

Producer: Frank Ross. Director: Sam Wood. Screenplay: Noman Krasna. Music: Roy Webb. Photography: Harry Stradling. Production Designer: William Cameron Menzies. Art Director: Van Nest Polglase. Associate: Albert D'Agostino. Editor: Sherman Todd. Production: Frank Ross-Norman Krasna, Inc. Distribution: RKO-Radio. Release Date: April 11, 1941. Running Time: 91 minutes. Cast: Jean Arthur, Robert Cummings, Charles Coburn, Edmund Gwenn, Spring Byington, S. Z. Sakall, William Demarest, Walter Kingsford, Montagu Love, Richard Carle, Charles Waldron, Edwin Maxwell, Edward McNamara, Robert Emmett Keane, Florence Bates, Charles Irwin, Matt McHugh, Julie Warren, Ilene Brewer, Regis Toomey, Pat Moriarity.

## Kings Row

Executive Producer: Hal B. Wallis. Associate Producer: David Lewis. Director: Sam Wood. Based upon the novel by Henry Bellamann. Screenplay: Casey Robinson. Music: Erich Wolfgang Korngold. Photography: James Wong Howe. Special Effects: Robert Burks. Production Designer: William Cameron Menzies. Art Director: Carl Jules Weyl. Editor: Ralph Dawson. Production and Distribution: Warner Bros. Release Date: April 18, 1942. Running Time: 127 minutes. Cast: Ann Sheridan, Robert Cummings, Ronald Reagan, Betty Field, Charles Coburn, Claude Rains, Judith Anderson, Nancy Colman, Kaaren Verne, Maria Ouspenskaya, Harry Davenport, Ernest Cossart, Ilka Gruning, Pat Moriarity, Minor Watson, Ludwig Stossel, Erwin Kalser, Egon Brecher, Ann Todd.

## The Pride of the Yankees

Producer: Samuel Goldwyn. Director: Sam Wood. Story: Paul Gallico. Screenplay: Jo Swerling, Herman J. Mankiewicz. (Uncredited: Vincent Lawrence, Dorothy Parker.) Music: Leigh Harline. Photography: Rudolph Maté. Special Effects: Jack Cosgrove, R. O. Binger. Production Designer: William Cameron Menzies. Art Director: Perry Ferguson. Associate: McClure Capps. Editor: Daniel Mandell. Production: Samuel Goldwyn. Distribution: RKO Radio Pictures. Release Date: March 5, 1943. Running Time: 129 minutes. Cast: Gary Cooper, Teresa Wright, Babe Ruth, Walter Brennan, Dan Duryea, Elsa Janssen, Ludwig Stossel, Virginia Gilmore, Bill Dickey, Ernie Adams, Pierre Watkin, Harry Harvey, Robert W. Meusel, Mark Koenig, Bill Stern, Addison Richards, Hardie Albright, Edward Fielding, George Lessey, Edgar Barrier, Douglas Croft, Gene Collins, David Holt.

## Mr. Lucky

Producer: David Hempstead. Director: H. C. Potter. Based upon the story "Bundles for Freedom" by Milton Holmes. Screenplay: Milton Holmes, Adrian Scott. (Uncredited: Charles Brackett, Dudley Nichols, Kenneth Earl, M. M. Musselman.) Music: Roy Webb. Photography: George Barnes. Special Effects: Vernon L. Walker. Production Designer: William Cameron Menzies. Art Directors: Albert S. D'Agostino, Mark-Lee Kirk. Editor: Theron Warth. Production and Distribution: RKO Radio Pictures. Release Date: July 2, 1943. Running Time: 96 minutes. Cast: Cary Grant, Laraine Day, Charles Bickford, Gladys Cooper, Alan Carney, Henry Stephenson, Paul Stewart, Kay Johnson, Erford Gage, Walter Kingsford, Florence Bates.

## For Whom the Bell Tolls

Producer-Director: Sam Wood. Based upon the novel by Ernest Hemingway. Screenplay: Dudley Nichols. (Uncredited: Louis Bromfield, Jeanie MacPherson.) Music: Victor Young. Photography: Ray Rennahan (Technicolor). Special Effects: Gordon Jennings, Jan Domela, Irmin Roberts. Process Photography: Farciot Edouart. Production Designer: William Cameron Menzies. Art Directors: Hans Dreier, Haldane Douglas. Editors: Sherman Todd, John F. Link. Production and Distribution: Paramount. New York premiere: July 14, 1943. Running Time: 166 minutes. Cast: Gary Cooper, Ingrid Bergman, Akim Tamiroff, Katina Paxinou, Arturo de Cordova, Vladimir Sokoloff, Mikhail Rasumny, Fortunio Bonanova, Eric Feldary, Victor Varconi, Joseph Calleia, Lilo Yarson, Alexander Granach, Adia Kuznetzoff, Leonid Snegoff, Leo Bulgakov, Duncan Renaldo, Frank Puglia, Pedro de Cordoba, Michael Visaroff, Martin Garralaga, Jean Del Val, Jack Mylong, Feodor Chaliapin.

## The North Star

Producer: Samuel Goldwyn. Associate Producer: William Cameron Menzies. Director: Lewis Milestone. Story and Screenplay: Lillian Hellman. (Uncredited: Edward Chodorov.) Music: Aaron Copland. Lyrics: Ira Gershwin. Photography: James Wong Howe. Special Effects: Ray Binger, Clarence Slifer. Art Director: Perry Ferguson. Associate: McClure Capps. Editor: Daniel Mandell. Production: Samuel Goldwyn. Distribution: RKO Radio Pictures. Release Date: November 1943. Running Time: 106 minutes. Cast: Anne Baxter, Dana Andrews, Walter Huston, Walter Brennan, Ann Harding, Jane Withers, Farley Granger, Erich von Stroheim, Dean Jagger, Eric Roberts, Carl Benton Reid, Ann Carter, Esther Dale, Ruth Nelson, Paul Guilfoyle, Martin Kosleck, Tonio Selwart, Peter Pohlenz, Robert Lowery, Gene O'Donnell, Frank Wilcox, Loudie Claar, Lynn Winthrop, Charles Bates.

### Address Unknown

Producer-Director: William Cameron Menzies. Assistant Producer: Lonnie D'Orsa. Based upon the story by Kressmann Taylor. Screenplay: Herbert Dalmas. Music: Ernst Toch. Photography: Rudolph Maté. Art Directors: Lionel Banks, Walter Holscher. Editor: Al Clark. Production: Address Unknown, Inc. (Sam Wood). Distribution: Columbia Pictures. Release Date: June 1, 1944. Running Time: 72 minutes. Cast: Paul Lukas, Carl Esmond, Peter van Eyck, Mady Christians, Morris Carnovsky, K.T. Stevens, Emory Parnell, Mary Young, Frank Faylen, Charles Halton, Erwin Kalser, Frank Reicher, Dale Cornell, Peter Newmeyer, Larry Joe Olsen, Gary Gray.

### Duel in the Sun

Producer: David O. Selznick. Director: King Vidor. (Uncredited: William Dieterle.) Second Unit Directors: Otto Brower, Reaves Eason. (Uncredited: William Cameron Menzies.) Based upon the novel by Niven Busch. Adaptation: Oliver H. P. Garrett. Screenplay: David O. Selznick. Music: Dimitri Tiomkin. Photography: Lee Garmes, Hal Rosson, Ray Rennahan (Technicolor). Additional Photography: Charles P. Boyle. Special Effects: Clarence Slifer. Production Designer: J. McMillan Johnson. (Uncredited: Josef von Sternberg.) Art Director: James Basevi. Associate: John Ewing. Editor: Hal C. Kern. Associates: William H. Ziegler, John Faure. Production: Vanguard Films. Distribution: United Artists. World Premiere: December 31, 1946. Running Time: 144 minutes. Cast: Jennifer Jones, Joseph Cotten, Gregory Peck, Lionel Barrymore, Herbert Marshall, Lillian Gish, Walter Huston, Charles Bickford, Harry Carey, Joan Tetzel, Tilly Losch, Butterfly McQueen, Scott McKay, Otto Kruger, Sidney Blackmer, Charles Dingle.

NOTE: According to Lee Garmes, Menzies designed and co-directed the barbecue sequence. Studio records show he worked a total of five days on this film, on loan from RKO.

### Spellbound

Producer: David O. Selznick. Director: Alfred Hitchcock. Based upon the novel *The House of Dr. Edwardes* by Frances Beeding. Adaptation: Angus MacPhail. Screenplay: Ben Hecht. Music: Miklós Rózsa. Photography: George Barnes. Special Effects: Jack Cosgrove, Clarence Slifer. Art Director: James Basevi. Associate: John Ewing. Editor: Hal C. Kern. Associate: William H. Ziegler. Production: Vanguard Films. Distribution: United Artists. Release Date: December 28, 1945. Running Time: 110 minutes. Cast: Ingrid Bergman, Gregory Peck, Michael Chekhov, Leo G. Carroll, Rhonda Fleming, John Emery, Norman Lloyd, Bill Goodwin, Steven Geray, Donald Curtis, Wallace Ford, Art Baker, Regis Toomey, Paul Harvey.

NOTE: Menzies consulted on the dream sequence, which was based on designs by Salvador Dalí.

### Deadline at Dawn

Executive Producer: Sid Rogell. Producer: Adrian Scott. Director: Harold Clurman. (Uncredited: William Cameron Menzies.) Based upon the novel by William Irish. Screenplay: Clifford Odets. Music: Hanns Eisler. Photography: Nicholas Musuraca. Special Effects: Vernon L. Walker. Art Directors: Albert S. D'Agostino, Jack Okey. Editor: Roland Gross. Production and Distribution: RKO Radio Pictures. Release Date: March 1946. Running Time: 83 minutes. Cast: Susan Hayward, Paul Lukas, Bill Williams, Joseph Calleia, Osa Massen, Lola Lane, Jerome Cowan, Marvin Miller, Roman Bohnen, Steven Geray, Joe Sawyer, Constance Worth, Joseph Crehan.

*It's a Wonderful Life*

Producer-Director: Frank Capra. Based upon the story "The Greatest Gift" by Philip Van Doren Stern. Screenplay: Frances Goodrich, Albert Hackett, Frank Capra. Additional Scenes: Jo Swerling. (Uncredited: Marc Connelly, Dalton Trumbo, Clifford Odets, Michael Wilson.) Music: Dimitri Tiomkin. Photography: Joseph Walker, Joseph Biroc. (Uncredited: Victor Milner.) Art Director: Jack Okey. Editor: William Hornbeck. Production: Liberty Films. Distribution: RKO Radio Pictures. Release Date: January 7, 1947. Running Time: 120 minutes. Cast: James Stewart, Donna Reed, Lionel Barrymore, Thomas Mitchell, Henry Travers, Beulah Bondi, Frank Faylen, Ward Bond, Gloria Grahame, H. B. Warner, Todd Karns, Samuel S. Hinds, Mary Treen, Frank Albertson, Virgina Patton, Charles Williams, Sarah Edwards, Bill Edmunds, Lillian Randolph, Argentina Brunetti, Bobbie Anderson, Ronnie Ralph, Jean Gale, Jeanine Anne Roose, Danny Mummert, Georgie Nokes, Sheldon Leonard, Frank Hagney, Ray Walker, Charlie Lane, Edward Kean, Carol Coomes, Karolyn Grimes, Lary Simms, Jimmy Hawkins.

NOTE: Menzies consulted on selected sequences, and was present for at least some of the filming.

*Ivy*

Producer: William Cameron Menzies. Director: Sam Wood. Based upon the novel *The Story of Ivy* by Marie Belloc Lowndes. Screenplay: Charles Bennett. Music: Daniele Amfitheatrof. Photography: Russell Metty. Special Effects: David S. Horsley. Art Director: Richard H. Riedel. Editor: Ralph Dawson. Production: Inter-Wood Productions. Distribution: Universal-International. Release Date: June 1947. Running Time: 98 minutes. Cast: Joan Fontaine, Patric Knowles, Herbert Marshall, Richard Ney, Sir Cedric Hardwicke, Lucile Watson, Sara Allgood, Henry Stephenson, Rosalind Ivan, Lilian Fontaine, Molly Lamont, Una O'Connor, Isobel Elcom, Alan Napier.

*Arch of Triumph*

Producer: David Lewis. Associate Producer: Otto Klement. Director: Lewis Milestone. Based upon the novel by Erich Maria Remarque. Screenplay: Lewis Milestone, Harry Brown. (Uncredited: Irwin Shaw.) Music: Louis Gruenberg. Photography: Russell Metty. Production Designer: William Cameron Menzies. Art Director: William E. Flannery. Editor: Duncan Mansfield. Production: Arch of Triumph, Inc. (Enterprise). Distribution: United Artists. Release Date: March 1948. Running Time: 120 minutes. Cast: Ingrid Bergman, Charles Boyer, Charles Laughton, Louis Calhern, Ruth Warrick, Roman Bohnen, J. Edward Bromberg, Ruth Nelson, Stephen Bekassy, Curt Bois, Art Smith, Michael Romanoff.

*The Tell-Tale Heart*

Director: William Cameron Menzies. Based upon the story by Edgar Allan Poe. Production: Menzies-Finney. Distribution: Telepak. Running Time: 17 minutes. Cast: Richard Hart, Allen Wells.

NOTE: *The Tell-Tale Heart* was nominated for a 1948 Emmy Award in the category of Best Film Made for Television. It first aired as an episode of ABC's *Actors Studio* on February 20, 1949. In October 1949, it was released to the 16mm noncommercial market by Post Pictures Corp.

*A Terribly Strange Bed*

Director: William Cameron Menzies. Based upon the story by Wilkie Collins. Production: Menzies-Finney. Distribution: Telepak. Running Time: 16 minutes. Cast: Richard Greene, Roman Bohnen.

NOTE: This film first aired as part of NBC's *Fireside Theatre* on June 21, 1949. In October 1949, it was released to the 16mm noncommercial market by Post Pictures Corp.

## The Marionette Mystery

Director: William Cameron Menzies. Screenplay: Ashmead Scott. Photography: William O'Connell. Production and Distribution: Telepak. Running Time: 21 minutes. Cast: John Hoyt, Regis Toomey, Lois Moran, Gale Gordon, Janet Scott, Gloria Holden, Tony Barrett, Earl Lee.

NOTE: No air date has been established for this film. In October 1949, it was released to the 16mm noncommercial market by Post Pictures Corp.

## Reign of Terror

Producer: William Cameron Menzies. Associate Producer: Edward Lasker. Director: Anthony Mann, Lewis Milestone. Story: Robert E. Kent, Alfred Neumann. Story and Screenplay: Philip Yordan, Aeneas MacKenzie. Music: Sol Kaplan. Photography: John Alton. Art Director: Edward Ilou. Editor: Fred Allen. Production: Walter Wanger Pictures, Inc. Distribution: Eagle-Lion Films. Release Date: February 1949. Running Time: 89 minutes. Cast: Robert Cummings, Richard Basehart, Richard Hart, Arlene Dahl, Arnold Moss, Norman Lloyd, Charles McGraw, Beulah Bondi, Jess Barker.

NOTE: Although produced and initially released under the title *Reign of Terror,* this film was retitled *The Black Book* prior to its New York opening in October 1949.

## The Whip Hand

Executive Producer: Sid Rogell. Producer: Lewis J. Rachmil. (Uncredited: Stanley Rubin.) Director: William Cameron Menzies. (Uncredited: Stuart Gilmore.) Based upon the story "The Man He Found" by Roy Hamilton. Screenplay: George Bricker, Frank L. Moss. (Uncredited: Stanley Rubin.) Music: Paul Sawtell. Photography: Nicholas Musuraca. Production Designer: William Cameron Menzies. Art Directors: Albert S. D'Agostino, Carroll Clark. Editor: Robert Golden. Production and Distribution: RKO Radio Pictures. Release Date: October 1951. Running Time: 82 minutes. Cast: Carla Balenda, Elliott Reid, Edgar Barrier, Raymond Burr, Otto Waldis, Michael Steele, Lurene Tuttle, Peter Brocco, Lewis Martin, Frank Darien, Olive Carey.

NOTE: Bobby Watson's scenes as Adolf Hitler were removed from this film prior to its release.

## Drums in the Deep South

Producers: Maurice King, Frank King. Assistant to the Producers: Arthur Gardner. Director: William Cameron Menzies. Second unit Director: B. Reeves Eason. Story: Hollister Noble. Screenplay: Philip Yordan, Sidney Harmon. Music: Dimitri Tiomkin. Photography: Lionel Lindon (Super Cinecolor). Production Designer: William Cameron Menzies. Art Director: Frank Sylos. Editor: Richard Heermance. Production: King Bros. Productions, Inc. Distribution: RKO Radio Pictures. Release Date: October 1951. Running Time: 87 minutes. Cast: James Craig, Barbara Payton, Guy Madison, Barton MacLane, Robert Osterloh, Tom Fadden, Robert Easton, Louise Jean Heydt, Craig Stevens, Taylor Holmes, Lewis Martin, Peter Bocco, Dan White.

## The Zayat Kiss

Producer: Herbert Swope, Jr. Director: William Cameron Menzies. Based upon the story by Sax Rohmer. Adaptation: Sax Rohmer, Elizabeth Knox. Screenplay: John L. Gerstad, Herbert Swope, Jr.

Photography: Edward Hyland. Art Director: Dick Sylbert. Production: Herles Enterprises. Running Time: 26 minutes. Cast: Cedric Hardwicke, John Carradine, John Newland, Colin Keith-Johnston, Melville Cooper, Rita Gam, Frank Daily, Bob Wing, Mike Ma.

NOTE: No air date has been established for this film, which was made in New York in April 1952.

## The Wild Heart

Producers: Alexander Korda, David O. Selznick. Directors: Michael Powell, Emeric Pressburger. (Uncredited: Rouben Mamoulian, William Cameron Menzies.) Based upon the novel *Gone to Earth* by Mary Webb. Screenplay: Michael Powell, Emeric Pressburger. Music: Brian Easdale. Photography: Chris Challis. Production Designer: Hein Heckroth. Art Director: Arthur Lawson. Editor: Reginald Mills. Production: London Film Productions, Vanguard Films. Distribution: RKO Radio Pictures. Release Date: July 1952. Running Time: 82 minutes. Cast: Jennifer Jones, David Farrar, Cyril Cusack, Sybil Thorndike, Edward Chapman, Esmond Knight, Hugh Griffith, Joseph Cotten.

NOTE: According to documents in the Selznick collection, Menzies made retakes and directed added scenes for this film in February 1951. The original British production had been released in September 1950 under the title *Gone to Earth*.

## We're Not Married!

Producer: Nunnally Johnson. Director: Edmund Goulding. Story: Gina Kaus, Jay Dratler. Adaptation: Dwight Taylor. Screenplay: Nunnally Johnson. Music: Cyril Mockridge. Photography: Leo Tover. Art Directors: Lyle Wheeler, Leland Fuller. Editor: Louis Loeffler. Production and Distribution: 20th Century-Fox. Release Date: July 1952. Running Time: 85 minutes. Cast: Ginger Rogers, Fred Allen, Victor Moore, Marilyn Monroe, David Wayne, Eve Arden, Paul Douglas, Eddie Bracken, Mitzi Gaynor, Louis Calhern, Zsa Zsa Gabor, James Gleason, Paul Stewart, Jane Darwell.

NOTE: Menzies was montage director. At his request, he was uncredited and received no publicity for his work on this film.

## Androcles and the Lion

Producer: Gabriel Pascal. Associate Producer: Lewis J. Rachmil. Director: Chester Erskine. (Uncredited: H. C. Potter, Nicholas Ray.) Based upon the play by George Bernard Shaw. Adaptation: Chester Erskine, Ken Englund. (Uncredited: Noel Langley.) Music: Frederick Hollander. Photography: Harry Stradling. Special Effects: Linwood Dunn. Production Designer: Harry Horner. (Uncredited: William Cameron Menzies.) Art Directors: Albert S. D'Agostino, Charles F. Pyke. Editor: Roland Gross. Production: G. P. Productions, Inc., RKO Radio Pictures. Distribution: RKO Radio Pictures. Release Date: January 9, 1953. Running Time: 98 minutes. Cast: Jean Simmons, Victor Mature, Robert Newton, Maurice Evans, Alan Young, Elsa Lanchester, Reginald Gardiner, Gene Lockhart, Alan Mowbray, Noel Willman, John Hoyt, Jim Backus, Lowell Gilmore.

## Invaders from Mars

Producer: Edward L. Alperson. Associate Producer: Edward L. Alperson, Jr. Director: William Cameron Menzies. Screenplay: Richard Blake. (Uncredited: John Tucker Battle.) Music: Raoul Kraushaar. Photography: John Seitz (color). Special Effects: Jack Cosgrove. Production Designer: William Cameron Menzies. Art Director: Boris Leven. Editor: Arthur Roberts. Production: National Pictures Corp. Distribution: 20th Century-Fox. Release Date: May 1953. Running Time: 78 minutes. Cast: Helena

Carter, Arthur Franz, Jimmy Hunt. Leif Erickson, Hillary Brooke, Morris Ankrum, Max Wagner, Bill Phipps, Milburn Stone, Janine Perreau.

## The Maze

Executive Producer: Walter Mirisch. Producer: Richard Heermance. Director: William Cameron Menzies. Based upon the story by Maurice Sandoz. Screenplay: Dan Ullman. Music: Marlin Skiles. Photography: Harry Neumann (3-D). Special Effects: Augie Lohman. Production Designer: William Cameron Menzies. Art Director: David Milton. Editor: John Fuller. Production and Distribution: Allied Artists. Release Date: July 26, 1953. Running Time: 81 minutes. Cast: Richard Carlson, Veronica Hurst, Katherine Emery, Michael Pate, John Dodsworth, Hillary Brooke, Stanley Fraser, Lillian Bond, Owen McGiveney, Robin Hughes.

## A String of Beads

Executive Producer: Don W. Sharpe. Producer: William Frye. Associate Producer: Ann Marlowe. Director: William Cameron Menzies. Based upon the story by W. Somerset Maugham. Adaptation: Don Ettlinger. Photography: George E. Diskant. Art Director: Duncan Cramer. Editorial Supervisor: Bernard Burton. Editor: Samuel E. Beetley. Production: Everest Productions. Running Time: 25 minutes. Cast: Ronald Colman, Angela Lansbury, Branda Forbes, Ron Randell, Nigel Bruce, George Macready, Sean McClory, Sarah Selby, Ben Wright, Dorothy Green.

NOTE: This pilot for a projected series first aired as an episode of CBS's *Four Star Playhouse* on January 21, 1954. It was later syndicated as part of the series *The Star and the Story.*

## Star Studded Ride (Universal-International Color Parade)

Producer: Thomas Mead. (Uncredited: Sol Lesser.) Director: William Cameron Menzies. Screenplay: Alan Kitchel, Jr. Music: Jack Shaindlin. Art Director: Perry Ferguson. Editor: Ed Bartsch. Distribution: Universal-International. Release Date: 1954. Running Time: 10 minutes. Cast: Ben Hogan, Gussie Moran, Dave Gillam, Pat McCormick, Stubby Kruger. Narrator: Tex Antoine.

NOTE: This short subject was assembled from material originally shot in Palm Springs for the "Fun in the Sun" segment of Sol Lesser's *Three-D Follies.*

## Autumn in Rome

Producer: David O. Selznick. Associate Producer: Arthur Fellows. Director: William Cameron Menzies. Music: Paul Weston. Lyrics: Sammy Cahn. Arranger: Joe Reisman. Photography: James Wong Howe. Editor: Morrie Roizman. Production: Selznick Releasing Organization. Distribution: Columbia. Release Date: May 10, 1954. Running Time: 8 minutes. Cast: Patti Page.

NOTE: This short film, considered a "prologue" to the Columbia release *Indiscretion of an American Wife,* featured Patti Page singing "Autumn in Rome" and "Indiscretion." Both songs were derived from Alessandro Cicognini's score for the feature.

## It's News to Me

Producers: Mark Goodson, Bill Todman. Director: Jerome Schnur. Host: Walter Cronkite. Panelists: Nina Foch, Quentin Reynolds, Anna Lee, John Henry Faulk. CBS, Fridays, July 9–August 27, 1954.

NOTE: Menzies was witness to a historic event, the first Academy Awards dinner, on one episode.

## The Halls of Ivy

Executive Producer: Leon Fromkess. Producer: William Frye. Directors: William Cameron Menzies, Norman Z. McLeod. Created by Don Quinn. Teleplays: Barbara Merlin, Milton Merlin, Don Quinn. Music: Henry Russell. Photography: Robert Pittack, Alfred Gilks. Art Director: Perry Ferguson. Editor: Otto Meyer. Production: Television Programs of America. Running Time: 28 minutes. Cast: Ronald Colman, Benita Hume, Mary Wickes, Ray Collins, Herbert Butterfield, James Todd.

NOTE: Menzies directed approximately half of the thirty-nine episodes that made up this series. It debuted on CBS on October 19, 1954.

## Johnny and the Gaucho

Producer: Abner J. Greshler. Director: William Cameron Menzies. Screenplay: Parke Levy. Music: Vincente Gomez. Cast: Señor Wences.

NOTE: This pilot for a daytime television series featuring ventriloquist Señor Wences and his characters was reportedly filmed in February 1955.

## Around the World in 80 Days

Producer: Michael Todd. Associate Producer: William Cameron Menzies. Director: Michael Anderson. (Uncredited: John Farrow, Michael Todd.) Based upon the novel by Jules Verne. Screenplay: James Poe, John Farrow, S. J. Perelman. Music: Victor Young. Photography: Lionel Lindon (Technicolor/Todd-AO). Special Effects: Lee Zavitz. Production Designer: William Cameron Menzies. Art Directors: James Sullivan, Ken Adams. Editors: Gene Ruggiero, Howard Epstein. (Uncredited: Paul Weatherwax.) Production: Michael Todd Co. Distribution: United Artists. World Premiere: October 17, 1956. Running Time: 178 minutes. Cast: David Niven, Cantinflas, Robert Newton, Shirley MacLaine, Finlay Currie, Robert Morley, Ronald Squire, Basil Sydney, Noel Coward, Sir John Gielgud, Trevor Howard, Harcourt Williams, Martine Carol, Fernandel, Charles Boyer, Evelyn Keyes, José Greco and Troupe, Gilbert Roland, Luis Dominguin, Cesar Romero, Alan Mowbray, Sir Cedric Hardwicke, Melville Cooper, Reginald Denny, Ronald Colman, Robert Cabal, Charles Coburn, Peter Lorre, George Raft, Red Skelton, Marlene Dietrich, John Carradine, Frank Sinatra, Buster Keaton, Col. Tim McCoy, Joe E. Brown, Andy Devine, Edmund Lowe, Victor McLaglen, Jack Oakie, Beatrice Lillie, Glynis Johns, Hermione Gingold, John Mills, Edward R. Murrow, A. E. Matthews, Ronald Adam, Walter Fitzgerald, Frank Royde.

# INDEX

Page numbers in *italics* refer to illustrations.